The Realms of Verse
1830–1870

The Realms of Verse
1830–1870

*English Poetry in a
Time of Nation-Building*

MATTHEW REYNOLDS

OXFORD
UNIVERSITY PRESS

OXFORD

UNIVERSITY PRESS

Great Clarendon Street, Oxford OX2 6DP

Oxford University Press is a department of the University of Oxford.
It furthers the University's objective of excellence in research, scholarship,
and education by publishing worldwide in

Oxford New York

Athens Auckland Bangkok Bogotá Buenos Aires Calcutta
Cape Town Chennai Dar es Salaam Delhi Florence Hong Kong Istanbul
Karachi Kuala Lumpur Madrid Melbourne Mexico City Mumbai
Nairobi Paris São Paulo Shanghai Singapore Taipei Tokyo Toronto Warsaw
with associated companies in Berlin Ibadan

Oxford is a registered trade mark of Oxford University Press
in the UK and in certain other countries

Published in the United States
by Oxford University Press Inc., New York

© Matthew Reynolds 2001

The moral rights of the author have been asserted
Database right Oxford University Press (maker)

First published 2001

British Library Cataloguing in Publication Data

Data available

Library of Congress Cataloging-in-Publication Data
Reynolds, Matthew.
The realms of verse, 1830-1870: English poetry in a time of nation-building/Matthew Reynolds.
p. cm.
Includes bibiogaphical reference and index.
1. English poetry—19th century—History and criticism. 2. Nationalism and
literature—Great Britain—History—19th century. 3. Nationalism in literature. 4. Politics
and literature—Great Britain—History—19th century. 5. Imperialism in literature. 6. Great
Britain—Intellectual life—19th century. I. Title.
PR585.N27 R49 2001   821'.809358—dc21   00-046945

ISBN 0-19-818712-2

1 3 5 7 9 10 8 6 4 2

Typeset in Bembo by
Cambrian Typesetters, Frimley, Surrey
Printed in Great Britain
on acid-free paper by
Biddles Ltd, Guildford and King's Lynn

For

Dr M. L. & Prof. E. O. R. Reynolds

ACKNOWLEDGEMENTS

I am grateful to Trinity College, Cambridge and to St Anne's College, Oxford for providing environments in which it was possible to begin and continue work on this book; and to the Arts and Humanities Research Board for funding the sabbatical which made possible its completion.

Early attempts at formulating some of the arguments in this volume were published in *Journal of Anglo-Italian Studies*, vol. 4 (1995); *Times Literary Supplement*, 4891 (1996); and John Woolford (ed.), *Robert Browning in Contexts* (Winfield, Kan.: Wedgestone Press, 1998).

Of the many people to whom I am indebted for information, stimulus and support, I would like to thank in particular Kate Clanchy, David Forgacs, Eric Griffiths, Robin Kirkpatrick, Jeremy Maule, Adrian Poole, and Christopher Ricks.

CONTENTS

A NOTE ON THE TEXT

In line with my conviction that the poems at the heart of this book are best understood in relation to a 'time of nation-building', rather than more local and immediate historical contexts, I have quoted them, unless otherwise stated, not from their first-published texts but from the final texts as printed in the following editions:

Elizabeth Barrett Browning:
Aurora Leigh, ed. Margaret Reynolds (Athens, Oh.: Ohio University Press, 1992).
Casa Guidi Windows, ed. Julia Markus (New York: Browning Institute, 1977).

Robert Browning:
The Poetical Works of Robert Browning, general ed. Ian Jack (Oxford: Clarendon Press, 1983–).
The Ring and the Book, ed. Richard D. Altick (Harmondsworth: Penguin, 1981).

Arthur Hugh Clough:
The Poems of Arthur Hugh Clough, 2nd edn., ed. F. L. Mulhauser (Oxford: Clarendon Press, 1974).

Alfred Tennyson:
The Poems of Tennyson, 2nd edn., ed. Christopher Ricks, 3 vols. (Longman, 1987).

Poets who have not yet been securely edited are quoted from first editions or (when there is a question of influence) from texts widely available in the mid-nineteenth century.

In the footnotes, full title and publication details are given on a work's first appearance; these are repeated in the List of Works Cited. Place of publication is London unless otherwise stated. Authors of writings published anonymously appear in parentheses; for Victorian periodicals, attributions of authorship follow those in

The Wellesley Index to Victorian Periodicals: 1824–1900, ed. Walter E. Houghton and Jean H. Slingersland, new edn., CD-ROM (Routledge, 1999). Writing in foreign languages is rendered into English unless its foreignness matters to my argument (as, for instance, in works which the Brownings read in French or Italian). Translations are my own unless indication is made to the contrary.

ABBREVIATIONS

AL	*Aurora Leigh*
AV	*Amours de Voyage*
B	*The Bothie of Tober-na-Vuolich*
CGW	*Casa Guidi Windows*
Memoir	Hallam, Lord Tennyson, *Alfred Lord Tennyson: A Memoir: By his Son*, 2 vols. (Macmillan, 1897)
OED	*Oxford English Dictionary*, CD-ROM (Oxford: Oxford University Press, n.d.)
P	*The Princess*
RB	*The Ring and the Book*

PART I

ORIENTATIONS

I

POETRY AND ITS TIMES

When Garibaldi visited Britain in 1864, he found time to call on the Poet Laureate. For Tennyson's son Hallam, then 11 years old, this was 'the great event of the year'; the poet himself was still proud of the occasion two decades later, mentioning, in some verses about his garden, the 'waving pine' planted by 'the warrior of Caprera'.[1] In their admiration for their visitor, the Tennysons were not alone. Garibaldi had become famous throughout Europe as the commander of two key enterprises in the Italian Risorgimento: the defence of republican Rome in 1849 and, in 1860, the extraordinary conquest of Sicily and southern Italy by 'the Thousand'.[2] As the *Illustrated London News* observed, these exploits had provoked remarkable enthusiasm in British hearts: 'the name of Garibaldi exerts a talismanic influence of unprecedented potency over all classes of society, and inspires a common sentiment of affectionate, we may even say passionate, admiration into the bosoms of the nobility, the middle classes, and the toiling millions.'[3] Lurking beneath such unanimous acclaim was some disagreement as to quite what Garibaldi was being applauded for. Whigs and Tories emphasized his loyalty to the King of Piedmont—and later of Italy—Vittorio Emmanuele II, and interpreted Italian unification as an assertion of British-style constitutional monarchy. Radicals, on the other hand, took comfort from his humble background and his association with the republican

---

[1] Hallam, Lord Tennyson, *Alfred Lord Tennyson: A Memoir: By his Son*, 2 vols. (Macmillan, 1897: cited as *Memoir* hereafter), ii. 2; Alfred Tennyson, 'To Ulysses', 25–6. Tennyson's poems are quoted from *The Poems of Tennyson*, 2nd edn., ed. Christopher Ricks, 3 vols. (Longman, 1987).
[2] See Giorgio Candeloro, *Storia dell'Italia Moderna*, 2nd edn., 11 vols. (Milan: Feltrinelli, 1988–91), iii. 425–53; iv. 427–526; G. M. Trevelyan, *Garibaldi's Defence of the Roman Republic* (Longmans, Green and Co., 1907) and *Garibaldi and the Thousand* (Longmans, Green and Co., 1909).   [3] *Illustrated London News*, 44/1256 (23 Apr. 1864), 382.

revolutionary Mazzini: for them, Italian unification was at once an instance and a symbol of the shift of European (including British) politics towards self-determination and democracy. These conflicting views came face to face in 1864 when Garibaldi's presence in Britain caused such popular agitation that he was encouraged by powerful friends to curtail his trip.[4] Not, however, before he had met the Tennysons.

Mrs Tennyson recorded the event in her diary, where she begins by describing Garibaldi as 'a most striking figure in his picturesque white Poncha [*sic*] lined with red, his embroidered red shirt & a coloured tie over it. His face very noble powerful & sweet, his forehead high & square. Altogether he looks one of the great men of our Elizabethan age . . .'. Here, her imagination seems quite untroubled as it assimilates Garibaldi's uniform, with its republican associations, to the costume worn by subjects of one of the great English monarchs. As her account continues, however, ideological tensions become more marked:

A. T. and I went out to fix a spot where the Wellingtonia should be planted (given A. T. by the Duchess of Sutherland, and raised by her from a cone that had been shot from a tree three hundred feet high in California) . . . People on foot and on horseback and in carriages had waited these two hours for him [Garibaldi]. Some rushed forward to shake hands with him. He stood up and bowed. A. T. and I and the boys were in the portico, awaiting his arrival . . . Garibaldi admired the primroses with which the rooms were decked, and liked the view, and said to A. T., 'I wish I had your trees in Caprera.' A. T. and Garibaldi went up to A. T.'s study together and they talked on politics, and A. T. advised the General not to talk politics in England. They repeated Italian poetry to each other . . . Then we went to plant the Wellingtonia. A. T. had the large screen made of old *Punches* put up to protect Garibaldi from the cold east wind. Several strangers were there, and when the tree was planted, they gave a shout.[5]

The admirable primroses and the pleasant view were safe topics of conversation, as well as being suited to Garibaldi's halting English

---

[4] Derek Beales, 'Garibaldi in England: The Politics of Italian Enthusiasm', in John A. Davis and Paul Ginsborg (eds.), *Society and Politics in the Age of the Risorgimento* (Cambridge: Cambridge University Press, 1991), 199–208. On divergent understandings of the Risorgimento, see below, Chapter 2.

[5] Emily, Lady Tennyson, *Lady Tennyson's Journal*, ed. James O. Hoge (Charlottesville, Va.: University Press of Virginia, 1981), 196–7.

and Tennyson's unconversational Italian; but the pine tree they planted together brought with it a shadow of disagreement, for— certainly in Garibaldi's hands—it risked calling to mind the trees of liberty which revolutionaries had set up throughout France in 1790.[6] Mrs Tennyson opens the way for this connotation when she remarks that the pine cone had been shipped over from that other revolutionary republic, the United States; but she blocks it by noting that the tree had been raised by an aristocrat and bore the name of the soldier who was as much a hero for English conservatives as was Garibaldi for European liberals: Wellington. The Wellingtonia planted by Garibaldi in the garden of the English Poet Laureate might stand as a emblem of that limited, monarchical version of Italian freedom for which Tennyson, a devoted subject of Queen Victoria, could call himself an 'enthusiast', but which Mazzini (for one) considered to be a betrayal of the national cause.[7]

The poems which the Laureate and the revolutionary recited to one another in private were, no less than the Wellingtonia, linked in to politics by filaments of implication. Tennyson chose Manzoni's ode 'Il Cinque Maggio', which mourns the death of Napoleon, paying homage to his greatness but offering no comment as to the political value of his career. Like its author's great novel, *I promessi sposi*, the poem adopts an attitude of Catholic resignation before the troubles of this world: as Mazzini remarked, 'the destiny of man on this earth, as regards society, forms no part of the moral aim contemplated by the disciples of this school.'[8] The records do not reveal whether Tennyson voiced Manzoni's Italian or the English of Gladstone, by whom the ode had been translated; either way, if he had hoped that Garibaldi might enjoy the implied comparison between himself and the French Emperor, and that the poem would add reinforcing sentiments to the judicious advice 'not to talk politics in England', he appears to have been mistaken. 'I don't know whether he relished it', Tennyson recalled, 'but he began immediately to speak of Ugo Foscolo', and quoted 'with great fervour, a fragment of his "I Sepolcri" '.[9]

---

[6] Simon Schama, *Citizens: A Chronicle of the French Revolution* (Harmondsworth: Penguin, 1989), 491; see also *Illustrated London News*, 44/1257 (30 Apr. 1864), 422.

[7] *Memoir*, ii. 1; Denis Mack Smith, *Mazzini* (New Haven: Yale University Press, 1994), 159.

[8] Giuseppe Mazzini, *Life and Writings of Joseph Mazzini*, 6 vols. (Smith, Elder and Co., 1864–7) ii. 179.

[9] *Memoir*, ii. 3.

Foscolo was an active nationalist who had fought for Napoleon against Austria, and had spent a decade of exile in London before his death in 1827. His poem, 'Dei sepolcri', is indebted to Gray's 'Elegy'—it is located imaginatively in a graveyard and dwells on thoughts of the buried—but it draws from its ruminations hope of a political resurrection. The lines Garibaldi selected tell of the ghosts of Athenians and Persians who every night contest the battle of Marathon anew. With a typically circular nationalist interpretation of history, past greatness, whether Greek or Italian, is presented as a spur to contemporary agitation and a promise for the future. If Tennyson ever looked through the whole text of Foscolo's poem, which Garibaldi later sent him from London, he may have noticed something it had in common with his own latest work, the first collection of *Idylls of the King*. The *Idylls* share with 'Dei sepolcri' the assumption that ancient heroism is an ideal towards which the present should aspire; that the past is, in this sense, a mirror of the future. Maybe it was some such recognition of similarity which prompted Tennyson to send Garibaldi the *Idylls* in return. Perhaps also it was a desire to continue the ideological debate which had begun in his study at Farringford. From one point of view, he thought Garibaldi close to being a modern embodiment of the heroism which is celebrated in the *Idylls*: 'what a noble human being! . . . One cannot exactly say of him what Chaucer says of the ideal knight, "As meke he was of port as is a maid"; he is more majestic than meek, and his manners have a certain divine simplicity in them . . .'. Going simply on his manners, Tennyson might have written for him the lines he later penned in tribute to Prince Albert: 'He seems to me | Scarce other than my king's ideal knight'.[10] On the other hand, Garibaldi was possessed of radical opinions which looked set to imperil monarch and aristocracy, and which the example of Arthur, the hero-king, may have been expected to combat. Tennyson may have hoped that Garibaldi, like Guinevere, would come to see in Arthur, not Mazzini, 'the highest and most human too'. Then again, perhaps he was recognizing the fondness of that hope when he remarked that his gift to Garibaldi was one 'which I do not suppose he will care for'.[11]

---

[10] *Memoir*, ii. 3; 'Dedication [Idylls of the King]', 5–6.
[11] 'Guinevere', 644–5; *Memoir*, ii. 3.

The encounter of Tennyson and Garibaldi on the Isle of Wight suggests two factors that a historically sensitive approach to the *Idylls*, and to other mid-nineteenth-century English poems, should keep in view. First, their interest in and relevance to the politics and literature of the continent, of which I will have more to say in the next chapter. Secondly, that there was greater continuity between poetry and high politics than there is today, and that people active in the two kinds of endeavour treated each other with more respect. It was not only that poets thought of themselves as being politically engaged: their claims to be, in some more or less figurative way, legislators, were taken seriously by those men (they were of course all men) who were involved in the day-to-day business of actual legislation. As Gladstone observed, recalling 'Love thou thy land' and its companion poems at the beginning of his review of the 1859 *Idylls*: 'never has political philosophy been wedded to the poetic form more happily than in the three short pieces on England and her institutions, unhappily without title, and only to be cited, like writs of law and papal bulls, by their first words.'[12] The *Illustrated London News* recalled the same group of poems when it remarked:

If we know Tennyson and Garibaldi, they could not long confer together without speculating on the prospects of a successful assertion of the liberty of nations . . . No other English poet has so thoroughly comprehended the public spirit of this country; in none is the love of freedom more richly tempered with a loyal respect for the ancient laws, customs, and institutions of old England, and her venerable traditions of 'the storied past';

> Where freedom broadens slowly down
> From precedent to precedent.[13]

The choice of quotation suggests just how much Tennyson's and Garibaldi's thoughts on the liberty of nations are likely to have differed, for the phrasing 'from precedent to precedent' contrives to envisage the progress of freedom as a return into the past, and the generally calmative rhetoric ('broadens slowly down') now

---

[12] W. E. Gladstone, *Gleanings of Past Years, 1843–78* (John Murray, 1879), ii. 133.

[13] *Illustrated London News*, 44/1256 (23 Apr. 1864), 398. 'The storied past' is from 'Love thou thy land, with love far-brought', 2; the succeeding two lines are 'You ask me, why, thought ill at ease', 11–12, with altered indentation: Tennyson wrote 'Past' and 'Freedom' with initial capitals.

seems almost comical in its determination to shut out any hint of
the kind of revolution (a quick rising from below) in which
Garibaldi was a specialist.

As even a brief look at the readings which Tennyson and
Garibaldi exchanged in shared appreciation and guarded disagreement makes clear, nineteenth-century poetry was, in its political
bearings, often considerably more subtle and enquiring than the
skillfully versified opinions of 'Love thou thy land'. *Idylls of the
King* is typical of the poems which are the focus of this book in
that it both requires and resists insertion into contemporary
debates. The Round Table clearly has some connection with
Prince Albert and also some doubtless more tenuous link to
Garibaldi. But to suggest that the work was simply about these
contemporary figures would be to make it a travesty, as Swinburne
well knew when he proposed the alternative title *Idylls of the Prince
Consort*.[14] The ambivalent imaginative and conceptual location of
much Victorian poetry has been well described by Isobel
Armstrong: 'Art occupied its own area, a self-sufficing aesthetic
realm over and against practical experience . . . And yet it was at
once apart and central, for it had a mediating function, representing and interpreting life.'[15] *Idylls of the King*, like many mid-nineteenth-century poems, was designed both to speak to the practical
concerns of its times, and to hold itself apart from them so as to
make itself available to more wide-ranging and multivalent interpretations.

The title of Professor Armstrong's own wide-ranging volume,
Victorian Poetry: Poetry, Poetics and Politics, appears to herald a
consideration of the overlaps between Tennyson's realms of activity and those of Gladstone or Garibaldi. In fact, the word 'politics',
as it appears in the book, takes on a partial and specialized definition: 'the task of a history of Victorian poetry is to restore the
questions of politics, not least sexual politics, and the epistemology
and language which belong to it.'[16] In practice, 'not least' often
hardens into 'that is to say'. The virtue of this approach is that it
allows even the most apparently uncommitted of works to be

[14] John D. Jump (ed.), *Tennyson: The Critical Heritage* (Routledge and Kegan Paul, 1967),
339.
[15] Isobel Armstrong, *Victorian Poetry: Poetry, Poetics, and Politics* (Routledge, 1993), 4.
[16] Ibid. 7.

placed in relation to political issues. Of Tennyson's 'The Kraken', Armstrong remarks—having adduced a variety of contexts—that 'according to which of the myths are activated, utopian or conservative, the Kraken is the principle of transformation, of mindless destruction, or evil, or the helpless victim of external forces', and suggests that this multifariousness is the sign of 'a peculiarly radical conservatism, which dreads change and sees its necessity, even the necessity of violence'. Such observations support her claim that 'one of the subliminal themes' of Tennyson's 1830 *Poems, Chiefly Lyrical* is 'what revolutionary change is, how it comes about and what its consequences are'.[17] The shortcoming of this line of argument, however, is that it tends to reduce, even annihilate the distance between imaginative changes registered in the seclusion of the page, and the developments that were debated in the public space of Parliament, or that were demonstrated for and fought over in the even more public streets of London, Dublin, Paris, Milan, and elsewhere. To emphasize that sexual relations, epistemology, and language are—as we now think—themselves intrinsically 'political' is to play down the question of how they connect with what people in the nineteenth century generally meant by politics: 'the science and art of government . . . Political affairs or business . . . The political principles, convictions, opinions, or sympathies of a person or party' (*OED*). Indeed, such an emphasis makes it possible to write a book about poetry and 'politics' without taking parliamentary debates and such like into consideration at all. Armstrong has little to say about politicians—she mentions neither Gladstone nor Garibaldi —and barely comments on the works in which Victorian poets most obviously confronted politics in the public sense, and which will, for that reason, be at the heart of this volume: *Aurora Leigh*, *Amours de Voyage*, *The Ring and the Book*, *The Princess*, and *Idylls of the King*. Her book virtually concurs with the old view that the Victorian poetry which matters is confined to the personal life; with this difference, that the personal is now understood to be political.

If private life is already shot through with political implications, the possibility of conflict between a realm thought of as 'private', and a 'public' realm which is the location of politics, will disappear; with the result that everything will be seen to have a political

---

[17] Ibid. 56, 51.

aspect. The very mysteriousness of 'The Kraken', the difficulty of associating it with any political attitude, itself makes the poem the embodiment of a political position. However, it has long been recognized that in the mid-nineteenth century the disjunction between 'private' and 'public', although neither fixed nor unbridgeable, was strongly maintained, and was fundamental to people's experience of their lives.[18] The contrast was felt with particular acuity by poets, for poetry, though not simply 'private' discourse, was not straightforwardly 'public' either. Sometimes coinciding, and sometimes contrasting with the paradox 'at once apart and central', was another paradox: at once private and public. Awareness of this double status appears throughout Tennyson's 1830 volume, and registers most creatively in the poems' allusions to the transfer out of the private realm which they themselves undergo upon publication. Tennyson's unease about what the public will make of his work brings him, in 'The Poet's Mind', to the point of insulting them:

> Vex not thou the poet's mind
> With thy shallow wit:
> Vex not thou the poet's mind;
> For thou canst not fathom it.

It is only at the beginning of the second stanza that we are offered the possibility of deflecting this tirade onto a 'dark-browed sophist' who threatens to invade and blight a flourishing garden of the mind, hedged (aptly enough) with 'laurel-shrubs', where a 'merry bird chants' and a 'fountain . . . springs', 'drawn | From the brain of the purple mountain' which, in its turn, 'draws it from Heaven above'. This endearing ecology of the imagination prompts us to configure the sophist, in whose 'eye there is death', and 'frost' in his 'breath', as a rationalistic psychologist, someone like James Mill, whose *Analysis of the Phenomena of the Human Mind* appeared in 1829.[19] However, we cannot escape so easily, for to advance such an interpretation is itself to claim to have fathomed the work, and so to make us again vulnerable to the abuse launched in the opening four lines. Even so slight a creation as 'The Poet's Mind',

[18] Karl Marx, *Critique of Hegel's Philosophy of Right*, ed. Joseph J. O'Malley (Cambridge: Cambridge University Press, 1970), 32; John Tosh, *A Man's Place: Masculinity and the Middle-Class Home in Victorian England* (New Haven: Yale University Press, 1999), 27–31.

[19] 'The Poet's Mind', 1–4, 8, 14, 22, 24, 31, 28–9, 32, 17–18.

a poem which appears to tell you its interpretation in its title, turns out not only to resist understanding but to make a demonstration of resistance. It is in the paradoxical situation of having been published but wanting not to be understood, perhaps not even to be read.

The unease about exposure which is dramatized in 'The Poet's Mind' continues to be manifest throughout Tennyson's career. Forty years later he was to complain about interpreters of *Idylls of the King*, 'I hate to be tied down to say, "*This* means *that*," because the thought within the image is much more than any one interpretation'.[20] His remark suggests how the familiar story of the conflict between the two Tennysons, aesthete and prophet, gives rise, at the level of text, to a question about the multivalence or otherwise of his writing. If, as he insisted, 'poetry is like shot-silk with many glancing colours', it cannot straightforwardly have a public voice, for it is not, in the usual sense of the phrase, saying something.[21] On the other hand, as 'The Palace of Art' and the many laureate poems make clear, Tennyson was determined that his verse should assume a civic role. As we will see, works such as *The Princess* and *Idylls of the King* operate a tug of war between these two imperatives, so as to be 'political poems' with the full weight of both those words. This duality, and the internal conflict which it engenders, is shadowed forth in the poem which anticipates so much of the later narrative writing: 'The Lady of Shalott'.

When Lancelot irrupts into the Lady's consciousness she is liberated and energized: such at least is the implication of the sudden burst of movement, and profusion of active verbs: 'She left the web, she left the loom, | She made three paces through the room', and so on.[22] As Tennyson remarked, 'the new-born love for something, for some one in the wide world from which she has been so long secluded, takes her out of the region of shadows into that of realities'.[23] However, this vigorous adoption of a subject position is also a 'curse', and results in the attenuation and eventual loss of her existence.[24] If, as readers have generally agreed, the lonely weaving in the first, predominantly lyric half of the poem has as its main implication the self-sufficing activity of

---

[20] *Memoir*, ii. 127.   [21] Ibid.
[22] 'The Lady of Shalott', 109–10.   [23] *Memoir*, i. 117.
[24] 'The Lady of Shalott', 116.

the artistic imagination, the second, narrative half in which the Lady floats along the river to the town of Camelot, dying on the way, suggests the process by which poetic imaginings are written down and made available to the public. 'Singing in her song she died', whereupon she becomes no longer the origin of a melody that was heard occasionally echoing in the distance, but an object to be observed with the eye, and whose name is written and can be read: '*The Lady of Shalott*'. Lancelot's judgement at Camelot that she has 'a lovely face', and the action of the crowd, who cross themselves 'for fear', are not presented with so unequivocally negative a spin as the endeavours of the sophist in 'The Poet's Mind'.[25] Nonetheless, as acts of interpretation they seem unsatisfactory, and hint to us that we should make our readings different from them by travelling, as it were, back up the river and entrancing ourselves in the poem's weave. This, the geography of the work implies, is a matter of momentarily leaving behind our social roles with all their commitments and opinions. The poem relies on the fact that its readers, when they are reading, will generally be alone, silent, imaginatively alert and comparatively abstracted from their usual duties. It asks them, therefore, to identify more with the Lady than with Lancelot. On the other hand, it also recognizes that it is destined to have its spell broken by being summed up and thought 'lovely' or otherwise as it becomes a counter in the intellectual and commercial exchanges of society at large.

As a poem, 'The Lady of Shalott' moves between the two extremes represented by Shalott and Camelot. It is not so much 'at once apart and central' as a journey from one position to the other and then perhaps back again. Its two locations are not unlike the two places which figure prominently in Garibaldi's descent on Farringford: the isolated study, where the latter-day Lancelot retired with the poet to indulge in shared aesthetic delight and private conversation, and the crowded garden where they adopted their civic roles and conducted a public ceremony. Like the visit, the poem helps us to understand the kind of relationship which much of Tennyson's writing—and indeed that of his contemporaries—has with its social and political context. *The Princess* and *Idylls of the King* are located away from their times in a mythical elsewhere. To read anything is, in some degree, to abstract one's

[25] 'The Lady of Shalott', 152, 162, 169, 166.

attention from one's immediate surroundings; but what is special about these poems is the extent to which they make readers aware that what we are doing in reading is departing from the real and inhabiting a place of the imagination. When Leavis wrote that 'nineteenth-century poetry . . . was characteristically preoccupied with the creation of a dream-world' he was right; but only in part.[26] What Tennyson's contemporaries found in that other place continually threw light back on the circumstances they were encouraged to think they had left behind them. This does not happen in any systematic way: it would be wrong to think of the works as being allegorical. One might rather say, as Tennyson did of the *Idylls*, that they have a 'parabolic drift', meaning that they are in the nature of a parable, and also that they have a tangential relation to the present, like a parabola.[27] The parabolic mode allowed him, and with variations some of his contemporaries, to produce writing that was politically relevant and yet avoided the simplicities and stridencies of direct address. In order to understand this kind of poetry, we must give full weight to both aspects of the dilemma that Tennyson felt himself to be in: he had to speak to his contemporaries, so as to be politically relevant; and he had to hold himself apart from them, so as to be a poet.

If, in Isobel Armstrong's argument, Victorian verse is all Shalott, with the proviso that Shalott is inherently political (the Lady's predicament, she suggests, is like that of workers in the recently mechanized weaving industry),[28] the other dominant understanding of the relationship between poetry and politics in the nineteenth century sees nothing but Camelot. For the critics of this school, 'every poem is a social event', which 'organizes communication oriented toward reciprocal action, and itself reacts'. The significance of a poem's 'communication' can be deduced by attention to the context of its 'point of origin'—which is sometimes the moment of composition (if that can be identified) and sometimes the date of first publication. Thus, in Jerome McGann's opinion, Keats's 'To Autumn', is a direct reaction to Peterloo: 'the poem's autumn is an historically specified fiction dialectically

---

[26] F. R. Leavis, *New Bearings in English Poetry: A Study of the Contemporary Situation* (1932; Harmondsworth: Penguin, 1972), 14.   [27] *Memoir*, ii. 127.
[28] Armstrong, *Victorian Poetry*, 84–5.

called into being by John Keats as an active response to, and alteration of, the events which marked the late summer and early fall
of a particular year in a particular place.' Being an 'active response'
it has a clear polemical significance: 'its message is that the fine arts,
and by extension imagination generally, are more humanly
productive than any of the other more practical sciences of the
artificial.' Critics who adopt this point of view have little truck
with the multiplicities of meaning which are so subtly drawn out
in Professor Armstrong's book. As Tom Paulin remarks, approvingly: 'this makes the poem look less like an urn in a national
museum and more like a pamphlet or a piece of journalism.'[29]

What we might call the poetry-as-journalism approach adopts for
literature the practice of historical contextualization pioneered by
Quentin Skinner for the history of political thought. Skinner's
methodology considers works of political theory to be analogous to
speech acts, whose meaning can be gauged only in relation to a
detailed reconstruction of the context for which they were
produced: 'any statement . . . is inescapably the embodiment of a
particular intention, on a particular occasion, addressed to the solution of a particular problem, and thus specific to its situation in a way
that it can only be naïve to try to transcend.' Works of political
theory lend themselves to this kind of analysis because they generally respond to contemporary political problems and engage in a
debate whose terms have been laid down by their predecessors. But
works of literature are not to the same degree bound in to a definable context, as Professor Skinner recognizes when he observes that
'any example of the application of this rule to a work of literature is
liable either to look very crude or to be very complicated'.[30] In the
first place, the kind of intention which poets can be thought to
embody in their writing is usually different from that which may be
extrapolated from a work of political thought. We find it quite
reasonable that a poet should declare 'I hate to be tied down to say,
"*This* means *that*" '; such an admission would, however, be fatal to
a political theorist. Correspondingly, poems do not on on the whole
address themselves to 'the solution of a particular problem'. The

---

[29] Jerome J. McGann, *The Beauty of Inflections: Literary Investigations in Historical Method
and Theory* (Oxford: Clarendon Press, 1985), 24, 19, 59, 61, 60; Tom Paulin, *Minotaur:
Poetry and the Nation-State* (Faber and Faber, 1992), 137.
[30] James Tully (ed.), *Meaning and Context: Quentin Skinner and his Critics* (Cambridge:
Polity Press, 1988), 65, 77.

stimuli to which they are responses and the questions upon which they bear are usually various and not easily definable. What are the issues confronted by 'The Lady of Shalott', or for that matter 'My Last Duchess'? Certainly they are more wide-ranging than those tackled by, say, Hobbes in his chapter 'Of the RIGHTS of Soveraignes by Institution'.[31]

Admittedly, some pieces of writing which we are accustomed to call 'poems' do not differ very greatly from journalism. Tennyson's lines entitled 'The Third of February, 1852'— published four days later in the *Examiner*—are a versified argument against a House of Lords' decision rejecting a Bill for the organization of a militia to defend Britain against a supposed threat from France:

> We love not this French God, the child of Hell,
> Wild War, who breaks the converse of the wise;[32]

—it proclaims. This work does have a particular intention which is specific to its occasion. For that very reason, it announces itself as possessing a particular generic character as just one of the many distinguishable kinds of writing covered by the word 'poetry': it is an 'occasional poem', or a 'polemical poem'. A text's genre determines how it should be taken by a reader: as comedy or journalism or a piece of abstract logical reasoning or a lyric; in recognizing how it should be taken, we make a judgement about how it relates to its context, and what that context is. 'The Lady of Shalott' is of a different genre from 'The Third of February, 1852', and asks to be read according to other expectations: its symbolic mode and its rhetorical distance from the immediate circumstances of its composition let readers know that it is not likely to be making a direct response to contemporary political developments; rather, it has to do with longer-running questions about subjectivity, gender, interpretation, and so on, as its extensive critical history makes clear.[33] The poetry-as-journalism approach assumes that, whatever a poem's genre, its defining

---

[31] Thomas Hobbes, *Leviathan* (1651), ed. Richard Tuck (Cambridge: Cambridge University Press, 1991), 121.

[32] 'The Third of February, 1852', 7–8.

[33] See Edgar F. Shannon, 'Poetry as Vision: Sight and Insight in "The Lady of Shalott" ', *Victorian Poetry*, 19 (1981), 207–8; Kirk H. Beetz, *Tennyson: A Bibliography, 1827–1982* (Scarecrow, 1984).

context is always provided by its immediate historical surroundings. On this view, if only you look closely enough, all poems are
like 'The Third of February, 1852'.

Certainly there may be illumination to be gained from recon-
structing the historical circumstances of any piece of writing,
perhaps even (very occasionally) a mathematical equation.
However, the degree of illumination will vary according to the
contextual requirements of the work's genre. 'The Lady of
Shalott' was written at a time of rural agitation: in consequence,
its peaceful vision of 'reapers, reaping early | In among the
bearded barley' may well have given Tennyson a specially calmative pleasure of the sort Keats is supposed to have found in
composing 'To Autumn' soon after Peterloo.[34] The poem cannot
therefore satisfactorily be described as an 'active response' to this
circumstance with a 'message' to deliver. The rural connection is
one element in the work's multifarious and uncertain range of
concern.

The poems which I will be discussing characteristically maintain
a generic distance from their immediate historical surroundings.
Yet they did not thereby turn their back on politics, for by
abstracting themselves from the present, so as to open up a longer
timescale for the imagination, they brought themselves into proximity with perhaps the most momentous political concept in the
nineteenth century: 'nation'. As Edmund Burke had explained: 'a
nation is not an idea only of local extent, and individual momentary aggregation; but it is an idea of continuity, which extends in
time as well as in numbers and in space'.[35] In the mid-nineteenth
century, 'poetry', like 'nation', was strongly felt to be an 'idea of
continuity'. Benedict Anderson has written perceptively of the
importance of language in creating a sense of national community
subsisting through time:

No one can give a date for the birth of any language. Each looms up
imperceptibly out of a horizonless past . . . If English-speakers hear the
words 'Earth to Earth, ashes to ashes, dust to dust'—created almost four-
and-a-half centuries ago—they get a ghostly intimation of simultaneity

---

[34] Robert Bernard Martin, *Tennyson: The Unquiet Heart* (Oxford: Clarendon Press,
1983), 125; 'The Lady of Shalott', 28–9.
[35] Quoted in Raymond Williams, *Culture and Society: Coleridge to Orwell* (1958; Hogarth
Press, 1993), 11.

across homogeneous, empty time. The weight of the words derives only
in part from their solemn meaning; it comes also from an as-it-were
ancestral 'Englishness'.[36]

As Anderson's choice of quotation implies, nationhood is fostered,
not only by continuity of language, but by the persistence in a
culture of particular usages of that language. An extract from a
sixteenth-century broadside pamphlet would not carry quite the
same weight as those very familiar words from the Book of
Common Prayer.

The lifetime of canonical poetry in Western culture is not
dissimilar to that of liturgy. In consequence, when, in the late
eighteenth and early nineteenth centuries, the idea of nationhood
began to command the thoughts of intellectuals and the hopes of
revolutionaries, poets were ascribed a central role. In his very
influential lectures *On Heroes and Hero-Worship* (1840), Carlyle
declared: 'poor Italy lies dismembered, scattered asunder, not
appearing in any protocol or treaty as a unity at all; yet the noble
Italy is actually *one*: Italy produced its Dante; Italy can speak!'[37] A
fantastical claim, one might think. However, more recent theorists
have attributed to creative writers a no less significant part in the
construction of nationhood—although they have generally
eschewed the idealist terminology adopted by Carlyle. 'Who,
more than poets, musicians, painters and sculptors, could bring the
national ideal to life and disseminate it among the people?'—asks
Anthony D. Smith:[38] not only living poets, he might have added,
but dead ones also, and perhaps more effectively. Generations of
Italian schoolchildren who have been under the happy obligation
of reading through the *Divine Comedy* one canto per week at
school would testify to the persistence of such ideas in contemporary practice.

Mid-nineteenth-century English poets were excited by the new
conception of poetry's nation-building power. If the realms of
verse were also the dwelling-places of a national spirit, the
commitment to generic abstraction and the desire for political

[36] Benedict Anderson, *Imagined Communities: Reflections on the Origin and Spread of
Nationalism*, 2nd edn. (Verso, 1991), 144–5.
[37] Thomas Carlyle, *On Heroes, Hero-Worship and the Heroic in History* (1840; Chapman
and Hall, 1897), 114.
[38] Anthony D. Smith, *National Identity* (Harmondsworth: Penguin, 1991), 92.

influence might be reconciled. In order to understand what poets made of this possibility, we must precisely not limit ourselves to asking how their work may have reacted to and altered 'the events which marked . . . a particular year in a particular place'. Poets were attracted by the thought of creating comparatively general and enduring myths or archetypal narratives which, while having relevance to contemporary affairs, might also throw light on many other, past and future events—in the way that, to give a small example, Tennyson found the 1859 *Idylls* to be apposite to Garibaldi in 1864. It is not so much that the book would have taken on a different implication in that particular context, as that the book is offered as being itself a context, in relation to which Garibaldi and many other people can be understood and judged: the *Idylls* present themselves as occupying 'homogeneous, empty time', the time of 'Englishness'. Equally, however, poets were—to differing degrees—suspicious of the potential for coercion in such writing, and uncertain about the large claims for national unity made by propagandists such as Mazzini. Browning gained critical purchase on the ideas of 'as-it-were ancestral' nationhood and of poetry's role in its evocation, by setting his verse in a different else-where: Italy. Even Tennyson was creatively aware of the large element of make-believe in the myths which he nonetheless continued to produce. The challenge for a historically sensitive criticism is to trace the filaments by which these works are linked to contemporary political matters, while not flattening their enquiring and expansive textures into the blankness of a 'message'—as it were, to lay bare the roots of Tennyson's Wellingtonia, without killing the tree.

2

POETS AND NATIONS

COMMON SYMPATHIES

Many mid-nineteenth-century writers would have agreed with George Eliot's view that 'the greatest benefit we owe to the artist, whether painter, poet, or novelist, is the extension of our sympathies'.[1] Opinions of this kind go back at least to Wordsworth's 1800 'Preface', but they took on fresh urgency after 1829, when, in his famous essay 'Signs of the Times', Carlyle proclaimed that human relations based on sympathy were being destroyed by the 'Age of Machinery'.[2] Introducing his new magazine, *Household Words* (1850), Dickens wrote of his desire 'to bring the greater and the lesser in degree together' on the 'wide ground' of imagination.[3] In the aftermath of Carlyle's essay, even Tennyson had received a letter from an undergraduate friend J. W. Blakesley which urged him to put his writing at the service of the community so as to combat 'the selfish spirit which pervades the whole frame of society at present' by implanting 'another principle with which selfishness cannot co-exist'.[4] Tennyson's immediate reaction to this proposal may perhaps be indicated by the tradition in the Blakesley family that their forebear was the original of the 'dark-browed sophist' in 'The Poet's Mind';[5] nonetheless, such notions exerted a compelling influence on his writing and that of his contemporaries.

Like Eliot and Dickens, Tennyson sought—with varying

---

[1] George Eliot, 'The Natural History of German Life' (1856), *George Eliot: Selected Critical Writings*, ed. Rosemary Ashton (Oxford: Oxford University Press, 1992), 263.

[2] Thomas Carlyle, *Critical and Miscellaneous Essays*, 5 vols. (Chapman and Hall, 1899), ii. 59.

[3] Charles Dickens, *The Nonesuch Dickens: Collected Papers*, ed. Arthur Waugh *et al.*, 2 vols., (Nonesuch Press, 1937), i. 223.   [4] *Memoir*, i. 69.

[5] *Poems of Tennyson*, ed. Ricks, i. 246.

degrees of directness and felicity—to nurture the growth, within the boundaries of the United Kingdom of Britain and Ireland, of shared sympathies. That is to say, he quite consciously fostered the development of 'nationhood' or 'nationality'; terms which had shifted definition radically over the previous hundred years. What they had come to signify by the mid-nineteenth century was explained with characteristic clarity by J. S. Mill:

A PORTION of mankind may be said to constitute a Nationality, if they are united amongst themselves by common sympathies, which do not exist between them and any others—which make them co-operate with each other more willingly than with other people, desire to be under the same government, and desire that it should be government by themselves, or a portion of themselves exclusively.

The definition echoes Eliot's 'extension of our sympathies', although Mill does not mention novels in his account of factors contributing to the development of a nationality:

This feeling of nationality may have been generated by various causes. Sometimes it is the effect of identity of race and descent. Community of language, and community of religion, greatly contribute to it. Geographical limits are one of its causes. But the strongest of all is identity of political antecedents; the possession of a national history, and consequent community of recollections; collective pride and humiliation, pleasure and regret, connected with the same incidents in the past. None of these circumstances however are either indispensable, or necessarily sufficient by themselves.[6]

As a definition, this paragraph is far from satisfactory, for Mill's 'causes' are not kept separate from the 'feeling' which they are meant to generate: 'community of recollections' might better be said to be a constituent of 'common sympathies' than a cause of them, while the suggestion that 'the possession of a national history' contributes to the feeling of nationality is circular. However, these uncertainties are due, not so much to any failing of Mill's, as to an intrinsic haziness in the modern idea of nationhood which, in the last two centuries, has required the presence of both what are now generally called 'subjective' and 'objective' factors (roughly, Mill's 'feeling' and 'causes' respectively). A putative movement for the

---

[6] John Stuart Mill, *Considerations on Representative Government* (1861), *On Liberty and Other Essays*, ed. John Gray (Oxford: Oxford University Press, 1991), 427.

national independence of Essex would not carry much conviction because Essex lacks many of Mill's 'causes'. On the other hand, a region such as Catalonia is possessed of most of Mill's 'causes' (more, certainly, than Switzerland), yet most Catalans do not for the time being think of themselves as members of a Catalan nation which has a right to independence—although one day their views may change.

Objective factors such as geographical unity or a common language were therefore not sufficient. It was necessary for nationals to recognize their nationhood; and that is the reason why nineteenth-century nationalism ascribed so important a role to imaginative writers. Such recognition was itself the fundamental component of nationality: it was, in both senses of the word, a 'realization' of it. At a time when much of the population of Europe was illiterate, national self-awareness among the people at large could be no more than an ideal. Nonetheless, the feeling that bourgeois intellectuals had when they read, say, *Middlemarch*, that they were being brought into contact with different sections of society and taught to understand and relate to them, was, it could seem, generalizable. As literacy spread, and readership grew, people would find reflected in their national literatures images of themselves as, precisely, nationals.[7] What Coleridge had so influentially defined as being the tendency of imagination 'to unify' took on an importantly social aspect.[8] Implicitly, for Eliot and Dickens, the mirror of art has become concave: it draws people together.

There is more to be said about the detail of nineteenth-century ideas of nationhood; but, for the moment, consider how different is Mill's definition from the account of the fundamental unit of political sovereignty in John of Gaunt's famous speech in *The life and death of Richard the second*:

> This royall Throne of Kings, this sceptred Isle,
> This earth of Maiesty, this seate of Mars,
> This other Eden, demy Paradise,

[7] On the growth of literacy in Britain, see Raymond Williams, *The Long Revolution* (Harmondsworth: Penguin, 1965), 177–94.

[8] Samuel Taylor Coleridge, *Biographia Literaria: Or Biographical Sketches of My Literary Life and Opinions*, 2 vols., ed. James Engell and W. Jackson Bate (Princeton: Princeton University Press, 1984,) i. 304.

> This Fortresse built by Nature for her selfe,
> Against infection and the hand of warre,
> This happy breed of men, this little world,
> This precious stone set in the siluer sea,
> Which serues it in the office of a wall,
> Or as a Moat defensiue to a house,
> Against the envie of lesse happier Lands.
> This blessed plot, this earth, this Realme, this England,
> This nurse, this teeming wombe of Royal Kings,
> Fear'd by their breed, and famous for their birth,
> Renowned for theyr deedes as farre from home,
> For Christian seruice, and true Chiualrie
> As is the sepulcher in stubburne *Iury*
> Of the Worlds ransome blessed *Maries* Sonne.
> This Land of such deere soules, this deere-deere Land,
> Deere for her reputation through the world,
> Is now Leas'd out (I dye pronouncing it)
> Like to a Tenement or pelting Farme.[9]

England, here, is imagined primarily as a place: a 'throne', an 'isle', an 'Eden', a 'fortress', and so on. Thoughts of the country as a residence ('seate') and as a garden lead into its personification as 'nurse', and then as mother, or rather womb, the origin of the passage's second dominant patriotic image, the 'Royal Kings'. These chivalrous monarchs bring in a third idea, that of England as defender of the Faith, as important a bastion of Christianity as the sepulchre of Christ. The speech identifies three focal points of loyalty: monarch, land, and Church. There is no hint of 'common sympathies', and no suggestion of any difference between England, Scotland, and Wales; indeed, the only mention of the people at large, 'This happy breed of men', is quickly elided into the 'Royall Kings, | Fear'd by their breed', which makes it seem as though the island is inhabited only by monarchs. There is nothing about language, and no mention of history as such, for the renowned deeds and the reputation which results from them appear in a continuous present. By the mid-nineteenth century, all the motives of Gaunt's eloquence have dwindled to three items in Mill's list of 'causes': 'geographical limits', 'religion', and 'pride'.

---

[9] William Shakespeare, *The life and death of Richard the second*, II. i: *Shakespeare's Comedies, Histories, & Tragedies: Being a Reproduction of the First Folio Edition, 1623* (Oxford: Clarendon Press, 1902), 350.

Gaunt's words express the vision of a particular, aristocratic character at a moment of special strain. Nevertheless, the three focuses of his patriotism—land, monarch, and religion—were recurrent and central in descriptions of English identity during Shakespeare's lifetime, and for at least the following two hundred years.[10] After 1688 they were frequently joined by 'liberty', as for example in Pope's presentation of Windsor Forest as, not only the 'Seat' of monarchy but the place where 'Fair *Liberty, Britannia's* Goddess, rears | Her chearful Head, and leads the golden Years'.[11] During the eighteenth century, under the pressure of war, consciousness of, and adherence to, these patriotic values grew.[12] However, it was not until sometime after the French Revolution that the shift of understanding which so radically separates Mill's conception of political identity from Shakespeare's can truly be said to have occurred. Before then, the word 'nation' had generally been used to signify something like what we today would mean by 'ethnic group'.[13] Take, for instance, the exchange between a Welshman, Fluellen, and an Irishman, MacMorris in *The Life of King Henry the Fift*:

Welch. Captaine *Mackmorrice*, I thinke, looke you, vnder your correction, there is not many of your Nation.

Irish. Of my Nation? What ish my Nation? Ish a Villaine and a Basterd and a Knaue and a Rascall? What ish my Nation? Who talks of my Nation?[14]

As the defensiveness of Mackmorrice's reply suggests, taunts based on putative national characteristics were already well established. However, this is a long way from the view, widely accepted by the mid-nineteenth century, that it is the right, even destiny, of a nation to achieve political independence. Fluellen's Welshness and Mackmorrice's Irishness do not preclude them from being loyal to their English King. Shakespeare may well have been presenting a

---

[10] Richard Helgerson, *Forms of Nationhood: The Elizabethan Writing of England* (Chicago: University of Chicago Press, 1992), 132; Linda Colley, *Britons: Forging the Nation, 1707–1837* (New Haven: Yale University Press, 1992), 17–18, 212.

[11] Alexander Pope, *Windsor-Forest*, 91–2. Quoted from *The Poems of Alexander Pope*, ed. John Butt (Methuen, 1963). [12] Colley, *Britons*, 364–75.

[13] Aira Kemilainen, *Nationalism: Problems Concerning the Word, the Concept and Classification* (Jyväskylä: Studia Historica Jyväskyläentia 3, 1964), 13–15.

[14] *The Life of King Henry the Fift*, III. ii: *Shakespeare's Comedies, Histories, & Tragedies*, 432.

rosy picture of multi-ethnic harmony under Henry's rule;[15] but it remains true that in his time, as throughout the age of what came to be known as the *ancien regime*, political legitimacy was not thought of as being rooted in nationhood. Rulers' titles to their possessions were determined by conquest and inheritance.[16] Even where these principles were tempered, as at the Glorious Revolution, the deciding factor was religion, not nationality. Subjects owed fealty, not to any national will, but to their lords.

In many respects, the political community known as Britain in the Renaissance and the eighteenth century was continuous with the Britain of the Victorians. From one angle Hugh Seton-Watson is clearly right to say that 'the doctrine of nationalism dates from the age of the French Revolution, but nations existed before the doctrine was formulated'.[17] Yet such a statement needs qualifying because part of the meaning of the word nation in the nineteenth century (as Mill's definition makes clear) was for nationals to be aware of themselves as constituents of a nation, and to share something of what Seton-Watson calls 'the doctrine'—roughly, the view that nationality should coincide with statehood. It is not enough to note, as John Armstrong does of the entities he christens 'nations before nationalism', that 'of course, they were not expressed in the terms of nineteenth-century nationalism',[18] for the terms in which a nation is 'expressed', what people think of it as being, the claims they think of it as making, are a large part of what it 'is'. As Benedict Anderson has so fruitfully demonstrated, nations are above all imagined communities; and what they were imagined as being, and therefore into being, in the nineteenth century was new. For the generation of Tennyson and Browning part of the meaning of 'nation' was still what Shakespeare's Mac Morris had meant by the word; but in addition it had taken on all the claims to political coercion which, for Shakespeare's Gaunt, were the property of the 'Realme'.

When Dickens selected the title *Household Words*, he chose to

[15] See Stephen Greenblatt, *Shakespearean Negotiations: The Circulation of Social Energy in Renaissance England* (Oxford: Clarendon Press, 1988), 56–7.

[16] Anderson, *Imagined Communities*, 19.

[17] Hugh Seton-Watson, *Nations and States: An Enquiry into the Origins of Nations and the Politics of Nationalism* (Methuen, 1977), 6.

[18] John A. Armstrong, *Nations Before Nationalism* (Chapel Hill, NC: University of North Carolina Press, 1982), 10.

echo Shakespeare. By doing so he created a small instance of community of sympathy analogous to that which he hoped to promote with the magazine, although community through time rather than between classes. The allusion also marks out a contrast between two distinct conceptions of shared social identity. The phrase 'household words' was first written to be spoken by Henry V on the eve of Agincourt, when he predicts that each soldier, looking back, will feel that he has been brought together with others on the wide field, not of imagination, but of battle:

> . . . Then shall our Names,
> Familiar in his mouth as household words,
> *Harry* the King, *Bedford* and *Exeter*,
> *Warwick* and *Talbot*, *Salisbury* and *Gloucester*,
> Be in their flowing Cups freshly remembered.[19]

This vision of a 'community of recollections' might certainly be called proto-nationalist. However, it is no more than that, for it happily separates the 'greater and lesser in degree'. When, a few lines further on, Henry proclaims that 'he to day that sheds his blood with me, | Shall be my brother', the fraternity he has in mind is not national but aristocratic: 'be he ne're so vile, | This day shall gentle his Condition'.[20] In the world Henry imagines, the people—whatever their ethnicity—identify with their local aristocrats, who in turn are loyal to the King. This is a different principle of community from the imaginative acquaintance and mutual understanding which Dickens proposed to foster with his *Household Words*.

During the nineteenth century, the doctrine of nationhood—in this new sense—spread throughout Europe and beyond. It held that the borders of the 'nation', a group of people supposedly united by common sympathies and capable of sustaining political independence, should coincide with those of the State. Mazzini, the loudest advocate of 'the principle of nationality' gave the new conception a sharply democratic twist when he declared in the early 1830s: 'the nation is the universality of the citizens speaking the same tongue, and associated in equality of civil and political

---

[19] *The Life of King Henry the Fift*, IV. iii: *Shakespeare's Comedies, Histories & Tragedies*, 441.
[20] Ibid.

rights, in the pursuit of a common aim—the progressive development, improvement, and free exercise of all the social forces.'[21]
However, its presence can no less clearly be discerned in a poem
by Tennyson written at about the same time. 'Love thou thy land'
starts out in the vicinity of Gaunt's vocabulary of patriotism ('land'
belonging with 'plot' and 'Realme') but it soon moves on to
another concern:

> Love, that endures not sordid ends,
> For English natures, freemen, friends,
> Thy brothers and immortal souls.[22]

That nationality was a kind of fraternity, uniting people forever
('immortal') in common love; that it deserved independence
('freemen'); and that a poet's business might be to promote such
views and feelings: all this would have been strange to Pope and
Shakespeare. Tennyson was of course no democrat, as the rest of
the poem shows; but it is only therefore the more significant
that, here, he elides social difference in a vision of shared sympathies. The lines say that be they dukes or paupers all the English
are in spirit, and should recognize themselves to be, 'friends' and
'brothers' simply by virtue of their nationality. This, in the full
nineteenth-century significance of the term, is a nationalist
vision.

Tennyson, the Brownings, and Clough did not blindly propa-
gate such visions. A commitment to the 'extension of our sympathies', though in many ways it harmonizes with nationalism, must
also in the end come into conflict with it, for the idea of distinct
national identities entails, not only that the requisite sympathies
should be shared by the members of a group, but that they should
be limited to that group alone. This contrariety was brought home
to mid-nineteenth-century writers by the fact that they lived, not
in a nation-state, but in a multinational empire: the United
Kingdom of Great Britain and Ireland. The awkwardness of this
amalgam became apparent as they observed, and occasionally in a
small way participated in, the nationalist movements on the continent: above all, the Italian Risorgimento.

---

[21] Mazzini, *Life and Writings*, i. 167.
[22] Tennyson, 'Love thou thy land, with love far-brought', 6–8.

BRITAIN AND EUROPE

As they watched the progress of nationalist movements on the continent, one thing British people thought they were observing was the legacy of the French Revolution. It was the Declaration of the Rights of Man and of the Citizen (1789) which had first proclaimed 'the Nation is essentially the source of all sovereignty'. At that early stage, defining the limits of 'the Nation' had not seemed problematic. As John Breuilly observes, 'this idea of the nation did not refer to a special group of people with a common cultural identity': it simply meant citizens of the French State.[23] Since the French revolutionaries were taking over a pre-existing political unit, there was at first no reason to worry about who should count as French: the citizens of the new state were those who had been subjects of the old. However, for a liberal in (say) Milan after the restoration, the question of what might be the boundaries of any future republic was a pressing one. Italy was divided between numerous different absolutist States: Sicily and the south formed the Kingdom of the Two Sicilies; the Pope exerted autocratic control over Rome and large tracts of central Italy; then there was the Kingdom of Sardinia, which included Piedmont; the Grand Duchy of Tuscany; the Dukedoms of Parma and Modena; while Lombardy and Venice were ruled from Vienna. The Milanese were, therefore, subjects of the Austrian Empire; but for cultural, linguistic, and logistical reasons, overthrow of that regime throughout its dominions would not have seemed practicable. A State of Lombardy, then? It was a possibility; but many revolutionaries, among them Mazzini, held out for that emotive word which had been placed by Dante and Petrarch, and more recently Alfieri and Foscolo, at the centre of a high literary tradition: 'Italia'.[24] One reason why nationalism spread so quickly in the early nineteenth century was that it offered a workable solution to a fundamental problem: if governments were to be democratic, quite whom should any one of them represent?

Conservative opinions about European nationalism were haunted by memories of 1789 and the ensuing decades of war. For

---

[23] John Breuilly, *Nationalism and the State* (Manchester: Manchester University Press, 1982; repr. with amendments, 1985), 60.

[24] Stuart Woolf, *A History of Italy 1700–1860: The Social Constraints of Political Change* (Methuen, 1979), 248–55, 303–16.

Tories, the great bulwark against the return of such disasters was
the Vienna settlement of 1815, which had restored the *ancien regime*
monarchs and re-established the old system of hereditary right: as
the *Quarterly Review* declared (optimistically) in 1848, it seemed to
ground the existing governments and their territories in 'those
international laws which never can be violated with impunity, and
which even tyrants are obliged to respect'.[25] By contrast, 'the principle of nationality' was in the Tory view (as Matthew Arnold
reported) 'chimerical'.[26] The slightest compromise with its
demands, such as the secession of Belgium from Holland in 1830,
threatened a resurgence of chaos. In the aftermath of the 1830
uprisings, the *Foreign Quarterly Review* warned its readers 'that there
is in the Romagna, as well as in other Italian States, and indeed in
most countries of Europe, a set of men . . . who defile the fair
name of liberty by using it as a watchword for the foulest passions,
who aim at the destruction, not only of all monarchies, but of
society itself as at present constituted over Europe'.[27] For conservatives, nationalism was the monstrous twin of socialism, yoked
with it in opposition to political and moral law.

Democratic radicals typically celebrated European nationalism
for the same reasons that motivated Tory condemnation. In their
view, nations were 'the natural organization of Humanity', as
opposed to 'the arbitrary divisions of kings'.[28] Whigs, however,
took an altogether different line. They tended to associate
European nationalism not with revolutionary democracy, but with
British-style constitutional freedom. In 1832, the *Edinburgh Review*
found in the success of Belgian independence a reason for advo-
cating the national unifications of Poland and Italy:

---

[25] (Edward Cheney), 'Whiteside on Italy', *Quarterly Review*, 83/166 (Sept. 1848), 569.
See *The Wellesley Index to Victorian Periodicals*, ed. Walter .E. Houghton and Jean H.
Slingersland, new edn., CD-ROM (Routledge, 1999) for the political complexion of the
Quarterly and other periodicals.

[26] Matthew Arnold, *England and the Italian Question* (1859), *The Complete Prose Works of
Matthew Arnold*, iii: *Lectures and Essays in Criticism*, ed. R. H. Super (Ann Arbor: University
of Michigan Press, 1962), 65.

[27] (André Vieusseux), 'Modern Rome and the Papal Government', *Foreign Quarterly
Review*, 11/21 (Jan. 1833), 71.

[28] (W. J. Linton), 'The Liberty of Rome', *Westminster and Foreign Quarterly Review*,
53/104 (Apr. 1850), 83; see also Eugenio F. Biagini, *Liberty, Retrenchment and Reform:
Popular Liberalism in the Age of Gladstone, 1860–1880* (Cambridge: Cambridge University
Press, 1992), 42–50.

A political existence implies a body politic . . . Vitality can be breathed into it only by a community of interests and of feelings. Before it can live and move and have its being, there must be formed in it the life-blood of public opinion, to circulate through the parts, connect them as a whole, and inspire them with one common character and principle of action. Where one or other of these preliminary facts is wanting, as in the case of . . . unamalgamating races, like the inhabitants of Holland and of Belgium, it passes the power . . . of all diplomacy . . . to create a real political life.

Both Italy and Poland, on the other hand, retained the necessary 'spirit and love of country' despite both having undergone partition.[29] For Whigs—and, later, moderate liberals—the principle of nationality was neither 'chimerical' nor simply 'natural', but was rather a version of the body politic, and belonged in a tradition which went back through Coleridge and Burke at least to Hooker in the sixteenth century. The *Edinburgh* saw the Belgian uprising as an echo of 1688, not 1789; a vindication of communal political life against the unnatural requirements of arbitrary power.

As a generalization, during the 1830s and the early 1840s the kinds of opinion which were put forward by the *Quarterly* and the *Foreign Quarterly* predominated among the governing classes in Britain. Although it was known that there were also moderate variants of nationalism on the continent, these appear to have been outweighed by the spectre of Mazzinian revolution. In the 1850s, however, it seems that arguments like the one advanced by the *Edinburgh* began to gather more support. English observers were impressed by the strength of Italian resistance during the revolutions of 1848–9. In 1851, the *Edinburgh* expressed its 'satisfaction' at the 'honourable valour' of the Italians, and opined that 'the time is come, we admit, for present endurance; but also, we believe, for future hope'.[30] In the same year, Gladstone's *Two Letters to the Earl of Aberdeen on the State Prosecutions of the Neapolitan Government* made evident the cruelty of the regime of 'King Bomba' in the south of Italy; and soon afterwards Cavour became prime minister of Piedmont, focusing the Risorgimento around a real constitutional monarchy instead of Mazzini's democratic ideal: Cavour

[29] (William Empson), 'Political Condition of the Italian States', *Edinburgh Review*, 55/110 (July 1832), 363–4.

[30] (Henry Lushington), 'The Defeat of Italy', *Edinburgh Review*, 93/190 (Apr. 1851), 528, 531.

'scarcely ever made a speech or wrote a paper . . . in which he does not show that he was thoroughly imbued with the spirit of the English constitution', as the *Quarterly* was later to observe.[31] By 1859, even the *Quarterly* printed (under the usual veil of anonymity) an article by Gladstone which argued that 'the conduct of Austria towards Italy at large has involved a glaring and systematic contempt of liberty and of public right'.[32]

In the 1860s, the appropriation of nationalist ideologies by established governments continued, following the example of Bismarck, whom the *Quarterly* approvingly differentiated from Mazzini: 'nobody ever took Prussia for a realm of ideology, nor Count Bismarck for a dreamer of dreams or seer of visions. What he sees and handles is men and things in the concrete; he is no devotee of "Geist," no professorial apostle of "the Idea".'[33] For liberals, however, this latest development in the proclivities of nationalism was to be deplored. As George Gissing reflected on his travels by the Ionian Sea in 1900: 'how can one greatly wish for the consolidation and prosperity of Italy, knowing that national vigour tends more and more to international fear and hatred.'[34]

Because of the long evolution of continental nationalism, and the variety of positions which British observers adopted towards it, the term 'nationalism' itself gathered a range of contrasting implications. At one end of the scale was what the word generally means for historians of the period today: 'devotion to one's nation; national aspiration; a policy of national independence', a sense which the *OED* first records in 1844. In this usage, the word sits happily alongside liberty, equality, fraternity. At the other extreme is what might now be defined as 'narrow nationalism', as for instance when Mazzini wrote in 1834 of 'that spirit of nationalism (I do not say of nationality, a thing sacred with us all) . . . which retards the progress of our intellectual life by isolating it from the

---

[31] (A. H. Layard) 'Cavour', *Quarterly Review*, 110/219 (July 1861), 216.

[32] (W. E. Gladstone), 'Foreign Affairs—War in Italy', *Quarterly Review*, 105/209 (Apr. 1859), 544.

[33] (John Wilson), 'Count Bismarck, Prussia, and Pan-Teutonism', *Quarterly Review*, 130/259 (Jan. 1871), 87.

[34] George Gissing, *By the Ionian Sea: Notes of a Ramble in Southern Italy* (Chapman and Hall, 1901), 151.

universal life'.[35] This is what Gissing would have meant by the word, and also what Denis Mack Smith must have had in mind when he made the otherwise surprising remark that 'Mazzini . . . condemned nationalism as absolutely wrong'.[36] The two opposing connotations imply different optics. In the first case, 'nationalism' is seen as it were from inside: it brings people together, extends sympathies, creates community. From the second, exterior angle of view it holds people apart, creates prejudice, and initiates conflict.

As they pondered the evolving situation in Europe, British observers gauged the implications which events there might have for the multinational State in which they themselves lived. Lord Acton responded to the Italian Risorgimento by grouping the United Kingdom with the Austrian Empire. Explicitly attacking the Risorgimento, and implicitly defending the union of England with Ireland, Scotland, and Wales, he presented national identity as a prejudice, and argued that true political liberty was possible only in a State which included several different nationalities and thereby obliged them to overcome their ethnic predilections in debate.[37] A more influential calibration was originated by Matthew Arnold in his pamphlet *England and the Italian Question* (1859). Like Acton, he had one eye on the United Kingdom when he observed that 'the principle of nationality, if acted upon too early, or if pushed too far, would prevent that natural and beneficial union of conterminous or neighbouring territories into one great state, upon which the grandeur of nations and the progress of civilisation depends'. In consequence, he proposed a mitigated nationalism which formalizes the two contrasting implications mentioned above. In Arnold's view, which was later adopted by J. S. Mill, only 'great' nationalities whose unification would contribute to 'the progress of civilization' should be allowed to achieve independence. The nationalism of 'small' nationalities was

---

[35] Mazzini, *Life and Writings*, iv. 68. This usage dates from 1843: Eric Hobsbawm is therefore mistaken when he writes that 'the term "nationalism" was actually invented in the last decade(s) of the nineteenth century' in order to express 'a sharp shift to the political right of nation and flag', *Nations and Nationalism since 1780: Programme, Myth, Reality*, 2nd edn. (Cambridge: Cambridge University Press, 1992), 102.

[36] Smith, *Mazzini*, 12.

[37] John Emerich Edward Dalberg Acton, First Baron Acton, 'Nationality' (1862), in *Essays on Freedom and Power* (1956), 166, 168.

atavistic and should be opposed. Small nations should be encouraged to 'merge' with their greater neighbours.[38]

For Arnold, Mill, Tennyson, and many others, the United Kingdom of Great Britain and Ireland was a single great nationality in the process of formation. It was like Italy. Indeed, in the end, even the Empire might somehow be brought into the amalgam, so as to form, in Tennyson's words, an 'ever-broadening England'.[39] From this point of view, it was quite easy to reconcile support for the Risorgimento with hostility to Irish nationalism, for Ireland had no more of a claim to independence than Sicily. Yet, as Mill recognized, British treatment of Ireland was hardly conducive to 'natural and beneficial union'. In the parliamentary debate of 1844 on the motion that 'Ireland is occupied, and not governed', the Irish liberal MP Thomas Wise adduced a different analogy from Europe, comparing Britain's treatment of Ireland with the 'policy . . . of Russia, in regard to Poland. It pretends to nothing but annihilation . . . to obliterate nationality itself'.[40]

NATURAL AND BENEFICIAL UNION?

As Arnold was aware, there can be no rules for distinguishing between 'great' and 'small' nationalities. Deciding whether Ireland was analogous to Belgium or to Sicily was a matter of gauging the pragmatic weight of a whole range of different factors—a process which, evidently, left a good deal of room for the operations of prejudice. There is a similar problem with differentiating Arnold's 'natural and beneficial union' from Wise's 'annihilation'. Some kind of *rapprochement* between distinct nations gathered into a single State may often be a humane and reasonable thing to hope for (it is, after all, arguably, the aim of the European Union); but the obliteration of one nationality by another is not. Since the matter at issue is so personal and nebulous as cultural identity, it is, in the general terms of public rhetoric or political theory, impossible to draw a line between the two. One Scot may view the cultural and economic dominance of England as an opportunity, another as a threat. In the present intellectual climate, few would

---

[38] Arnold, *England and the Italian Question*, 71; Mill, *On Liberty and Other Essays*, 431.
[39] Tennyson, 'To the Queen [Idylls of the King]', 30.
[40] *Hansard's Parliamentary Debates*, 3rd series, vol. 72 (1844), col. 730.

make the mistake of simply eliding cultural imperialism with 'the progress of civilization' in the manner of Arnold. However, it is equally possible to sentimentalize the 'different' and the 'local'. Mid-nineteenth-century poets were alive to this difficulty: their imaginative representations of people living on the faultline between two nations, or between the regional and the national, can help us to grasp the significance, for particular people, of the abstract distinction between 'union' and 'annihilation'.

In the spring of 1848, Arthur Hugh Clough visited revolutionary Paris. Soon after his return he began a poem in which he imagines how French-style aspirations towards democratic national unity might take shape within the British Isles. *The Bothie of Tober-na-Vuolich* narrates the successful courtship of an English undergraduate and a Scottish crofter's daughter, treating it as a typical instance of the relationship between their two classes and ethnic groups. Here, Elspie, the Scottish woman, is speaking to her betrothed:

No, nor do *I*, dear Philip, I don't myself feel always,
As I have felt, more sorrow for me, these four days lately,
Like the Peruvian Indians I read about last winter,
Out in America there, in somebody's life of Pizarro;
Who were as good perhaps as the Spaniards; only weaker;
And that the one big tree might spread its root and branches,
All the lesser about it must even be felled and perish.
No, I feel much more as if I, as well as you, were,
Somewhere, a leaf on the one great tree, that, up from old time
Growing, contains in itself the whole of the virtue and life of
Bygone days, drawing now to itself all kindreds and nations,
And must have for itself the whole world for its root and branches.
No, I belong to the tree, I shall not decay in the shadow;
Yes, and I feel the life-juices of all the world and the ages
Coming to me as to you, more slowly no doubt and poorer;
You are more near, but then you will help to convey them to me.[41]

Some readers might discover in this representation of Elspie's love for an English academic, and for the cultural forces to which he exposes her, nothing more than an act of ventriloquism, a glaring instance of what has been called 'the cultural imperialism that

---

[41] *B* VIII. 82–97. Clough's poems are quoted from *The Poems of Arthur Hugh Clough*, 2nd edn., ed. F. L. Mulhauser (Oxford: Clarendon Press, 1974).

underlies most of the British Romantic and Victorian writers'.[42]
Such a view might be contested by an appeal to historical evidence
which shows that many Scots in the period were eager to assimi-
late themselves to English culture[43] (although resolute defenders of
cultural difference would interpret even that eagerness as a product of the invading ideology). However, simply to show that
Elspie's feelings were in general terms shared by some actual
people who were in a roughly similar situation is not enough, for
it leaves untouched the question of how thoroughly the poem
represents the pressures which Elspie is under, and how sympathetically it describes her response to them.

Elspie is imagined alluding, as Thomas Wise had done in the
House of Commons, to an analogy from international politics,
comparing Philip's presence in Scotland to Spanish imperialist—
and ultimately genocidal—incursions in South America. The text
does not gloss over her feelings of repulsion. Next, when she
abandons this threatening comparison in favour of the one great
tree, of which all individuals are but leaves, and all nations
branches, the verse draws attention to the hegemonic drive of the
developing world culture by the insistent repetition 'in itself . . . |
. . . to itself . . . | . . . for itself . . .'. Now, though, Elspie's attitude
to the invasive force has modulated into an acceptance which, in
the rather prurient last sentence, with its mingling of 'life-juices',
is compared to and shown to have its origin in her erotic feelings
for Philip. Even readers who still judge that they are being urged
to buy into this unifying drive (and by the very act of reading we
cannot help but feel to some extent at one with the loving couple),
must recognize that, by its clear-sightedness, the text offers them
ample opportunity to demur. The poem weighs up the pros and
cons of a decision such as Elspie's in a way which neither celebrates cultural imperialism nor sentimentalizes resistance to it.
Elspie neither quite abandons the 'annihilation' view nor
absolutely espouses the idea of 'natural and beneficial union': as
she says, it is not that she now never feels like the exterminated
Indians, only that she does not feel like them 'always'.

---

[42] David Lloyd, *Nationalism and Minor Literature: James Clarence Mangan and the Emergence of Irish Cultural Nationalism* (Berkeley: University of California Press, 1987), 209.

[43] Linda Colley, 'Whose Nation? Class and National Consciousness in Britain, 1750–1830', *Past and Present*, 113 (Nov. 1986), 97–118.

In its handling of the discourses of nationalism, the *Bothie* does something similar to what Martha Nussbaum has said to be the ethical function of art in general:

Great art plays a central role in our political lives because, showing us the tangled nature of our loves and commitments, showing us ourselves as flawed crystals, it moderates the optimistic hatred of the actual that makes for a great deal of political violence, moderates the ferocious hopefulness that simply marches over the complicated delicacies of the human heart.[44]

This remark does not seem apposite to all 'great art' (think of *The Faerie Queene* or the sculptures of Giacometti); but it is the case that Clough's poem, like the novels of Henry James which Nussbaum primarily has in mind, helps us to imagine the relation between a political ideal and the particular changes to individual lives which it comes down to in practice. By tracing Elspie's mixed feelings, the poem makes us see that her situation is an instance neither of the 'progress of civilization' nor of the 'anni-hilation' of one nationality by another, but of something more complicated. However, there is a further aspect to the poem's explorations of nationalist 'hopefulness', which is that it was written, and asks to be read, with the recognition that it is itself part of the cultural developments which are its subject. Nussbaum's theory is in the tradition of art as mirror. It tends to present literature as being informative about, but nonetheless distinct from, the real business of living. Reading, you step aside from loves and commitments, but always with the aim of return-ing to the active life illuminated, so that all novels have the func-tion referred to in that sardonic title *La Vie mode d'emploi*. However, works of literature do not only reflect life; they are also an element within it. Each one of them is itself (as Dickens said) a 'wide ground' on which its readers are brought together. The significance of this fact about books will of course vary in different times and places. Much has been and still could be said about its importance for nineteenth-century novels, but, if anything, it had a greater effect on poems, for it presses in on all those elements of diction, rhythm, and form which command closer attention in poetry than in prose, with the effect that, in

---

[44] Martha C. Nussbaum, *Love's Knowledge: Essays on Philosophy and Literature* (New York: Oxford University Press, 1990), 213.

the words of T. S. Eliot, 'no art is more stubbornly national than poetry'.[45]

In writing the *Bothie*, Clough sought to expand the lexis of poetry so that more readers would feel at home in the work: he hoped, as he said, to build them a 'real house to be lived in' instead of the 'Ionic portico' constructed by most verse.[46] As they enter into this new dwelling-place for their imaginations, readers discover Scottish words such as 'claymore' and 'speat' rubbing shoulders with Oxbridge slang like '*topping*' and '*clippingest*', classical mythology ('Hyperion', 'Antinoüs'), Latin epigraphs, phrases in dog-Gaelic ('*Slan leat . . . Caleg Looach*') and a single word of French: '*égalité*'.[47] The poem welcomes its readers into a liberal polity of diction. This fact is complicated, however, by the verse-form into which the multi-cultural words are disciplined: an accentual version of the classical hexameter. On the one hand, this metre is exceptionally flexible, allowing lines to vary in length from thirteen to seventeen syllables and take on a wide variety of rhythms, thereby making possible the *Bothie*'s linguistic liberties; on the other, it carries a weight of tradition. Tom Paulin proposes that the hexameters 'rest on the Athenian ideal of free citizenship in a free state';[48] but since Clough's most frequent point of reference in the poem is Virgil (the epigraphs are mostly from *Eclogues* and *Georgics*) we might better take them as hinting at the diffuse presence of imperial power, the British Empire figuring, in line with one of its more common self-imaginings, as the new Rome. The hexameters are a formal counterpart to the undergraduates' invasion of the Scottish countryside. From one point of view, they domesticate the idea of empire, making it seem no more threatening than a party of students reading the classics; but they might also be understood as representing the traces of *realpolitik* which are to be discerned in even so gentle an activity as a walk in the highlands.

Locating a poem in its historical context does not, as the poetry-as-journalism school would have us believe, necessarily reveal it as being the equivalent of a speech-act conveying a 'message'. The *Bothie* draws our attention to the workings of

---

[45] T. S. Eliot, *On Poetry and Poets* (Faber and Faber, 1957), 19.

[46] *Selected Prose Works of Arthur Hugh Clough*, ed. Buckner B. Trawick (University, Ala.: University of Alabama Press, 1964), 145.

[47] *B* I. 150, 90, 24; III. 146, 187; II. 171.   [48] Paulin, *Minotaur*, 72.

national or international unification, and itself, to a degree, enters into them. Readers who enjoy the poem will find their sympathies extending to new characters and (if they are from the south) places, and their tastes happily adapting to a newly various lexis and liberal form. Friendly critics will note that this process requires an overcoming of prejudices and a loosening of cultural identity as Englishness stretches into Britishness, in rather the same way as the work itself challenges and relaxes preconceptions about what it is to be a poem. Even judges hostile to such a broadening of minds must recognize the extent to which the *Bothie* itself provides them with ammunition against what is in many respects its own enter-prise, and leaves them at liberty to think that Elspie is, after all, more like the Peruvian Indians than not. As Isobel Armstrong has observed, novels do not hold the monopoly on dialogism. To adopt her useful phrase, the *Bothie* is (like much other mid-nine-teenth-century verse) 'a double poem': it can be taken in two opposed ways at once, and with any number of gradations in between.[49] The contrasting possibilities are present throughout, and nowhere more clearly than in the final twist of the narrative. When we are told that Philip and Elspie have 'rounded the sphere to New Zealand', should we think this a serious option (after all there was during the 1840s a boom in emigration),[50] perhaps a new stage in the spread of mutual understanding?—or rather a way of poking fun at the newly married couple and all they represent, lumping them together with the Micawbers? The poem comes comes down conclusively on neither side, for its business is not to strike political attitudes but rather to bring them into relation with the stuff of people's lives, asking readers to feel and understand their repercussions.

'ME, YOU, ALL OF US I MEAN, ITALY'

Simply by the act of using English, poets were brought to ask themselves how widely or otherwise their writing was representa-tive of the many diverse people who might be thought to make up *the* English. The question became especially acute when their work (like the *Bothie*) was set identifiably within the British Isles. A serious poem of that kind could hardly fail to come to grips with

---

[49] Armstrong, *Victorian Poetry*, 13.   [50] Williams, *The Long Revolution*, 83–4.

contemporary anxieties about nationhood. When, as was often the case, mid-nineteenth-century English poets were writing about Italy, nationalism appears in their work with similar insistence, although for different reasons and in a distinct form. For British people in general, the Risorgimento was the grandest and most involving instance of nation-building in this period. There was the fervent propaganda of Mazzini, the frequent rebellions which culminated in the revolutions of 1848–9; then, during the 1850s the development of constitutional government in Piedmont, the revolutions and wars of 1859–60 which resulted in the unification of most of the peninsula, and, finally, the incorporation of Rome and Venice into the new State in 1866 and 1870 respectively.[51] These events were of special appeal to poets because Italy had long figured in British conceptions of things as a land of the imagination. The Tory view that the 'principle of nationality' was 'chimerical' was urged with particular vehemence in the case of Italy, because Italians were, in the general view, constitutionally prone to be carried away by fanciful notions. As *Blackwood's* proclaimed (with singularly bad timing) in 1859: 'the existing state of Europe, and the present aspect of civilization, are . . . undoubtedly adverse to the genius, no less than to the frailty of Italy . . . Dearly bought experience has overthrown baseless and visionary theories; facts are stronger than political fiction; the enacters of plain prose have conquered the mere dreamers of poetry.'[52] To observers more sympathetic both to Italy and to that variety of 'genius' which it had come to represent, the progress of the Risorgimento could look like a version of poetic composition. Byron thought it 'the very *poetry* of politics'; Mazzini, a great admirer of Byron's, proclaimed that 'poetry has forsaken ancient Europe to animate the young and lovely Europe of the peoples'.[53] Alternatively, as the entity which previously had existed only in books took on political life, the Risorgimento could seem a proof of Shelley's claim that 'poets are . . . the mirrors of the gigantic

---

[51] The most authoritative account of the Risorgimento is Candeloro, *Storia dell'Italia Moderna*, vols. i–v; in English, see Woolf, *A History of Italy*; Denis Mack Smith, *The Making of Italy, 1796–1866* (Macmillan, 1968); Derek Beales, *The Risorgimento and the Unification of Italy* (George Allen and Unwin, 1971).

[52] (J. B. Atkinson), 'Italy: Her Nationality or Dependence', *Blackwood's Edinburgh Magazine*, 85 (Mar. 1859), 361–2.

[53] *Byron's Letters and Journals*, 12 vols., ed. Leslie A. Marchand (John Murray, 1973–82), viii. 47; Mazzini, *Life and Writings*, i. 150.

shadows which futurity casts upon the present'.[54] If the central issues for poets thinking about the United Kingdom were the borders of nationhood and the prospect of the merging or cohabitation of nations, the Risorgimento was for them a key example of the relation between imagined ideals and political practice.

Italy's first prime minister, Massimo D'Azeglio, registered the challenge of giving substance to the ideal of Italian nationhood when, at the opening of the first Italian Parliament, he asked: 'we have made Italy, but who now will make Italians?'[55] The problem is amusingly illustrated in Giovanni Verga's *I Malavoglia* (1881), when the Sicilian peasants who form the novel's cast hear news of the battle of Lissa (1866):

—They say it's been a bad business; we've lost a great battle, said don Silvestro . . . Everyone's saying we lost! . . .
—Who's lost?
—Me, you, all of us I mean; Italy, said the shopkeeper.
—I ain't lost nothing! replied Campana di legno, shrugging his shoulders.[56]

Of rural France in the mid-nineteenth century, a traveller noted: 'every valley is still a little world that differs from the neighbouring world as Mercury does from Uranus. Every village is a clan, a sort of state with its own patriotism.'[57] National consciousness in polyglot and long-fragmented Italy was probably even rarer: 'even at the present day', reported one exile in 1851, 'nineteen out of twenty among the living Italians are ignorant of their own appellation, and use it with hardly any discrimination or precision'.[58] There is an almost-believable anecdote that when Vittorio Emmanuele II entered Naples in 1860 many of the crowd took 'Italia' to be the name of his wife.[59] English observers were prone to similar uncertainties: in 1859 Thomas Adolphus Trollope (Anthony's brother) thought of Tuscany as being a 'nation', while

---

[54] 'A Defence of Poetry', in *Shelley's Prose: or, The Trumpet of a Prophecy*, ed. David Lee Clark, (Albuqerque N. Mex.: University of New Mexico Press, 1966), 297.

[55] Edward Latham, *Famous Sayings and their Authors*, 2nd edn. (Swan Sonnenschein, 1906), 234.

[56] Giovanni Verga, *I Malavoglia*, ed. G. Carnazzi (Milan: Rizzoli, 1978), 253–4.

[57] Quoted in Walker Connor, 'When is a Nation?', *Nationalism*, John Hutchinson and Anthony D. Smith (eds.), (Oxford: Oxford University Press, 1994), 154–5.

[58] Luigi Mariotti (pseudonym of Antonio Gallenga), *Italy in 1848* (Chapman and Hall, 1851), 5. [59] Breuilly, *Nationalism and the State*, 81.

a draft title for the first part of Elizabeth Barrett Browning's *Casa Guidi Windows* (1851), had been 'A Hope in Tuscany', although 'Italy' was soon substituted in line with the expansion of her hopes.[60]

Historians have given much attention to the processes by which people like Campana di legno were turned into Italians. The nationalist view that nations have always existed, so that nationalism is simply a matter of discovering what was always there, has now been thoroughly exposed as a myth. Indeed, Thomas Adolphus Trollope had already recognized as much in 1860: 'Italian nationality is the creation of modern circumstances,' he wrote.[61] More recently, Eric Hobsbawm has stressed 'the element of artefact, invention and social engineering which enters into the making of nations': 'nations do not make states and nationalisms but the other way round'.[62] Mazzini's 'Idea' of Italy, *Blackwood's* 'visionary theory', has rightly been renamed an ideology. Yet Hobsbawm's vigorous formulation, intent as it is on overturning nationalism's self-image, is in danger of replacing a myth of naturalness with a myth of artificiality. No forms of polity are without some element of artefact, while, on the other hand, the present condition of Somalia and the former Yugoslavia (and indeed in its own small way the United Kingdom) suggests that there are limits to the power of States to fabricate nations. If a nation is in essence an 'imagined community', it must nonetheless be one which people are able and comparatively content to imagine. In the case of Italy, there was a groundswell of peasant unrest which, though not itself consciously nationalist, still fed into the Risorgimento.[63] There was long-standing bourgeois hostility to foreign rule; and, although only a minority of Italians spoke the language of Italian literature, there was a family relation between Italian dialects which did not exist between them and German.[64] All these factors combined with economic pressures to make the Italian Peninsula

---

[60] Thomas Adolphus Trollope, *Tuscany in 1849 and in 1859* (Chapman and Hall, 1859), 317; Elizabeth Barrett Browning, *Casa Guidi Windows*, ed. Julia Markus (New York: Browning Institute, 1977), 72.

[61] Thomas Adolphus Trollope, *Filippo Strozzi: A History of the Last Days of the Old Italian Liberty* (Chapman and Hall, 1860), 124.

[62] Hobsbawm, *Nations and Nationalism*, 10.

[63] Franco della Peruta, *Società e classi popolari nell'Italia dell'ottocento* (Palermo: EPOS, 1985), 111.

[64] Martin Maiden, *A Linguistic History of Italian* (Longman, 1995), 3–4, 233–7.

a place which was susceptible to nationalist ideology because many of its inhabitants found that Italian unification answered to their interests and feelings. To varying degrees, the same was true of Germany, Ireland, Poland, Hungary, and so on.

Because of their preconceptions about Italy, and their comparatively detached point of view, English poets were especially prone to interpret the Risorgimento as a work of imagining. Some of them, such as Swinburne, gave themselves over to hymning the national ideal:

> Yea, even she as at first,
>   Yea, she alone and none other,
>   Shall cast down, shall build up, shall bring home;
> Slake earth's hunger and thirst,
>   Lighten, and lead as a mother;
>   First name of the world's names, Rome.[65]

Like much else in *Songs Before Sunrise* (1871), this poem, 'Dedication to Joseph Mazzini', enthusiastically amalgamates inspiration, motherhood and the Italian State in a rhetoric that was later to be echoed by Mussolini. A source for such visions is to be found in the work of Elizabeth Barrett Browning, whom Swinburne greatly admired. In *Casa Guidi Windows*, the first-person narrator calls for a leader to

> Teach, lead, strike fire into the masses, fill
>   These empty bladders with fine air, insphere
> These wills into a unity of will,
>   And make of Italy a nation—dear
> And blessed be that man! . . .[66]

Alliteration and assonance carry the force of the narrator's eagerness: 'fire . . . fill | . . . fine'; 'Teach, lead, insphere . . '. (etc); at 'dear', it is as though she turns to address, to implore, the man whose intervention she is imagining. National inspiration is thought of as being continuous with the inspiration of the poet. Individuals, the empty bladders, are—literally—fulfilled by their obedience to the leader; alone, they have no strength, no shape; they realize their potential only when they are made 'into' the greater unity. With 'insphere | These wills into a unity of will' the

[65] A C. Swinburne, 'Dedication: To Joseph Mazzini', *Songs Before Sunrise* (F. S. Ellis, 1871), p. vi.   [66] Barrett Browning, *Casa Guidi Windows*, I. 837–41.

people are elided into a whole by ambiguity: each will is insphered into circular unity with itself; and/or all the wills are insphered into a greater unity, which is itself a sphere. This vision looks hardly less totalitarian than Swinburne's. The difference is that, whereas the lyrics of *Songs Before Sunrise* offer themselves as gospel, the lines from *Casa Guidi Windows* are located within a particular context. They are presented as being uttered in the heat of the moment by a person who is watching the uprising in Florence from the windows of her home, aware that, as a (quite frail) woman and a foreigner she cannot participate actively, but nonetheless sympathizing, and desiring to provide for Italy a prophetic voice in the manner of that which Carlyle and Mazzini heard in Dante. All these contextual factors are made quite clear in the poem itself, so that the voice is always dramatized; in Part II, which is set after the failure of the revolutions, it is subjected to irony. The way is therefore left open for readers both to feel and to gain a critical purchase on the emotional appeal of 1848.

Of all the English poems about Italy, it is Clough's *Amours de Voyage* which conducts the most acute and thorough enquiry into the seductions of nationalist rhetoric. The work is set in Rome during Mazzini's revolutionary rule of 1849. In the following passage, the central character, Claude, ponders why he has not joined up to fight for the good of Italy:

> DULCE it is, and *decorum*, no doubt, for the country to fall,—to
> Offer one's blood an oblation to Freedom, and die for the Cause; yet
> Still, individual culture is also something, and no man
> Finds quite distinct the assurance that he of all others is called on,
> Or would be justified, even, in taking away from the world that
> Precious creature, himself. . . .[67]

The passage is teasingly ambivalent. To begin with, the sentiments couched in the strong dactylic rhythm of the first two lines are made to sound pompous: 'no doubt' is odd in alliteration with 'DULCE' and '*decorum*', while '—to', at the line end, seems cheekily to inscribe a pause for breath as a preliminary to the more ranting tones of 'Offer one's blood an oblation', where the alliterative stress hints at the shambolic bludgeoning by which that classical ideal of an 'oblation' might well turn out to be realized. This puts

---

[67] Clough, *Amours de Voyage*, II. 30–5.

implicit inverted commas around 'Freedom' and 'the Cause', and makes 'yet | Still', as it interrupts the fulsome beat of the verse, appear to usher in a counsel of common sense. Then, however, the exactness of 'quite distinct' and 'would be justified even' looks like quibbling; a suggestion which is made more explicitly by 'that | Precious creature', where the narrator's ironic gaze turns back on to his own self, as he offers precious, perhaps specious, arguments in defence of individuality (among others, his own). On the one hand, patriotic solidarity has a feel of rodomontade about it; on the other, 'individual culture' looks finicky. Claude offers criticism of the clichés of national solidarity, but is equally cutting about the clichés of individualism. Finally, his own relentessly critical habit of mind is itself put into a critical light by the narrative, in which his inability to commit himself to anything at all leaves him stranded and solitary:

> I, who refused to enfasten the roots of my floating existence
> In the rich earth, cling now to the hard, naked rock that is left me.[68]

Such an attitude might well be presented as laudably stoic, but Claude refuses that seduction likewise. The poem shows us both the dangers of bowing to coercive social and political rhetoric and the costs of not doing so.

The Bothie of Tober-na-Vuolich and *Amours de Voyage* both come to grips with nationalism in a way which is quite clear to see. The one is set on the borders of England and Scotland; the other in Italy in a time of revolution. The intersections with nationalism of other mid-nineteenth-century poems are, though no less important, more oblique, and therefore harder for us to recognize. If we are to understand works such as *The Ring and the Book* and *The Princess*, we need first to grasp what their authors thought of three types of unity—political, conjugal, and aesthetic—and how they drew correlations between them.

---

[68] Ibid. V. 66–7.

3

THREE TYPES OF UNITY

Clough's *Amours de Voyage* dwells in the shadow of the most famous practitioner of 'amours de voyage' in the nineteenth century: Byron. Visitors to Rome were likely to have called Byron to mind under any circumstances, let alone a revolution: quotations from *Childe Harold* graced Murray's *Guide*, which is perhaps a source of the bourgeois Mrs Trevellyn's conversation in Clough's work: 'she . . . | Quotes, which I hate, Childe Harold' (as Claude remarks).[1] Claude's own predicament might roughly be defined as the inability to resemble Don Juan in any way—or perhaps, more charitably, the determination not to be like him. He will not be 'circumscribed . . . into action' and he shuns everything 'factitious': to put it bluntly, he neither seduces nor fights.[2] The overlaps and interferences between his two possible areas of commitment—the courtship of Mary and the siege of Rome—likewise both recall and ask to be distinguished from the mingling of private and public in *Don Juan*.

In Byron's poem, the personal tribulations of the hero continually verge into matters of public, political significance. His romance with Haidée on a paradise island in the Aegean prompts thoughts about ideal polities and Greek independence. His involvement in the siege of Ismael gives rise to a satire on the possibility of heroism in an age of mechanical warfare. Most apposite to *Amours de Voyage*, however, is the encounter with Gulbeyaz in Canto V.

As wife to the Sultan, Gulbeyaz is accustomed to being obeyed, a disposition which makes itself apparent in her every movement:

---

[1] *Handbook for Travellers in Central Italy including the Papal States, Rome, and the Cities of Etruria* (John Murray, 1843), 286; *AV* I. 206–9.   [2] *AV* III. 124; V. 98.

'Her very nod was not an inclination'.[3] Among the suggestions produced by the linkage of 'nod' and 'inclination' is the thought that her nodding, which is literally an inclination of her head, should not be taken as a hint of any sort of obedience (moral inclination). There is room also for the sense of inclination as desire: Gulbeyaz gets whatever and whomever she wants, but only at the cost of turning her whole world into a shelf of commodities. When Juan caught her eye, 'She order'd him directly to be bought'.[4] Can such an attitude really be called desire (or even 'inclination')?—the pun nudges readers to enquire.

The episode constructs a series of arabesques on the old theme that in a tyranny no one is free, not even the rulers:

> Something imperial, or imperious, threw
> A chain o'er all she did; that is, a chain
> Was thrown as 'twere about the neck of you,—[5]

The side-step from 'imperial' to 'imperious' associates her personal demeanour with her official status by means of a play on words: as someone of 'imperial' rank she could throw you in literal chains whenever the whim took her; the knowledge of this fact, which she shares with everyone around her, makes her 'imperious', and covers everything with figurative constraint. These lines hint that she too is restricted by her position, which is after all only that of a 'bride'. Perhaps she is no more than a link in the imperial 'chain':

> . . . and to complete
> Her state, (it is the custom of her nation),
> A poniard deck'd her girdle, as the sign
> She was a sultan's bride, (thank Heaven, not mine.)[6]

Here, the collocation of 'state' and 'nation' adds a glitter of political suggestion to lines which are in any case dazzling with ambiguity. On the one hand the 'poniard' might be a sign of subservience, making clear that her 'state' in the sense of grandeur is only the result of her state of sexual submission to the sultan. On the other, the closing parenthesis implies that Gulbeyaz is not likely to be submissive to any man, not even a sultan. From this angle, the phallic poniard looks like a symbol of her prestige, not

---

[3] *Don Juan*, V. 882. Byron's poems are quoted from *Lord Byron: The Complete Poetical Works*, 7 vols., ed. Jerome J. McGann (Oxford: Clarendon Press, 1980–93).
[4] *Don Juan*, V. 907.   [5] Ibid. 873–5.   [6] Ibid. 885–8.

his. The uncertainty here goes to the crux of the episode, which is the relation between political and sexual power. Gulbeyaz has both: Byron wickedly sees them embodied in her breasts, those 'charms which seldom are, if e'er | By their possessors thrown into the shade', and which seem to give her 'a double "right divine" '.[7] However, as Juan is still grieving for Haidée, and is therefore not really in the mood, he finds that her imperiousness destroys her eroticism, and takes the opportunity to make a fine declaration of principle:

> 'The prison'd eagle will not pair, nor I
> Serve a sultana's sensual phantasy.'[8]

It is only when she loses her 'state' and weeps that Gulbeyaz begins to gain control of Juan's heart.

Gulbeyaz is offered as an *exemplum* of the mentality created by a tyrannical political system. She reproduces for others the oppression to which she is subject: she buys Juan as a slave, has him appear before her dressed as a concubine, and expects him to submit himself to her desire at a word of command. The implication is that under despotism everyone has the status of a concubine. This arrangement is presented as being unnatural, firstly as regards gender identity, for in matters of the heart (it is assumed) submission is the woman's role, and only by the act of submitting does she gain her rightful power; and secondly for the more comprehensive reason that, as Juan announces, 'Love is for the free!'[9] The narrative prompts readers to extrapolate from its specifics in a way that might be illustrated by some words of the young Karl Marx: 'the immediate, natural and necessary relationship of human being to human being is the relationship of man to woman . . . Thus, from this relationship the whole cultural level of man can be judged.'[10]

In the Gulbeyaz episode, as throughout *Don Juan*, a personal relationship is made to echo with issues of large political principle. Puns and the manipulation of ambiguity are central to this technique: 'imperious' brings in 'imperial'; 'state' means grandeur but implies government, and so on. Such words are continually

---

[7] *Don Juan*, V. 1029–31.   [8] Ibid. 1007–8.   [9] Ibid. 1012.
[10] *Karl Marx: Selected Writings*, ed. David McLellan (Oxford: Oxford University Press, 1977), 88.

moving between smaller and larger scales of reference, inviting readers to expand and contract their thoughts accordingly. The alteration of focus from personal to public and back again offered a provocative model for mid-nineteenth-century poets. Analogous techniques are to be found, not only in the works of Clough, but in Barrett Browning's *Aurora Leigh*, Browning's *The Ring and the Book*, Tennyson's *The Princess* and *Idylls of the King*, to mention only the most imposing instances. For this generation of poets, the relation between the personal and the public was more troubling than it seems in *Don Juan*. As we saw, Clough's *Bothie* does offer a personal relationship as an *exemplum* for the consideration of larger political issues; but *Amours de Voyage* presents difficulties to a reader who might want to take the failure of Claude's courtship (if it can be called by so vigorous a name) as being, say, symptomatic of the collapse of the 1848 revolutions. Although Claude discovers a kind of liberty in Mary's company ('for the first time in life I am living and moving with freedom'),[11] his emancipation relies on the continuance of class divisions. What he is enjoying, as he realizes, is 'the horrible pleasure of pleasing inferior people'; if the Trevellyns like him it is because, with their 'reverent worship of station', they think him 'superior'.[12] In some respects, the tentative beginning of a love between Claude and Mary asks to be understood, like the marriage of Philip and Elspie in the *Bothie*, as socially redemptive: it reaches across class barriers, and Claude employs whole forests of organic imagery to describe his feelings. In others, it seems a perpetuation of the old ways of class interest—something rather like the marriage, again between an aristocrat and a bourgeoise, which is at the centre of Browning's *The Ring and the Book*. Indeed, the uncertainty as to which of these possible interpretations is right contributes to Claude's loss of nerve, which leaves him in the end both mourning the loss of Mary and reflecting that 'After all perhaps there was something factitious about it'.[13]

Clough uses the partial correspondences between Claude and Mary's *amour* and the siege of Rome to bring into focus the large problem of the relationship between individuals and the socio-political groupings to which they belong. A loud theme of Mazzinian rhetoric was the need for absolute national unity; for

---

[11] *AV* I. 216. [12] *AV* I. 214, 137, 269. [13] *AV* V. 164.

individuals to be ready, nay, happy to sacrifice themselves for the national cause. Claude is attracted by such ideas but cannot manage to take them seriously. Like love, they seem to him 'factitious'. He is too much of an individual to lose himself in the mass, and, mostly, he likes himself that way. If he were triumphantly to marry Mary, or, better, elope with her, and join up with Garibaldi, his personal life would be continuous with, and could be seen as symbolic of, the revolutionary drive towards unity and freedom, in the same way as, in the *Bothie*, the marriage between Philip and Elspie is offered (however carefully and thoughtfully) as an instance of the merging of nationalities. This is exactly the problem, for if Claude were to behave in such a manner he would— as he sees it—be less entirely himself: his life would resonate with political significance, like the encounter between Juan and Gulbeyaz. The fundamental difference between the signifying practices of *Amours de Voyage* and Book V of *Don Juan* is that in Clough's poem the relationship between individuals and the larger political whole within which they live, and of which they might be thought to be exemplary, is itself complicated and made significant. To suggest that Claude's personal life is 'typical' of his revolutionary times, as Gulbeyaz is typical of despotism, would be to take for granted an identity between the individual and the whole which it is the point of the work to put in question.

Don Juan is presented as an everyman. Widely promiscuous, he is also Protean. He gets along with everyone in many different countries and, correspondingly, his personality is not distinct. One might say of him, as Tennyson's Ulysses remarks of himself, that he is a part of all that he has met; and indeed that all that he has met is a part of him. He is perpetually being 'circumscribed into action' and adapting himself to the commonplaces of different times and locations. This energetic vacuousness makes him a target for the narrator's irony. Juan thinks that he is being grand and brave when he exclaims 'Love is for the free!', a declaration which attracts the weary narratorial remark, 'This was a truth to us extremely trite'.[14] Claude, by contrast, feels happily at one with nobody, and is therefore individual to an acute degree. The play back and forth between irony and involvement which in *Don Juan*

[14] *Don Juan*, V. 1017.

provides enlightenment and comedy is in *Amours de Voyage* the source of an unhappy dilemma, for Claude combines Byronic protagonist and Byronic narrator in one person: he both chants the 'Marseillaise' and thinks himself ridiculous for doing so.[15] By a further twist of the knife, the evolution of events makes satirical individualism look no more satisfactory than active political or amorous commitment. The achievement of *Amours de Voyage*, then, is that it is, not merely satire, but a satire on satire.

The anxiety about the relation between private and public which is at the heart of *Amours de Voyage* is the same anxiety which beset the young Tennyson. Clough's poem is in this respect an elaboration of 'The Lady of Shalott'. Indeed, all mid-nineteenth-century poets who wanted to write about contemporary politics were in a position similar to that of Claude in revolutionary Rome: the risk of adopting a public voice was that it would get caught up in the gusts of rhetoric and so become 'factitious'. As I suggested in Chapter 1, the poets often responded to this difficulty by placing their work at a distance from public affairs, by locating it in the past, or in a realm of myth, and, as in *Amours de Voyage*, focusing it on a narrative about two characters. The relationship between those characters and the political events by which they are surrounded, and in which they are to various degrees involved, thus reproduces the predicament that the poets felt themselves to be in as they wrote about politics. And that predicament was itself only a special case of the central question which was newly raised by nationalism: the relation between the individual and the mass. If the dominant model of community is that of a people 'united by common sympathies', what is to be done with the person whose sympathies are uncommon?

In *Amours de Voyage*, Claude refuses to identify himself with the Roman revolution or with Mary, and the work as a whole backs him up by not attributing any symbolic meaning to his actions. To adopt Jakobson's seminal usage, his relation to the people and places which surround him is primarily metonymical: he recognizes his contiguity with them, but no more. As he says, 'it is only juxtaposition'.[16] Correspondingly, readers of Clough's poem

---

[15] *AV* II. 59–60, 156–60.

[16] Roman Jakobson, *Language in Literature* (Cambridge, Mass.: Harvard University Press, 1987), 109–11; *AV* I. 225.

cannot straightforwardly identify with Claude: his vertiginous ironies reject sympathy by the same token as they attack his nascent feelings of community with the Trevellyns and the Roman Republic. There is a similar emphasis on individuality, and consequently on the difference between fictional characters and their readership, in the work of Robert Browning—although, as we will see in Chapter 7, this generalization is rather complicated by his view of the relation of the past, in which his poems are mostly set, to the present inhabited by his readers. Elizabeth Barrett Browning's *Aurora Leigh* likewise has much in common with *Amours de Voyage*. She thought of the work as a 'novel-poem', and shared with Clough the desire to write about realistic characters in comparatively demotic language. However, her central characters also have symbolic functions of the sort which Claude was anxious to escape. Aurora is presented as Poet, as Woman; even (in Romney's words) as an 'Italy of Women', while Romney is Utilitarian Social Reformer, is Male, is English.[17] Their initial conflict and ultimate *rapprochement* are a matter, not only of their relationship as individuals, but of the compatibility or otherwise of the abstract qualities which they represent. In *Idylls of the King* and *The Princess*, the central characters are more symbolic still. Arthur was variously described by Tennyson as representing 'the soul', 'the conscience of a saint', and 'the complete man', while the Prince and Princess divide between them the qualities of North and South, Male and Female, Law and Rebellion, Narrative and Lyric (etc.).[18]

As these characters' mode of signification is different from Claude's, so is the relationship which a reader can form with them. Clough's characters might be said to be representative of their potential readers—which is to say, roughly but significantly, of Britain—in that they are recognizable individuals. Romney and Aurora Leigh are exceptional personages, and therefore appear as the embodiments of abstract qualities (Imagination, Social Reform, etc.). They might be said to be representative in the same way as an athletics team or an ideal selected House of Lords: they

[17] *The Brownings' Correspondence*, ed. Philip Kelley, Ronald Hudson, and Scott Lewis (Winfield, Kan.: Wedgestone Press, 1984–), ix. 293; *Aurora Leigh*, ed. Margaret Reynolds (Athens, Oh.: Ohio University Press, 1992), VIII. 358.

[18] *Poems of Tennyson*, ed. Ricks, iii. 260; 'Guinevere', 634; *William Allingham's Diary*, ed. Geoffrey Grigson (Centaur, 1967), 150.

are the best examples of different disciplines or walks of life. The central characters in the *Idylls* and *The Princess* are all royals, and, furthermore, exist in the parallel realm of myth. Living apart from us, they manifest our interests and our characteristics (the hope is) symbolically. Jerome McGann acutely remarks that *The Princess* 'offered Victorian readers a place where they would find their differences reconciled';[19] one should add that the manner in which it does this is implicitly royalist. Readers are invited to become imaginative subjects of either the Southern or the Northern State, and then to watch the Prince and Princess negotiating on our behalfs, until we are all joined with one another by their dynastic marriage.

Poets of the generation of Browning and Tennyson did not open up in their writing a uniform perspective on contemporary life. Rather, they all created different realms of verse, populated by different kinds of characters who institute different patterns of relationship with their readers. Those patterns of relationship were themselves felt to be of political significance. Hayden White's observation that: 'a society narrativizes itself, constructing a cast of social "characters" or "roles" for its members to play'[20] needs to be modified by a recognition that divergent political beliefs imply, not only distinct plot-lines, but varying modes of signification. As they entered into a Clough poem, readers could find themselves represented democratically: they would see there tradespeople, crofters, even academics: people like themselves. In *Amours de Voyage*, the attempt to provide an all-embracing narrative for these different people is made to look 'factitious', and even in the *Bothie* the central narrative is left vulnerable to irony. Not so in *The Princess*, where the central, symbolic narrative is supposed to gather everyone into itself, thereby implying an organically united, hierarchical national community in the tradition of Burke. The poetry of the Brownings is located both politically and aesthetically between the two extremes.

In all these different sorts of poem the different kinds of central character are brought into relationship with one another by the possibility or reality of marriage. This focus on wedlock is one of the defining characteristics of the generation of Browning and

---

[19] McGann, *The Beauty of Inflections,* 179.
[20] Hayden White, *The Content of the Form: Narrative Discourse and Historical Representation* (Baltimore: Johns Hopkins University Press, 1987), 158.

Tennyson. Yet marriage too could be understood in diverse ways, both in itself, and as an image of that other kind of union, the 'married calm of states'.[21]

CONJUGAL UNION AND NATIONAL UNITY

The title of Browning's great volume, *Men and Women*, might well stand as the heading of all mid-nineteenth-century verse, for thoughts and imaginings of marriage are all-pervasive in the poetry of the time. One reason for this pre-eminence is that marriage was widely thought to be the fundamental social relation. Unlike a sibling or parent–child relationship, marriage joins together people who must not be (except very distantly) related by blood. In contrast to friendship, however, the attachment between a married couple had legal force. As a contract, marriage could readily be brought into comparison with the social contract, which in this period was generally held to be—whether historically or only logi-cally—at the origin of political communities. As a sacrament, it offered an image for more mystical understandings of the relation between individual and nation or State.

A marriage created a little society. This might be set apart from society at large—as it is, famously, when 'Little Dorrit and her husband', at the end of Dickens's novel, walk out of the church and down into the 'roaring streets', 'alone', 'inseparable and blessed', preserved in quiet isolation from 'the noisy and the eager, and the arrogant and the froward and the vain', who fret and chafe and make 'their usual uproar'. The vision recalls the end of *Paradise Lost* where, expelled from Paradise, Adam and Eve 'hand in hand with wandring steps and slow, | Through *Eden* took thir solitarie way'—only in Dickens's imagining the fallen world finds its epit-ome in the city, and the married couple, as they emerge from the garden of sexual inexperience, nonetheless remain untainted by the relations of 'commerce' (in the largest sense of that word) which constitute civil society.[22] Similar idealization of the private life of a married couple was, of course, very common in the

---

[21] *Troilus and Cressida*, I. iii. 100. Quoted from *The Riverside Shakespeare*, 2nd edn. ed. G. Blakemore Evans (Boston: Houghton Mifflin, 1997).

[22] Charles Dickens, *Little Dorrit* (1855–7) ed. Harvey Peter Sucksmith (Oxford: Clarendon Press, 1979), 801–2; John Milton, *Paradise Lost*, XII. 648–9. *The Works of John Milton*, general ed. Frank Allen Patterson (New York: Columbia University Press, 1931–8).

Victorian period, and Dickens was its master-purveyor; its inevitable counterpart appears in *The Tenant of Wildfell Hall*, where because of the supposed sanctity and (for most people, and especially most women) the legal inviolability of the marriage-bond, Mrs Huntingdon has no means of securing protection from her brutal husband except flight. The Matrimonial Causes Act of 1857 did little to diminish such abuses: by 1872 there were still hardly more than two hundred divorces per annum.[23]

Not only two individuals are connected by marriage, but also two sets of relations; and—as the marriage service made clear—'It was ordained for the procreation of children' and therefore the increase of family.[24] From this point of view, a marriage appears no longer as a private refuge from people in general, but as one of the many knots which make up the web of a community, and as the first step towards involvement in society proper. Burke elaborated this conception in some famous words:

We begin our public affections in our families. No cold relation is a zealous citizen. We pass on to our neighbourhoods, and our habitual provincial connections. These are inns and resting-places. Such divisions of our country as have been formed by habit, and not by a sudden jerk of authority, were so many little images of the great country in which the heart found something which it could fill. The love to the whole is not extinguished by this subordinate partiality. Perhaps it is a sort of elemental training to those higher and more large regards, by which alone men come to be affected, as with their own concern, in the prosperity of a kindom so extensive as that of France.[25]

E. C. Gaskell's *North and South* ends with a couple's delighted recognition of the people other than themselves who will be joined together at their wedding:

'How shall I ever tell Aunt Shaw?' she whispered, after some time of delicious silence.
'Let me speak to her.'
'Oh, no! I owe to her,—but what will she say?'
'I can guess. Her first exclamation will be, "That man!" '

[23] K. Theodore Hoppen, *The Mid-Victorian Generation, 1846–1886* (Oxford: Clarendon Press, 1998), 200.

[24] The Book of Common Prayer, Solemnization of Matrimony (Oxford University Press, n.d.).

[25] Edmund Burke, *Reflections on the Revolution in France* (1790), ed. Conor Cruise O'Brien (Harmondsworth: Penguin, 1968), 315.

'Hush!' said Margaret, 'or I shall try to show you your mother's indignant tones as she says, "That woman!" '[26]

Here the prejudices to be overcome by the spread of affection are social and provincial, as well as familial: Aunt Shaw dislikes Mr Thornton because he is, and has the manners of, a northern industrialist, while Mrs Thornton thinks Margaret to be a hoity-toity young lady typical of the south. As the book's schematic title makes clear, their wedding is offered as a little image of the great country, a sign, not so much of 'the mystical union which is betwixt Christ and his Church' (as the Form of Solemnization of Matrimony would have it) as of the imaginative union which joins different places into one nation.[27] Many other people are brought to participate in that union (if more loosely) by the marriage of minds which occurs between a book and its reader.

Marriage had of course been thought of as an emblem of social harmony for several centuries before the Victorian period and probably ever since its inception. Its symbolism was important in the French Revolution, as Michelet records in his *History*: 'several of our confederations had thought of a touching symbol of union: the celebration of marriages at the altar of the fatherland. Confederation itself, that union of France with France, seemed to be a prophetic symbol of the future marriage of the peoples, the general wedding of the world.'[28] These ceremonies share with the endings of Shakespearean comedies an all-encompassing aura of unification whose vagueness doubtless contributed to their efficacy as political symbols. During the nineteenth century, the relation between marriage and society was subjected to more precise scrutiny, in the explicit terms of political writing no less than in the imaginings of novels. Wilhelm von Humboldt argued that married couples combined 'personal independence with the intimacy of the common bond', and that they should therefore be seen as a model for the reconciliation of liberty and unity in political associations.[29]

[26] Elizabeth Gaskell, *North and South* (1855), ed. Angus Easson (Oxford: Oxford University Press, 1982), 436.

[27] The Book of Common Prayer, Solemnization of Matrimony.

[28] Jules Michelet, *Histoire de la Révolution francaise*, 5 vols. (Paris: Chamerot, 1847–50), ii. 180.

[29] Wilhelm von Humboldt, *Ideen zu einem Versuch, die Gränzen der Wirksamkeit des Staats zu bestimmen* (Breslau: Eduard Trewendt, 1851), 11; trans. J. Coulthard as *The Sphere and Duties of Government* (Chapman, 1854), 13.

Lord Acton advanced a similar but more elaborate comparison in his essay 'Nationality', where marriage appears as an image of the mixture of spontaneous feeling and legal constraint which he thought to be characteristic only of multinational states: people's national loyalties, he maintains, are held in check by their obligations as citizens, so that 'the love of country, like married love, stands at the same time on a material and a moral foundation'.[30] In other words, a citizen's connection to the State is legal as well as emotional, and so must override his or her regional or national attachments (to Yorkshire, say, or Wales) in the same way as the obligations of marriage could be enforced by law where those of friendship could not. J. S. Mill, by contrast, assimilated the legal element of marriage to political absolutism. Wedding vows, he thought, were a licence for the husband to domineer over his wife, so that the law of marriage was a law of tyranny. In his account, Burke's idea that 'we begin our public affections in our family' is a sad truth, for since children learn social behaviour from the example of their parents, 'the family is a school of despotism'.[31] The socialist Robert Owen took a similar view.[32]

Readers of *Blackwood's Edinburgh Magazine* would, then, have been quite familiar with the terms in which, in 1861, it sneered at the beginnings of the women's movement: ' "Social Science', we understand, takes as one of its bases the equal rights of woman side by side with man. This startling attitude on the part of the ladies, analogous, we presume, to the uprising of certain oppressed nationalities on the continent of Europe . . .'[33] Readers would also have been aware that the analogy could work in different ways. Poets, in particular, had noticed its various possibilities. In *Idylls of the King* Guinevere's violation of the marriage bond symbolises (and indeed appears to cause) the fragmentation of Arthur's realm. In *The Ring and the Book*, however, it is Pompilia's relationship, not with her aristocratic husband, but with her beloved Caponsacchi which takes on implications of national unity. Where for Tennyson, as for Acton, marriage connotes a just and happy polity, for Browning, as for Mill, it does the opposite.

---

[30] Acton, *Essays on Freedom and Power*, 163.

[31] John Stuart Mill, *The Subjection of Women* (1869), *On Liberty and Other Essays*, 501, 518.

[32] Barbara Taylor, *Eve and the New Jerusalem: Socialism and Feminism in the Nineteenth Century* (Virago, 1983), 39–40.

[33] (J. B. Atkinson) 'Social Science', *Blackwoods Edinburgh Magazine*, 90 (Oct. 1861), 468.

Tennyson's ideal of marriage is avowed in the Prince's speech to
his future wife in part VII of *The Princess*. Like Michelet, the
Prince looks forward to the 'statelier Eden' which is the end of all
the world's progress: 'Then reign the world's great bridals chaste
and calm'. He proposes that he and Princess Ida should 'type them
now' in their own lives, presenting their equality in marriage as an
example to their people and a model of 'the crowning race of
humankind' which is to come:

> '. . . seeing either sex alone
> Is half itself, and in true marriage lies
> Nor equal, nor unequal: each fulfils
> Defect in each, and always thought in thought,
> Purpose in purpose, will in will, they grow,
> The single pure and perfect animal,
> The two-celled heart beating, with one full stroke,
> Life.'[34]

The Prince had earlier envisaged the woman of the future setting
'herself to man | Like perfect music unto noble words':[35] here,
the harmonies of his verse conspire to animate his vision, the pairs
of words ('equal' | 'unequal', 'thought' | 'thought', 'purpose' |
'purpose', 'will' | 'will', 'pure' | 'perfect') building up pressure
until the compound 'two-celled' initiates a fusion which reaches
its consummation in the single, free-standing monosyllable: 'Life'.
Unlike Mill, Tennyson takes for granted the existence of irreducible natural differences between the characters of men and
women. Indeed, such disparities are essential to his vision, for the
point of this marriage is precisely that it should be a symbol for the
reconciliation of difference. The Prince and Princess come from
separate countries known (pre-empting Gaskell's novel) only as
the 'North' and the 'South'. Because of the mythical nature, and
therefore indeterminate reach, of Tennyson's narrative, his imagined unification extends tentacles of relevance throughout Britain
and beyond, to the different subject-nations of the Empire.

Even when he is not writing in a mythical or 'parabolic' mode,
Tennyson always presents marriage as a reconciliation of differ-
ence. His poem of welcome for the Grand Duchess Marie
Alexandrovna of Russia imagines her wedding to Alfred, Duke of

---

[34] *P* VII. 277–9, 281, 283–9.   [35] *P* VII. 270.

Edinburgh in terms which hark back to the dynastic unions of the ancien regime. It heralds

> Between your peoples truth and manful peace,
> Alfred–Alexandrovna![36]

The hyphen links the obviously disparate English and Russian names into something like a 'two-celled heart' which, Tennyson might fancifully have imagined, shows signs of a propensity for 'beating, with one full stroke | Life' in the identity of the two pairs of first letters, 'Al'. In the description of a private wedding, too, at the end of *In Memoriam*, he focuses attention on the process by which disparities are overcome:

> . . . The ring is on,
> The 'wilt thou' answered, and again
> The 'wilt thou' asked, till out of twain
> Her sweet 'I will' has made you one.[37]

(*Her* 'I will' because she is the second of the pair to speak those words.) The verse prompts us to notice the gentle steps by which the repeated questions and answers bring the couple together, modulating from their separate pronouns in the middle two lines to the plural 'you' of the last. Here, as in *The Princess*, the words themselves co-operate in the unifying ritual—'thou' moved by assonance on to 'out'; 'wilt' into 'till', and on into 'will'; and then 'will' linked by phonetic alliteration to 'one'—to the extent that the verse seems to be describing the process of its own formation, and marriage appears as a special case of that unifying power of the imagination described by Coleridge.

When Browning thought of marriage, he saw it as a union, not primarily between two individuals, but between love and the law.[38] The importance of a wedding was, not so much that it joined people together, as that it gave legal form to a pre-existing relationship. What fired his imagination was the seeming paradox of vowing to love someone, a vow being an act of will, while love is by definition not subject to the will. At its worst, as in *The Ring and the Book*, a marriage consists only of legal obligation. This

---

[36] 'A Welcome to Her Royal Highness Marie Alexandrovna, Duchess of Edinburgh', 49–50. [37] *In Memoriam*, [Epilogue], 53–6.
[38] Here I am indebted to Eric Griffiths, *The Printed Voice of Victorian Poetry* (Oxford: Clarendon Press, 1989), 236–60.

thought is given a lurid cast in 'Mesmerism', where the deranged or supernaturally powerful speaker summons a woman to 'inform the shape' he has created for her, a shape which, it is suggested by his iterative play on the phrase 'to have and to hold', is not least that instituted by the marriage service:

> Having and holding, till
> I imprint her fast
> On the void at last
> As the sun does whom he will
> By the calotypist's skill—[39]

His desire to stamp the woman into a prepared outline appears in the way the rhymes are thrown into relief by the violent but uncertain pulse of the verse (the last four lines each begin with an anapaest, but their rhythm otherwise hesitates between iambs and spondees): it is as though he imagines his lines to be locking like manacles around her. A quieter version of this impulse to force someone into the image of a marriage figures in 'Andrea del Sarto', where the speaker persuades his wife to sit with him so that they will at least seem (above all to himself) to be fulfilling the agreement which, although it has not preserved their love, still structures their relationship:

> . . . let me sit
> Here by the window with your hand in mine
> And look a half-hour forth on Fiesole,
> Both of one mind, as married people use,[40]

In these poems the idea—which so animated Tennyson—that in marriage two people are made 'one' turns into an excuse for oppression, whether in the form of Gothic fantasy or uxorious wheedling. *The Princess*'s imaginings of amorous unity take shape in many memorable lines, such as:

> Now lies the earth all Danaë to the stars,
> And all thy heart lies open unto me.[41]

—lines which are astonishing not only for the shift of scale by which a couple's love appears to contain all space (the stars) and all

---

[39] 'Mesmerism', 52, 41–5. Browning's poems other than *The Ring and the Book* are quoted from *The Poetical Works of Robert Browning*, general ed. Ian Jack (Oxford: Clarendon Press, 1983–).   [40] 'Andrea del Sarto', 13–16.
[41] *P* VII. 167–8.

time (the reach back to the myth of Danaë's impregnation by Zeus in a shower of gold), but for the way in which sex and emotion are melded by the comparison of 'Danaë' and the 'heart'. Browning's poem 'Two in the Campagna' recollects Tennyson's lines, but gives them a contrary twist:

> How say you? Let us, O my dove,
>   Let us be unashamed of soul,
> As earth lies bare to heaven above!
>   How is it under our control
> To love or not to love?

The perhaps fulsome imaginings of unity in *The Princess* are then exposed to criticism:

> IX.
> I would I could adopt your will,
>   See with your eyes, and set my heart
> Beating by yours, and drink my fill
>   At your soul's springs,—your part my part
> In life, for good and ill.
>
> X.
> No. . . .[42]

The words in which the desire is phrased prepare for its collapse: 'drink my fill' is oddly greedy; 'set my heart | Beating' makes a heart sound like a clock. The lines beg to differ from the vision with which they echo, that of a 'two-celled heart beating, with one full stroke, | Life'. The paradox which Tennyson delights in—that of being two and yet also one—seems to Browning either meaningless or impossible. Unity of wills is irretrievably a matter of one will lording it over the other, so that what Tennyson takes to be a glorious consummation, Browning sees as tyranny.

Perhaps Browning's most compelling dramatic character is at once a husband and a tyrant. Where Andrea del Sarto creates a tableau of a happy marriage, holding hands with his wife and framed by the window, the Duke of Ferrara goes one better, doing away with the living, speaking woman and substituting for her a portrait whose story can be told only by himself. Like 'Two in the Campagna', 'My Last Duchess' is about a lover's desire to be one with his or her partner, but where the speaker of 'Two in the

---

[42] 'Two in the Campagna', 31–5, 41–6.

Campagna' imagines giving himself or herself up, the Duke wants only to command, to make his wife adopt his will, see with his eyes. His ambition is more insidious than that of Gulbeyaz in *Don Juan*, for Byron's despot views her man as a sexual object and cares nothing for his inner life, whereas Browning's wants to compel not only his wife's physical submission but her love. The poem connects forcefully with the potential for oppression in marriage in mid-nineteenth-century Britain. It is an imaginative counterpart to the argument later put forward by Mill, that the 'law of marriage' is a 'law of despotism'. Equally, it makes manifest the erotic ambitions of political tyrannies, their need, if they are to endure, to control not only the bodies but the desires of their subjects. There are several reasons for preferring the possibility that the Duchess has been shut up in a dungeon or a convent over the thought that the Duke has simply had her murdered. Bigamy is a more exquisite crime than murder, and compelling a woman to take the veil was, in nineteenth-century imaginations, one of the most refined forms of cruelty (see the story of Gertrude in Manzoni's *The Betrothed*).[43] Most persuasive of all is the suggestion that the Duchess represents those stirrings of sexuality—the great democrat, indeed, the great anarchist—which the Duke must suppress if his regime is to survive, but which are, in the long view, unkillable. The Duchess is another 'madwoman in the attic', whose fate is to be, not buried, but confined in dark places of the State and of the mind. As Freud made clear, such imprisonments are necessary not only to absolutisms.[44]

For Tennyson, each wedding is a miniature unification, a bringing together of different people who maintain their individualities and yet also become one: so many marriages are therefore 'so many little images of the great country'. Browning has a grimmer view, in which marriage epitomizes the necessary constraint, and sometimes cruelty, which society exerts upon its individual members and their desires. The stories about marriages which are at the centre of so much of mid-nineteenth-century literature have a wider and more intricate range of implications than has been understood by critics who suggest that the function of such narratives is merely to

---

[43] Alessandro Manzoni, *I promessi sposi* (1840–2), trans. as *The Betrothed and History of the Column of Infamy*, ed. David Forgacs and Matthew Reynolds (J. M. Dent, 1997), 127–54.

[44] See Sigmund Freud, *Civilization and its Discontents*, ed. James Strachey (Hogarth Press, 1975).

promote social homogeneity. A statement such as Franco Moretti's, that 'in marriage, conquest becomes *consent* and is thus fully legitimized' holds true of *The Princess*; but many other works from the period—including Tennyson's *Idylls of the King*—use their imaginings of marriages to enquire into the nature and possibility of such consent, and to question the desirability of such legitimation. To recognize this is to put pressure on Moretti's claim that 'literature . . . has a problem-solving vocation: to make existence more comprehensible, and more acceptable. And, as we shall see, to make power relations more acceptable too—even their violence.'[45] The difficulty of maintaining such a conviction is suggested by the looseness of its phrasing: does it mean '(a) more comprehensible and (b) more acceptable'? or 'more comprehensible and therefore more acceptable'? 'My Last Duchess' certainly helps us to comprehend power relations both in English marriages and Italian politics, but it would be a strange reader who thought it urged us to accept them.

THE LAW OF THE VERSE AND THE FREEDOM OF THE LANGUAGE

When Sordello, in Browning's poem, first experiences the civil strife which beset thirteenth-century Italy he feels chosen for a political mission. 'On me it lights | To build up Rome . . . !' he exclaims; and

> . . . forth he sprung
> To give his thought consistency among
> The very People—let their facts avail
> Finish the dream . . .[46]

But he fails to embody his vision in political reality, as he had failed previously to realize a similar 'dream' in language: 'the whole', he explains of the first disappointment, cannot adequately be represented 'By parts, the simultaneous and the sole | By the successive and the many'.[47] The reason for this repeated falling-short, and for the comparison between poetry and statecraft which it implies, is that, according to the broadly Hegelian view of things

---

[45] Franco Moretti, *Modern Epic: The World System from Goethe to Garcia Marquez*, trans. Quintin Hoare (Verso, 1996), 27, 6.   [46] *Sordello*, IV. 1025–6, 1028–31.
[47] Ibid. II. 593–5.

adopted by *Sordello,* history expresses ideals which previously had
shown glimpses of themselves in art. Here just as much as in
Shelley—who was an overwhelming influence on the young
Browning—today's poem is a shadow of tomorrow's polity.

The language of Hegelian idealism is extremely adaptable, and
it quickly spread into many different areas of enquiry. In particular, descriptions of the State and of poems began to look similar.
'An organic life requires in the first place One Soul, and in the
second place, a divergence into differences, which become organic
members, and in their several offices develop themselves to a
complete system; in such a way, however, that their activity
reconstitutes that one soul.'[48] That passage concerns the life of
political communities; yet at about the same time as Hegel spoke
the German equivalent of those words, Coleridge was defining a
poem as 'a harmonious whole', 'proposing to itself such delight
from the whole as is compatible with a distinct gratification from
each component part'. Every element of a poem, he explains,
fulfils its particular office and, in so doing, contributes to the
complete system, so that the reader is 'carried forward . . . by the
pleasurable activity of mind excited by the attractions of the journey itself'.[49] Here, as in *Sordello*, failures in poetry and in politics
have common symptoms. Hegel argues that 'the Persians . . .
could not "inform" the conquered lands with their principle, and
were unable to make them into a harmonious Whole, but were
obliged to be content with an aggregate of the most diverse individualities'; Coleridge claims that one must deny 'the praises of a
just poem . . . to a series of striking lines or distichs, each of which
absorbing the whole attention of the reader to itself disjoins it from
its context and makes it a separate whole, instead of a harmoniz-
ing part' (a remark which lies behind Sordello's bafflement at how
to reconcile 'the whole' with 'the successive and the many').[50] In
both cases the opposite extreme—monolithic unity—is equally to
be deplored.

The striking overlap between the discourses of political and

[48] G. W. F. Hegel, *Vorlesungen über die Philosophie der Geschichte*, ed. T. Litt (Stuttgart:
Philipp Declam, 1989), 218; trans. J. Sibree as *The Philosophy of History* (1899; repr. New
York: Dover Publications, 1956), 144.

[49] Coleridge, *Biographia Literaria*, ii. 13–14.

[50] Hegel, *Vorlesungen*, 318–19: *The Philosophy of History*, 222; Coleridge, *Biographia
Literaria*, ii. 13–14.

poetic theory in this period does not of itself tell us anything about poetic practice. But it does make clear a network of interrelations and correspondences which were available for poets to explore if they so desired. When Coventry Patmore wrote, in his influential 'Essay on English Metrical Law' (1857), of 'the co-ordination of life and law, in the matter and form of poetry', he invited readers to see in his own and other poets' versification a little image of that larger co-ordination of life and law which is the task of politics.[51]

The shape of such an analogy—if it appears in practice—will vary according to the precise terms in which the institutions of government, and of verse, are conceived. At the beginning of *Considerations on Representative Government*, J. S. Mill distinguished two opposing views of the State: 'by some minds, government is conceived as strictly a practical art . . . Forms of government . . . are regarded as wholly an affair of invention and contrivance'; while by others 'the fundamental political institutions of a people are considered . . . as a sort of organic growth from the nature and life of that people: a product of their habits, instincts, and unconscious wants and desires, scarcely at all of their deliberate purposes'.[52] The first model had been developed by Bentham and James Mill, who were influences on the young Browning.[53] The second had been most influentially formulated by Burke: the British political system, he contended, preserves 'the method of nature in the conduct of the state', while 'the very idea of the fabrication of a new government is enough to fill us with disgust'.[54] This position was maintained by a line of conservative thinkers which included Coleridge and Carlyle, and it was attractive to Tennyson. However, Mill's distinction, although useful, is too simple. Political institutions are presented as 'a sort of organic growth' not only in the Burkean tradition but in German idealism; and while Coleridge and Carlyle happily splice Hegelian thoughts into predominantly Burkean arguments, idealist theories were also adopted by Mazzinian republican nationalism. This meant that the

---

[51] *Coventry Patmore's 'Essay on English Metrical Law': A Critical Edition with Commentary*, ed. Sister Mary Augustine Roth (Washington: Catholic University of America Press, 1961), 7; cf. Dennis Taylor, *Hardy's Metres and Victorian Prosody* (Oxford: Clarendon Press, 1988), 5–32.

[52] Mill, *Considerations on Representative Government* (1861), *On Liberty and Other Essays*, 205–6. [53] Armstrong, *Victorian Poetry*, 25–40, 112–26.

[54] Burke, *Reflections on the Revolution in France*, 120, 117.

terms employed by conservatives to depict the British constitution could reappear bizarrely transposed in the declarations of radicals. Coleridge described the opposing kinds of form as follows: 'the form is mechanic when on any given material we impress a predetermined form, not necessarily arising out of the properties of the material . . . the organic form, on the other hand is innate, it shapes as it developes [*sic*] itself from within',[55] and he gave a detailed account of what he thought to be organic form in politics in *On the Constitution of Church and State*.[56] John Sale Barker—a supporter of Mazzini—echoed Coleridge's words when, in 1860, he wrote of the contrast between nationalism and the 'artificial' despotic governments imposed on Europe by the treaties of 1815: 'these states, thus existing by no law from within, are only maintained artificially in existence by pressure from without'; Mazzini's programme of national unity, on the other hand, 'implied Italy self-created, its outward political organization as one nation, to be worked out by a force from within, arising from the consciousness in the people of national individuality as one collective life'.[57] Mill, by contrast, thought of republican nationalism as a movement seeking to replace the supposedly organic institutions of the *ancien regime* with forms of government which were rationally contrived to be representative.

A poet who was interested in a struggle between, say, established state institutions and a movement for national liberty might sometimes want to give that conflict form in his or her writing by making 'the law of the verse' (in Patmore's words) do battle with 'the freedom of the language'.[58] Someone with a rosier view might want to make that freedom live happily in the company of that law, so as to represent, by what George Saintsbury called 'ordered liberty' in verse,[59] an organic interrelation between law and what it controls. Someone like Tennyson:

> Love thou thy land, with love far-brought
> From out the storied Past, and used

[55] Quoted in *Biographia Literaria*, ii. 84.

[56] *On the Constitution of Church and State: The Collected Works of Samuel Taylor Coleridge*, vol. *10*, ed. John Colmer (Princeton: Princeton University Press, 1971), 107.

[57] John Sale Barker, 'Italian Unity and the National Movement in Europe', *Macmillan's Magazine*, 3 (Nov. 1860), 72, 76.

[58] *Coventry Patmore's 'Essay on English Metrical Law'*, 9.

[59] Taylor, *Hardy's Metres and Victorian Prosody*, 32.

> Within the Present, but transfused
> Through future time by power of thought.[60]

'Storied' means 'in layers' as well as 'full of history and legend': correspondingly, the distinct steps of time are here embodied in the stanza, past, present, and future each occupying a separate line. This conceptual and structural break between the ages is elided in the flow of the language: the line-ends always fall before a preposition where there would naturally be a slight pause; but the stronger grammatical hiatuses before the conjunctions 'and' and 'but' are smoothed over by being placed within the lines. The rhyme 'used | . . . transfused' seems therefore less to mark the form of the stanza than to sound within the movement of the sentence, enacting the continuity which subsists through the changing words, and which is carried by assonance from 'transfused' on into 'through' and 'future'. This representation of a people's enduring love for its 'land' urges against any rejection of political tradition like that attempted by the French Revolution. The structure of the verse seems to grow out of the natural motion of the language, and not to be a distinct form: it resembles what for Burke were the organic British political structures, rather than the rationally 'fabricated' French constitution.[61]

Elizabeth Barrett Browning draws on the more radical possibilities of organicism when she imagines the thoughts of Aurora Leigh:

> What form is best for poems? Let me think
> Of forms less, and the external. Trust the spirit,
> As sovran nature does, to make the form;
> For otherwise we only imprison spirit
> And not embody. Inward evermore
> To outward—so in life, and so in art
> Which still is life.[62]

This differs from Burke—and resembles Barker—in that it emphasizes the distinction between 'spirit' and 'form' which Tennyson aims to elide. In harmony with Aurora's resolution to 'think | Of forms less', her verse is unrhymed, and the language saunters casually across the metre with much elision ('th'external', 'onl'imprison') and

---

[60] 'Love thou thy land, with love far-brought', 1–4.
[61] I am here indebted to Isobel Armstrong, *Language as Living Form* (Brighton: Harvester, 1982), ch. 1.   [62] *AL* V. 223–9.

colloquial syntax. The one end-rhyme, of 'spirit' with itself, seems, with its sudden reminder of the verse-form, to represent that confinement of which Aurora is speaking, while a more liberal structure is suggested by the relation of 'form', at the end of the third line quoted, to its half-rhyme two lines later, in 'Inward evermore | To outward'. 'Form' appears transformed in the last syllable of 'evermore', as though it were caught up in the swell of the enjambment and reformed as part of a process of continual revolution which, Aurora tells us, is the habit no less of life than of art. The likely consequences for governments are hinted at by the words 'sovran' and 'imprison'.

As we will see in the next chapter, Barrett Browning trusted to 'spirit' over 'form' just as much in her political views as in her artistic practice. Her husband, on the other hand, was preoccupied by conflicts between form and spirit, and bodied these forth in his writing in the relation between 'the law of the verse' and 'the freedom of the language'. The following lines, from 'Old Pictures in Florence', are addressed to ancient Greeks who—it is imagined— are gazing at classical statues:

> So, you saw yourself as you wished you were,
>   As you might have been, as you cannot be;
> Earth here, rebuked by Olympus there:
>   And grew content in your poor degree
> With your little power, by those statues' godhead,
>   And your little scope, by their eyes' full sway,
> And your little grace, by their grace embodied,
>   And your little date, by their forms that stay.[63]

The sculptures are seen as absolutist rulers (the next stanza cites Theseus, Hector, and Alexander), reigning as though from Olympus and sanctioned by the laws of hereditary right ('forms that stay'). The language, like their subjects, feels oppressed: the last four lines quoted are fixed into the rigid forms of anaphora and parison, the people on the left separated from their rulers on the right by the repeated strong caesuras, locked with them into a structure of confrontation. Later, the revolution comes:

> On which I conclude, that the early painters,
>   To cries of 'Greek Art and what more wish you?'—

Replied, 'To become now self-acquainters,
And paint man man, whatever the issue!
Make new hopes shine through the flesh they fray,
New fears aggrandize the rags and tatters:
To bring the invisible full into play!
Let the visible go to the dogs—what matters?'[64]

Like *Aurora Leigh*, they resolve to think less of forms and the external as they aim at a fuller realization of spirit. Here, though, we may well feel that as it reports their ambition the verse simultaneously subjects it to criticism. The artists are made to sound reckless—most strongly in the tongue-twister 'through the flesh they fray'—in their sloganizing and desire that everything should be 'new ... | New' without a thought for the consequences. Where the lines describing the tyrannical Greek statues were heavily articulated with conjunctions and prepositions, here the grammar loosens up, perhaps too much so, with its succession of varied infinitives, suddenly veering into a dismissive imperative at 'Let'. The handling of the language itself implies the speaker's later judgement that these revolutionaries were 'daring so much, before they well did it'.[65] This writing suggests that the organic form advocated by *Aurora Leigh* may turn out to be no form at all.

Browning's imagination was fascinated by such conflicts between law and freedom, whether in art, in sexual relations, or in politics. Many of the terms in which 'Old Pictures in Florence' contrasts Greek sculpture to early Italian painting reappear in the antithetical portrayals of the uxorious Andrea del Sarto, whose devotion to form is indicated by his sobriquet, 'The Perfect Painter', and the licentious, innovative Fra Lippo Lippi. While readers have traditionally been most impressed by the rebellious verve of Browning's work, to the extent that Fra Lippo has been considered 'really a kind of spokesman for the poet',[66] in fact reflections of his own artistic persona can be glimpsed in the controlling characters no less than the impetuous ones. 'Mesmerism' (from which I quoted above) with its talk of the 'the calotypist's skill' most immediately taps into a nervousness about the exciting new technique, photography; for

---

[64] Ibid. 145–52.   [65] Ibid. 154.
[66] *Robert Browning: The Poems*, ed. John Pettigrew, 2 vols. (Harmondsworth: Penguin, 1981), i. 1110.

many shared—and share—something of the superstition, usually attributed to primitive tribespeople, that a photograph steals something of our souls. However, the poem also guides us to observe that the process by which this character desires to 'imprint' someone 'on the void' is not unlike that by which Browning himself summons his men and women into his mind, and then has them printed on blank paper. The same thought is at the heart of 'My Last Duchess', for the Duke, in addition to being a husband and a ruler, is an aesthete. Barbara Everett has suggested that he sounds 'something very like a highly successful and established Victorian artist, Ferrara, RA, receiving in his studio, the 'introduction' of his wife commuting to the Private View'.[67]

However, if art, as Patmore thought, is a negotiation between life and law, the Duke does nothing more than impose the law. He represents the triumph of the critical over the inventive. As he represses his subjects and refuses to enter into the give-and-take of anything that might be called a relationship with his wife, so in art he does not stoop to involve himself in the processes of creation but merely collects, observes, expounds, and judges. He is therefore not so much Ferrara, RA, as Ferrara of the _Quarterly Review_. Indeed, in the retrospective light of Burckhardt's famous chapter-heading in his _History of the Renaissance in Italy_, 'The State as a Work of Art', we might say that Browning offers us the absolutist State as a work, not so much of art, as of criticism. Readers have long admired the Duke's eloquence, and he is himself as much under the sway of his own judgement as all the other pieces in the private gallery to which he and the envoy have withdrawn. The quality of his self-control is put across to us by the relation between freedom and law in the verse with which Browning represents his voice:

> That's my last Duchess painted on the wall,
> Looking as if she were alive. I call
> That piece a wonder, now: Frà Pandolf's hands
> Worked busily a day, and there she stands.[68]

Here at the opening there is a momentary tension between the iambic metre of the lines and the varying accentuation required by

---

[67] Barbara Everett, _Poets in their Time: Essays on English Poetry from Donne to Larkin_ (Oxford: Clarendon Press, 1991), 162.

[68] 'My Last Duchess', 1–4.

the spoken rhythm of the words and suggested by the dramatic context. Our expectation of an iambic pulse encourages us to stress the first few words

× / × / ×
That's my last duchess . . .

—an emphasis which suitably brings out the importance of the first person pronoun for the Duke, whose last words are 'for me!' However, the dramatic situation, as soon as we have apprehended it, suggests a second pattern:

× × / × ×
That's my last duchess . . .

—for the Duke, as we discover, is deep in conversation about his next one. After this momentary disturbance, the poem settles down into a movement which is about as regular as it is possible for verse to be without becoming monotonous. The most remarkable aspect of the versification is the coexistence of couplet rhymes, which mark the borders of the form very clearly, with predominant enjambment. Commonly in English poetry, pentameter couplets have been end-stopped in the manner of Pope; when Keats departed from this tradition, following in the feet of Chaucer and William Browne, he allowed his enjambed couplets frequently to include unaccented, extra-metrical syllables at the ends of lines, as in 'A thing of beauty is a joy for ev_er_'.[69] Browning drew on Keats when he launched his own version of the enjambed couplet in *Sordello*; but he denied himself the liberty of the odd additional syllable, writing more incisive rhymes against which the flow of syntax struggles. In 'My Last Duchess', the same form has a different feel, for here the language and the rhymes seem utterly at ease with one another, the words relaxed in their total submission to the shape which is being imposed on them, or perhaps rather the shape itself rising up inevitably through the words. This is something like what Tennyson achieved with his manipulation of enjambment across rhyme in 'Love thou thy land', only here the discipline of the writing is stricter. The dramatic context created in the poem prompts us to wonder

---

[69] *Endymion*, I. 1. Quoted from *The Poems of John Keats*, ed. Miriam Allott (Longman, 1970).

whether this curious meld of ease and control may not have something to do with Ferrara's understanding of political rule; whether
his speech may not seem at home in such tight bonds because he
is himself the law, as his first wife has discovered.

The formal discipline which is so marked a feature of
Browning's poem has its final cause in what it represents to us: the
character of the Duke. And he is himself the representative or ideal
manifestation of the State which (we are told by the subtitle indication of speaker and location) bears his name: Ferrara. In his
person and in his domain—which, under absolutism, is only an
extension of his person—he will allow no murmur of liberty;
when Browning represents his speech, the freedom of the
language is similarly placed in utter subjugation. This feeling of
absolute command is part of what is attractive about the poem, but
it is also stifling. The very triumph of formal law nudges readers to
long for liberty, liberty such as had appeared in the smiles of the
Duchess, and which may still be present in the potential freedom
of thought and action of the Duke's silent interlocutor. Yet almost
as soon as that possibility appears, it closes off, for the envoy is the
vassal only of that inferior sort of aristocrat, a Count. To him,
hearing the Duke's confession is like being entrusted with a secret
by a mafia godfather: it entrammles him further in his power.

It is possible that the envoy may go on to risk his life and
obstruct the second marriage; but the main thought which his
presence suggests is the contrast between his situation and that of
the reader. In his immediate circumstances, the envoy can obviously voice no objection, and having grown up in a sixteenth-
century absolutist regime it may not even occur to him that
anything is wrong. Most readers, however, are at liberty to differ
from the Duke. The poem is located in a secluded environment,
above and away from 'the company below', a space, in fact, not
unlike that inhabited by the Lady of Shalott.[70] Like Tennyson's
work, 'My Last Duchess' asks us to move back and forth between
what, in Chapter 1, we saw to be the imaginative attitudes Shalott
and Camelot represent. We must both feel the charm of the
Duke's rhetoric, and resist it. However, where Tennyson appears
to dread the necessity of publication, Browning seems to relish it,
for what makes the difference between us and the envoy is that we

----

[70] 'My Last Duchess', 48.

are readers, and, for all that the solitude of our reading is echoed in the location of the poem, still we are aware that the Duke's hidden machinations have now been published and are available to everyone. How different it would be if his designs were addressed to us in a personal letter. In this respect the poem is the Duchess's revenge. Like her looks, his words now go 'everywhere'.[71] He has been brought to book.

The imaginations which created 'The Lady of Shalott' and 'My Last Duchess' were acutely sensitive to their work's relationship with its readers, and aware that that relationship was made possible and limited by the structure of interaction between people in society more widely. In Tennyson's poem, publication lines up with encroachment, even murder; in Browning's, it does the opposite. Browning's woman (the Duchess) is silenced so that she can be kept private, Tennyson's (the Lady) as she goes out before the public. Both works extend filaments of suggestion towards the spread of political representation in the period, but with contrasting force. Tennyson's aristocrat is an enigma to the crowd at Camelot, who are incompetent to judge her. Browning, however, gladly lays his aristocrat open to the adjudication of the free. When 'My Last Duchess' was written (even more than is the case today) not everyone in the world was at liberty to read it—and especially not in Italy. The poem therefore operates a subtle variant of the calibration between Italy and England which I discussed in Chapter 2. The real Dukes of Ferrara had not outlasted the sixteenth century; but Italy was still under the absolutist rule of their imaginative (and indeed actual) relations, people like the Duke of Modena and the Grand Duke of Tuscany. Readers who recognize the difference between their own political circumstances and those of the envoy were (and are) also prompted to see that other people do not share their liberties, not least the liberty to read.

For the Duke, despotism in art, in politics, and in wedlock is all of a piece, and is everywhere admirable. When, with his final, designedly casual gesture, he offers an image of himself and what he has done in the bronze of 'Neptune . . . | Taming a sea-horse', he must want the envoy to take the beauty of the sculpture's stilled vigour as a justification of his rule.[72] Browning's poem is likewise

---

[71] Ibid. 24.   [72] Ibid. 54–5.

a triumphant artistic representation of the triumph of art over life, but it is offered to its audience in a different way. As readers, we have the liberty to observe that in the real world sea-horses cannot be tamed, and to remember the lesson taught by King Canute.

'My Last Duchess' is the most concentrated synthesis of three types of unity—marital, aesthetic, and political—which in the work of Browning, Tennyson, and their contemporaries are brought into many, variously harmonious and awkward combinations. Where Ferrara institutes a threefold tyranny, other poems, notably long works such as *The Ring and the Book*, present us with more accommodating realms, in which, as we will see, life and law interact and conflict in the verse and the larger form no less than in the narrative. In the same way as Princess Ida and her Prince are offered as 'types', in the biblical sense of hazy symbol or precursor, of 'the world's great bridals', so the three types of unity may be thought of as types of one another, a central marriage relationship shadowing the accommodation of liberty to law in the handling of poetic form, whose discipline (or contrived lack of it) may have an analogue in politics. The links between the different types are neither uniform, not consistently strong. Sometimes, a work, or part of it, is shaped so as to suggest an explicit parallel between its own structure and political arrangements; on other occasions, verse may be handled so as to create a 'feel'—of oppressiveness, say, or liberty—which the imagined context encourages us to trace back to social or political causes; in yet other instances, the time of nation-building exerts a pressure on the imagining of a relationship between two people, or two elements of verse, in more diffuse and partly subliminal ways. To notice these varying interactions is to see why mid-nineteenth-century poems so often set stories about courtship or separation in a context of public, political activity, whether making the one sphere symbolic of the other, as in *Idylls of the King*, or having them conflict, as in *Amours de Voyage*. And to recognize the perceived relation between national and artistic unity is to understand why so many of these works fail to cohere in any obvious fashion, presenting themselves rather as groups, series or collections: not so much unities, perhaps, as communities. To follow these observations through is to discover that mid-nineteenth-century poets were writing an exceptionally inquisitive variety of civic poetry, to the details of which we may now turn.

PART II

THE INSPIRATION OF ITALY

4

FROM ELEGY TO PROPHECY

The young Elizabeth Barrett was as boisterous as she was poetical. Aged 10, in the summer of 1816, she wrote from her family's mock-oriental mansion in Herefordshire:

Oh dearest Grandmamma, Hope End is so beautiful, Nature here displays all her art, the ivy that droops upon the ground, she fastens up to some majestic tree, without the aid of nails, or <an> active gardener—We have played at a new game lately, we have each been Queen, or King of some country, or island, for example I and Arabella are the empresses of the Hyeres, Bro and Henrietta are the emperor and empress of Italy, Storm is the Prince of Rome, and Sam is the Emperor of Oberon . . .

Not satisfied with shared control of a small town in the Riviera, the diminutive ruler soon advanced on the Empire of Italy: 'we sometimes have Battles, the other day Henrietta and I fought, I conquered, took her prisoner and tied her to the leg of the table . . .'[1] To the imaginations of the mid-nineteenth-century English, Italy was a uniquely attractive land, and often it was transformed by them into a realm of fantasy no less involving—and hardly more connected to the realities of the peninsula—than Bro and Henrietta's empire. In *Little Dorrit*, Flora—a living 'Dictionnaire des idées reçues'—has never been there; but she is nevertheless able to give a vivid summary of the country's significance in English culture: 'the grapes and figs growing everywhere and lava necklaces and bracelets too that land of poetry with burning mountains picturesque beyond belief . . . and is she really in that favored land with nothing but blue about her and dying gladiators

---

[1] *Brownings' Correspondence*, i. 25.

and Belvederas . . .'.[2] As that list suggests, Italy was for the English rich in implication.

Above all—and more than is the case today—Italy meant a landscape ('burning mountains') which, by comparison with the highly-cultivated, chilly countryside of Britain, seemed Eden-like in its fertility ('grapes and figs growing everywhere'). In consequence, it was perhaps of all countries the one most thoroughly personified as mother: 'ah Italy, fair Italy! Many have come to thee in hatred and defiance, lance in rest, who, no sooner had they tasted the sweet milk of thy breast, than they laid down their arms, blessed thee, and called thee "Mother".'[3] Those words, from a novel by the exile Giovanni Ruffini, would not have surprised English readers, although English writers frequently took a sterner view of the emasculating influence of the land which, here, subdues the aggressively positioned lances of its invaders, making them subside from the role of rapist to that of child. A cradle of nature, Italy was also a fountain of culture: 'parent of our religion', as Byron had declared, and 'mother of Arts'.[4] Indeed, the natural and the artificial seemed to merge. The English had usually first encountered Italy in pictures and, primarily, in poetry: *Childe Harold's Pilgrimage*, supplemented by Shelley, Tasso, Ariosto, Dante, as well as by Samuel Rogers's *Italy* (1822–8), numerous verses in magazines and annuals, and for the more dedicated of them—like Elizabeth Barrett—John Edmund Reade's enormous and derivative *Italy: A Poem in Six Parts* (1838). When they reached the peninsula, tourists were impressed by the sheer volume of treasures, as well as by the frequent melodiousness of their guides, and often had the idea that art came to the Italians with the spontaneity of nature—a thought which had been developed in fiction into the improvisatory heroines of Madame de Staël's *Corinne ou l'Italie* (1807) and Letitia Landon's *The Improvisatrice* (1824). Conversely, the Italian landscape was discovered to have the beauty of a work of art: it was, as Flora says, 'picturesque beyond belief'. There (Landon wrote) 'earth and sky, | Are picture both and poetry', while Henry James observed that

---

[2] Dickens, *Little Dorrit*, 598.

[3] (Giovanni Ruffini), *Dr Antonio: A Tale: By the Author of Lorenzo Benoni* (Edinburgh: Thomas Constable, 1855), 231.

[4] Byron, *Childe Harold's Pilgrimage*, IV. 419, 417.

'a month's rides in different directions will show you a dozen prime Claudes'.[5] That ancient paradoxical idea—of which even the 10-year-old Elizabeth Barrett was aware—that 'Nature' is most herself when she most 'displays . . . art' found its incarnation in Italy.

One thing English travellers understood themselves as doing in this compound realm of nature and culture was, straightforwardly, consuming it. In 1840 John Kenyon sent Elizabeth Barrett a poem inviting her—or anyone—to join him there: 'And feed thy soul with glorious art, | And drink again of classic lore!' Kenyon was rather a foodie, and he presents the delights of Italy, ideal holiday destination, 'very Kenyonianly', as Barrett remarked.[6] For other tourists, the richness of the place gave rise to feelings of a more mysterious cast. At Pisa in 1843 Frederick Faber, a leading member of the Oxford movement, indulged in a 'delicious dream of art and history'. Dickens felt something similar when he visited Parma and Piacenza: 'what a strange, half-sorrowful and half-delicious doze it is, to ramble through these places gone to sleep and basking in the sun!' Dickens's impression (and doubtless Faber's) will have been fostered by the weather and that un-English habit of taking siestas; and perhaps—the word 'delicious' hints—also by the food. No less important, however, is the fact that all the sights were some hundreds of years old, so that the country seemed to be stuck in history. In Dickens, this prompted apocalyptic thoughts, 'that there is no more human progress, motion, effort, or advancement of any kind beyond this. That the whole scheme stopped here centuries ago, and laid down to rest until the Day of Judgement'. To step into what one of his chapter-headings calls 'An Italian Dream' is to step out of the march of time. Faber soon recoiled from his moment of Childe Harold-esque musing: 'this voluptuous and silent poetry which Italy engenders in so many, is just what I have been arming myself against beforehand as effeminate, sensual, literary'.[7] Perhaps he associated the 'poetry' of Italy with

---

[5] Letitia Elizabeth Landon, *The Improvisatrice and Other Poems* (Longman, Rees, Orme, Brown and Green, 1831), 1; Henry James, 'Roman Rides' (1873), *Italian Hours*, ed. John Auchard (University Park, Pa.: Pennsylvania State University Press, 1992), 149.

[6] *Brownings' Correspondence*, iv. 243.

[7] John Pemble, *The Mediterranean Passion: Victorians and Edwardians in the South* (Oxford: Clarendon Press, 1987), 67; Charles Dickens, *Pictures from Italy* (1846), ed. Kate Flint (Harmondsworth: Penguin, 1998), 65, 77.

the elaborate practices of the Roman Catholic Church, for in 1843 he was still clinging to Anglicanism (he went over to Rome two years later). Certainly, religious considerations were uppermost in the mind of the unitarian Frances Power Cobbe when she denounced 'the lotos-eater life of the South': 'to quit the field and wander away to dream, and gaze, and ponder; and live as perhaps man may have earned the right to live in centuries to come when Giant Despair and Giant Sin are dead'.[8] In such remarks we can doubtless feel the weight of a culture ill at ease with leisure;[9] but we can also see that for impressionable observers Italy created a kink in time. The beauty of the countryside recalled Paradise, and therefore also provided a glimpse of the distant future, the Last Day, when everywhere would cease progressing as Italy seemed to have done already, and when, surely, the entire world would revert to the climate of Eden, i.e. the climate of Italy. The works of art likewise appeared to exist in a stopped, or at least a slower, timescale. Travellers in the mid-nineteenth century were less excited by ruins than their Romantic forebears had been: often, their key image of Italy was provided by classical sculptures such as the Dying Gladiator and the Apollo Belvedere mentioned by Flora, which were hard to distinguish from Renaissance works and still provided an ideal for contemporary artists such as William Wetmore Story. The tourist experience configured the whole peninsula as an object of observation, and the comparative lack of industrial or other economic activity there made the country seem ready-made for that role. What Victorians characteristically found in Italy was, not the 'organic . . . time', 'measured by the pleasures and labour of the vital human life' which, as Bakhtin acutely pointed out, Goethe discovered there,[10] but a plenitude of time, which could equally be understood as its absence. Italy, then, was placed broadly in the category of the aesthetic: eternal, beautiful, politically quiescent. Sandra M. Gilbert is largely right when she suggests that during this period Italy was felt to be a 'text . . . a palimpsest of western history',[11] but the activities

[8] Pemble, *Mediterranean Passion*, 53.

[9] See Peter Bailey, *Popular Culture and Performance in the Victorian City* (Cambridge: Cambridge University Press, 1998), 13–29.

[10] M. M. Bakhtin, *Speech Genres and Other Late Essays*, trans. Vern W. McGee (Austin, Tex.: University of Texas Press, 1986), 31–2.

[11] Sandra M. Gilbert, 'From *Patria* to *Matria*: Elizabeth Barrett Browning's Risorgimento', Angela Leighton (ed.), *Victorian Women Poets: A Critical Reader* (Oxford: Blackwell, 1996), 27.

of English tourists there were frequently less vigorous than reading or interpretation: they dreamed.

The eternal triumphs of Italy's landscape and artistic heritage were in sad contrast to its political abjection in the mid-nineteenth century. Much of the north belonged to the Austrian Empire; the south was an absolutist State, the Kingdom of the Two Sicilies; the centre was governed in despotic fashion by the Pope; the Grand Duchy of Tuscany and the Duchies of Parma and Modena were ruled without the help of representative assemblies, as (before 1848) was the Kingdom of Sardinia, which included Piedmont. No parliaments, no free press and (a matter of particular irritation to tourists) intrusive customs officers.[12] Although Tuscany and Sardinia were comparatively enlightened absolutisms, the condition of Italy was sufficiently uniform for visitors to attempt a peninsula-wide diagnosis. Madame de Staël, whose novel-cum-travelogue *Corinne* set the tone of much English rumination, blamed the pleasures of the countryside: 'la nature leur offre tant de jouissances, qu'ils se consolent facilement des avantages que la société leur refuse.'[13] A similar thought was at the root of Ruskin's explanation of the contrast between Gothic (i.e. northern) and Renaissance (i.e. southern) styles of architecture: 'imagine the difference between the action of a man urging himself to his work in a snowstorm, and the action of one laid at his length on a sunny bank among cicadas and fallen olives, and you will have the key to a whole group of sympathies which were forcibly expressed in the architecture of both . . .'[14] Ruskin developed this opinion with considerable subtlety and power; but it appears elsewhere in English culture in remarkably simple forms. A quick shuffling of centuries made Gothic the style of Protestantism and political liberty. That languid, effeminate group of sympathies which manifested itself in the domes and rounded arches of the Renaissance was quite happy to forgo the erected conscience of Protestantism, and give itself up to the sensuality and spiritual tyranny of Rome. In an unusually strident formulation, 'the religion of the north is suited to northern sternness, and the chill of a northern climate,

---

[12] G. K. Chesterton, *Robert Browning* (Macmillan, 1913), 90.

[13] Madame de Stael, *Corinne ou l'Italie* (1807; Paris: Gallimard, 1992), 161.

[14] *The Works of John Ruskin*, 39 vols., ed. E. T. Cook and Alexander Wedderburn (George Allen, 1903–12), ix. 186.

but cannot pass the southern boundaries of the Alps and the Pyrenees. The lands of the olive and of the vine, of Ceres and of Bacchus, are doomed, we fear, to revel in a religion of *festas* and of orgies.'[15]

Such views had difficulty accounting for those key *loci* of active virtue and civic freedom, the medieval city-states (perhaps the climate was chillier then?), let alone for the archetypally Gothic figure of Dante. Nonetheless, there was available in mid-century English culture a seductively coherent amalgam of ideas about the relation between Italy's landscape, its past, the character of Italians, their religion, and their political capabilities. The perfection of nature and the perfection of art belonged together. Living in the company of such glories, the Italians were corrupted by them. It was as though the entire population had lost themselves in Faber's 'delicious dream of art and history' and given themselves up to Cobbe's 'lotos-eater life of the South'. Hence their Catholicism. Being, apparently, leisured, being set apart from 'progress', 'effort', and 'advancement', Italians seemed feminine; being voluble and enjoying silly pursuits such as opera, they were childish. For the mid-century English, the typical Italian was no longer a villain à la Mrs Radcliffe, but a fanciful, gentle, smiling creature like Dickens's Cavalletto: 'in his submission, in his lightness, in his good humour, in his short-lived passion . . . a true son of the land that gave him birth'.[16] Elizabeth Barrett Browning took a similar line: 'they are an amiable, refined, graceful people, with much of the artistic temperament as distinguished from that of men of genius—effeminate, no, rather *feminine* in a better sense—of a fancy easily turned into impulse, but with no strenuous and determinate strength in them.'[17] She found much to admire in this national character, but many observers, especially before 1848, thought it unlikely that such people merited political liberty any more than English women and children. Defenders of the Risorgimento sought to divert blame for the Italians' supposed deficiency of moral fibre onto their oppressors: 'it cannot be denied that the defects of character, attributable to the Italians of the upper and middle classes of society, spring in a considerable

---

[15] (J. B. Atkinson), 'Italy: Her Nationality or Dependence', *Blackwood's Edinburgh Magazine*, 85 (Mar. 1859), 360.   [16] Dickens, *Little Dorrit*, 14.
[17] *The Letters of Elizabeth Barrett Browning*, 2 vols., ed. Frederick G. Kenyon (Smith, Elder and Co., 1897), i. 388.

degree from the despotic form of government to which they are subjected.'[18] For opponents, however, the Italians were self-condemned to life under absolutism both religious and political: 'such a people must be ruled as children of larger growth—kindly, but firmly.'[19] Like an English household, Italy required paternal government.

Serving, as it often did, to justify foreign political control, the English cultural formation 'Italy' may be understood as a variant of orientalism or colonial discourse. To take a representative definition: 'the objective of colonial discourse is to construe the colonized as a population of degenerate types on the basis of racial origin, in order to justify conquest and to establish systems of administration and instruction.'[20] However, for several reasons this description does not exactly fit the English imagining of Italy. Obviously enough, Her Majesty's Government had no direct political control of the peninsula, and neither was there any established trading connection which might be thought of as 'informal empire'. Although tourism was an economic relationship, and one which encouraged Italians to live up to English expectations,[21] still it exerted nothing like the negative, stereotyping pressure that power relations did in, say, Jamaica. English opinions of Italy were therefore comparatively malleable and free-floating. In the 1830s and 1840s, tourists generally experienced the peninsula as being markedly what we would now call 'Other', consistently setting it in opposition to their own identities, and implicitly reinforcing these by means of the contrast. However, during the 1850s things changed. Gladstone's denunciation of the Neapolitan legal system in 1851 helped to turn public opinion against the absolutist regimes supported by Austria, while the constitutional reforms instituted by Cavour meant that Piedmont-Sardinia, at least, came to be seen as a younger England, all the more so when it fought alongside Britain in the Crimean War. Speakers in the Lords and the Commons in 1855 largely agreed that the Piedmontese-Sardinians were 'a gallant and spirited people' with 'a faithful and

[18] Mabel Sherman Crawford, *Life in Tuscany* (Smith, Elder and Co., 1859), 119.
[19] (J. B. Atkinson), 'Italy: Her Nationality or Dependence', 353.
[20] Homi K. Bhabha, *The Location of Culture* (Routledge, 1994), 70.
[21] Pemble, *Mediterranean Passion*, 263–4.

upright king'.[22] Italy, now, was not the converse of Britain, but a relation, albeit an unreliable and backward one. Cavour, according to his obituary in the *Quarterly Review*, 'was thoroughly embued with the spirit of the English constitution'.[23]

This alteration during the 1850s exploited a possibility which had been available in English images of Italy even before 1848. Colonial discourse fixes the identity of the colonized, but English metaphors for Italy included a capacity for change. If the Italians were children, they could grow up; if Italy was asleep, it could wake; if it was dead, even, it could be resurrected. Although the word 'race' does appear in discussions of Italians, it has none of the defining force that it assumed when applied to the inhabitants of Africa and India. Though 'southern', Italy was nonetheless in Europe, and the English did not forget (in Disraeli's words) 'how much we owe to that country, that in ancient times it gave us our laws, and in modern times our arts . . .'.[24] The British Empire's highest aspiration was to be a new Rome. One could never be absolutely certain that people who had had so grand a past might not enjoy a comparable future.

A third distinguishing feature of what might therefore be called 'Italianism', as distinct from orientalism, is that there was considerable cultural circulation between the representers and the represented. The English fuelled their imaginings of Italy with readings of Italian writers. They found laments for the peninsula's sad political condition in Dante (*Purgatorio*, 6) and Petrarch (*Canzoniere*, 128); the sonnet by Filicaia which Byron incorporated into Canto the Fourth of *Childe Harold's Pilgrimage*, and which deplores Italy's 'fatal gift of beauty', was well known.[25] The literary forebears of English Italianism in the nineteenth century, therefore, were also key sources for the Italians' imaginings of themselves. Foscolo and Leopardi were as eloquent as Byron on the subject of Italy's ancient splendour, although in 'Dei sepolcri' (1807) and 'All'Italia' (1818) respectively they configure this more as a goad to action than as a motive of woe.[26] Byron himself was incorporated into

[22] *Hansard*, vol. 137, col. 1080. The words are Frederick Denison's; cf. Gladstone, col. 1085, and Lord Shaftesbury, col. 1054.

[23] (A. H. Layard), 'Cavour', *Quarterly Review*, 110/219 (July, 1861), 216.

[24] *Hansard*, vol. 143 (1856), col. 764.   [25] *CGW*, ed. Markus, 73.

[26] See Carolyn Springer, *The Marble Wilderness: Ruins and Representation in Italian Romanticism, 1775–1850* (Cambridge: Cambridge University Press, 1987), 3–14.

Risorgimento myth-making: for Mazzini, his death in Greece symbolized 'the holy alliance of poetry with the cause of the peoples': 'all that is now the religion and the hope of the party of progress throughout Europe, is gloriously typified in this image.'[27] The conception of Italy as a land of the past, so fundamental to English and indeed European imaginings of the peninsula, is adopted, polemically, in Giuseppe Giusti's sparkling satiric poem, 'La terra dei morti' (1842), which draws its title from the description of Italy by Lamartine, the French republican, as 'la terre des morts':

> O mura cittadine,
> Sepolcri maestosi,
> Fin le vostre ruine
> Sono un'apoteosi.
> Cancella anco la fossa
> O barbaro inquïeto;
> Ché temerarie l'ossa
> Scuotono il sepolcreto.[28]

[O city walls, | Majestic tombs, | Even your ruins | Are an apotheosis. | Lock up the burial-place as well | O nervous barbarian | For the intrepid bones | Are rattling the graveyard.]

Like Leopardi and Foscolo, Giusti reverses the purport of an image of Italy which had come down to him as much from native sources as from foreign ones.

In many respects, then, English Italianism is continuous with the Italians' understanding of themselves. Some of its elements, however, are not shared with Risorgimento self-images, and cannot be understood in the same way. Italians as children, Italians as effeminate: these tropes are absent from the indigenous cultural heritage, and seem rather to be driven by a need on the part of the English to establish the Italians as Other than themselves, and thereby to define their own identity. Usually such tacit comparisons were to the detriment of the Italians; but not always, as Barrett Browning's description of them as 'refined' and 'graceful' indicates. How different (this comment implies) from the brutal English working and criminal classes, kidnappers of Flush, whom

[27] Mazzini, *Life and Writings*, vi. 93.

[28] Giusti, 'La Terra dei Morti', 97–104. Quoted from *Opere di Giuseppe Giusti*, ed. Nunzio Sabbatucci (Milan: UTET, 1976).

she was soon to describe in *Aurora Leigh*. James Whiteside, defender of O'Connell and future lord chief justice of Ireland, likewise opined, on a visit to Florence, that 'it is singular to find oneself among a people all of whom seem to be equally civilized'.[29] Such remarks are based to a large degree on ignorance, for social intercourse between English and Italians was distinctly limited.[30] For that very reason they are all the more evidently indications of a social ideal which was felt to be unrealized in the British Isles.

Italianism is, then, more than a fantasy of poetical tourists. In so far as it overlaps with Italian self-images, it forms part of a cultural quickening which contributed the Risorgimento. In this time of nation-building, the 'dreams' of artistic production emerged as motive forces in the realm of high politics. Even in Britain, English literary imaginings of Italy both epitomized and helped to guide public opinion, and therefore may take some credit for shaping the moderately supportive foreign policy of 1859–60.[31]

In so far as it offered an anti-image of Britain, Italianism was no less significant. A reason for its enduring appeal was the range and complexity of contrasts which it offered: Italy as past, southern, feminine, gentle, egalitarian, fanciful; Britain as future, northern, masculine, blunt, hierarchical, practical, etc. This set of imaginative antitheses was of particular interest to poets because, as Flora says, Italy was also the 'land of poetry'.

LAND OF POETRY

From the 1820s to the 1840s, obvious options for versifiers who wanted to write about Italy were to bewail the country's fallen condition, or to trumpet Britain's, and therefore their own, superiority. 'The Briton's Lament for Italy' printed anonymously in the *New Monthly Magazine*, 1821 (where Elizabeth Barrett herself published a poem about Greece), notes that in the peninsula 'Nature her gifts in gay profusion yields', and asks: 'Why does her bosom's lavish state deny | The heav'n-born plant—celestial

---

[29] Pemble, *Mediterranean Passion*, 145.   [30] Ibid. 161–2.
[31] For which, see Derek Beales, *England and Italy, 1859–60* (Thomas Nelson and Sons, 1961).

Liberty!' The answer turns out to be that Italy is unfortunately not inhabited by Britons with 'glowing breasts' and 'pow'r divine': true wealth, the rhyme concludes, is of the spirit: 'That land is rich . . . | Where glows the free-born breast with freedom's fire', etc.[32] Writing of that kind makes no room for the idea that Italy's pleasures might be akin to those of poetry itself.

The fact that Italy was so common a topic for verse led more resourceful poets to approach the country in roundabout ways. Robert Browning concentrated on the Italy of the Renaissance and the seventeenth century; Arthur Hugh Clough wrote poems of ironic resistance to the Italian dream and its progeny, the dream of the Risorgimento. However, it was also possible to exploit the association between Italy, poetry, and dreaming for an artistic end. An early instance of this manœuvre is Felicia Hemans's 'Naples: A Song of the Syren', in which the famous beauties of the Bay of Naples sing:

> 'Queen of the day and the summer sea,
>   Forget that thou art not free!'

> So doth the Syren sing, while sparkling waves
> Dance to her chant. But sternly, mournfully,
> O city of the deep! from Sybil grots
> And Roman tombs, the echoes of thy shore
> Take up the cadence of her strain alone,
> Murmuring—*Thou art not free!*[33]

The shift from a rhyming stanza to the blank verse of the final six lines, together with the gathering of syntax and strengthening of rhythm, urges us to agree that the voice of the grots and tombs sings in the manner we are explicitly told it does: 'sternly, mournfully'. On the other hand, we are no less clearly informed that the apparently vigorous words which, marked as an exclamation, conclude the poem are merely 'echoes', and only 'murmur'. These contradictory signals prompt us to wonder what happens to the example of past greatness when it is perceived by a musing visitor and expresses itself in verse; and to surmise that it may become hardly less of a contribution to elegiac feeling than the song of the

---

[32] 'The Briton's Lament for Italy', *New Monthly Magazine*, 2 (1821), 17.
[33] *The Works of Mrs Hemans*, 7 vols. (Edinburgh: William Blackwood and Sons, 1839), vi. 322.

bay. Whether or not she was aware of it, Hemans's poem makes
plain the contradiction of sympathizing with the Italians *in poetry*,
for what Italy needed to be freed from was precisely the condition
of being 'poetical', i. e. voluptuous, effeminate, backward-look-
ing. Barrett Browning's comment on the general run of Hemans's
writing has a special aptness to this poem: 'we say "How sweet &
noble" & then we are silent & can say no more—perhaps,
presently, we go to sleep, with angels in our dreams'.[34] However
stern and mournful the voice of the past might be elsewhere (say
in the prose of Ruskin or Carlyle), in a lyric set in Naples it cannot
but sing a lullaby.

Tennyson was awake to this tendency of poems about the land
of dreams. The subtitle of 'The Daisy' tells us that the work was
'Written in Edinburgh': it consists of recollections prompted by
the discovery of a pressed daisy picked in Italy some time before.
The speaker gives himself up to a series of tableaux: 'orange-blos-
som', 'sandy beaches', 'distant colour', 'long galleries', 'Sun-smit-
ten Alps' . . .

> And I forgot the clouded Forth,
> The gloom that saddens Heaven and Earth,
>   The bitter east, the misty summer
> And grey metropolis of the North.
>
> Perchance, to lull the throbs of pain,
> Perchance, to charm a vacant brain,
>   Perchance, to dream you still beside me,
> My fancy fled to the South again.[35]

As in 'A Song of the Syren', Italy's charms urge a forgetting of
the unpleasant and the real. Here too—and more distinctly than
in the Hemans poem—their influence seems to be held up crit-
ically to the light, so that it is recognized as being no more than
a 'dream' even while it is being indulged in. The last stanza is
woven out of recollections of Keats's 'Ode to a Nightingale',
with its 'beaker full of the warm South', its 'dull brain', its
'fancy' and its desire to 'forget . . . | The weariness, the fever
and the fret'.[36] Tennyson's adoption of this pointedly romantic

---

[34] *Brownings' Correspondence*, vi. 165–6.
[35] Tennyson, 'The Daisy', 3, 15, 27, 42, 62, 101–8.
[36] Keats, 'Ode to a Nightingale', 15, 34, 73, 21–3.

vocabulary asks us to see that the description of Italy provoked by the daisy is a reverie meeting the needs of people in the North to be lulled, to be charmed and to forget. In its last line, the poem announces itself to be a work of 'fancy', a faculty which, by the time Tennyson was writing, although not when Keats used the same word in his 'Ode', had become thoroughly separated from the truly inventive power, the imagination. When Coleridge made his famous distinction, he defined the fancy as being merely 'a mode of Memory'.[37] 'The Daisy' takes language which for Keats had been the vehicle of creativity and presents it as the idiom of reminiscence; it is located in the country which for the previous generation of poets had been a source of inspiration—the romantic country *par excellence*—but finds in it material for nothing greater than a daydream. Finally, it associates itself with this diminution, offering itself—a poem of landscape, of recollection, of elegy—as a work of fancy, not imagination.

'The Daisy' is not Italianist in the brute sense because it prompts its readers to notice the fact that the dream of Italy in which it indulges includes a large element of wish-fulfilment. In so doing, it identifies itself as a work which is knowingly pleasant, but no more than that: a poem of elegiac feeling located in the land of memory. This kind of verse was never the sort of thing that appealed to Elizabeth Barrett Browning. As an adult writer she was no less vigorous than she had been as a 10-year-old empress. For her, poetry was 'the enthusiasm of the understanding', and poets should adopt a prophetic, social role of the kind proclaimed by Shelley, Mazzini, and Carlyle.[38] When the first gains of liberalism in Florence in 1847 inspired her to start her first poem about Italy, she exploited a different possibility of Italianism: not self-consciously to indulge in the Italian dream, but to turn it round, as Foscolo, Leopardi, and, in his more acid way, Giusti had all sought to do. The opening of *Casa Guidi Windows* makes this revolutionary ambition quite clear: it denounces poets whose work revelled in the usual Italian themes, calling the country 'childless among mothers, | Widow of empires' etc. Such writers created a

---

[37] Coleridge, *Biographia Literaria*, i. 305.
[38] Margaret Forster, *Elizabeth Barrett Browning* (Vintage, 1998), 32.

> . . . personating Image, wherein woe
>   Was wrapt in beauty from offending much,
> They called it Cybele, or Niobe,
>   Or laid it corpse-like on a bier for such,
> Where all the world might drop for Italy
>   Those cadenced tears which burn not where they touch,—
> 'Juliet of nations, canst thou die as we?'

Although the passage includes references to Filicaia and the French poet Auguste Barbier, the main target is Byron, for in Canto the Fourth of *Childe Harold's Pilgrimage* Italy occasions what was to become the definitive example of the beautiful indulgence of woe. The declamatory verve of *Casa Guidi Windows* doubtless owes something to Byron, but it is deployed to opposite effect:

> Too many of such complaints! Behold, instead,
> Void at Verona, Juliet's marble trough.
>   As void as that is, are all images
> Men set between themselves and actual wrong,
>   To catch the weight of pity, meet the stress
> Of conscience,—since 'tis easier to gaze long
>   On mournful masks, and sad effigies,
> Than on real, live, weak creatures crushed by strong.[39]

The triple rhyme is kept up throughout the poem: in combination with habitual enjambment and general looseness of rhyme (e.g. 'stress'—'effigies') it produces a careering impetus. In the lines quoted, this collaborates with marked rhythmical emphasis to put across to a reader the 'weight of pity' felt by the narrator. There is heaviness in the repetition of 'void', in the dull trudge of the enjambment 'meet the stress | Of conscience', and in the growing ictus which culminates at the end of the passage. The penultimate line, 'on mournful masks, and sad effigies' has only nine syllables, and sounds feeble like the sad artifices it describes; this contrasts with the heavy strike of the last line, with its alliteration ('cr'), internal rhyme ('ea'), four successive stressed syllables and the bucking rhythm that takes off from them:

>   × × / /   /   / × /   × /
> Than on real, live, weak, creatures crushed by strong.

Italy, events suggest, is 'awake at last': the image of it as a nation

[39] *CGW* I. 40–8.

asleep and a land of dreams no longer fits. Likewise the manner of elegy, of recollection: the narrator sneers at 'rhymers sonneteering in their sleep' and announces that she will 'sing with these who are awake'.[40] In 1845 Theodosia Garrow had written a lyric on a similar theme which Barrett Browning certainly knew. 'She is not Dead, but Sleepeth' opens in the usual way, with Italy 'Spell-bound upon her couch of glittering sea', and then goes on to urge awakening: 'who may defy | A nation link'd in vast conspiracy?'[41] However, Garrow's poem achieves no stylistic vigour of its own to correspond with that which it seeks to encourage in Italy: for all its aggressive sentiments it still sounds like a song of the syren. The achievement of *Casa Guidi Windows* is that it presents Italy in a new style.

SIGNS OF PROMISE

The first part of *Casa Guidi Windows* was composed in late 1847, a time of political agitation in Italy. The previous year had seen the election of a comparatively young and supposedly liberal-minded Pope, Pio IX, who soon announced an amnesty for political prisoners and exiles. This act appeared to corroborate the ideas of the moderate reformer, Vincenzo Gioberti, whose *Primato morale e civile degli Italiani* (1843) had argued that the Pope was the figure best placed to lead any political and economic development in the peninsula. The amnesty initiated a period of heightened liberal activity—for Mazzini and his followers were eager to force the pace of change—as well as some concessions on the part of the established governments, such as a relaxation of press censorship in Tuscany, and preliminary negotiations towards a customs union between Tuscany, Piedmont-Sardinia, and the Papal States. On the other hand, repressive measures had also been taken: Austrian troops had occupied the Papal dominion of Ferrara, and on 8 September a demonstration in Milan had been violently suppressed. The parade described in *Casa Guidi Windows*, Part I, which celebrated the Grand Duke of Tuscany's concession to his subjects of the right to form a civic guard, took place only four days later.[42] The historical events which gave rise to Barrett

[40] *CGW* I. 219, 148, 155.
[41] Countess of Blessington (ed.), *The Keepsake for 1846* (1845), 27, 29; *Brownings' Correspondence*, xi. 163–4.
[42] Candeloro, *Storia dell'Italia Moderna*, iii. 9–92.

Browning's work were therefore not simply a 'wave of liberalism', as Julia Markus suggested in her pioneering edition, and as critics of the poem have since reiterated.[43] Major revolutionary activity did not occur until January 1848; the preceding months, in which Part 1 was written, were marked by some change, but also disappointment, and economic depression. There was no clear indication as to what, if anything, would happen next, or who would take the lead. An awareness of the uncertain context of *Casa Guidi Windows* can help us make sense of what has often been judged its strident, even 'frantic' style.[44]

Reading the introductory passage, with its dismissal of the 'personating Image', one might expect the poem then to describe or give voice to the neglected 'real, live, weak creatures crushed by strong' as Barrett Browning had done already in 'The Cry of the Children' and was to do again in *Aurora Leigh*. However, *Casa Guidi Windows* forgoes documentary realism, and indeed personifies Italy just as much as the precursor poems which it begins by spurning. The difference is that it presents its own images, not as the currency of a subjective, elegiac response (Niobe, Juliet, etc.), but as glimpses of a spiritual truth which inhabits material reality. Like Dickens's Flora, the narrator speaks of mountains, but describes them as animate beings: 'the mountains from without | In silence listen for the word said next'. The products of civilization likewise have metaphysical significance: Giotto's campanile is 'an unperplexed | Fine question Heaven-ward, touching the things granted | A noble people', while Michelangelo's sculptures are a 'sign' of future liberation.[45] As, more obviously, are the events of 1847: 'the signs | Are good and full of promise'.[46] Like Moses when Israel has passed through the Red Sea and faces the uncertainty of the wilderness of Shur, or like Zaccaria at the analogous moment in Verdi's great Risorgimento opera *Nabucco* (1840),[47] the narrator of *Casa Guidi Windows* stands forward as a

---

[43] *CGW*, p. xv. Cf. Helen Cooper, *Elizabeth Barrett Browning, Woman and Artist* (Chapel Hill, NC: University of North Carolina Press, 1988), 126; Linda M. Lewis, *Elizabeth Barrett Browning's Spiritual Progress: Face to Face with God* (Columbia, Miss.: University of Missouri Press, 1998), 94.

[44] 'Frantic' is in William Irvine and Park Honan, *The Book, the Ring and the Poet: A Biography of Robert Browning* (Bodley Head, 1974), 254.

[45] *CGW* I. 66–7, 69–71, 142.   [46] *CGW* I. 546–7.

[47] Robert had mentioned *Nabucco* to Elizabeth in a letter of 1846: *Brownings' Correspondence*, xii. 257.

prophet. 'Prophet and Poet', Carlyle had said in his famous lecture, are 'fundamentally . . . still the same', in that they can penetrate 'that divine mystery, which lies everywhere in all Beings, "the Divine Idea of the World", that which lies at "the bottom of Appearance", as Fichte styles it; of which all Appearance, from the starry sky to the grass of the field, but especially the Appearance of Man and his work, is but the *vesture*, the embodiment that renders it visible'.[48] Those words precisely anticipate the mode of vision which Barrett Browning offers the reader in *Casa Guidi Windows,* Part I: Italy becomes, no longer a dream of art and history, but a Fichtean or Hegelian Idea which is moving towards realization in the future. She writes, not an elegy, but a prophecy. Critics who have condemned this part of the work for 'rash optimism' or for being 'idealistic, unrealistic', have not taken sufficient account of its genre.[49] The poem has assumed the prophet's task: to identify and to hymn an Ideal.

As things stood, the Campanile was but a promise, a sign whose referent did not yet exist. Similarly, the concession granted by the Grand Duke—the right of citizens to form an armed Civic Guard—is an indication of greater changes in the future: of the guards' uniforms, we are told: 'if not the sign | Of something very noble, they are nought'.[50] The genre of prophecy requires first the noticing, and then the interpretation of such signifiers; and finally the urging of their significations into being. In *Casa Guidi Windows*, this shifting of rhetorical mode takes place through the development of imagery. Barrett Browning had always had a vigorous way with images, as for instance in some lines from 'Lady Geraldine's Courtship': 'the silence round us flinging | A slow arm of sweet compression'.[51] In all her verse it is common for the vehicle of a metaphor to be more physically solid than its tenor. Silence is described again in 'Bertha in the Lane', where it 'audibly did bud, and bud'; in 'The Romaunt of the Page' the heavens 'are leaning down': such images might well be described—in

[48] Carlyle, *On Heroes*, 80.

[49] Alethea Hayter, *Mrs Browning: A Poet's Work and its Setting* (Faber, 1962), 131; Cooper, *Elizabeth Barrett Browning*, 135.   [50] *CGW* I. 752.

[51] 'Lady Geraldine's Courtship', 169–70. Barrett Browning's works other than *Aurora Leigh* and *Casa Guidi Windows* are quoted from *The Complete Works of Elizabeth Barrett Browning*, ed. Charlotte Porter and Helen A. Clarke (New York: Thomas Y. Crowell and Co., 1900).

Barrett Browning's own words—as reaching 'o'er | The window-sill of metaphor'.[52] In *Casa Guidi Windows* this tendency hardens into a programme. At one point, the Arno is seen as an arrow, which 'shoots away | Through Florence' heart', while the bridges 'strain . . . like bows'.[53] In so far as the image alludes to Cupid, it suggests a polity struck by the love of freedom; in the context of potential revolution it implies battle. On both counts, it challenges the melancholy visions—of tears, of the passing of time—often provoked by rivers, and thereby contributes to the reimagining of Italy as a place of action. We might object that the metaphor is not very carefully considered, for if the arrow has pierced Florence's heart, the city may be dead. But then we should also recognize that, as a prophecy, the work does not ask for such careful attention.

Nonetheless, it is surprising that Barrett Browning did not make more of the word 'heart' in her lines about the Arno, for hearts, blood, and the pulse are recurrent figures in the work. Elegiac verse about Italy, she says, 'touched the heart of us | So finely that the pity scarcely pained';[54] her intent, by contrast, is to set our pulses racing:

> . . . Shall I say
> What made my heart beat with exulting love,
> A few weeks back?–
>
> . . . . The day was such a day
> As Florence owes the sun. The sky above,
> Its weight upon the mountains seemed to lay,
> And palpitate in glory, like a dove
> Who has flown too fast, full-hearted!–take away
> The image! for the heart of man beat higher
> That day in Florence, flooding all her streets
> And piazzas with a tumult and desire.[55]

The narrator sets off in the usual Italianate direction—sky, mountains, etc.—and arrives at the distinctly picturesque image of the dove. Then, however, she repeats the gesture with which the work opened, and turns back in favour of the human drama which is being enacted in the city. This, too, gives rise to an image; one

---

[52] 'Bertha in the Lane', 77; 'The Romaunt of the Page', 36; 'A Vision of Poets', 653-4.
[53] *CGW* I. 53–5.　　　　[54] *CGW* I. 18–19.　　　　[55] *CGW* I. 444–53.

which appears, no longer as a product of fancy, but as a revelation of the spirit of liberty which animates the crowd and unites them, so that collectively they form 'The first pulse of an even flow of blood, | To prove the level of Italian veins'.[56] Given that some real blood had already been spilt, and in the campaign against Austria much more was soon to flow, this choice of metaphor may well be judged cavalier. Worse follows:

> So let them die! The world shows nothing lost;
> Therefore not blood. Above or underneath,
>   What matter, brothers, if ye keep your post
> On duty's side? . . .[57]

Her assumed fraternity with the revolutionaries consorts oddly with her willingness to see them dead, the more so as she is not herself in danger. Doubtless the exhortation would have seemed less callous to someone who had a firm belief in personal immortality. Possibly we might argue that it shows Barrett Browning's awareness of the importance of martyrdom in programmes of nationalist myth-making such as Mazzini's: 'the seed that we have sown . . . will . . . germinate beneath the soil sanctified by the blood of our martyrs; . . . You may kill men; you cannot kill a great idea', as he had written in *Ricordi dei Fratelli Bandiera* (1844), a book she knew.[58] Nonetheless, the lines seem forced. In a later poem, 'Mother and Poet', Barrett Browning was to write movingly of the pain occasioned by self-sacrifice for the nationalist cause. Such considerations are shut out of *Casa Guidi Windows* by the genre of prophecy which she has assumed. In consequence, many readers today will justifiably think the work strident and headlong. However, those very characteristics show how vigorously Barrett Browning has set about overturning the old images of Italy. If *Casa Guidi Windows* is often strained, it is with the vehemence of opposition.

THE PULSE OF THE VERSE

Casa Guidi Windows is written in a variant of *terza rima* and therefore recalls Dante, the first canto of whose *Commedia* Barrett

---

[56] *CGW* I. 468–9.　　　　[57] *CGW* I. 1210–13.
[58] Mazzini, *Life and Writings*, iii. 316; *Brownings' Correspondence*, xi. 180–1.

Browning had translated not long before.[59] Judging Italy to be in
need of 'Dante's soul', she presents the country with at least an
echo of his rhymes.[60] The provenance of the form, however, is
less remarkable than her handling of it.

Rhythm had always excited her imagination. In 1826 her
youthful self had remarked on a line of Milton:

I feel strongly the exquisite effect of the first amphibrach & subsequent
trochees—like the heaving of the half formed elements.

'Confusion heard his voice and—

And I feel no less strongly the sudden cessation of confusion, the sudden
firmness, & 'standing fast' produced *by* what appear to me the five successive long syllables—when

'wild uproar

Stood ruled'.[61]

Certainly the writer of that passage would have meant something
by the sequence of long, stressed syllables which I mentioned
earlier:

> . . . since 'tis easier to gaze long
> On mournful masks, and sad effigies,
> Than on real, live, weak creatures crushed by strong.

Here, though, the emphasis makes sense as impulse, not restraint.
It puts across to us the 'weight of pity', the 'stress of conscience'
by which the narrator has been moved; writing it, Barrett
Browning might have thought something like the words which
she later composed for Aurora Leigh: 'I felt | My heart's life
throbbing in my verse to show | It lived'.[62] The throb of life
keeps up throughout the first part of *Casa Guidi Windows*, driving
the sentences on from line to line, pausing only at the ends of the

[59] Elizabeth Barrett Browning, *Hitherto Unpublished Poems and Stories*, 2 vols. (Boston:
Bibliophile Society, 1914), 236–43.
    [60] *Letters of Elizabeth Barrett Browning to Mary Russell Mitford, 1836–54*, ed. Meredith B.
Raymond and Mary Rose Sullivan, 3 vols. (Winfield, Kan: Wedgestone Press, 1983), iii.
250.
    [61] *Brownings' Correspondence*, i. 258–9. The editors insert an inverted comma between
'and' and '—' in the first indented quotation.   [62] *Aurora Leigh*, III. 338–40.

long, irregular verse-paragraphs. This is a poem which aims, not to 'lull the throbs of pain' but to amplify them, and it does that by making the pulse of the verse beat loudly.

The opening of Part II sounds different:

> I wrote a meditation and a dream,
>> Hearing a little child sing in the street.
> I leant upon his music as a theme,
>> Till it gave way beneath my heart's full beat,
> Which tried at an exultant prophecy
>> But dropped before the measure was complete—
> Alas for songs and hearts! . . .

Here the movement is more controlled, the reason being that the ends of these lines always coincide with breaks between syntactic clauses, while the rhythm is comparatively regular: only line two ('Hearing a little child sing in the street') and the end of line four ('heart's full beat') are markedly not iambic. In the last line quoted it seems that the narrator is so discouraged that her pulse will not keep up even to the end of the line, her words dropping before their measure is complete, re-enacting in microcosm the failure of her prophecy. Later on, when she describes the return of Florence's old absolutist ruler accompanied by an Austrian garrison in May 1849, her voice is even more depressed:

> From Casa Guidi windows, gazing, then,
> I saw and witness how the Duke came back.
>> The regular tramp of horse and tread of men
> Did smite the silence like an anvil black
>> And sparkless. . . .[63]

As at the opening of Part II, the line-ends broadly correspond with syntactic breaks, while the general semantic flabbiness ('then', 'and witness', 'Did') makes the writing seem weary. Even the marked run-on from the fourth to the fifth line contributes to the general deadening of the verse: if you take lines three and four by themselves the sentence looks as though it comes to an end at 'black', so that '. . . | And sparkless' appears as a dull afterthought. 'Regular' is odd, introducing as it does an irregularity of rhythm, but perhaps we are meant to think of even that word as being oppressed by the general monotony, reduced to the pronunciation

---

[63] *CGW* II. 286–90.

'reg'lar'. We might imagine the narrator's subdued heart beating
in time with the 'tread' of the famously methodical Austrian army
(Mrs Wetmore Story was similarly struck by its 'stony, solid
aspect')[64] and communicating that flattened pulse to the feet of her
verse. Support for this idea comes from one of Barrett Browning's
essays, where she wrote of Dryden: 'he established finally the reign
of the literati for the reign of the poets—and the critics clapped
their hands. He established finally the despotism of the final
emphasis . . . And so, in distinctive succession to poetry and inspiration, began the new system of harmony "as by law established." '[65] What she dislikes about Dryden's use of the heroic
couplet is that it introduces a new law to restrict poetic liberty:

> Among the elder poets, the rhyme was only a felicitous adjunct, a musi-
> cal accompaniment, the tinkling of a cymbal through the choral
> harmonies . . . But the new practice endeavoured to identify in all possi-
> ble cases the rhyme and what may be called the sentimental emphasis;
> securing the latter to the tenth rhyming *syllable* . . . And not only by this
> unnatural provision did the emphasis minister to the rhyme, but the
> pause did it also. 'Away with all pauses,'—said the reformers,—'except
> the legitimate pause at the tenth rhyming syllable.'[66]

Political metaphors are central to the thought of this passage: the
new 'despotism' follows the old 'reign' of liberty by 'succession',
and is declared 'legitimate'; emphasis is presented as being rhyme's
'minister'. There is also a thread of theological implication: minis-
ters belong in churches as well as courts, and the phrase 'as by law
established' seems to allude to the Church of England. 'Choral
harmonies' has a similar drift. While they do not converge into a
clear argument, these metaphors do show how strongly Barrett
Browning associated verse-form with religious and political structures. Indeed, their vagueness, together with the insistence with
which they are advanced, suggests a conviction which runs deeper
than reason. Dryden's couplets, she implies, derive from and
represent the Restoration, while the hint of theology brings in the
thought that he may have been especially prone to use that rhyme-
scheme because after the accession of James II he became a
Catholic. Of the style of her youthful work 'An Essay on Mind'—

---

[64] Henry James, *William Wetmore Story and his Friends*, 2 vols. (Thames and Hudson,
1903) i. 141.   [65] *Complete Works of Elizabeth Barrett Browning*, vi. 285.
[66] Ibid. 280.

which is in couplets—Barrett Browning commented that it was 'written . . . when the mind was scarcely free in any measure from trammels & *Popes*'.[67] As the title of the work suggests, the Pope she most had in mind was Alexander, the poet; yet the fact that the word is made plural and appears alongside trammels and lack of freedom points in the direction of the Pope of Rome, for the great aim of the leader of the Catholic Church, *Casa Guidi Windows* informs us, is to prevent minds from becoming free: 'he must resent | Each man's particular conscience, and repress | Inquiry, meditation, argument'.[68] The onomastic pun was there for the taking, since, like Dryden, Alexander Pope was a Catholic.

Europe, including Italy, had suffered a Restoration too (in 1815), one which, like that of 1660, favoured the Roman Catholic Church. Incorporated into an 'An Essay on Mind' is a vehement declaration of support for the movement which first challenged the 1815 settlement: Greek nationalism. In Barrett Browning's twenties Greece was for her more or less what Italy was to become in her forties: 'My other country—country of my soul!'—she declares, adopting and adapting the phrase Byron coined for Rome.[69] When she apologized for the poem, it seems that she was thinking particularly of the contrast between its traditional form and libertarian intent. In *Casa Guidi Windows*, her mature command of her craft lets her bring her style into harmony with her pro-Risorgimento campaign, and to write in opposition to '*Popes*'.

Throughout Part I, the main hope is that Italy will (in the terms of the letter which I quoted towards the beginning of this chapter) turn its 'fancy' into a strong 'impulse', that it will feel a shock of revolt like that which beats in the rhythm of 'real, live, weak creatures crushed by strong'. Part II aims to get over the revolutions' failure with a course of discipline. The Italians have much to learn from the Austrians: 'cognisant of acts, not imageries', their invaders do not suffer from that fancifulness which was so often thought to be Italy's main shortcoming. As it gathers rhetorical force, the passage which prophesies the development of similar mental control among the Italians builds into the rhythmical impetus of Part I the formal restraint which has become the sound of Austria:

---

[67] *Brownings' Correspondence*, v. 202.　　[68] *CGW* I. 995–7.
[69] 'An Essay on Mind', II. 1147.

> That having learnt—by no mere apophthegm –
> Not just the draping of a graceful stuff
> About a statue, broidered at the hem, –
> Not just the trilling on an opera stage,
> Of 'libertà' to bravos—(a fair word,
> Yet too allied to inarticulate rage
> And breathless sobs, for singing, though the chord
> Were deeper than they struck it!) but the gauge
> Of civil wants sustained, and wrongs abhorred, –
> The serious, sacred meaning and full use
> Of freedom for a nation,—then, indeed,
> Our Tuscans, underneath the bloody dews
> Of some new morning, rising up agreed
> And bold, will want no Saxon souls or thews,
> To sweep their piazzas clear of Austria's breed.[70]

The sprawling articulation of this sentence suggests that Barrett Browning was concentrating on matters other than syntax; the rhythm, however, commands attention. The first half of the passage is rhythmically tepid: the opening four lines stop and start, and the verse in parentheses has no marked beat. With 'but', as the diction becomes more exalted, the movement changes: there are stresses on 'gáuge', 'cívil', 'sustáined', 'wróngs', 'abhórred', and this declamatory pulse rolls on to the end of the pasage, kept from stiffening into a sclerotic clatter by the variation of mid-line pauses, until it achieves its purpose in the resounding strike of the last line. The 'wrongs abhorred' which at the start of the work had provoked the momentary throb of life in 'creatures crushed by strong' here contribute to the development of a regular beat. The rhymes, chiming across the enjambed clauses, are, as Barrett Browning would say, like a 'cymbal through the choral harmonies', harmonies which sound loudly as assonance (e.g., 'me̱aning . . . fre̱edom . . . inde̱ed . . . underne̱ath') and alliteration (e.g., 'su̱stained . . . s̱erious, s̱acred . . . us̱e . . . S̱axon s̱oul s̱ . . . s̱weep'). In Part I the Italians were described as 'A noble people who, being greatly vexed | In act, in aspiration keep undaunted';[71] here in Part II we are to imagine that visionary nature developing, through endurance, the northern practicality of 'Saxon souls or thews' so as to bring its dreams to fruition.

---

[70] *CGW* II. 223–37.   [71] *CGW* I. 71–2.

In its own gathering of rhetorical force, its marrying of imaginative impulse to formal discipline, the writing offers its readers an aesthetic analogue of the wished-for political development. This verse bears the marks of Italian liberty in the same way as Dryden's poetry—in Barrett Browning's view—bore the marks of the Restoration; but with the difference that her work is in advance of the facts. Like Giotto's Campanile, it is a sign of things that ought to come. Part II hopes that an echo, nay, more than an echo of its own forceful pulse will appear in the 'heart of man'; and finds the beginnings of such a development in that most Austrian of Italian States, Piedmont, where, the poem asserts towards its end, 'life throbs'.[72]

A POLICY OF ENTHUSIASM

Even if Barrett Browning had wanted to have her poem published or distributed in Italy, censorship—after the restoration of absolutism in 1849—would have prevented her. In 1848, when she finished Part I—then thought of as an independent work and entitled 'A Hope in Italy'—she did not agitate to have it printed (perhaps in translation) by a revolutionary press in Florence, but instead sent it to *Blackwood's*, who rejected it.[73] The completed poem was published in London in 1851. Like all her writing, *Casa Guidi Windows* is directed primarily at an English audience. In consequence, exhortations such as 'Will, therefore, to be strong, thou Italy!'[74] have an odd status: not in practice addressed to Italians, but offered to the English as an example of cosmopolitan solidarity. Nonetheless, she did have a polemical design on her audience: she sought to promote greater political support for the Risorgimento and perhaps some kind of international intervention. 'Help, lands of Europe!' cries Part I, having an eye to French revolutionaries as well as English liberals.[75] When the whole work finally appeared in 1851, Part II made a similar though longer-term claim, denouncing the Great Exhibition and asking 'gracious nations' to support 'poor Italia, baffled by mischance'.[76]

However, as the long interpretation of Italian art history in Part I suggests, the poem's field of relevance is not confined to this

---

[72] *CGW* II. 731.
[74] *CGW* I. 661.
[75] *CGW* I. 1104.
[73] *CGW*, ed. Markus, 116–18.
[76] *CGW* II. 651–2.

immediate intent. Michelangelo's statues have languished for three centuries in 'that small chapel of the dim St. Lawrence', but they are nonetheless still freighted with political meaning. In Barrett Browning's view, works of art are vitally connected to politics, but they do not have the limited and specific application of speeches or pamphlets. Instead, they record the (broadly Hegelian) Idea which it is then the business of politics to enact. At one stage she asks for a poet to step forward whose work will be 'Annunciative, reproving, pure, erect, | To show which way your first Ideal bare | The whiteness of its wings'.[77] *Casa Guidi Windows* is her own bid at replying to that appeal. Critics who have defended what they take to be the work's pragmatic approach to its political circumstances,[78] therefore, risk misapprehending it almost as much as those who have condemned it for 'rash optimism'. *Casa Guidi Windows* is an exercise in resolute idealism. To read the relevant parliamentary debates in 1848–9 is to see that the call for active British support of Italy had absolutely no prospect of being answered.[79] Barrett Browning's appeal is knowingly, and wilfully, 'idealistic', for she thought the voicing of ideals to be a central task of poetry. This belief coincided with what appears to have been a more general tendency to, and enjoyment of enthusiasm, a tendency of which she was perfectly well aware: 'I have strong credulity, say my friends', she writes in a letter, while after some particularly vehement declamation she concludes with cheery bathos: 'see what a republican you have for a . . . Ba'.[80] Something of the same knowingness appears occasionally in Part I of *Casa Guidi Windows*, for instance when, having been carried away on the subject of Dante, she pulls herself up short; 'What do I say? I only meant . . .'.[81] Such moments of self-correction bring into the texture of Part I a recognition that the happy prospect it announces might very well not be realized, as indeed it was not. The consequent 'discrepancy between the two parts', the 'Advertisement to the First Edition' explains, exemplifies 'the interval between aspiration and performance, between faith and dis-illusion, between hope and fact' which is one of 'the conditions of our nature'.[82] *Casa Guidi*

---

[77] *CGW* I. 81, 1096–8.

[78] *CGW*, xx; Forster, *Elizabeth Barrett Browning*, 215.

[79] See *Hansard*, vol. 96, cols. 662–3, 665; 97, col. 1198; 98, col. 138, etc.

[80] *Letters of Elizabeth Barrett Browning to Mary Russell Mitford*, iii. 386; *Brownings' Correspondence*, xii. 207.   [81] *CGW* I. 637.   [82] *CGW*, p. xli.

Windows is all about the discovery and assertion of 'hope'. Although Part II records and explains the failure of the aspirations of Part I, it then goes on to assert a new hope of its own.

The knowingly credulous productions of Barrett Browning's imagination, therefore, took their place in a perpetual dialectic betweeen the ideal and the real, between 'hope and fact'. This policy of enthusiasm had special aptness in a time of revolution: a time, that is, when ideals took on manifest political force; and when—for whatever combination of reasons—people announced themselves as being willing to die for Freedom, or Italy. As Barrett Browning will have read in Lord Lytton's *Rienzi*, 'the prudent man may direct a state; but it is the enthusiast who regenerates it,—or ruins'.[83] In such circumstances the callousness of 'So let them die!' may be necessary. It all comes down to a question of genre. Henry James regretted the lack— in Barrrett Browning's poems about Italy—of 'that saving and sacred sense of proportion, of the free and blessed *general* that great poets . . . give us the impression of even in emotion and passion, even in pleading a cause and calling on the gods'; reading her we are, he goes on, 'less edified than we ought to be'.[84] To which one may reply that *Casa Guidi Windows* does not aim to edify, and as for losing her sense of proportion, Barrett Browning did that willingly as being the cost of her commitment. However, it must also be admitted that the poem is one kind of work and not another. It has the shortcomings of its virtues. In being vigorous it is not careful; in being committed it necessarily makes no attempt at impartiality.

The limitations of *Casa Guidi Windows* help us to see why many other mid-nineteenth-century poems come to grips with politics in a less direct fashion. Writers who wish to enquire into revolutionary enthusiasm—its costs, its virtues—must not themselves be carried away by it, at least, not in the act of composition. As we will see, Clough, Robert Browning, and—in *Aurora Leigh*— Elizabeth Barrett Browning herself help us to understand and judge the claims of nationalism (and much else) in poems which concentrate on particular characters, involving them in dramatic situations or narratives which connect with politics whether

---

[83] Lord Lytton, *Rienzi* (1835; J. M. Dent, 1911), 65.
[84] James, *William Wetmore Story*, ii. 54–5.

explicitly or by implication. Focusing on individuals, the poems necessarily take account of that variety of human values and commitments which *Casa Guidi Windows* in its campaigning vigour necessarily forgets. They maintain something like that 'sense of proportion' which mattered to Henry James.

From the perspective of a work by Clough or by Browning (though he would never have admitted it), *Casa Guidi Windows* stands as an example of how not to write poetry about politics. For Clough, and for Browning during the period of the great monologues, an essential requirement of poetry was that it should resist enthusiasm. Arnold recognized this when he called Clough 'a d—d depth-hunter in poetry', as did Browning when he said of his wife, 'the simple truth is that *she* was the poet, and I the clever person by comparison'.[85] In their writing, issues which in *Casa Guidi Windows* are trumpeted—the need for unity, inspiration, self-sacrifice, a great leader—appear as questions.

In some respects, then, *Casa Guidi Windows* was a dead end for poetry about politics. Barrett Browning herself resurrected its prophetic mode in *Poems Before Congress* (1860); thereafter, of serious writers, only Swinburne continued in its vein. However, the work does mark a turning point for English imaginings of Italy, although the degree to which it is responsible for this, rather than the events to which it alludes, cannot be determined. In the 1850s, magazine verse characteristically portrayed the Italians as a people who were, albeit slowly, preparing for change, and who therefore needed advice. One John Ashford, in a work entitled *Italy's Hope* (1857) adopted the usual stance:

> Italians! . . .
> O'ercome low sloth, which, after all,
> Is deadliest tyrant, and its thrall
> Wears weightiest fetters; of alloy
> Refine your faith, but not destroy.[86]

In later recollections of 1848, Barrett-Browningesque images quite frequently appear, as for instance in 'Ugo Bassi' (1873), by Harriet

---

[85] *The Letters of Matthew Arnold to Arthur Hugh Clough*, ed. H. F. Lowry (Oxford University Press, 1932), 81; *Dearest Isa: Robert Browning's Letters to Isabella Blagden*, ed. Edward C. McAleer (Austin, Tex.: University of Texas Press, 1951), 365.

[86] John Ashford, *Italy's Hope: A Tale of Florence* (J. F. Hope, 1857), 9.

Eleanor Hamilton King, where they are phrased—oddly—in the style of Tennyson's *Idylls*:

> But higher than the note of trumpet swelled
> The heart of Italy, and faster beat
> The heart of Italy than all the bells
> That pealed on one another through the air.[87]

To read these works, though, is to become newly appreciative of how thoroughly *Casa Guidi Windows* brings the resources of poetry to bear in support of its prophetic aim. As they explored other modes of writing, Barrett Browning's great contemporaries shared her feeling that the shift from a Europe of kingdoms to a Europe of nations had repercussions both for the language of English poetry and for its forms.

[87] Harriet Eleanor Hamilton King, *The Disciples* (Henry S. King and Co., 1873) 124.

5

THE SCOPE OF NARRATIVE: *AURORA LEIGH*

LIBERTY THROUGH UNION

The Brownings were surprised by a convergence between personal union and political unity when, in 1847, their first wedding anniversary coincided with the procession to mark the birth of the Florentine civic guard—the same celebration which was later to be described in Part I of *Casa Guidi Windows*. Elizabeth Barrett Browning recorded the event in a letter:

The fact was, that our Italians had resolved to keep our day for us on a most magnificent scale; an intention which we, on our parts, not only graciously appropriated, but permitted in return to perfect the glory by keeping at the same time the establishment of the civic guard & prospect of the liberty of Italy through union— . . . for above three hours the infinite procession filed under our windows with all their various flags & symbols, into the Piazza Pitti where the Duke & his family stood in tears at the window to receive the thanks of his people. Never in the world was a more affecting sight . . nor a grander, if you took it in its full significance—. . .[1]

The public, in its 'infinite procession', files between two domestic spaces: the home of the bourgeois married Brownings, and the palace of 'the Duke & his family', hereditary rulers of German descent. In each case, the boundary between private and public is asserted only to be blurred as the observers look out (like the narrator of *Casa Guidi Windows*) through windows. The aristocrats are made to seem united in feeling with the people by their tears (which in *Casa Guidi Windows* are filled out into 'good warm human tears'); this, it seems, is paternal government of a thoroughly

---

[1] *Brownings' Correspondence*, xiv. 300.

benign order. The married poets, on the other hand, feel a diffuse similarity between the 'liberty . . . through union' which they have achieved in marriage, and the liberty through union which they hope will be the end of political developments in Italy. As it turned out, of course, the Duke's display of sympathy did not lead to corresponding actions. In retrospect, the contrast between the two publicly resonant private relationships, the old established ruling family and the new escapee marriage of poets, prefigures similar contrasts in the work of both Brownings: the propertied match offered Aurora at the start of *Aurora Leigh* as against her coming together with a chastened, poorer Romney in Italy at the end; and the arranged marriage of Pompilia and Guido in *The Ring and the Book*, as against Pompilia's unconventional, liberating alliance with Caponsacchi.

Barrett Browning had long hazarded comparisons between household and national governance. Aged about 12, she had written in the following terms to her father: 'say inexorable monarch of Hope End can no intreaties mortal or immortal prevail upon you to command the crested chariot to be linked to the four high mettled steeds to bear us to Kinnersly'.[2] By the 1840s, Mr Barrett's increasingly strict notions of domestic order were no longer a joking matter. In her correspondence with her future husband, Elizabeth Barrett describes her father's 'patriarchal ideas of governing grownup children': 'he takes it to be his duty to rule like the Kings of Christendom, by divine right.'[3] Before she met Browning, she was already investigating in her poetry the connections between wedlock and broader issues of social and economic power: in 'Lady Geraldine's Courtship', questions about the relative value of intellectual accomplishment and class status are brought into focus by a marriage, while 'The Romaunt of the Page' attacks the view that wives should be confined to domestic duties, canvassing instead a more active, public role. As her relationship with Browning developed, the prospect of marriage to him took on the traits of a political struggle: 'I love thee freely, as men strive for Right', she wrote in *Sonnets from the Portuguese*, implicitly contrasting this democratic

---

[2] *Brownings' Correspondence*, i. 50.
[3] Daniel Karlin, *The Courtship of Robert Browning and Elizabeth Barrett* (Oxford: Clarendon Press, 1985), 27, 98.

'Right' with the 'divine right' represented by her father, and anticipating *Casa Guidi Windows*, where Italians likewise 'strive for right'.[4]

Appearing in a love sonnet, or murmured in the beloved's ear, such images have an erotic charge, something like Donne's 'Oh my America, my new found lande', or 'She'is all States, and all Princes, I'.[5] In the context of *Sonnets from the Portuguese*, 'I love thee freely, as men strive for Right' need not make any very precise political calibration, for the main point of the simile is, rather, the shift of scale: her love is as great as the ardour of a revolutionary movement; her desire as lawless as a crowd. Nonetheless, when, as at the Florentine demonstration of 1847, such habits of mind are brought into contact with a real freedom struggle, the comparisons which they engender may well become more specific. Looking forward, on her wedding anniversary, to the liberty of Italy through union, Barrett Browning links the Risorgimento to the story of her escape through marriage from her father's patriarchal realm. 'Union', as applied to Italy, alluded most immediately to a customs union between Tuscany and other northern states which was being proposed in 1847, and, following on from that, some kind of administrative unification. There are only the weakest grounds for a comparison between matrimony and the Risorgimento here. Marriage does, however, have more relevance to the other, less material kinds of union on which, according to *Casa Guidi Windows*, the progress of Italy would depend. There is union in the moral sense—self-discipline, devotion to an aim—which is figured as the joining of 'Italian aspiration' to 'Saxon souls or thews'; and 'union' as meaning devotion to a leader: 'if *thou* invite me forth, | I rise above abasement at the word', she wrote in *Sonnnets from the Portuguese*, a declaration which echoes in *Casa Guidi Windows*, with its calls for a 'teacher' to 'strike fire into the masses' and ready them for 'rising up agreed | And bold'.[6] As we saw, these kinds of union have an aesthetic counterpart in the hybrid style of the work itself, which at least one reader understood in terms of marriage, as a balancing of

---

[4] *Sonnets from the Portuguese*, XLIII. 7; *CGW* I. 428.

[5] John Donne, 'Elegie: To his Mistris Going to Bed', 27; 'The Sunne Rising', 21. Quoted from John Donne, *The Elegies and The Songs and Sonnets*, ed. Helen Gardner (Oxford: Clarendon Press, 1965).

[6] *Sonnets from the Portuguese*, XVI. 12–13; *CGW* I. 795, 837; II. 235–6.

'womanly faith and trust' with 'a manly power of analyzing events and facing disagreeable truths'.[7]

Critics who have noticed the pattern of imaginative interrelation between Italian politics and Barrett Browning's personal life have generally viewed it with disdain: 'it is hardly surprising' that she 'entangled the cultural myths of the nation's survival and rebirth with the personal myths of her own'. In this line of reasoning, her work is solipsistic, so that the only risorgimento which really interests her is 'the triumphant risorgimento of the woman poet'.[8] Such arguments neglect the fact that domestic metaphors have been a constant of political rhetoric and theory since at least Plato. Even in the broadest terms, marriage is as apt an image of political community as Leviathan or brotherhood: as we saw in Chapter 2, it implies that States should have an affective (rather than, say, legal) origin and that their members should freely consent to belong to them (rather than, say, being conquered). These suggestions may well be thought both vague and contentious, but they are no more so than the inherent implications of the metaphors adopted by Hobbes and Marx. What matters is the intelligence and circumspection with which such images are deployed and elaborated. One unease which readers of *Casa Guidi Windows* may justifiably feel is that the poem too readily configures political allegiance as desire. An electric touch may be a desirable attribute in a lover, but a leader who wants to 'strike electric influence through a race' is likely therefore to distrust the exercise of that personal 'Individuality' which Barrett Browning elsewhere holds sacred.[9] Because it remains implicit, the governing idea that Italian nationalism was heading towards a kind of marriage is not opened up for examination within the work itself. The heated circumstances of the poem's composition provide an explanation for this, and may be taken to justify it: as we saw in the last chapter, *Casa Guidi Windows* is a prophetic work and therefore not given to self-criticism. In the mid-1850s, when the

---

[7] *The Spectator*, 24/1200 (28 June 1851), 616–17; quoted in Sandra Donaldson's *Elizabeth Barrett Browning: An Annotated Bibliography of the Commentary and Criticism, 1826–1990* (G. K. Hall, 1993), 45.

[8] Flavia Alaya, 'The Ring, the Rescue, & the Risorgimento: Reunifying the Brownings' Italy', *Browning Institute Studies*, 6 (1978), 19; Gilbert, 'From *Patria* to *Matria*', 35.

[9] *CGW* I. 729; *Letters of Elizabeth Barrett Browning to Mary Russell Mitford*, iii. 235.

prospect of change in Italy seemed distant, Barrett Browning returned to her idea and framed it more explicitly, writing a narrative focused on individuals which develops comparisons between marriage and political unity in remarkably subtle and enquiring ways.

A UNIFICATION IN ITALY

Her first thoughts about the work that was to become *Aurora Leigh* occurred to Barrett Browning more than ten years before its completion. The popularity of 'Lady Geraldine's Courtship' (1844) had encouraged her to plan a longer poem along the same lines, combining her own habitual 'mysticism' with the 'realism' which she admired in books by her friend Mary Russell Mitford, as well as in the French novels which the two women enthused about in their letters. The projected opus would be 'a sort of novel-poem',[10] and would treat subjects often considered unsuitable for poetry, while linking them to 'noble ideal apprehensions' like those which made Balzac seem to Barrett Browning the most poetic of novelists.[11] Her thoughts about subject-matter soon merged into considerations of structure: 'having unity, as a work of art,—& admitting of as much philosophical dreaming & digression (which is in fact a characteristic of the age) as I like to use'.[12] The contrary poles of 'novel' and 'poem' here lose focus: poems doubtless generally have more 'unity', while novels allow more digression; 'philosophical dreaming', however, looks distinctly poetical. Nonetheless, it remains clear that the ruling idea at the origin of *Aurora Leigh* was that of the unification of generic opposites: of the material with the ideal, of liberty with form.

When the 1848 revolution took hold of Barrett Browning's imagination, her early ideas about a 'novel-poem' found some scope in the generic hybridity of *Casa Guidi Windows*. By 1853, when the composition of *Aurora Leigh* began in earnest, Italian politics were less involving. Although, with the rise of Cavour, constitutional reforms were under weigh in Piedmont (where 'life throbs', as *Casa Guidi Windows* had affirmed), any immediate upheaval seemed unlikely. Barrett Browning herself wrote: 'poor,

---

[10] *Brownings' Correspondence*, ix, 304, 293; see *AL*, ed. Margaret Reynolds, 21–6.
[11] *Brownings' Correspondence*, ix. 189.   [12] Ibid. 304.

poor Italy! Not dead yet, no—let her be ever so despised &
scorned & forgotten ... I have faith for the future .. sooner or
later, .. & probably later indeed'.[13] In her correspondence, the
space previously occupied by Italy is now taken up with domestic
happiness and with her child. Similarly, in *Aurora Leigh*, Italy
figures as a location, less of revolution than of retirement, and
much attention is given to childhood and mothering. The opposites which had always been central to the idea of the work are
now divided between the genders and embodied in two individuals: Aurora, a half-Italian woman poet, and Romney, a wholly
English male social reformer.

The first two books of the work resound with echoes of *Casa
Guidi Windows*. Falling in love with an Italian, Aurora's father
experiences the beginnings of something like a revolution:
'suddenly' he had 'thrown off the old conventions'; but his wife
dies before it can be fully accomplished: he 'Had reached to free-
dom, not to action, lived, | But lived as one entranced, with
thoughts, not aims'. This recalls the Tuscans in 1848–9 who had
failed to establish a new regime because of 'aims dispersed'.[14] Left
an orphan, the young Aurora is transported to England and
subjected to the Saxon discipline of her Aunt, whose 'narrow forehead' (like that of the treacherous Grand Duke whose 'forehead's
build | Has no capacious genius') is 'braided tight' against 'possi-
ble pulses' such as the beats and throbs which sound throughout
Casa Guidi Windows.[15] Where the raised hopes of 1848 had been
like the 'upspringing | Of ... a nimble bird to sky from perch',
Aunt Leigh lives a 'cage-bird life'; Aurora, by contrast, is 'A wild
bird scarcely fledged'.[16] This impetuous nestling is greeted by her
aunt 'Imperiously': she 'held me at arm's length, | And with two
grey-steel naked-bladed eyes | Searched through my face,—ay,
stabbed it through and through'. Aurora, therefore, shares in the
metaphorical condition of 'corpse-like' Italy under Austrian imperial control.[17] Subjected to her Aunt's domestic regime, she is
schooled in her social role, being taught to draw, dance, and
model flowers in wax. Secretly, though, she embarks on an intellectual adventure in her father's library, expanding her identity by

[13] *Letters of Elizabeth Barrett Browning to Mary Russell Mitford*, iii. 326; for a thorough
survey of the political situation, see Candeloro, *Storia dell'Italia moderna*, iv. 7–152.
[14] *AL* I. 176–7, 181–2; *CGW* II. 528.   [15] *AL* I. 273, 275; *CGW* I. 564–5.
[16] *CGW* I. 5–6; *AL* I. 305, 310.   [17] *AL* I. 326–8; *CGW* I. 33.

plunging 'Soul-forward, headlong, into a book's profound, |
Impassioned for its beauty and salt of truth' and 'hard-swimming
through | The deeps' of intellectual inquiry. This is like the
Renaissance in *Casa Guidi Windows*, where the 'swimmers'
Giotto, Fra Angelico and Raffael 'through the blue Immense, |
Strike out'.[18] When he happens upon her first efforts at verse,
Romney repeats the strictures which in the earlier poem were
heaped upon the aimless play of fancy: 'work for ends' he admon-
ishes, not for the 'sleek fringes' of 'baldaquins'—an image which,
though in itself somewhat obscure, certainly recalls the 'draping of
a graceful stuff | About a statue, broidered at the hem' scorned by
the narrator of *Casa Guidi Windows*.[19] 'Give art's divine', he says,
'Direct, indubitable, real as grief', echoing the earlier work's
commitment to revealing 'actual wrong'.[20]

Such echoes manifest, and tend to inculcate in a reader who
notices them, a habit of mind which continually moves back and
forth between the particular and the general, seeing in a local
instance of cruelty the shadow of systematic political oppression,
while also imagining how large forces ('despotism', 'Renaissance')
manifest themselves in the lives of individuals. In the terms I
suggested in Chapter 1, it holds Shalott and Camelot together, and
sets up patterns of comparison between them. This double vision
owes something to the example of Byron which I discussed in
Chapter 3: Barrett Browning wanted her poem to be 'a Don Juan,
without the mockery & impurity, ... under one aspect'.[21]
However, the connections which can be drawn between Aurora's
history and Italy's are more persistent and methodical than
anything in *Don Juan*. Perhaps, then, Aurora and Romney should
be thought of as figures of their respective nations, like their coun-
terparts in the work's most important source, Madame de Staël's
Corinne, ou l'Italie, a novel in which (as the title suggests) Corinne
embodies essential Italianness, by contrast with Lord Nelvil, the
epitome of England. De Staël is not interested in the vagaries of
individual personality, but offers the reader a study in what she
takes to be the essence, the Idea, of contrasting national temperaments. Opening as it does with an account of the disparity

---

[18] *AL* I. 707–8, 795–6; *CGW* I. 398–9.
[19] *AL* II. 137–8, 140; *CGW* II. 224–5.   [20] *AL* II. 154–5; *CGW* I. 44.
[21] *Brownings' Correspondence*, ix. 304.

between England and Italy, and quickly linking this to the conflict between Aurora (poetical, impulsive, etc.) and Romney (political, methodical), *Aurora Leigh* certainly gestures in the direction of *Corinne*: at one point, Romney calls Aurora an 'Italy of women'.[22] The resulting combination of the symbolic with the particular in the central characters has puzzled critics: Deirdre David dismisses them as 'emblematic sketches'; Virginia Woolf more fairly judged them to have been drawn with 'something of the exaggeration of a caricaturist'.[23] Without doubt, one aim of Barrett Browning's work was, by means of this emblematism, to suggest the compatibility and even mutual dependence of national dispositions which, in *Corinne*, are condemned to separation.

However, while it courts such generalizations, the poem also warns against them. Throughout, great importance is given to the development of individuality: it is made clear that Aurora is right to assert her own desires against Aunt Leigh's expectations, and later she finds that the most important function of poetry is to defend 'individualism' against its twin enemies, social 'conventions' and the 'universal' ambitions of Romney's socialist schemes for reform.[24] The shortcomings of Romney's way of thinking are presented most dramatically in his plan to marry the working-class girl Marian. As the wedding guests understand, the match is conceived as an allegory for the healing of social division: 'A contract . . . 'twixt the extremes | Of martyrised society', intended 'By symbol, to instruct us formally | To fill the ditches up 'twixt class and class'.[25] This is a bad thing because the pair conceive of themselves and one another, not as unique individuals, but as instances of a general case, and therefore do not feel for each other the love which should lead to marriage. His emotion is but a piece of the universal charity which is his social ideal: 'to wed | Requires less mutual love than common love', he says; hers is worship: 'a simple fealty on one side, | A mere religion'.[26] One polemical implication is that, because of the divisions in contemporary society, someone like Romney and someone like Marian are unlikely honestly to fall in love as the distance between them is too great. The more fundamental contention, though, is that

---

[22] *AL* VIII. 358.
[23] Deirdre David, *Intellectual Women and Victorian Patriarchy: Harriet Martineau, Elizabeth Barrett Browning, George Eliot* (Macmillan, 1987), 115.   [24] *AL* II. 478–9; I. 480.
[25] *AL* IV. 690–4, 754–5.   [26] *AL* IV. 330–1; IV. 193–4.

there is in each person an irreducible core of individuality, which makes itself manifest through the feelings, and which will always offer resistance to universalist prescriptions for human well-being.

The importance of this emphasis in the work is indicated by the fact that even Aurora, always the proponent of 'individualism', must have her theory brought home to her by experience. In the Sixth Book, soon after her arrival in Paris, she claims rather proudly that she and Romney, poet and philanthropist, 'both stand face to face with men, | Contemplating the people in the rough'.[27] This echoes Barrett Browning's own ambition, in her early thoughts about the 'novel-poem', to meet 'face to face & without mask, the Humanity of the age'.[28] However, what happens to Aurora next constitutes an attack on the generalized form of that claim. Absorbed in her musings on 'the people', 'Virtue', 'a poet's word', etc., she wanders through Paris until (like the Lady of Shalott at her weaving) she is interrupted:

> God! what face is that?
> . . .
>   What face is that?
> What a face, what a look, what a likeness! Full on mine
> The sudden blow of it came down . . .[29]

A single face, Marian's, whose impact shatters Aurora's grandiose ruminations. 'That face persists', she finds, a hundred lines later; 'in very deed a face | And not a fancy . . . | 'Twas a real face'; and she urges herself, 'Confront the truth, my soul'.[30] The truth in question turns out to be that Marian was carrying a child and must therefore, according to Aurora's preconceptions (which here are distinctly conventional), be 'damned'.[31] This hasty judgement is challenged when, a little further on, she is herself confronted by that face again, together with the irreducible individual to whom it belongs:

> 'Marian, Marian!'—face to face—
> 'Marian! I find you. Shall I let you go?'[32]

These two lines, with their tense doublings, the second line divided by its full stop into syllabically equal halves, suggest the

[27] *AL* VI. 201–2.

[28] *Brownings' Correspondence*, x. 103.

[29] *AL* VI. 202, 218, 221, 226, 231–3.

[30] *AL* VI. 308, 311–12, 331, 342.

[31] *AL* VI. 366.

[32] *AL* VI. 441–2.

tension of facing up, in the rough, to one particular person. In the end, Marian's life story overcomes Aurora's previously untested notions about the culpability of unmarried mothers:

> . . . but I, convicted, broken utterly,
> With woman's passion clung about her waist
> And kissed her hair and eyes,—'I have been wrong,
> Sweet Marian' . . .[33]

Aurora stands, not just convinced of Marian's innocence, but 'convicted' of her own presumption.

In its immediate historical and national context, the conclusion of this part of the plot is socially daring, for unlike the single mother in Mrs Gaskell's *Ruth* (1853), Marian is allowed to remain alive, and is adopted by Aurora into her household. The work takes this instance of charity as an illustration of its wider argument about the importance of individual development and one-to-one relationships. Dissatisfied with the impersonal rewards of a literary career, and chastened by the events in Paris, Aurora travels on to Italy, where she sets up home with Marian and her child in the hills above Florence. There she rejoices in the fact that, although she can wander through streets crowded with people, she is

> . . . possessed by none of them! no right
> In one, to call your name, inquire your where,
> Or what you think of Mister Some-one's book,
> Or Mister Other's marriage or decease[34]

Released from social expectation, she discovers in herself what is presented as a more authentic identity based on her family, both old and newly adopted. In the 'land of all men's past' her thoughts turn back to her own history, her childhood with her father: she hears his 'step on that deserted ground, | His voice along that silence', the words ' "My child," "my child" '.[35] In turn, she loves Marian's baby, yet she is 'sorrowful' because of her estrangement from Romney.[36] What a falling-off from her youthful commitment to be a 'Moses' and to 'move the masses'—to write verse, presumably, in the manner of *Casa Guidi Windows*.[37] The domestic pleasures and melancholies of this life in Italy contrast with the

---

[33] *AL* VI. 778–81.
[35] *AL* VII. 1157, 1111–12, 1116.
[37] *AL* II. 172, 481.

[34] *AL* VII. 1203–6.
[36] *AL* VII. 958.

earlier descriptions of Britain, both the contrived social whirl in Mayfair and the massed, undifferentiated working classes, 'The humours of the peccant social wound'.[38] Italy figures, therefore, less as a 'Matria' (as Sandra Gilbert would have it) than as a place where one discovers the importance of personal relationships and, above all, of family.

When Romney appears and confesses the failure of his socialist reform schemes, even he now agrees that 'the love of all . . . | Is but a small thing to the love of one'.[39] The one he loves is Aurora, and she loves him, and as they expound their feelings for each other they also declare that it is wrong to 'talk by aggregates | And think by systems'.[40] It looks as though the work will end by narrating the triumph of domestic satisfaction over public endeavour, and by abandoning the realm of politics completely. Yet, astonishingly, what happens next is that the decision which Romney and Aurora have taken to reject the general is itself generalized. If only everyone will do as they have done, personal connections will eventually spread out across the whole world. 'God's love' finds its 'counterpart' in 'the love of wedded souls', which joins with a 'multitude of leaves' into a 'social rose':

> Loves filial, loves fraternal, neighbour-loves
> And civic—all fair petals, all good scents,[41]

In this vision, the broadly Hegelian ideas which animated *Casa Guidi Windows* reappear in an unusually personalized form. Here, 'Spirit' manifests itself, not in the State, but in individuals, each of whom collaborates freely with the others to form a community: 'Genuine government | Is but the expression of a nation . . . even as all society . . . | Is but the expression of men's single lives'.[42] On this view, there is no contrast between public and private; the gulf between the crowds outside Casa Guidi and the two married poets within has been bridged. This is the sort of moment which Barrett Browning's critics condemn as being 'idealistic' and 'impractical'; and certainly, in the context of industrial revolution and the expansion of empire the image of the social rose looks (precisely) rosy. However, at least two factors ask to be borne in mind.

---

[38] *AL* IV. 544.   [39] *AL* V. 479–81.
[40] *AL* VIII. 801–2.   [41] *AL* IX. 881, 883, 882, 887, 892, 888–9.
[42] *AL* VIII. 83–7.

Firstly, the vision is quite emphatically shown to be an ideal: as the echoes of Revelation in the closing lines of the work make clear, it is a prophecy of the millennium. In relation to contemporary politics, therefore, it stands not as an image of an actual political possibility, but as the paragon towards which politics should always aspire, and in comparison with which it will always be found wanting. Secondly, the idea of the worldwide spread of personal, and therefore spiritual relationships has a particular aptness in a book of poetry for, as we found in Chapter 1, poetry in the mid-nineteenth century was significantly ambivalent between public and private voices. *Aurora Leigh* had a readership of tens of thousands, yet it was written by one person, and almost every reader will have come face to face with the text and its story of three individuals in a private location and a private frame of mind. As we will see, this fact exerts a creative pressure on the work's narrative, and on its style.

SWEET POISE OF VOWELS

A reader who begins *Aurora Leigh* soon comes across the following:

> ... I who have written much in prose and verse
> For others' uses, will write now for mine,—
> Will write my story for my better self
> As when you paint your portrait for a friend,
> Who keeps it in a drawer and looks at it
> Long after he has ceased to love you, just
> To hold together what he was and is.[43]

The 'better self' may be a later self, the Aurora who, in the future, will read over her younger words; it may be the present Aurora when her thoughts are concentrated in the act of composition or of reading; it may be another person, a future loved one (her better half) or someone like the 'cousin and friend' John Kenyon to whom Barrett Browning's book is dedicated; or it may be a composite of all these possibilities. For whomever she writes, this narrator does not present herself to a public, but welcomes the reader—which is to say, reader after reader after reader—into her

---

[43] *AL* I. 2–8.

personal circle. Doing so, she asks for a particularly individual kind
of attention, even indulgence. Implying that we might like to
occupy the role of 'a friend', she compares our ignorance of her to
his dead love: our reading, it appears, is to have something like the
inwardness to us, the importance to our identity, of the remem-
brance of an old flame. The echo of 'My Last Duchess' which is
sounded by the 'portrait', kept not behind a curtain but in a
drawer, reinforces this suggestion: here we have, not a commis-
sioned picture, but a self-portrait, offered up, not to a hostile
appraisal like that of the Duke, but to sympathetic understanding.
Barrett Browning's very first book, *The Battle of Marathon*,
privately printed at the expense of her father, was dedicated to
him, as was her mature collection *Poems* (1844). Apart from them,
all her volumes had been introduced, never by a dedication, but,
if by anything at all, by a 'Preface' or 'Advertisement' offering her
work 'to the world'.[44] The dedication to *Aurora Leigh* addresses
Kenyon as 'cousin and friend, in a sense of less equality and greater
disinterestedness than "Romney's" ', and asks him to 'accept, in
sight of the public, this poor sign of esteem, gratitude, and affec-
tion from | your unforgetting | E.B.B.'.[45] The public therefore
receives the book as-it-were 'in sight of' the private, being introduced to the text through a series of personal relationships, Barrett
Browning and Kenyon, Aurora and Romney, Aurora and her
'better self'.

As with any first-person narrative, on beginning the story we
are introduced to the printed voice of an individual. However,
Aurora Leigh has an unusual, perhaps unique narrative structure
which distinguishes it from contemporary works narrated in the
first person such as *The Prelude* (1850), *Great Expectations* (1859),
and *Villette* (1853). In the fiction of the poem, Aurora writes her
autobiography from the First Book to half-way through the Fifth
Book as an uninterrupted narrative, until at V, line 579 it catches
up with her as she describes a party earlier the same day. The end
of the Fifth Book looks to the future as she departs for Italy. The
Sixth and Seventh Books are composed at several different times:
first, when she has just caught sight of Marian in Paris and immediately lost her (VI. 1–389); then when long weeks have passed

---

[44] *An Essay on Mind, With Other Poems* (James Duncan, 1826), p. iii.
[45] *AL*, ed. Margaret Reynolds, 161.

without news (VI. 390–411); then after she has found Marian, but
before they leave for Italy (VI. 411–VII. 374); and lastly when they
have reached Italy but before the final appearance of Romney
(VII. 375 to the end of VII). The Eighth and Ninth Books are
written continuously after the events which they describe.[46]
Unlike Pip and Lucy Snowe, the Aurora who begins telling her
story has not herself already got to the end of it; and neither does
she present herself as setting out, like the narrator of *The Prelude*,
on a journey of self-discovery. Perhaps, to start with, she believes
herself to be in the position of Dickens's and Brontë's protagonists:
in that case, she will think that she is recounting a tale about the
isolation of a woman who has dedicated herself to her career. At
the end of the Fifth Book, though, she turns into someone more
like Wordsworth's narrator, escaping, like him, from 'the vast
city', and looking forward to the 'prospect' of a more pastoral existence which, in her case, is located in Italy. However, she has
nothing of Wordsworth's trust in the future, no 'heart | Joyous,
nor scared at its own liberty'; and rightly so, for the sequel of
events repeatedly shows her to have been mistaken: about Marian,
Romney, Lady Waldemar, and, finally, herself.[47] Unlike the
narrating Pip and the narrating Lucy, Aurora-the-narrator is not in
command of her own story. This gives the work's conclusion a
markedly different feel from the end of *Jane Eyre*, to which it is
otherwise so much indebted. Aurora's disillusionment with her
career is like Jane's rejection of a missionary life in the company of
St John Rivers; the reunification with Romney, blinded in the fire
which has destroyed his ancestral home, is like Jane's return to
Rochester, and with its description of Romney as a 'sea-king'
appearing by moonlight has something of the same fairy-tale
aura.[48] The difference is that Romney's arrival is as much of a
surprise to Aurora-the-narrator, who by now has converged with
Aurora-the-character, as it is to the reader. Aurora relates to us,
not as someone who has established her place in life and is now
offering her story to the public, but as a person who is still in the
process of becoming, and who shares the reader's ignorance about

[46] I here depart slightly from the accounts of *Aurora Leigh*'s narrative form in Cora
Castan, 'Structural Problems and the Poetry of *Aurora Leigh*', *Browning Society Notes*, 7/3
(1977), 73–81 and *AL*, ed. Margaret Reynolds, 30–1.
[47] William Wordsworth, *The Prelude* (1850), ed. J. C. Maxwell (Harmondsworth:
Penguin, 1971), I, 7, 27, 14–15.   [48] *AL* VIII. 60.

what will happen to her. The ending appears before us, not as a secret which the narrator has all along held in reserve, but as an unforeseen event which breaks in upon the story. When the narrative arrives at the present and fragments, it dramatizes for the reader that experience of confronting the real which is so important to both Romney and Aurora. By doing so, it puts Aurora in a position more like ours than would ever be possible in a narrative told straight through from beginning to end. When, in the Fifth Book, she struggles to make sense of the encounter with Marian, and asks '—A child! what then?', she has no more idea of the answer than we do; when the news comes to us, 'I have found her!', it has been news to her too only hours before.[49] The narrative structure of *Aurora Leigh*, then, institutes a peculiar closeness between reader and narrator, prompting us to recognize that relationship as itself being one of the 'petals' in the 'social rose'.

As readers get to know Aurora, they become familiar with her narrative voice and attuned to her enthusiasms and dislikes. One thing she particularly loves is the Italian landscape:

> My multitudinous mountains, sitting in
> The magic circle, with the mutual touch
> Electric, panting from their full deep hearts
> Beneath the influent heavens, and waiting for
> Communion and commission. . . .[50]

Here the verse enters fully into the community of feeling, its repeated enjambments circling round the line-ends, the flow of the verse suggesting the narrator's own emotion and therefore asking the reader to be moved in sympathy. The inspiriting thought of the mountains releases a metaphorical verve in Aurora's writing: the circle is at once a séance and a conspirators' meeting (Barrett Browning had punningly conflated the two kinds of circle in 1853: 'the *circoli* at Florence are as revolutionary as ever, only tilting over tables instead of States, alas!');[51] the spiritualists longing for a manifestation, and the revolutionaries for that 'soul' who in *Casa Guidi Windows* it was prophesied would run 'from God down with a message'.[52] The English countryside has the opposite

---

[49] *AL* VI. 370, 412.
[51] *Letters of Elizabeth Barrett Browning*, ed. Kenyon, ii. 117.
[50] *AL* I. 622–6.
[52] *CGW* I. 803.

effect on Aurora's feelings and on her verse: Dover's cliffs are 'frosty'; and further inland,

> The ground seemed cut up from the fellowship
> Of verdure, field from field, as man from man;
> The skies themselves looked low and positive,
> As almost you could touch them with a hand,
> And dared to do it they were so far off
> From God's celestial crystals; . . .[53]

These lines nearly rhyme: 'fellowship' has the same rhythm and final vowel-sound as 'positive', while 'man' sounds a clear half-rhyme with 'hand'. The weight that falls on the line-ends—natural pauses being emphasized by these partial rhymes—collaborates with the social divisions in Britain by cutting up the lines from one another, impeding the rhythmic flow of the verse. The language, rhythmically hangdog and predominantly monosyllabic, is itself depressed and static, and, as for the mode of description, it is the opposite of personification: the Italian mountains were made spiritual, but the English sky is solidified ('positive' hints at Positivism, the materialist 'religion' developed by Auguste Comte). Here, the law of the verse seems to impose itself heavily on the language, as it did in the description of the arrival of the Austrians, with their 'despotism of the final emphasis', in *Casa Guidi Windows*. The verse recreates for the reader what one can only call the 'feel' of the different countries to Aurora. As we read on, there appears in the texture of the poem a drama of relationship between an aspiring, affective use of language which carries with it the atmosphere of Italy, and a flatter, more subjugated kind of writing which is associated with England.

Brought to England, the young Aurora is taught to discipline her 'copious curls' into 'braids' like those worn by her aunt, and is subjected to analogous linguistic restraint:

> I left off saying my sweet Tuscan words
> Which still at any stirring of the heart
> Came up to float across the English phrase
> As lilies (*Bene* or *Che che,*) because
> She liked my father's child to speak his tongue.[54]

'My father's child' evokes the voice of Miss Leigh ('don't forget you are your father's child', one can imagine her saying), who

---

[53] *AL* I. 251, 260–5.   [54] *AL* I. 387–91.

seeks to excise the influence of Mrs Leigh, Aurora's Italian mother, by repressing the Italian words which Aurora had learnt from her, and which, as narrator, she can once more allow to float up in the air-bubble of their parentheses across the English phrase. The suppression of Italian words is important to Miss Leigh's designs on Aurora because Italian was, for Barrett Browning, the pre-eminently poetical language. It has to do with 'stirring of the heart' and, like the Italian mountains, it possesses a 'magic circle':

> . . . how the Tuscan musical
> Vowels do round themselves as if they planned
> Eternities of separate sweetness . . .[55]

The vowel most suggested here is 'o'—the letter with which Italian words most commonly end—as we can tell from the rhymes 'h<u>o</u>w', 'v<u>o</u>wels', 'r<u>o</u>und', (note also how the verse is itself rounded by the strong enjambment 'musical/Vowels'). This feeling was not new to Barrett Browning: in 1843, before she had heard much spoken Italian, she had written of Carlyle's prose style, 'if the consonants were everywhere in a heap, like the "pots and pans" of Bassano,—classic or not, English or not,—it was certainly a true language—a language "μερόπων ἀνθρώπων,"—the significant articulation of a living soul: God's breath was in the vowels of it'.[56] Breath, for her, meant freedom: she had difficulty with the English atmosphere, but in Italy she could breathe easily; 'there's something vital about this Florence air.'[57] (She also transferred the feeling to politics: 'newspapers breathe heavily just now, that's undeniable', as she wrote of press censorship in France after the coup, echoing her own predicament in London's 'heavy air').[58] Vowels, on this view, are the aspiring element of the language, continually hinting at infinity; consonants are the material reality which repeatedly cuts them short. Seen in this way, Italian is, like its landscape, more spiritual than English, whose divisive consonants drag it down.

When Aurora moves to Italy, her verse comes to sound more Italian, giving greater weight to vowels as when, on the boat, she

> . . . felt the wind soft from the land of souls;
> The old miraculous mountains heaved in sight,[59]

[55] *CGW* I. 1187–9.   [56] *Complete Works of Elizabeth Barrett Browning*, vi. 314.
[57] *Letters of Elizabeth Barrett Browning*, ed. Kenyon, ii. 192.   [58] Ibid. 108, 18.
[59] *AL* VII. 467–8.

It is as though the spiritual breeze breathes through the circle of the virtual rhyme 'souls' and 'old'. Often Barrett Browning's feeling for vowels modulates itself through words that sound vocalic and Italian because they have 'feminine'—dactylic or trochaic—rhythm. She hears Italians speaking with '*issimo* and *ino* and sweet poise | Of vowels' and uses the softness of those Italian cadences in her own verse.[60] For example, when Romney appears at Aurora's villa:

> . . . There he stood, my king!
> I felt him, rather than beheld him. Up
> I rose, as if he were my king indeed,
> And then sate down, in trouble at myself,
> And struggling for my woman's empery.
> 'Tis pitiful; . . .[61]

The toll of monosyllables in the first line, which announces Romney's kingship, is responded to by the isolated and emphatic 'up' of Aurora's movement, standing up as Barrett Browning had so often urged Italy to do: but this resolution fails in the dying falls of the feminine words 'trouble', 'struggling', 'woman's empery', 'pitiful'. In the First Book, the heroine's soul, 'At poetry's divine first finger touch | Let go conventions and sprang up surprised':[62] by now, in the Eighth Book, her early promise seems empty to her, and though she rises up she fails to stand alone. Here, as in *Casa Guidi Windows*, linguistic Italianness conveys Italianate characteristics: sympathy, weakness, aspiration.

Towards the end of *Aurora Leigh*, similar feelings are frequently imparted to the verse by the introduction of pauses immediately after trochees or dactyls. In her critical work, *The Book of the Poets*, Barrett Browning had noticed in the poetry of Stephen Hawes,

passages of thoughtful sweetness and cheerful tenderness, at which we are constrained to smile and sigh, and both for 'pastyme'.

> Was never payne but it had joy at laste
> In the fayre morrow.
There is a lovely cadence![63]

The cadence will have struck her as lovely because the rhythm of 'morrow' seems to fall short as though in disagreement with the

[60] *AL* VII. 1176–7.   [61] *AL* VIII. 61–6.
[62] *AL* I. 851–2.   [63] *Complete Works of Elizabeth Barrett Browning*, vi. 253.

paraphrasable content of the lines, imparting an air of melancholy and uncertainty to the speaker's hope. This melody, with the caesura placed after the fifth, unaccented syllable, sounds often in the last three books of *Aurora Leigh*; and as it moved Barrett Browning herself 'to smile and sigh', so it seems designed to appeal to the reader. 'I am lonely in the world', says Aurora to Marian, asking her to come with her to Italy:

> And thou art lonely, and the child is half
> An orphan. Come,—and henceforth thou and I
> Being still together will not miss a friend,
> Nor he a father, since two mothers shall
> Make that up to him. . . .[64]

The faltering movement of Aurora's loneliness ('and thou art lonely'), the tentativeness and sadness of it, marks also her hopes for the child: 'Nor he a father' (remembering the father that she herself had lost), 'Make that up to him'; can two mothers, after all, she feels, fill up the father's place? The cadence echoes with loss and disappointed expectations in this part of the work: 'Than all I have failed in', 'I thought "my father!" '—and contrasts with the rarer, more resolute movement of verse which pauses after the fourth or sixth syllables ('The soul's the way', 'Like that Aurora Leigh's').[65] In the letter Aurora receives in the Ninth Book, Lady Waldemar writes that Smith, her latest admirer, swears

> That I'm the typic She. Away with Smith!—
> Smith smacks of Leigh . . .[66]

Her scorn speaks out from the rhyme of the stressed sixth and fourth syllables, 'She' and 'Leigh'. How different is this brisk rhythm from the Italian cadence echoing through the conversation between Romney and Aurora which forms most of the work's last two books. Here is how it recurs during the course of about a hundred lines of the Eighth Book:

> Well, well! no matter. . . .
>
> It had not hurt me. . . .
>
> Which come too seldom. . . .
>
> Not so far saddened. . . .

---

[64] *AL* VII. 120–5.   [65] *AL* VII. 188, 491; VIII. 544, 517.
[66] *AL* IX. 134–5.

> And what, permitted. . . .
>
> For what had *I*, I thought, to do with *her*,
> Aurora . . Romney? . . .[67]

There is a lovely cadence, the way the rhythm of each of their individual sadnesses repeats itself in Romney's first tentative mention of the two of them. The melody is taken up by Aurora's avowal in the Ninth Book: ' "I love you, Romney," ' the half-line longing to be completed by a reciprocal declaration.[68] After a momentary overflow of passion, the poem arrives at its ending:

> I saw his soul saw,—'Jasper first', I said,
> 'And second, sapphire; third, chalcedony;
> The rest in order,—last, an amethyst.'[69]

Here, in a vision of the heavenly Jerusalem where (if anywhere) aspiration will finally meet its fulfilment, the Italian cadences, 'I saw his soul saw', 'And second, sapphire', 'The rest in order', are filled out into whole lines by words which broadly reverse their rhythm. This metrical marriage provides a formal echo to the new partnership of Aurora and Romney, who have come together at last as equals. All along, the destined union between the pair has been hinted at by the fact that, as cousins, they bear the same surname. Aurora's name contains a balance of implications: the expansive rhythm of the Italian word 'Aurora' (the dawn) being met by the stressed English monosyllable 'Leigh' (suggesting 'lee'—'shelter', 'sediment'). As Aurora carries what is presented as being characteristically Italian sympathy and imaginative *élan* into the formalistic house of Leigh, so Barrett Browning brings into her verse the cadences which she associates with that nationality and those qualities, reaching out with them to her English public so as to bring it into communion with her poem.

THE PERSONAL IS AND IS NOT POLITICAL

On entering into *Aurora Leigh* with their imaginations, readers find themselves in a work which is not in any secure sense an artistic unity. There is the division between different sorts of rhythm, and

---

[67] *AL* VIII. 484, 498, 505, 531, 590, 604–5.   [68] *AL* IX. 608.

[69] Cf. Revelation 21: 19.

the fact that the narrative is not presented from a uniform standpoint, while the subject-matter switches from abstruse metaphysical rumination to party chit-chat to slums and the diction varies accordingly. In a review, George Eliot configured this variety along the lines of gender, suggesting that the work amalgamated 'feminine subtlety of perception, feminine quickness of sensibility, and feminine tenderness' with 'masculine vigour, breadth and culture'.[70] In numerous ways, the novel-poem's own characteristics can be connected to the relationship between Romney and Aurora, and, like their story, the form of the work is less a unity than a process of unification.

Aurora and Romney recognize their love for one another after they have discarded their public roles. In Italy, Aurora is separated from her readership, and Romney from the English social divisions which he had sought to bridge. Narrating their reconciliation on a terrace beneath the stars, the work too develops unity of place and of tone. As with the two protagonists, this happens only as a result of moving away from the disparate, novelistic material across which the narrative has previously ranged. It is as though the Lady of Shalott has returned to her castle.

However, this private unification in Italy is then imaginatively expanded across the whole world by the image of the social rose, which draws into its metaphorical embrace all the personal jealousies and civil conflicts which we have read about, and transmutes them into love. The work which began with echoes of *Casa Guidi Windows* now returns to that poem and its prophetic mode, for the final vision of the New Jerusalem harks back to the earlier hope that God would rebuild the 'ruins' of the world 'With pillared marbles rare'.[71] Equally, the end of *Aurora Leigh* anticipates 'Italy and the World' (1860) which takes the Risorgimento to herald the demise of many wrongs. Italy will 'Rise; prefigure the grand solution | Of earth's municipal, insular schisms', thereby doing away with 'Churchman's charities, tender as Nero', 'Indian suttee', 'Service to rights divine' and 'Heptarchy patriotisms', and replacing them with

> —National voices, distinct yet dependent,
>   Ensphering each other, as swallow does swallow,
>   With circles still widening and ever ascendant,
>   In multiform life to united progression,—[72]

---

[70] Donaldson, *Annotated Bibliography*, 65.   [71] *CGW* II. 777–8.
[72] 'Italy and the World', 36–7, 123–30.

Like the social rose, the comparison of national voices to swallows makes the solution of civilization's ills seem spontaneously natural, although here the paradoxical reconciliation of unity and multeity is not implied by the image itself and has to be made clumsily explicit in the phrases 'multiform life' and 'united progression'. Nonetheless, by happy paranomasia, Italy's 'rise' marks the beginning of the 'rose'.

For all the evident imaginative continuity between the prophecy at its end and the hopes inspired in Barrett Browning by Italian politics, *Aurora Leigh* also prompts readers to resist the easy indulgence of such visions. There is the space given to the experiences which impress first on Romney and then on Aurora the importance of attending to individuals on their own terms. Moreover, there is the fact that the work markedly avoids explicit comment on the Risorgimento. Scattered political references in the Fourth Book date the failed wedding of Romney and Marian to 1848, a detail which may add symbolic weight to that fiasco, but which also makes the absence of any mention of the revolutions themselves, or of the Chartist demonstrations in Britain, the more surprising. In all her description of Italy, Aurora's only allusion to its politics is a bad joke about how Romney will doubtless turn his trip there 'to our Tuscan people's use', and help them against 'the Austrian boar'.[73]

To use Tennyson's word, though in a slightly different sense from his, *Aurora Leigh* stands in a 'parabolic' relation to the Risorgimento, not confronting it explicitly, but taking questions which were raised pre-eminently by Italian nationalism, and elaborating them imaginatively in a realm of verse which, while not locked into its immediate historical context as a newspaper article might be, nonetheless casts light on that context and is aware of itself as having an effect within it. In *Casa Guidi Windows*, as we saw, individuals were brusquely amalgamated into the idea of the nation by expressions such as 'insphere these wills | Into a unity of will'; the problem of 'How to our races we may justify | Our individual claims' is held over to be answered 'slowly'.[74] This, perhaps the most fundamental question raised by nationalism, is at the heart of *Aurora Leigh*: the work tells us the stories of three individuals whose claims are variously thwarted by the state of society

[73] *AL* VIII. 99–100.   [74] *CGW* I. 838–9, 698–9, 696.

in Britain, and who then achieve happiness when they escape from that society, abandon public ambition, and discover that personal relationships are what is most important to them. When she sets up house in Italy, the *Corinne*-style symbolism which had attached to Aurora's younger self as she was striving to become a poet drops away: we are told less of her ideals and learn more of her feelings. Among these is her love of the place where she was born: the closing books of the work include much moving description of what it is to feel at home. Now, Aurora's Italianness is conceived less in terms of abstractions such as 'aspiration' and more as a matter of particular attachment, and (as we have seeen) cadences of speech. What Aurora finds surviving beyond the various pretensions and prejudices that she leaves behind her are feelings of belonging to a country and to an unconventional sort of family. To an extent, this discovery harmonizes with the emphases of liberal nationalism, but it is striking that Aurora has no feeling of communion with the Italians at large, or indeed any Italian. We might speculate that this is really an indication of Barrett Browning's own feeling about her adoptive country; or, keeping within the logic of the work, we might take it as a sign of the estrangement that has been wrought upon Aurora by her time in England. Either way, *Aurora Leigh* is more circumspect about national unity than *Casa Guidi Windows* had been. It imagines three people coming together into a community of sympathy. Perhaps an indication that industrially advanced but socially divided Britain can learn from the example of Italy? Perhaps the beginnings of an ideal nation? Certainly the final vision suggests as much, but it suggests also the remoteness of that ideal, and the smallness of the contribution Aurora's life is likely to make towards it.

Further on in the letter which describes the demonstration on 12 September 1847, Barrett Browning ponders the contrast between the conviviality of that Italian political gathering and the frequent violence of similar events in Britain. In the Italian crowd, 'people were *embracing* for joy';

Our poor English want educating into gladness—they want refining, not in the fire but in the sunshine. How different a thing a crowd is here to an English crowd, you must come here to learn—yet whose is the fault, I wonder? And why should it be so, with all our advantages of a more scriptural instruction and larger constitutional rights?

She concludes that despite the concrete political and religious liberties which exist in Britain, something is lacking in the sphere of the arts: 'the narrowness which cuts down literature & refuses to accept Art into the uses of the Christian Life, is more rife with injury & desecration than you see at a first glance—of this I am more & more sure the more I see & live.'[75] In *Aurora Leigh*, Barrett Browing aimed to carry literature into the uses of life; and she succeeded: by 1860 the work was already in its fifth edition.[76] However, in order to spread among her readers something like that 'sympathy' which she had observed in the Tuscan crowd, she had precisely not to adopt the declamatory voice of *Casa Guidi Windows* or *Poems Before Congress* (1860), for to do that would be to configure her readers as a public, rather than as an expanding circle of friends.

In the event, and somewhat to her surprise, the work mainly struck reviewers and readers as a contribution to 'the woman question', an issue which, she said, was 'only a collateral object with my intentions in writing'.[77] Echoes of this impression appear in the name of M. E. Braddon's 'fast' heroine Aurora Floyd, and the poet L. S. Bevington's early pseudonym Arbor Leigh. However, Barrett Browning's friend Isa Blagden was no less responsive to the scope of *Aurora Leigh* when, in her novel *Agnes Tremorne* (1861) she has a group of Italian conspirators adopt the password '*Aurora*'.[78] The novel-poem has a similarly liberal and nation-building purpose, although a less secret and more tentative one: to pass from hand to hand and voice to voice, drawing reader after reader into its embrace.

---

[75] *Brownings' Correspondence*, xiv. 301.   [76] *AL*, ed. Margaret Reynolds, 105.
[77] *AL*, ed. Margaret Reynolds, 18.
[78] Isa Blagden, *Agnes Tremorne*, 2 vols. (Smith, Elder and Co., 1861), ii. 17.

6

REPULSIVE CLOUGH

SOLITARY VERSES

'I care not for Rome, nor | Italy'. That remark by Claude, the protagonist of *Amours de Voyage*, would have scandalized Elizabeth Barrett Browning, as would much else in the poem. With its satirically presented satirical voice, *Amours de Voyage* is the consummation of Clough's lifelong unease at the idea, so attractive to her, that poetry might be a socially unifying force. One of the work's epigraphs, '*Il doutait de tout, même de l'amour*', attributed ominously to a 'FRENCH NOVEL', turns out to be, not a quotation from anywhere, but a riposte, to Madame de Staël's *Corinne*, whose heroine writes when she is abandoned by her beloved, 'j'ai douté de tout, même de la vertu'.[1] The body of the poem expands upon this opening jibe against the affective, prophetic kind of writing which *Corinne* encouraged in Barrett Browning. *Amours de Voyage* contains all the elements for a grand synthesis à la *Aurora Leigh*— love, art, politics—but they remain unamalgamated. In Barrett Browning's poem, the 'rose of love' which Aurora bears for Romney expands into 'the social rose'; in Clough's, as its title announces, love is less comprehensive: it is multiple and therefore divided, its manifestations perhaps conflicting with one another; it occurs on holiday; above all, it is French, and therefore to be viewed with suspicion.[2]

Clough had begun to disagree with Barrett Browning when he was at Oxford earlier in the 1840s. Again and again in his poems of those years a possible step into community of feeling and obligation with other people—whether this be a religious community, as in 'The New Sinai', a friendship ('Sic Itur'), or a marriage

---

[1] *AV* V. 125–6; de Stael, *Corinne*, 571.   [2] *AL* IX. 691, 892.

('When Panting Sighs the Bosom Fill')—is suspended by the thought that to take it would be to betray one's true self. His characteristic plot-line is the opposite of *Aurora Leigh's*, which has the true self being discovered through companionship, above all through love. The most elusive of his antisocial verses is an untitled lyric beginning 'Why should I say I see the things I see not', in which the protagonist is unable to join a 'dance' because he cannot hear the music which animates it; later on, it turns out that there is in fact no music and the dancers have all along been shamming. As Clough was having religious doubts at this time, the dance may well allude most to the shared faith and rituals of the Anglican Church; certainly the final lines, where the speaker dedicates himself to 'the bare conscience of the better thing', suggest a quaker-like rejection of religious forms.[3] Nonetheless, the very generalized traits of the situation described allow the poem to bear on other kinds of group too, the most salient of which is the community promoted by poetry, or at least poetry of a particular kind, for the first line emphatically responds to a passage in Keble's *Tract 89: On the Mysticism Attributed to the Early Fathers of the Church* which claims (drawing on St Paul) that 'Poetical' vision involves making 'the things we see represent the things we do not see'.[4] This central tenet of Tractarian poetic theory, according to which the imagination should elaborate symbols of divine truths out of the matter of the natural world, describes the practice of Keble's own *The Christian Year* (1827) in which 'Every wave in every brook, | Chanting with a solemn voice, | Minds us of our better choice' and the drooping of a willow tree mysteriously offers a lesson in 'Contentment's power'.[5] Clough was doubtless irritated by Keble's blurring-together of imagination and belief, but what he emphasizes by configuring the imagined or believed-in unseen as dance music is its role in animating and disciplining a community. As his letters and prose writings on the Irish famine and the 1848 revolutions have some similarities to Marx's, 'Why should I say I see the things I see not' might without too much violence be

---

[3] 'Why should I say I see the things I see not', 30, 34, 57–9.

[4] (John Keble) *Tract 89: On the Mysticism Attributed to the Early Fathers of the Church*, 2nd edn. (J. G., and F. Rivington, 1842), 143; I Corinthians 4: 18.

[5] (John Keble), *The Christian Year* (1827), 67th edn. (John Henry and James Parker, 1860), 49–50; see G. B. Tennyson, *Victorian Devotional Poetry: The Tractarian Mode* (Cambridge, Mass.: Harvard University Press, 1981), 158.

summarized as an investigation of ideology (which 'represents the imaginary relationship of individuals to their real conditions of existence') and of some poets' role in its production.[6]

In a draft, which later provided the title for the collection *Ambarvalia* (1849), Carlyle had been included among the poem's targets: 'the Ambarvalian brothers nine' who 'beat the bounds' of 'old Imperial Rome' were compared to poets in new imperial Britain, whose 'great prophetic song' enthrals 'the listening throng'.[7] Perhaps Clough judged this goad at the notion of poet as prophet to have been too obvious, but he did not change his mind about it completely, for a similar point is more gently introduced into the published version by means of an allusion to Barrett Browning. When he had read her 1844 *Poems*, he had found much to enjoy, admitting to have been 'disappointed' only by 'the Vision of Poets: it is all in support of the Painfulness and Martyrdom Poet-Theory, the which I don't agree to'.[8] The protagonist of this 1005-line work, after he has been through various rituals such as drinking from the pool of '*World's cruelty*', is afforded a mystical experience which is accompanied by 'measured thunders', 'concords of mysterious kind', and

> . . . wavelike sounds
> Re-eddying into silver rounds,
> Enlarging liberty with bounds:[9]

These wavelike sounds (perhaps combined with Keble's chanting waves) reappear in 'Why should . . .', where the speaker imagines joining in the social and/or religious whirl:

> Joyously take my part,
> And hand in hand, and heart with heart, with these retreat, advance;
> And borne on wings of wavy sound,
> Whirl with these around, around,
> Who here are living in the living dance![10]

An iambic pulse like that of Barrett Browning's poem here invades Clough's, imposing itself most thoroughly in the third and fourth

---

[6] Louis Althusser, *Essays on Ideology* (Verso, 1984), 36.

[7] *Poems of Arthur Hugh Clough*, 579.

[8] *The Correspondence of Arthur Hugh Clough*, ed. Frederick L. Mulhauser, 2 vols. (Oxford: Clarendon Press, 1957), i. 139.

[9] Barrett Browning, 'A Vision of Poets', 183, 742–3, 748–50.

[10] 'Why should . . .', 17–21.

lines quoted, which also imitate her rhymes. In 'A Vision of Poets'
the comparatively regular ictus collaborates with triple rhyme to
produce an air of solemnity: there, as often in Barrett Browning,
rhythm carries a redemptive, liberatory implication. In Clough's
poem, however, the iambs are rendered precarious by the unpredictable lengths of the lines: the rhythm is always being caught by
surprise, as though it is trying to dance without knowing the right
steps. One critic proposes that the verse here gives an affirmative
'image of real hearing and responsive movement', but its own
motion seems on the contrary to belie the speaker's claim that he
is moving 'Joyously' in 'the living dance'. After this picture of
awkward participation it is not a complete surprise to discover that
'all along | The music is not sounding'.[11]

Such sceptical handling of the attractive fluidities of rhythm and
imagery is typical of the poems collected in *Ambarvalia*. At one
point, a halo of desire is imagined 'transmuting, mingling, glorify-
ing' a lover's judgement of his beloved:

> Yet, is that halo of the soul?
> Or is it, as may sure be said,
> Phosphoric exhalation bred
> Of vapour, steaming from the bed
> Of Fancy's brook or Passion's river?[12]

The halo looks as though it has risen out of the centre of the word
'exhalation', while the collocation of 'bed', 'Passion', and 'bred'
suggests the mechanism of the halo's conception, half-concealed in
the verse as it is also in the lover's idealistic feelings. Such inves-
tigative writing, which always seeks for the root of an emotion,
was the sort of thing Matthew Arnold had in mind when he
attacked Clough for being 'a mere d—d depth hunter in poetry'.
Arnold himself repeatedly imagines separation and solitude, but
takes them as occasions more for the evocation of feeling than for
its analysis. When he laments that 'We mortal millions' are all
separated from one another by 'The unplumbed, salt, estranging
sea', the idea that the sea's depths are unplumbed, and therefore
beyond human knowledge and control, serves to build an
emotional climax. In his verse, it appears that alienation in no way
results from social conditions or intellectual developments but is

[11] Barbara Hardy, *The Advantage of Lyric: Essays on Feeling in Poetry* (Athlone Press, 1977), 38; 'Why should . . .', 27–8.   [12] 'When panting sighs the bosom fill', 55, 58–62.

universal and all the fault of 'A God, a God'. This is offered as a
consolation, suggesting as it does that although each of us may be
'*alone*' we are all in the same boat.[13]

Clough, by contrast, wrote so as to reproduce in the relation
between his poems and their readers the feeling of disjunction
which he observed between selves and others. He manipulated the
familiar elements of verse so as to make them discomfiting. In the
lines about phosphoric exhalation, simple rhymes and regular
rhythm—which in Arnold are generally a source of comfort—
mime the coercive power of the biological process described.
Similar uses of form in the *Ambarvalia* poems often imply unwel-
come obligation, as in the hard comedy of these well-known lines:

> DUTY—that's to say complying
> With whate'er's expected here;
> On your unknown cousin's dying,
> Straight be ready with the tear;[14]

Resistance to social convention, on the other hand, frequently
takes the shape of rhythmical uncertainty. There are the persistent
enquiries of 'The Questioning Spirit':

> Dost thou not know that these things only seem?—[15]

Or the ineffable sources of 'Wisdom' and 'Power', which, oddly
revising the volume's general hostility to liquid,

> Are welling, bubbling forth, unseen, incessantly?[16]

Just as much as Barrett Browning's verse, these poems suggest
recurrent analogies between social structure and verse-form. But
whereas, in her work, metrical pattern is habitually associated with
restrictive laws and conventions as against the liberating pulse of
the imagination, in Clough's early writings rhythmical drive and
metaphoric vigour collaborate with the prescriptions of metre to
threaten the sincerity of the individual. The self offers resistance to
these coercive forces by subjecting its own words to an analytic
variant of paranomasia ('halo . . . exhalation'), by clogging its lines
so as to hold back the impetus of rhythm ('<u>th</u>ou . . . <u>th</u>at <u>th</u>ese

---

[13] *Letters of Matthew Arnold to Arthur Hugh Clough*, 81; Arnold, 'To Marguerite—
Continued', 4, 24, 22: quoted from *The Poems of Matthew Arnold*, 2nd edn., ed. Kenneth
and Mirian Allott (Longman, 1979).   [14] 'Duty—that's to say complying', 1–4.
[15] 'The Questioning Spirit', 12.   [16] 'In a Lecture–Room', 11.

things'), by relishing unusual phonetic concords ('unseen, incessantly'). These pleasures are not of the kind that was usually offered by lyric verse: they do not conspire to draw the reader into sympathy with the imagined voice, but rather hold him or her at one remove. The layout of Clough's poems in the shared volume *Ambarvalia*, where they were printed mostly without titles, seems designed further to perplex the public: the reviewer in *Fraser's Magazine* asked 'why these mere scraps—very often without titles? Why were they not kept to be inserted as parts of some continuous whole?'—while the *Spectator* thought the layout showed the author's 'contempt of his reader'.[17] Clough's half of the book contains a poetry of opposition to the leading ideas which we have pursued in these pages so far: a poetry which is decidedly not prophetic, and which does not seek to build a community out of its readers, providing them with neither communal images nor choric rhythms. Unsurprisingly, when Elizabeth Barrett Browning read *Ambarvalia* she disliked 'its fragmentary, dislocated, unartistic character'. She much preferred a volume entitled *The Bothie of Toper-na-Fuosich* (altered to '. . . *Tober-na-Vuolich*' on its next publication) which, though composed later, had appeared earlier, in 1848: 'written in loose and more-than-need-be unmusical hexameters, but full of vigour and freshness, and with passages and indeed whole scenes of great beauty and eloquence . . . Oh, it strikes both Robert and me as being worth twenty of the other little book'.[18]

THE TIDE OF 1848

Many readers have agreed with Elizabeth Barrett Browning in admiring *The Bothie*'s 'vigour and freshness'.[19] It is easy to see why:

> Yes, it was he, on the ledge, bare-limbed, an Apollo, down-gazing,
> Eying one moment the beauty, the life, ere he flung himself in it,
> Eying through eddying green waters the green-tinting floor
> underneath them,
> Eying the bead on the surface, the bead, like a cloud, rising to it,
> Drinking in, deep in his soul, the beautiful hue and the clearness,[20]

[17] Michael Thorpe (ed.), *Clough: The Critical Heritage* (New York: Barnes and Noble, 1972), 88, 75.   [18] *Letters of Elizabeth Barrett Browning*, ed. Kenyon, i. 429.
[19] See Thorpe (ed.), *Clough: The Critical Heritage*, 28–71.   [20] *B* III. 76–80.

This verse makes sparkling use of imaginative elements which in *Ambarvalia* had always been resisted or entertained with suspicion. Attention to odd assonances ('<u>Eying</u> . . . <u>eddying green</u>') here collaborates with the rise of a compelling rhythm; there is vivid description which relishes the seductive uncertainty of the water rather than depth-huntingly getting to the bottom of it, and which seems designed (especially with the repetition of 'eyeing') to draw the reader into the verse, to make us dive in as this young 'Apollo' is about to do, and not hold ourselves at one remove as in 'Why should . . .'. The words are allowed to breed images: in the vicinity of water, one might expect 'drinking' to happen literally, but it turns out that what the character is imbibing is not the water itself but the look of it, 'the beautiful hue and the clearness'; when the pool is idealized as 'the beauty, the life' the writing makes 'the things we see represent the things we do not see' almost in the manner of Keble.

In many other ways too, *The Bothie* contrasts with *Ambarvalia*: it is a narrative poem, a 'continuous whole', and ends with a marriage. Indeed, as Barrett Browning will have noticed, it in several respects anticipates the novel-poem she was planning to write herself. It is of hybrid genre, and includes comparatively realistic characters; it is linguistically adventurous, and is set in the present day. She may even have taken some pointers from Clough's plot: the clan dinner with which the *Bothie* opens stands as a microcosm of the existing social order in rather the same way as Aunt Leigh's house; when Philip escapes into the highlands, his first amour with the farmer's daughter Katie is like Romney's plan to wed Marian; like Romney, he then comes temporarily under the influence of an aristocrat, and ends up discovering that he really loves a woman with whom he had been put in contact right at the outset.

More striking than these faint echoes, however, is the similarity in the symbolic scope of the two narratives, for in the *Bothie*, as in *Aurora Leigh*, we are prompted to understand some of the personal relationships as partial allegories of large-scale political arrangements. Philip's involvement with Katie is offered as an experiment in what the Piper calls 'that confounded *égalité*, French manufacture', and the reason for his breaking it off is put in similarly broad terms: he finds that he has been 'Letting drop from him at random as things not worth his considering | All the benefits gathered and put in his hands by fortune' (benefits such as education and the possibility of public influence).[21] What he has had to become in order to sustain the relationship is taken to indicate the fate of any intellectual in a strictly egalitarian society, so that his personal experience with Katie is made to tell against his political commitment to 'equality'. His subsequent crush on Lady Maria has consequences which are equally far-reaching: 'I yield to the laws and arrangements', he says, 'Yield to the ancient existent decrees: who am I to resist them?'[22] Readers may justifiably have developed some, possibly amused, feelings of incongruity as they are asked to draw serious political morals from the romantic vicissitudes of an Oxford undergraduate, and in the crowning relationship these irrupt explicitly into the text itself. Philip, true to form, understands his final choice of Elspie as embodying the quietist, liberal stance 'let each man seek to be that for which Nature meant him'.[23] Elspie herself, on the other hand, the first women in the poem to speak at length in her own voice, resists being seen as an embodiment of anything. Hobbes is on Philip's side of the question when he imagines, albeit humorously, that the couple will bring 'Democracy upon New Zealand'; however, the narrator's closing words tell only of domestic happiness: 'There he built him a home; there Elspie bare him his children . . .'.[24] With startling insouciance, Philip's marriage is described both as the embodiment of a political principle and as an escape from the error of viewing relationships as embodiments of political principles. This is a point to which I shall return.

The new imaginative verve which Clough manifests in the *Bothie* has an origin in a dual liberation he had experienced at Easter 1848. Having admitted his inability to subscribe to the Thirty-Nine Articles, he had resigned his Oxford fellowship, and had gone almost at once to revolutionary Paris, as though to investigate the coincidence between his personal emancipation and the new political liberties being asserted on the continent. Where Oxford was like 'bondage in Egypt', he wrote in his letters, Paris was 'Jerusalem', which he 'walked about . . . with wonderful delight'.[25] For John Goode, the *Bothie* is therefore 'a revolutionary poem . . . an affirmative . . . vision of the possibilities of historical change';

---

[21] *B* II. 171; IV. 114–15.   [22] *B* V. 120–1.
[23] *B* IX. 17.   [24] *B* IX. 162, 197.
[25] *Correspondence of Arthur Hugh Clough*, i. 199, 214.

Tom Paulin calls it 'a unique expression of the spirit of 1848'.[26]
These views have some foundation, for during the first few weeks
of his stay in Paris Clough had been struck by the appearance of
unity between different social groups, in contrast to the class
antagonism which had distressed him at home. The *Bothie* imagines the achievement of a similar unity (although across national
cultures as well as classes) in Britain and on a personal scale.
However, the work is also, and primarily, a story about some privileged Oxford undergraduates having a good time on a reading
party in Scotland. It describes them in a mock-heroic style which,
though affectionate, makes somewhat light of their experiences
and theories. There is, then, a marked, and comic, disparity
between the central matter of the narrative and the implications
which are attached to it. The work's jokey side was advertised by
the shape in which its first edition appeared. It was a paperback,
printed not by a mainstream London publisher but by an Oxford
bookseller: Clough's bibliographer notes that 'its original paper
covers show the kind of ephemeral impact intended'.[27] One
reviewer suggested that its distinctly 'Oxford' focus made it 'not
very intelligible, and hardly to be recommended, beyond the walls
of the University', a judgement which Clough pre-empted by
introducing the work as a 'TRIFLE' and dedicating it to 'MY LONG-
VACATION PUPILS'.[28] Although the *Bothie* may nonetheless have to
do with serious and large-scale political issues it is clearly not being
straightforwardly 'affirmative' or expressive in the manner of, say
Casa Guidi Windows. Throughout the poem, there runs a current
of self-parody, which is kept perpetually before the reader's eye by
an unusual metre: the accentual hexameter.

   Clough knew poems in accentual hexameters by Goethe and
Longfellow, and had taken part in a dispute carried on in the pages
of a journal called *The Classical Museum* about the right way of
translating Greek and Latin poetry.[29] A central issue was whether
it was possible to bring into English accentual verse anything like

---

[26] John Goode, '1848 and the Strange Disease of Modern Love', in John Lucas (ed.),
Literature and Politics in the Nineteenth Century (Methuen, 1971), 64; Paulin, *Minotaur*, 65.

[27] Patrick Greig Scott, *The Early Editions of Arthur Hugh Clough* (New York: Garland,
1977), 9.

[28] Thorpe (ed.), *Clough: The Critical Heritage*, 79; *Poems of Arthur Hugh Clough*, 593.

[29] Joseph Patrick Phelan, 'Radical Metre: The English Hexameter in Clough's *Bothie of
Toper-na-Fuosich*', *Review of English Studies*, NS vol. 50/198 (1999), 166–87.

the patterns of quantity (i. e. syllabic length) which were fundamental to the classics. Clough's view, as he made clear in a later
article, was that, to the extent that it is possible to distinguish
between 'long and short' in English, 'quantity' should be 'attended
to in the first place', and that 'in the second', 'natural accents'
should be 'very frequently laid upon syllables which the metrical
reading depresses' (i.e. which are scanned short). He then gives an
instance of translation carried out according to these principles:

> Tydides also fled with me, his company calling;
> Later, upon our track followed the yellow Meneläus;[30]

Upon resolving these lines into hexameters one discovers that
quantity is indeed the defining principle of the verse: 'followed' is
taken as short-long, as is 'yellow'; 'track followed the yellow
Menelaus' therefore scans spondee-dactyl-dactyl-spondee: if we
do not readily pick up on this structure it is because we are not
used to looking for patterns of quantity in English. The hexameters of the *Bothie*, however, rely on a different principle from
Clough's scholarly, unrhythmical translations. In the *Bothie*, the
metrical form is defined primarily by stress:

> Eying through | eddying green | waters
>
> the | green-tinting | floor under | neath them

Quantity does matter here, but only in the subsidiary, expressive
way in which it normally affects English verse: the long words
'through' and 'green' (at its first appearance) pull against their
unstressed positions, creating a hint of rhythmical wobble to
mimic the eddying that is being decribed. When Clough had his
scholarly hat on, he called this sort of verse 'lengthy, straggling,
irregular, uncertain slips of *prose mesurée*'.[31]

Prose mesurée provided him with great liberty. Not only could he
vary its length from thirteen up to seventeen syllables in the normal
way of hexameters, but he could have the spoken weight of the
words tell against an established rhythm in the usual manner of
English accentual-syllabic verse. This formal freedom makes possi-

---

[30] *Poems of Arthur Hugh Clough*, 557–8.
[31] *Selected Prose Works of Arthur Hugh Clough*, 182.

ble the remarkable dictional variety of the *Bothie*, at once in the basic sense that it allows such diversely unpoetical words as 'quadruped', '*clippingest*', and 'Méalfourvónìe' to be physically accommodated in a line of verse, and for the less demonstrable though equally important reason noted by William Whewell: 'the very novelty of the measure makes us willingly accept a style in which the usual conventional phrases and dim generalities of poetical description are replaced by the idioms and pictures of common life.'[32] Isobel Armstrong rightly celebrates the poem's combination of different dialects and idioms as making for 'a precise and self-conscious examination of language and power'.[33] However it is essential not to forget that the verse form also helps to produce the work's comic edge, as contemporary readers noticed. J. C. Shairp complained that Clough's hexameters had 'always a feeling of parody'; Henry Sidgwick more sympathetically observed that they were 'always suggestive of and allusive to the ancient serious hexameters, with a faint but deliberate air of burlesque, a wink implying that the bard is singing academically to an academical audience, and catering for their artificial tastes in versification'.[34]

When Clough describes the undergraduates plunging into the various currents of water and feeling and political resolution which they discover in Scotland, he does not abandon the worries about sincerity, about groundedness, by which he had been preoccupied in the *Ambarvalia* poems. Even in the most vigorous descriptions of swimming, he preserves for himself a dry location from which he can tip his readers a wink:

> How to the element offering their bodies, downshooting
>   the fall, they
> Mingled themselves with the flood and the force of imperious
>   water.[35]

Tom Paulin solemnly proposes that these lines 'take on the excitement of that year of revolutions', the association being hinted at by the word 'imperious'.[36] However, the tongue-in-cheekness of the writing evokes a more complex bundle of thoughts and feelings. With its rolling dactyls, the verse certainly takes on the

---

[32] *B* III. 61, 146, 180; Thorpe (ed.), *Clough: The Critical Heritage*, 68.
[33] Armstrong, *Victorian Poetry*, 181.
[34] Thorpe (ed.), *Clough: The Critical Heritage*, 123, 286.
[35] *B* III. 163–4.   [36] Paulin, *Minotaur*, 56.

impulse of the water, but does this in a way that is so obvious as to seem artificial: it suggests a narrator self-consciously, and camply, miming the undergraduates' exerience. In this context, the word 'imperious' seems to carry inverted commas: the self-awareness of the writing encourages us to appraise the word as well as be impressed by it; to remember that, although the swimmers feel the water to be imperious, and their feeling may be traced in the direction of politics, they are nonetheless youngsters in a stream; and to notice that there is a large difference between this small bucolic episode and the year of revolutions. The verse brings in the possibility of metaphor but simultaneously resists it by presenting the image as a joke. This technique is used throughout the poem so as simultaneously to invoke and to question that generalizing tendency of the imagination which is fostered by *Aurora Leigh*. It keeps before our eyes the disparity between the developments in Philip's personal life and the large political issues to which they are also shown to be connected. These contrary pulls reach their highest tension in the paradoxical account of the relationship with Elspie which I mentioned before.

John Goode proposes that 'the actualization of love' between Philip and Elspie 'envisages the potentiality of revolution, even though the potential remains unrealized except in terms of private escape'.[37] Philip's political ideal can issue in nothing grander than an unusual marriage followed by emigration, he suggests, because it has been stifled by the contemporary social structure in Britain: the *Bothie* is therefore all the more polemical for making this clear. On this view, Philip's love for Elspie is in essence the same thing as his commitment to liberal democracy, so that in their relationship 'the human forces which make for revolution are realized in personal terms'.[38] But what Elspie makes Philip see is that a personal relationship, though it includes issues of power (as her talk of American Indians makes clear),[39] is too complex to be understood as the realization of a political commitment. It brings different and sometimes contrary 'human forces' into play, so that the realm of love and the realm of politics cannot be mapped onto one another. Hence the puzzlement in Philip's long description of his emotions (IX. 73–108), where he first of all says that 'the old

---

[37] Goode, '1848 and the Strange Disease', 70.   [38] Ibid. 69.
[39] See above, Chapter 2.

democratic fervour' is returning into his 'soul of souls' like a 'tide' but then paradoxically realizes that 'the love of Elspie' has had the effect of reconciling him to 'the whole great wicked artificial civilized fabric' of society so that it 'Seems reaccepted, resumed to Primal Nature and Beauty'. He recognizes that his feelings have operated something like what modern critics of Romantic poetry call a 'displacement' of the political into the personal, but as in 'Tintern Abbey' and the final books of *The Prelude*, the question of whether his individual fulfilment is a beginning for political action or an alternative to it is left unresolved.

For Isobel Armstrong, the ambiguity of the ending, in which 'Philip's decision may constitute a bold political realism, or it may be a quixotic and romantic idealism' is itself politically radical because 'it is only through the linguistic inventiveness of ambiguity that transformation is possible'. Yet the *linguistic* ambiguity much attended to by Armstrong in the wake of Kristeva and Bakhtin is a different kind of uncertainty from the interpretive puzzle of the poem's conclusion. Armstrong suggests that by contracting his ambivalent marriage, 'Philip solves the problem of political action and intervention';[40] on the contrary, the reader is left with the difficulty of whether the marriage is politically significant at all. Like the meeting of Romney and Aurora in Italy, it seems importantly to be an escape from politics, an assertion of the self-sufficiency of personal relationships and the fulfilment that they offer. Barrett Browning, as we saw, proceeded to bridge the divide between personal and political by imagining the spread of such relationships around the world, a vision which, though consciously utopian, took some substance from the relationship of reading. Clough leaves us with a contradiction, a relationship which is greeted as the conclusion of a political quest while in itself refusing to take on anything other than personal significance. The two dimensions cannot be reconciled, and their paradoxical co-existence, appropriately enough in a comic poem, constitutes a large and serious joke. The issues which it raises are fundamental to understanding the actions of individuals who are members of a political community. The personal and the political are always connected—at moments of high pressure they may seem to be as one—but the personal also

[40] Armstrong, *Victorian Poetry*, 185, 191, 181.

offers resistance to political understanding, for its thoughts, sensa-
tions, and commitments may veer away from those that can be
expressed in a public role. In the *Ambarvalia* poems this difficulty
had appeared utterly stifling, to the extent that any commitment
to a group or even to another individual, had seemed impossible.
The *Bothie*, although more relaxed about the issue, is no less alive
to it, offering up for our understanding the various ways in which
Philip's actions are and are not revolutionary, do and do not have
public significance. A year later, in 1849, Clough went to Rome,
and what he found there gave him reason to pose these questions
again, in a less jovial style.

LOVE ON A ROMAN STAGE

'Oh Rome! my country! city of the soul!'[41] Primed by Byron and
the classics, Victorian travellers had high expectations of Rome.
Often, they were disappointed. As they approached the city on the
travels described in *Pictures from Italy* (1846), Dickens and his party
'began, in a perfect fever, to strain our eyes for Rome; and when,
after another mile or two, the Eternal City appeared, at length, in
the distance; it looked like—I am half afraid to write the word—like
LONDON!!!'[42] Claude's initial observations in *Amours de Voyage*,
therefore, would not have startled mid-nineteenth-century readers,
even if he elaborates on his disappointment with unusual verve:

> Rome disappoints me much; I hardly as yet understand, but
> *Rubbishy* seems the word that most exactly would suit it.
> All the foolish destructions, and all the sillier savings,
> All the incongruous things of past incompatible ages,
> Seem to be treasured up here to make fools of present and future.
> Would to Heaven the old Goths had made a cleaner sweep of it!
> Would to Heaven some new ones would come and destroy
>   these churches!
> However, one can live in Rome as also in London.[43]

A glimpse of the Coliseum in the midst of the modern city was
enough to restore Dickens's enthusiasm ('here was Rome indeed
at last; and such a Rome . . .'),[44] but in *Amours* it is precisely the

---

[41] Byron, *Childe Harold's Pilgrimage*, IV. 703.
[42] Dickens, *Pictures from Italy*, 115.   [43] *AV* I. 19–26.
[44] *Pictures from Italy*, 118.

coexistence of the residues of different ages and beliefs which leaves Claude nonplussed. Like George Eliot's Dorothea, in whom Rome produces a similar impression of 'stupendous fragmentariness', he does not assume the comprehensive view 'which breathes a growing soul into all historic shapes, and traces out the suppressed transitions which unite all contrasts'; only in his case this is the result, not of ignorance, but of a principled refusal to accept an idealist explanation of history as organic development.[45] As we discover towards the end of Canto I, *Amours de Voyage* is set in one of the two last bastions of revolution in 1849: republican Rome, which came under siege from a French army sent by Louis Napoleon to enforce the restoration of the Pope.[46] Like all nineteenth-century nationalism, Mazzini's doctrine of the Risorgimento assumed the existence of a national spirit, connecting past ages with the present and leading on into the future. Claude's early impression of the city therefore offers a pre-emptive challenge to the efforts of Mazzini's regime to resurrect the ancient Roman Republic as a step towards the unification of Italy.

In this Roman setting, hexameters take on newly apt and multifarious implications. Since they are a classical form, we might take them as conveying that '*spirit from perfecter ages*' which the introductory elegiacs in Canto II suggest may abide among the ruins and '*E'en in the people itself*'.[47] Perhaps we should think that as they draw resonant Latinisms such as 'superincumbent oppression' and slangy words of English origin like '*Rubbishy*' into the same verse texture they themselves accomplish what Mazzini wants to do and what Claude thinks to be impossible: 'Utter . . . the word that shall reconcile Ancient and Modern.'[48] However, it might equally be argued that Claude brings such different words together precisely so as to exhibit their incongruity. From this point of view, one might take the verse form as carrying the feel of his classically trained Oxford intellectualism, the very thing that stops him believing in the spirit from perfecter ages. Certainly, the fluidity of the hexameters allows his voice to be delineated with startling precision:

---

[45] George Eliot, *Middlemarch*, ed. David Carroll (Oxford: Clarendon Press, 1986), 187–8.
[46] See Candeloro, *Storia dell' Italia Moderna*, iii. 425–71; and Trevelyan, *Garibaldi's Defence of the Roman Republic*.   [47] *AV* II. 1, 8.
[48] *AV* I. 36, 200.

Seem to be treasured up here to make fools of present and future.

The predominantly dactylic pulse of the spoken weight of the words coincides almost exactly with the line's scansion, in which all the feet are dactyls apart from the fourth and sixth; a conjunction which gives Claude's argument the impetus of indignation. Then the movement changes:

Would to Heaven the old Goths had made a cleaner sweep of it!

If you resolve this into a hexameter, you find that 'Would to' and 'made a' are doing duty as spondees, while 'cleaner sweep' stands in for a dactyl, emphases which are at odds with the spoken rhythm. The consequent thickening of the line with possible stresses evokes a bursting-out into exclamation.

Since they show a character presenting himself in the first person, the hexameters' 'feeling of parody' turns against that character himself, and because the hexameters represent the comparatively considered form of letters (rather than speech or interior monologue) there is a persistent uncertainty about the degree to which Claude is himself aware of and responsible for this parodic feeling. When '*Rubbishy*' appears in that emphatic, perhaps self-admiring position at the start of the line, are we to take it that the implied author is poking fun at what Claude thinks to be his own daring?— or is it rather that the hexameters faithfully reproduce Claude's own emphasis as he writes with an air of slight self-mockery? Certainly by the time he gets to 'Would to Heaven some new ones would come and destroy these churches', he has worked his opinion up into an attitude, and is consciously adopting a scandalous posture which he then abandons in the line that follows. Too late, as it turns out, for the gods soon grant his unserious wish, making new Goths appear in the shape of the besieging French army.

Oxford scholar that he is, Claude at first occupies himself with visiting ancient remains and engaging in religious speculation. He makes clear that his journey to Rome is not an imitiation of Newman's ('No, the Christian faith . . . | Is not here, O Rome, in any of these thy churches'), and gathers evidence for his view of the incompatibility of the city's different ages, remarking of the Pantheon, which had long been consecrated as a church, 'No, great Dome of Agrippa, thou art not Christian'.[49] His enjoyment

[49] *AV* I. 70–1, 152.

of this a–social 'Eden' of contemplation is interrupted by that common holiday experience, shared by the undergraduates in the *Bothie*, of meeting people with whom he would not otherwise have associated. Where, to begin with, like Barrett Browning's Aurora, he appreciated his freedom in a foreign land from 'All the *assujettissement*' of his social identity in England, 'What one thinks one is, or thinks that others suppose one', now he finds himself having to put on a public face again:

> Curious work, meantime, re-entering society; how we
> Walk a livelong day, great Heaven, and watch our shadows!
> What our shadows seem, forsooth, we will ourselves be.
> Do I look like that? you think me that: then I am that.[50]

By his 'shadow', Claude must mean the person he is made out to be by others as they interpret his accent, dress, family, opinions, etc., which is to say the person he therefore becomes in their eyes. This might be taken to be a remarkable anticipation of Althusser's theory of the interpellation of the subject, were it not that Claude holds fast to the belief that, however much he acts his own shadow and enters into relationships with others, his real self persists high up above the sea of society on 'the great massy strengths of abstraction', to which, whatever happens, he will return.[51]

Like Elspie, Claude is aware that his developing feelings are conditioned by class and power. What he enjoys may be, it occurs to him, nothing more than 'the horrible pleasure of pleasing inferior people' (a thought which never entered Philip's head); yet, while accepting this possibility he nonetheless feels that 'for the first time in life I am living and moving with freedom'.[52] As in the *Bothie*, there appears the prospect of a love which will not only break through but in the end manage to ignore class boundaries, thereby allowing its participants to be in a relationship which is comparatively untrammelled by social constraints. Philip quickly became confident of being 'that for which Nature meant him', but Claude finds the reconciliation of sincerity and sociability, even the miniature sociability of love, to be more problematic.[53] What most attracts him in Mary is that she shares his view of the provisional status of his social persona:

---

[50] *AV* II. 277; I. 30–1, 83–6.   [51] *AV* I. 251.   [52] *AV* I. 214, 216.
[53] *B* IX. 17.

No, I could talk as I pleased; come close; fasten ties as I fancied;
Bind and engage myself deep;—and lo, on the following morning
It was all e'en as before, like losings in games played for nothing.[54]

As he acts out the social game of courtship, Claude arms himself against any 'malpractice of heart and illegitimate process', waiting for the impulse which will make his act real, unite his self and his shadow: 'Let love be its own inspiration!'[55]

Claude's amour is brought into a more specific and probing connection with politics than occurs in the *Bothie* because, as we soon discover, it is taking place during an episode of great political moment. A parallel between the two dimensions is lightly suggested by the fact that Georgina's enquiries about Claude in the last letter of Canto I are immediately followed in the first letter of Canto II by the news that the French army has arrived at the gates of Rome. The Republic and Claude's libertarian love come under siege together, from the forces of political reaction and social convention respectively.

As the double-plot unfolds, Italian nationalism and love for Mary line up together as perhaps-complementary or perhaps-alternative commitments which would put an end to Claude's detachment. A cancelled draft has him lumping the two together as he exclaims 'Oh, but I am in love; nothing else can account for the fervours | Of my republican heat' and proposes leaping into 'the great bridal bed of the combat and conflict of men';[56] in the published version they are brought more tentatively and amusingly into contact when, having swiftly decided not to fight for 'the Cause' of Rome, he asks himself whether Mary is worth defending:

Am I prepared to lay down my life for the British female?
Really, who knows? One has bowed and talked, till, little by little,
All the natural heat has escaped of the chivalrous spirit.[57]

('Female' is beautifully chosen because so un-chivalrous.) The defence of Rome, a battle for liberty against overwhelming odds, could easily be presented as the romantic cause *par excellence*: an article in the *Westminster Review* judged that it renewed the 'glorious strain of patriotism' first manifested in 'such hearts as those of

---

[54] *AV* III. 196–8.
[56] *Poems of Arthur Hugh Clough*, 638, 627.
[55] *AV* II. 272, 278.
[57] *AV* II. 31, 66–8.

Leonidas and Brutus, of Solon and Caius Gracchus'.[58] A hero in
the style of Sir Walter Scott would easily find a role for himself in
Claude's position: marry the girl, fight for liberty, make a daring
escape with Garibaldi. Claude is not immune to the attraction of
his circumstances:

> . . . Alas! 'tis ephemeral folly,
> Vain and ephemeral folly, of course, compared with pictures,
> Statues, and antique gems!—Indeed: and yet indeed too,
> Yet methought, in broad day did I dream,—tell it not in St. James's,
> Whisper it not in thy courts, O Christ Church!—yet did I, waking,
> Dream of a cadence that sings, *Si tombent nos jeunes héros, la*
> *Terre en produit de nouveaux contre vous tous prêts à se battre*;
> Dreamt of great indignations and angers transcendental,
> Dreamt of a sword at my side, and a battle-horse underneath me.[59]

As the mention of the aristocratic enclaves St James's and Christ
Church indicates, part of what excites Claude here is that he, a
gentleman, is being drawn into sympathy with republicanism. The
voice of individual culture is swept up into the public chorus of
the *Marseillaise*. Yet, for all the self-conscious daring with which it
is introduced ('and yet . . . Yet . . . tell it not . . .'), and for all the
intrinsic impact of the heroic French words and their historical
associations, Claude experiences the possibility of martial action as
no more than a dream. Anaphoric repetition often imparts deci-
siveness to a passage of verse, but not when the words involved are
'Dream . . . | Dreamt . . . | Dreamt'. This repetition makes the
vision seem less consequential the more it is asserted.

Claude's dream might be brought into relation with the feelings
of any of us who are not heroes when confronted with grand actions
on the world stage. However, it has a particular aptness in the Rome
of 1849, for the defence of the city organized by Mazzini and
Garibaldi was an exercise in the creation of a nationalist myth.[60]

[58] (W. J. Linton), 'The Liberty of Rome', *Westminster and Foreign Quarterly Review*,
53/104 (Apr. 1850), 77; for an elaboration of similar feelings in verse, see Ernest Myers,
'The Defence of Rome', *The Defence of Rome and Other Poems* (Macmillan, 1880).

[59] *AV* II. 54–62.

[60] John Goode, '*Amours de Voyage*: The Aqueous Poem', in Isobel Armstrong (ed.), *The
Major Victorian Poets: Reconsiderations* (Routledge and Kegan Paul, 1969), 284, followed by
Phelan, 'Elizabeth Barrett Browning's *Casa Guidi Windows*, Arthur Hugh Clough's *Amours
de Voyage* and the Italian National Uprisings of 1847–9', *Journal of Anglo-Italian Studies*, 3
(1993), 146.

When Clough visited Mazzini he found that he 'expects foreign intervention in the end, and of course thinks it likely enough that the Romana Reppublica [*sic*] will fall'.[61] The defenders of Rome were consciously enacting valour, so as to leave an example of Italian heroism to future revolutionaries in line with Mazzini's oft-repeated contention that—to quote the widely known *Records of the Brothers Bandiera* (1844)—'the seed that we have sown will remain; God will cause it to germinate beneath the soil sanctified by the blood of our martyrs; and should it blossom only over our graves— still, blessed be God—we shall rejoice elsewhere'.[62] To some observers, the doomed nature of the Roman enterprise made it seem all the more heroic; to others, the theatrical aspect introduced a possibility of comedy, as in the following rhyme from *Punch*:

> . . . Rome's old heroes from their spheres
> Shout, chiming in with British cheers,
> 'Bravo, MAZZINI!'[63]

Here, the dead metaphor of the 'theatre of conflict' is reanimated, with 'the gods' appropriately being occupied by ancient heroes. Claude's cheer at the spectacle of heroism in Canto III is similarly ironic, though more bitter:

> Meantime, pray, let 'em fight and be killed. I delight in devotion.
> So that I 'list not, hurrah for the glorious army of martyrs!
> *Sanguis martyrum semen Ecclesiae*; though it would seem this
> Church is indeed of the purely Invisible, Kingdom-come kind:
> Militant here on earth! Triumphant, of course, then elsewhere!
> Ah, good Heaven, but I would I were out far away from the
>   pother![64]

The verbal echoes of the passage from *Records of the Brothers Bandiera* are clear enough to suggest that Clough may have had it in mind. Whether he did or not, the rhetoric of national self-sacrifice which in the form of the 'Marseillaise' had previously tempted Claude, if only as a dream, now looks to him as false as the

---

[61] *Poems and Prose Remains of Arthur Hugh Clough*, ed. Blanche Clough, 2 vols. (Macmillan, 1869), i. 143.

[62] Mazzini, *Life and Writings*, iii. 316. For Clough's admiration of Mazzini, see *Correspondence of Arthur Hugh Clough*, i. 305–7.

[63] 'Bravo, Mazzini', *Punch*, 17 (1849), 35: quoted in Harry W. Rudman, *Italian Nationalism and English Letters* (G. Allen and Unwin, 1940), 82.

[64] *AV* III. 73–8.

Catholic slogan about martyrdom. To some extent this alteration in his view has been brought about by his feelings for Mary, for (as we later discover) he is mortified at having had his intentions about her questioned and miserable at her departure; but historical events will also have played their part, for the French, singers of the 'Marseillaise', themselves in revolution only a year before, are now actually attacking the Roman Republic on behalf of the Pope. Since they have switched causes without much diminution in their readiness to die, it seems to Claude that all such rhetorics are interchangeable.

As readers have often noted, Claude is much concerned to provide accurate witness of the events around him no less than of his feelings: indeed, because of this it is easy to date his letters against the historical record: II.i to 25 April, II.vi to 31st, etc. He not only resists Mazzinian declamation but corrects mistaken newspaper reports ('*The Times* . . . was slightly in error | When it proclaimed as a fact the Apollo was sold to a Yankee')[65] and painstakingly records his impressions, notably in letters II. v and II. vii which describe the French bombardment and what appears to have been the murder of a priest. The descriptive inflation which wars encourage and which Claude is committed to avoiding appears in a joke Clough makes with a letter of Georgina's:

ONLY think, dearest Louisa, what fearful scenes we have witnessed!

    ★   ★   ★   ★   ★   ★   ★   [66]

The asterisks suggest horrors an editor has had to excise (Claude, by contrast, notes 'the place is most peaceful').[67] The obvious accuracy of Claude's reporting has led several of the work's recent critics to suppose that he represents an exemplary consciousness whose attitude to the Risorgimento, indeed to the world, is held up for our admiration. Joe Phelan takes his final bitter comments about the siege to indicate that Clough himself saw 'the entire revolutionary interlude as . . . pointless and childish'; Goode thinks Claude's ratiocinations more generally show that 'Clough has retreated from the reconstructive rhetoric of Romantic and Victorian poetry to the chaos of the multiform, to the honesty of David Hume'.[68] What such brusquely paraphrastic interpretations

[65] *AV* II. 26–8.   [66] *AV* II. 217–18.   [67] *AV* II. 211.

[68] Phelan, 'Elizabeth Barrett Browning's *Casa Guidi Windows*', 151; Goode, '*Amours de Voyage*: The Aqueous Poem', 290–1.

neglect is that Claude is a dramatized character who goes through an emotional upheaval which he makes great efforts to conceal. As with any dramatic poem, the first requirement for reading *Amours de Voyage* is a readiness not to take its protagonist at his own valuation.

In Canto II we are given a strong hint of the disparity between Claude's ruminations in his letters and his actual behaviour, for his sarcasms about chivalry in relation to 'the British female' are soon followed by Georgina's account of his actions on the following day: 'Mary allows she was wrong about Mr. Claude *being selfish*; | He was *most* useful and kind on the terrible thirtieth of April'. In the delicately comic opening to the next letter but one, Claude writes, astonishingly, 'I AM in love', only to continue '. . . you think; no doubt you should think so'.[69] Why should Eustace now think Claude to be in love? Because Mary has not been mentioned at all in his last eight missives which are suddenly and (Eustace must think) suspiciously full of politics. There is a similar shape to Canto III, where we are surprised that Claude has not followed the Trevellyns to Florence, but do not find out the reason why until letter xii. This means that all the Canto's philosophical speculation about 'juxtaposition', 'Aqueous Ages', etc., interesting though it may be in the abstract, is in context primarily a way for Claude to talk about something other than his hurt, and implicitly to argue himself out of it. The Canto's political despair ('FAREWELL, Politics, utterly!'), including the comments on 'the glorious army of martyrs', must also draw some impetus from his personal misery.[70] To take pronouncements such as 'let 'em fight and be killed' or 'Let us seek knowledge;— the rest must come and go as it happens' and to erect them into either statements of Clough's own view or general philosophical principles is to ignore the specific circumstances which have led Claude to produce them.[71] By an idiotic misunderstanding he has been separated from the woman with whom he was falling in love: if this had not happened, he would not have been cast back on 'the hard naked rock' of solitude and observation; he would not have had to console himself by wondering whether 'perhaps there was something factitious' about his feeling; the circumstances which lead him to conclude

[69] *AV* II. 226–7; 250.   [70] *AV* III. 107, 97, 60.   [71] *AV* V. 199.

that love 'does pass . . . but Knowledge abideth' would have been different.[72]

Of the double plot in *Troilus and Cressida*, William Empson remarks:

The two parts make a mutual comparison that illuminates both parties ('love and war are alike') and their large-scale indefinite juxtaposition seems to encourage primitive ways of thought ('Cressida will bring Troy bad luck because she is bad'). This power of suggestion is the strength of the double plot; once you take the two parts to correspond, any character may take on *mana* because he seems to cause what he corresponds to or be Logos of what he symbolises.[73]

What is remarkable about the double plot of *Amours de Voyage* is that it presents us with a drama of which we may very well expect the two parts to correspond, but then refuses to satisfy that expectation. Admittedly, there is the vague analogy set up by the word 'freedom', the joke about being besieged, and the background possibility of a comparison between marital and national union; and certainly Claude's worries about 'factitiousness' have to do with both the rhetoric of national self-sacrifice and the conventionalities of love. But as the work develops these correspondences are either not followed up or are brought into conflict. Claude would absolutely resist the idea of taking on anything like *mana* (a Maori word for symbolic power), and the thought that by having a love affair during the siege of Rome he may do precisely that is probably one reason why he questions the sincerity of his emotions. In the end, the double plot separates into two incommensurable narratives:

ROME is fallen, I hear, the gallant Medici taken,
Noble Manara slain, and Garibaldi has lost *il Moro*;—
Rome is fallen; and fallen, or falling, heroical Venice.
I, meanwhile, for the loss of a single small chit of a girl, sit
Moping and mourning here,—for her, and myself much smaller.[74]

The heroic failure of the Italians' struggle for freedom and the ignominious end of his *amour* coincide, but are not connected, neither in his feelings ('I care not for Rome, nor | Italy')[75] nor in

---

[72] *AV* V. 67, 164, 198.
[73] William Empson, *Some Versions of Pastoral* (1935; Hogarth Press, 1986), 34.
[74] *AV* V. 113–17.   [75] *AV* V. 125–6.

any causal or symbolic way. This disparity appears again in the poem's concluding lines, which address the poem itself:

> Say, 'I am flitting about many years from brain unto brain of
> Feeble and restless youths born to inglorious days;
> But,' so finish the word, 'I was writ in a Roman chamber,
> When from Janiculum heights thundered the cannon of France.'

Between the '*Roman chamber*' of Claude's private life, and the '*Janiculum heights*' of political action (between, in the terms of Chapter 1, this Shalott and this Camelot) there is no connection apart from simultaneity. The poem presents us with the story of someone who ends up feeling that he cannot contribute to political change, and that in any case his unhappiness would in no way be alleviated by it. Claude's letters manifest the liberal disillusionment of late 1849 in a way that attacks the redemptive rhetoric spouted by all those who tell us that politics is the solution of our ills. However, *Amours de Voyage* does not offer Claude to its readers as the symbolic leader of a party of resistance—someone like Aurora Leigh—for to do that would be to create a rhetoric of individuality quite as liable to be 'factitious' as the rhetoric of nationalism.

AMOURS IN THE PUBLIC EYE

'Don't publish it', wrote J. C. Shairp upon reading the manuscript of *Amours de Voyage*, 'or if it must be published—not in a book—but in some periodical'. Shairp detected a degree of self-exposure in the work ('your nature ridding itself of long-gathered bile') which disturbed him and which he thought its author would live to regret. Clough energetically rebutted the suggestion: 'Gott und Teufel, my friend, you don't suppose all that comes from myself!—I assure you it is extremely *not* so.'[76] Nonetheless, Shairp's feeling that *Amours de Voyage* was not the sort of thing that should be published does have point, for what the poem lays out before the eyes of strangers is a representation of private letters. Contemporary readers' expressions of unease frequently carry the implication that the correspondence of Claude and the Trevellyns is none of their business. In a posthumous review, the *Athenaeum*

---

[76] Thorpe (ed.), *Clough: The Critical Heritage*, 122.

remarked of one of Mary's epistles that Clough should have found 'better use for his powers than committing to paper the boarding-school nonsense which passes in reams through the post-office every day'.[77]

Readers might well have had less difficulty with *Amours de Voyage* had it been written in prose, since, while the epistolary novel was an established—if outdated—form, there were few analogues for a work consisting primarily of familiar letters in verse. One of Clough's more important influences was Horace, yet his *Epistles* were all along written with an eye to public circulation. In them, as in nineteenth-century verse-letters such as Tennyson's 'To E. FitzGerald', there is no feeling of embarrassing self-betrayal: the impulse of such poems is to honour the personal relationships in question by raising them to the level of exemplarity. Clough's characters, however, would be shocked if they knew their letters were to become public knowledge: 'don't tell Mr. Claude, what I will tell you as a secret', as Mary at one point writes to Miss Roper.[78] Browning arranges betrayals of confidence in his dramatic monologues, but he generally avoids the suggestion of scandal-mongering which attaches to *Amours* by setting the poems in the past as well as in another country. The supposed writer of 'An Epistle Containing the Strange Medical Experience of Karshish, the Arab Physician' makes it clear that he expects his letter to be intercepted and therefore has not included any secrets; but in any case the imagined dating of the poem is such that, even if he had, he would be long past annoyance at their publication.

The one clear precedent for the indiscreet mode of *Amours de Voyage* is Thomas Moore's *The Fudge Family in Paris* (1818).[79] This collection of verse letters is mainly a satire on the social pretensions of their imagined writers, although Mr Fudge's reports to one Lord 'C————GH' make some hits at Castlereagh's diplomatic manœuvrings, while hostile political commentary is provided by Phelim Connor, an Irish revolutionary. Moore's characters are so straightforwardly comic that worries about their right to privacy are unlikely to arise in readers' minds. Nonetheless, the issue does appear in the preface, in a dark comment hinting at nefarious practices: 'in what manner the following Epistles came into my hands,

---

[77] Thorpe (ed.), *Clough: The Critical Heritage*, 138.   [78] *AV* III. 257.
[79] I am grateful to Jeremy Maule for alerting me to it.

it is not necessary for the public to know.'[80] *Amours de Voyage*
incites more anxiety about the invasion of private space. By the
time it was written, only three decades after *The Fudge Family in
Paris*, the epistolary novel was no longer in vogue. Among the
causes and consequences of this decline was the well-attested hard-
ening of the distinction between private and public spheres in the
mid-nineteenth century. Scandal had been caused by one particular breach of this boundary not long before the composition of
Clough's poem when, in 1844, it was discovered that the Home
Office had secretly been opening and reading the correspondence
of Mazzini. Radical MPs went on the attack: W. J. Linton
protested at 'the introduction into this country . . . of the odious
spy system of foreign countries', Thomas Duncombe asked 'were
the free subjects of a free state to be subject to such a system',
while Joseph Hume explained the obvious: 'many a statement
might be contained in a letter, which, although of no public
importance, might be of great importance to the individual to
whom it related, and no one would wish to see such letters
opened.'[81] Certainly there is some difference between what might
be of public importance in a political sense, and what might interest the public in a work of literature. Nonetheless, *Amours de
Voyage* seems designed to provoke something like the feeling that
Tennyson expressed in 'To—, After Reading a Life and Letters'
(1849), verses occasioned in part by the publication of a volume
which Clough had helped to prepare: the *Letters and Literary
Remains of Keats* (1848). 'Proclaim the faults he would not show:
| Break lock and seal: betray the trust: | Keep nothing sacred . . .'
runs the 'scandal and the cry' in Tennyson's poem.[82] Clough has
done exactly that to his characters.

In his account of the development of a 'public sphere in the
world of letters' during the eighteenth century, Habermas
proposes that in the 'intimate sphere' of private life individuals
understood themselves as being independent of their economic
and political roles: they were 'persons capable of entering into
"purely human" relations with one another'. The medium which

---

[80] (Thomas Moore), *The Fudge Family in Paris, edited by Thomas Brown, the Younger*, 2nd
edn., (Longman, Hurst, Rees, Orme and Brown, 1818), pp. v, 11.

[81] *Hansard*, vol. 75 (1844), cols. 895, 898, 904.

[82] Tennyson, 'To—, After Reading a Life and Letters', 17–19.

allowed ' "purely human" relations' to extend beyond the 'intimate sphere' was literature:

> On the one hand, the empathetic reader repeated within himself the
> private relationships displayed before him in literature; from his experi-
> ence of real familiarity (Intimität), he gave life to the fictional one, and
> in the latter he prepared himself for the former. On the other hand, from
> the outset the familiarity (Intimität) whose vehicle was the written word,
> the subjectivity that had become fit to print, had in fact become the liter-
> ature appealing to a wide public of readers.

The dominant literary form in this process, he suggests, was 'the
letter' which, when printed, establishes a continuity between
private and public, exposing the personal, or what pretends to be
the personal, to general view. Furthermore, the imaginative
centrality of the letter impacted upon other genres, so that 'the
first-person narrative', for example, 'became a conversation with
oneself addressed to another person'.[83]

Although these generalizations are applied to European society
in the eighteenth century, they have no less relevance to the
poems written by Clough and his contemporaries at a time when,
according to Habermas's account, belief in the possibility of
extending ' "purely human" relations' into the public sphere had
declined. 'A conversation with oneself addressed to another
person' is an exact description of the mode of address of *Aurora
Leigh*, a work which is introduced as being written 'for my better
self | As when you paint your portrait for a friend'.[84] As we saw
in Chapter 5, Barrett Browning's poem ends up rejecting both the
socialist political programme at first espoused by Romney, and
Aurora's social life in the Mayfair world of genteely intellectual
chat. Instead, it offers a vision of personal relationships spreading
out around the world so as to form a 'social rose', and makes its
own contribution towards this end by setting out to establish a
series of comparable relationships with its readers. In Habermas's
terms, *Aurora Leigh* might be understood as an attempt to re-estab-
lish the ideal of the public sphere at a time when this was under
threat: two existing conceptions of public life are dismissed, and
the possibility of maintaining ' "purely human" relations' on a

---

[83] Jürgen Habermas, *The Structural Transformation of the Public Sphere: An Inquiry into a Category of Bourgeois Society*, trans. Thomas Burger and Frederick Lawrence (Cambridge: Polity Press, 1989), 48–51.   [84] *AL* I. 4–5.

large scale is relocated in the liberal nationalist vision of each nation as a 'community of sympathies' coexisting harmoniously with others. The variety of first-person narrative which, in Habermas's account, is the unwitting vehicle of sociological development is employed by Barrett Browning explicitly to promote an alternative to the social and political status quo.

However, *Amours de Voyage* markedly does not bring readers into a harmonious imaginative relationship with its central characters. Comments such as Claude's 'Aн, what a shame, indeed, to abuse these most worthy people' impress upon us the disparity between his private opinion and public actions.[85] We are being confronted precisely not with a subjectivity which has 'become fit to print', but with one which should be kept secret if harmonious social relations are to be continued. Set at the highpoint of nationalist myth-making, *Amours de Voyage* resists the ideology of national unification and, in so doing, rejects all the means for the creation of imaginative community and direction which Barrett Browning had adopted in *Aurora Leigh*, and which Clough himself had canvassed in tongue-in-cheek fashion in the *Bothie*. The protagonist does not enter into the public field of narrative, does not in the end establish unity with another character or achieve a sense of continuity between his own life and the processes of world history. Correspondingly, he does not address himself to us as a friend; indeed, he does not address himself to us at all.

Mary notes, in some puzzlement, that she finds Claude 'repulsive' although she is not sure that she is using the word in its received sense; 'yet he does most truly repel me'. In the light of the poem's other vocabulary of scientific origin ('affinity', 'juxtaposition'), Mary may be grasping at the meaning of the word in physics, where particles repel one another so as to maintain their own identities. It is the counterpart of Claude's feeling of being left free by her: '*She* spoke not of obligations'.[86] Reading, you inevitably reach out to characters in imaginative sympathy, seeking to understand them and to share their feelings. In *Aurora Leigh*, this process is implicitly dramatized, so that readers are conscious of being drawn into intimacy with *Aurora*: we are encouraged to feel part of the family, like Romney and Marian. *Amours de Voyage* configures the reading process in the opposite way, so that we are

[85] *AV* I. 135.   [86] *AV* III. 28, 30, 151, 153, 205.

made to feel as uncomfortable about it as possible. We may think that we get to know Claude, but the satirical presentation of his satirical voice discourages us from feeling at one with him. In any case, he would spurn our sympathy. The voice of the passages in elegiac couplets which begin and end each canto is that of a generalized lyric narrator who draws readers into his point of view, even occasionally speaking in the first-person plural ('*Is it to Florence we follow . . . ?*'). But Claude would absolutely reject the idea of becoming a representative voice of a public ('Under those vulgar eyes, the observed of such observers!').[87] The achievement of the poem is that, in the age of the realms of verse, it precisely does not create a realm of verse for its readers to inhabit. Instead, we are cast in the role of spies trespassing on a private space like Home Office employees in 1845. Criticizing what he thought to be the socially homogenizing tendencies of modern life (precisely those tendencies which *Aurora Leigh* was designed to foster), J. S. Mill in 1859 wrote of the need to preserve 'Individuality' against the 'ascendancy of public opinion' and other kinds of 'assimilation'.[88] *Amours de Voyage* offers a force of repulsion against the assimilating claims of love, of national unity, and indeed of 'the extension of our sympathies' through reading: equally, it investigates the cost of so repelling them.

---

[87] *AV* II. 339; III. 279.   [88] Mill, *On Liberty and Other Essays*, 81-2.

7

BROWNING'S ALIEN PAGES

'I distrust all hybrid & ambiguous natures & nationalities', Robert Browning remarked when, after Elizabeth's death, he was hurrying back to England to find a tutor for his son Pen: 'if I delay this . . . I may lose the critical time when the English stamp (in all that it is good for) is taken or missed.'[1] Distrust could be a spur to Browning's imagination, for he invented many characters of ambiguous nature. Not of ambiguous *nationality*, though; and in this his anxiety about Pen signals a difference between his connection with Italy and that of his wife. She wrote in a letter, 'I do love Florence so! When Penini says, "Sono Italiano, voglio essere Italiano," I agree with him perfectly'; in her poetry, as we have seen, she makes Italianness and Englishness merge, inventing plot-lines that move from one country to the other, writing a distinctively Italianate variety of English, and creating a character of, precisely, hybrid nationality: Aurora Leigh.[2] In his work, by contrast, English people relate to Italy as observers or collectors: the appraising, appreciative voices of 'The Englishman in Italy', 'Old Pictures in Florence' and 'Two in the Campagna' accentuate the difference between the speakers and the foreign country upon which they gaze. Browning conceived of himself as occupying a similar position, as he explained in the letter about Pen: 'I find, by myself, that one leans out the more widely over one's neighbour's field for being effectually rooted in one's own garden' (or indeed, he might have thought subliminally, for being penned in one's own pen).[3] To put

---

[1] *Browning to his American Friends: Letters between the Brownings, the Storys and James Russell Lowell 1841–1890*, ed. Gertrude Reese Hudson (Bowes and Bowes, 1965), 76.

[2] *Letters of Elizabeth Barrett Browning*, ed. Kenyon, ii. 197.

[3] *Browning to his American Friends*, 76.

the matter bluntly: his wife identified with Italy; for him it was an object of interest.

What, then, of the monologues which represent in English verse the speech of Italian characters?—characters whom the poet, as he writes in 'One Word More' has contrived to 'Enter each and all, and use their service, | Speak from every mouth,—the speech, a poem'.[4] As this typically clinical (and implicitly sexual) description of the workings of his imagination suggests, Browning did not conceive of himself as merging with or domesticating his subjects: he uses them and casts them aside. The poems are thought of, not as creations of hybrid nationality, but as images of unmitigated Italianness, which ask English readers, as they incline over Browning's pages, to lean out over their neighbour's field. In letters to Julia Wedgwood about *The Ring and the Book*, he insists that she recognize the foreignness of his characters. 'Ay, but the man is Italian', he pleaded in defence of what she thought Caponsacchi's 'coarseness': 'all *great* (conventionally great) Italians are coarse—showing their power in obliging you to accept their cynicism.' 'Besides, it is Italian ignorance', he noted of Pompilia's lack of education; 'quite compatible with extraordinary insight and power of expression too'.[5] Critics were slow to accept this aspect of Browning's work: his preference for Italy, complained *Chamber's Journal* in 1863, 'is undisguised, and, to Englishmen, almost repulsive'. For many contemporaries, it was disconcerting to open a book of supposedly English verse and find there poems such as 'The Bishop Orders his Tomb at St Praxed's Church'. As the *Athenaeum* sighed in its review of *Men and Women*, 'why he should turn away from themes in which everyone can answer to his sympathies, and from modes of the lyre which find their echoes wherever hearts and ears know aught of music—is an enigma no less painful than perplexing, the unriddling of which is possibly reserved for no contemporary.'[6]

The *Athenaeum* hints at an answer to its own conundrum, for the words in which it complains about the lack of echoes awakened by Browning's verse themselves echo 'Two in the

---

[4] 'One Word More', 131–2.

[5] *Robert Browning and Julia Wedgwood: A Broken Friendship as Revealed in their Letters*, ed. Richard Curle (John Murray and Jonathan Cape, 1937), 161, 176.

[6] Boyd Litzinger and Donald Smalley (eds.), *Browning: The Critical Heritage* (Routledge and Kegan Paul, 1970), 205, 157.

Campagna': 'I would I could ... set my heart | Beating by yours
... | | No'.[7] In the light of that poem, which urges the impossi-
bility of being utterly in sympathy with any other person, the
Athenaeum's 'themes in which everyone can answer to his sympathies' look unattractive: it appears that they must be either coercive or delusory. Like Clough's 'repulsive' verse, Browning's
dramatic monologues purposely disappoint the widespread expectation that poetry should promote the growth of affective community: they offer resistance to 'the extension of our sympathies'.[8] As
a representation of the voice of a distinct, dramatically located
individual, each monologue compels each reader to notice
contrasts between it and him or her, to hear modes of the lyre
which may seem to him or her discordant. In Browning's first
creations in the form, 'Porphyria's Lover' and 'Johannes Agricola
in Meditation', the discord is very marked, for the speakers are
respectively mad and fanatical. However, the characters represented in later works are rarely such extreme cases. Robert
Langbaum neglects this development when, in his classic book on
dramatic monologues, he proposes that the essence of the form is
'tension between sympathy and moral judgement', and that therefore 'it is safe to say that most successful dramatic monologues deal
with speakers who are in some way reprehensible or odd, so as to
heighten the tension'.[9] The argument is in any case awkwardly
put: the qualifier 'most' destroys the claim that a tension between
sympathy and judgement is constitutive of the form, for if it were
it would have to be present in all monologues; while the slippage
from 'reprehensible' to 'odd' casts doubt on the kind of 'judgement' required, for oddness is not a moral category. Even these
fudges cannot accommodate the fact that Andrea del Sarto is no
more 'reprehensible' than many of us, while the speaker of 'Two
in the Campaga' cannot even be called 'odd'.

The 'tension' for which Langbaum seeks to account derives
from an ambiguity which is primarily rhetorical, not ethical, and
which is indicated by Browning's own term, 'dramatic lyric'.[10] On
the one hand, a comparatively short, non-narrative poem in the

---

[7] 'Two in the Campagna', 41–6.   [8] See above, Chapter 2.

[9] Robert Langbaum, *The Poetry of Experience: The Dramatic Monologue in Modern Literary Tradition*, 3rd edn. (Chicago: University of Chicago Press, 1985), 85.

[10] See Ralph W. Rader, 'The Dramatic Monologue and Related Lyric Forms', *Critical Inquiry*, 3/1 (Autumn, 1976), 135.

first person awakes expectations of lyric, and therefore of a kind of writing with which readers are intended to identify, of 'modes of the lyre which find their echoes wherever hearts and ears know aught of music'. On the other, the dramatic situation and distinctly characterized voice encourage readers to notice differences between themselves and the speaker, and to think of themselves as observers. The form pulls together the intimacy of reading and the detachment of spectacle. For the tension of the hybrid genre to be achieved, it is not necessary for the central character to be 'reprehensible or odd', only that he or she be marked out as significantly different from the reader. This may be done in a variety of ways. Very often in Browning the marker of otherness, the proscenium arch, as it were, which holds the poem away from the reader, is the foreignness, usually Italianness, of speaker or location. Walter Bagehot recognized this fact, without quite understanding it, when he lamented that 'so different is the material on which he has chosen to expend his poetical labour from all that we see around us, that we cannot regard the result otherwise than as a mere artistic product'.[11]

Browning may have taken some bitter comfort from that complaint, for the comparatively disinterested attitude of regarding something 'as a mere artistic product' was—he proclaims at the end of *The Ring and the Book*—exactly what his poems were designed to elicit. 'How look a brother in the face and say | "Thy right is wrong . . ." '—he asks, for a direct address of that kind is likely to cause offence or be attributed to some ulterior motive or in one way or another be taken wrongly:

> But Art,—wherein man nowise speaks to men,
> Only to mankind,—Art may tell a truth
> Obliquely, do the thing shall breed the thought,[12]

Eric Griffiths takes issue with these lines, protesting that they 'replace Wordsworth's hopeful man speaking to men with the altogether less believable man speaking to mankind, a definition of the poet which leaves us to wonder whether someone who speaks to mankind mustn't, now and again, also speak to men'.[13] Browning's point, though, has to do with the kind of hearing

[11] Litzinger and Smalley (eds.), *Browning: The Critical Heritage*, 301.
[12] *RB* XII. 841–2, 854–6.
[13] Griffiths, *The Printed Voice of Victorian Poetry*, 207.

which he intends his poems to attract. For him, the poet as defined
by Wordsworth, 'a man speaking to men', has come to seem a
partisan figure, someone like a politician addressing a crowd. In
that position, it is difficult to cast your listeners in a critical light;
rather, you give them what they want to hear, what they know
already, building an impression of group, perhaps national, solidarity. For 'men' read 'Englishmen'. Bagehot drew Wordsworth
in the same direction when, having censured Browning for
concentrating on 'Italian life' and 'Italian scenery' he praised
Tennyson for evoking 'the distinct consciousness that the poet
who speaks to us is one of ourselves, breathing the same atmosphere of inarticulate longing and tender hope, of unrest, and
indignation, and wonder over things that are' (surely one of the
strangest ever descriptions of English national character).[14] A
Browning poem which introduces someone who is distinctly not
'one of ourselves' challenges readers to abstract from the shared
habits of thought and feeling which constitute 'the same atmosphere', and to approach the represented character not as 'men', but
as far as possible as members of 'mankind'. The experience of
meeting otherness in this way will send readers' thoughts back to
their own case from a new perspective, thereby doing 'the thing
shall breed the thought'.

Wordsworth chose 'low and rustic life' as the location of his
poetry because he thought that there 'the essential passions of the
heart' were more apparent.[15] The surface strangeness of his pages
was a means for reflecting the real selves of his readers all the more
clearly. In 'The Complaint of a Forsaken Indian Woman' and
'The Mad Mother' he employs monologues to persuade his readers that they have sympathies in common with even these strange
people: that an 'Indian' is nonetheless a 'Woman'; that someone
who is 'Mad' can still have the feelings of a 'Mother'. The strangeness of Browning's verse goes deeper, for he was less sure of the
existence of 'essential passions' in which everyone could share.
Under his pen, the dramatic monologue develops into an instru-
ment for the recognition and exploration of human diversity.
Hence the importance of foreign countries to his imagination, for

---

[14] Litzinger and Smalley (eds.), *Browning: The Critical Heritage*, 302.
[15] William Wordsworth and Samuel Taylor Coleridge, *Lyrical Ballads 1805*, ed. Derek
Roper (Plymouth: Northcote House, 1987), 21.

the time of nation-building gave new salience to that kind of diversity which separated the members of distinct nationalities. Browning's foreign poems rely on, and draw attention to, the implicit nationalism of 'the extension of our sympathies': his Italian characters cannot readily be included in the community of feeling at which the plural pronoun 'our' vaguely and coercively gestures. Having used national difference to induce a critical attitude in his readers, he hopes that they will then extend that recognition of variousness to the people whom they think of as 'ourselves', giving attention to what separates each of 'us' from one another. To watch one's neighbour over the garden fence is to adopt a position of detachment which is usually taken to characterize the aesthetic point of view. In Browning, however, this appears as a moral imperative: only by observing people impartially can you gauge and understand their difference from you. Equally necessary, however, is the move to identify with the other person, to lean out over his or her field (perhaps even to shake hands). The adoption of Italy as a means for establishing the difference which must be both recognized and bridged is a remarkable variant of the widespread association of Italy with the aesthetic which I described in Chapter 4.

As we discovered, the average mid-nineteenth-century English poem about Italy locates an English person in the foreign country and has him or her muse upon it, especially its past. *Casa Guidi Windows*, *Aurora Leigh*, and *Amours de Voyage* are all distinguished variants of this scheme, as are Browning's 'Two in the Campagna', ' "De Gustibus—" ', 'Old Pictures in Florence', and 'The Englishman in Italy'. Browning's other Italian poems, though, reverse the national and also the temporal elements of the usual way of doing things: bringing 'the dead alive', they make past Italians speak in the present.[16] Not satisfied by the foreignness of his characters, he placed them a further, historical remove. 'His topic being thus alien, to begin with'—lamented *Chamber's Journal*—'he takes pains to deprive it still more of interest by selecting the period of action two or three hundred years back.'[17] More recent critics have explained this aspect of his verse by adducing

---

[16] *RB* I. 733.
[17] Litzinger and Smalley (eds.), *Browning: The Critical Heritage*, 205–6.

'the Victorian view of the past', which 'sees it . . . as standing in an evolutionary relation' to the present.[18] Different Victorians of course had varying ideas about the details of the present's emergence from antiquity. Nonetheless, in the wake not least of Sir Walter Scott, writers were able to exploit a feeling of connection to the past without necessarily having to decide between the differing historiographical assumptions of Sismondi, Macaulay, and Carlyle. Browning's play *Strafford* (1837) does this, presenting the assertion of parliamentary rights on the eve of the Civil War as an early victory in what one of the characters calls 'the advancing good of England', whose latest manifestation, it is implied, had been in the Reform Act of 1832. The view which triumphs in the drama is that 'the will of England' is better represented by Parliament than by the king: this stands in a (roughly) evolutionary relation to events of Browning's time because it is assumed that once the principle of parliamentary representation has been affirmed an enlargement of the franchise will inevitably follow.[19] Looking back to this earlier stage of progress, according to the historical work on Strafford which Browning co-wrote with John Forster, people could see 'the justification of the world's "appeal from tyranny to God" ': despite everything that separates the nineteenth century from the seventeenth, it is assumed that the 'principles of political conduct' are constant (a point that is neatly emphasized by the fact that 'appeal from tyranny to God' is a quotation, not from any Roundhead, but from Byron).[20] The play enlists seventeenth-century gentlemen on the side of a democratic agenda which in their time did not exist. By doing this, as the frequent patriotic exclamations make clear ('now shall England crouch', 'will Wentworth dare shed English blood', etc.), it promotes a radical version of English nationalism, for the past of the drama and the present of its public are linked, not only by shared 'principle', but by the idea of an England which subsists through history, and which therefore both audience and characters inhabit.[21]

However, the poems written in the same decade as *Strafford*

---

[18] John Woolford and Daniel Karlin, *Robert Browning* (Longman, 1996), 172.

[19] *Strafford*, I. i. 32; IV. ii. 75.

[20] *Robert Browning's Prose Life of Strafford*, introduction by C. H. Firth (Kegan Paul, Trench, Trübner and Co., for the Browning Society, 1892), 278.

[21] *Strafford*, I. i. 88, 212.

make more idiosyncratic assumptions about history, and employ them in a more self-critical manner. The protagonists of *Paracelsus* (1835) and *Sordello* (1840) are both historical figures; but since they are, respectively, Swiss and Italian, they cannot be brought into a myth of specifically national continuity. Both works depict their central characters as prophets in the Shelleyan style, 'mirrors of the gigantic shadows which futurity casts upon the present'; indeed, this is the justification, part-humorous, part-defensive, for Browning's propagation of their supposed thoughts in his verse: only in the nineteenth century (the idea goes) has humanity at last become able to understand them.[22] Yet the poems make it equally clear that Browning cannot have held such a view seriously, for if he did, he should either have produced faithful editions of Paracelsus and Sordello or have set about registering the future in his own verse. Instead, he attributes to his characters opinions which are nowhere recorded of them and which they could not possibly have formulated. The ruminations elaborated in both works are transparently his own, as the dedication appended to the revised *Sordello* of 1863 admits: 'the historical decoration was purposely of no more importance than a background requires.'[23] These poems, therefore, implicitly reject the theory of history upon which they present themselves as relying.

The monologues which Browning began writing in the 1840s likewise challenge easy assumptions of continuity between the present and the past. They are so committed to imagining the otherness of their central characters that they refuse to be brought into any clear alignment with the period of their composition, whether evolutionary or otherwise. When, on 18 February 1845, Browning submitted 'The Bishop Orders his Tomb at St Praxed's Church' for publication in *Hood's Magazine*, he made what appears to be a quite specific claim for its contemporary relevance: it was, he said, 'just the thing for the time—what with the Oxford business, and Camden society and other embroilments'.[24] Quoting this remark in their edition, John Woolford and Daniel Karlin present the poem (after the manner of the 'poetry-as-journalism' school) as a 'satire' which connects the 'Tractarian (or "Oxford")

---

[22] *Shelley's Prose*, ed. Clark, 297.
[23] *Browning: The Poems*, ed. Pettigrew, i. 150.
[24] *Brownings' Correspondence*, x. 83.

movement in England' with the 'Counter-Reformation' and, beyond that, 'the old, unregenerate Catholic Church'.[25] On this reading, the Bishop must represent the enduring essence of Roman Catholicism, the religion into which, as was widely expected in the winter of 1844–5, Newman was soon to be received.[26] However, although Browning was strongly anti-Catholic, his opposition to that Church in its nineteenth-century form emphasizes markedly different characteristics from those which are embodied in the Bishop. 'Christmas Eve' describes contemporary Catholicism as the religion of 'Love' in the absence of 'Intellect', and indeed in the absence of artistic discrimination, a point reiterated in 'The Englishman in Italy' with its mockery of a 'flaxen-wigged Image' of the Virgin.[27] This is a long way from the Bishop, with his delight in '*lapis lazuli*' and his insistence on 'Choice Latin'.[28] Newman was never attacked for being a sensualist or an aesthete: on the contrary, low-church Anglicans and Nonconformists criticized him for misplaced spirituality. Browning's own opinion of Newman is nowhere recorded; but it is likely to have coincided with that of Dr Arnold, who viewed the Oxford Movement as a manifestation of 'superstition' and 'fanaticism'.[29]

A closer look at the circumstances of the work's publication reveals a proliferation of ways in which readers could have felt it to be 'just the thing for the time'. On the day before he sent it to *Hood's Magazine*, Browning would have read in *The Times* of the dissolution of the Cambridge Camden Society, an organization whose declared object was 'to promote the study of Ecclesiastical Architecture and Antiquities, and the restoration of mutilated Architectural remains'.[30] The society's researches had led it to take

---

[25] *The Poems of Browning*, ed. John Woolford and Daniel Karlin (Longman, 1991–), ii. 260.

[26] Elizabeth Barrett Browning read a report that Newman could 'no longer remain a member of the English church' in the *Morning Chronicle*, 4 Nov. 1844. *Brownings' Correspondence*, ix. 214 n.

[27] 'Christmas Eve', 652, 658; 'The Englishman in Italy', 269.

[28] 'The Bishop Orders his Tomb', 42, 77.

[29] (Thomas Arnold) 'The Oxford Malignants and Dr. Hampden', *Edinburgh Review*, 63/125 (Apr 1836), 235.

[30] *Brownings' Correspondence*, x. 83 n.; *Report of the Cambridge Camden Society* (Cambridge: printed for the society, 1840), 30. See Robert A. Greenberg, 'Ruskin, Pugin, and the Contemporary Context of "The Bishop Orders his Tomb" ', *PMLA*, 84/6 (October 1969), 1590.

up a position like that of the Oxford Movement, asserting the substantial continuity of Anglicanism with the pre-Reformation Catholic Church; this caused some scandal, and consequently a decision was taken to disband.[31] On 18 February 1845, the relation between faith and church architecture was therefore much in the news.[32] The poem evidently takes on relevance in these circumstances, but it is not the straightforward relevance of a statement or a particular attitude, satirical or otherwise. The Bishop's interest in church furnishings might be understood as an analogue to the concerns of the Camden Society; but it might equally be taken as a contrast, for his tomb is to be a Renaissance work, whereas the society was preoccupied with the Middle Ages. His sensuality might have struck some readers as a typically Catholic trait; to others, it may have seemed a contrast to Oxford Movement 'superstition', a budding of those rebellious assertions of desire which Browning was later to explore in 'Fra Lippo Lippi'. As we saw in Chapter 1, 'The Lady of Shalott' achieves its fascinating polysemy by virtue of its comparatively abstracted, mythological location. Browning's poem employs opposite means to the same end. It is the historical specificity of 'The Bishop Orders his Tomb at St Praxed's Church' which prevents it from being drawn into a univocal relationship with Browning's time (or indeed with ours) and which makes it so tantalizing an object for the imagination.

When the poem first appeared in *Hood's Magazine*, March 1845, sandwiched between an article on Heidelberg in 1844 and an episode of 'The Patriot and his Son, A Tale of the Thirty Years War', it was entitled

The Tomb at St Praxed's
Rome, 15–
By Robert Browning [33]

That heading immediately raises questions about the time and place in which the poem should be located: is it the present inhabited by the author of this poetical 'Tomb at St Praxed's', or the

---

[31] Anon. *The Admirable Letter of the Count de Montalembert, to the Rev.—, Member of the Cambridge Camden Society, on the Architectural, Artistical, and Archaeological Investigations of the Puseyites* (Cambridge: J. B. Thompson, 1844), 3.

[32] *The Times*, 18/849 (17 Feb. 1845), 5.

[33] *Hood's Magazine*, 3/3 (Mar. 1845), 237.

past of the original description of the projected monument. Are the words Browning's or the Bishop's? Should we think of them as English or Italian? The poem delights in this uncertainty. It begins with a phrase as current in the nineteenth century as it had been for well over a millennium before:

> Vanity, saith the Preacher, vanity!

Those words are as much at home in the Roman Catholic Church as in the Anglican, unless (the first of many uncertainties) it strikes us that the idiom of the line as Browning renders it is identifiably that of the Authorized Version of the Bible, and not the Latin in which a Catholic Bishop in the nineteenth century as in the sixteenth was likely to have quoted it. If we feel ourselves being drawn into the poem by this opening, and readied for a generalized meditation on mortality—something, perhaps like Gray's 'Elegy Written in a Country Churchyard'—our expectation is immediately stymied:

> Draw round my bed: is Anselm keeping back?
> Nephews—sons mine . . . ah God, I know not! Well—

Are we happy to draw round also?—to think of ourselves as the Bishop's illegitimate children? Probably not, so that we are pushed away from the community of sympathy which the Bishop is endeavouring (and, we later surmise, failing) to create. Throughout the poem there is a toing and froing between expressions with which readers would have been willing to identify ('Life, how and what is it?') and comments which mark the speaker's inimical particularity ('Big as a Jew's head cut off at the nape').[34] As the work thereby shifts back and forth between the dramatic and lyric poles of its dual genre, it compels readers to recognize the challenge to their own identities of imagining themselves back into the past, or indeed of imagining themselves into complete sympathy with anyone. The awareness fostered by Browning's foreign and historical dramatic lyrics was particularly apposite in a time of nation-building. The poems refuse to satisfy the easy expectation of 'themes in which everyone can answer to his sympathies': what more universal topic can there be than death?—and yet the Bishop's response to it is far other than what

---

[34] 'The Bishop Orders his Tomb at St Praxed's Church', 10, 43.

'ours' is expected to be (for which, see Tennyson's *In Memoriam*). Equally, they attack the assertions of continuity with the past made by committedly nationalist works such as Foscolo's 'Dei sepolcri' (which, as we saw in Chapter 1, Garibaldi quoted to the Laureate) and Browning's own *Strafford*. Where Tennyson, like Elizabeth Barrett Browning, collaborated with the implicitly nation-building project of 'the extension of our sympathies', Robert Browning viewed it with unease. For him, as for J. S. Mill, uniformity of feeling was an enemy of liberty; and it was liberty that he valued. As, on a different plane of his imagination, we can see from the fact that, in narrative poems such as 'The Flight of the Duchess' and *The Ring and the Book*, happiness is to be found in separation, not marriage.

STORIES OF ART

The Bishop who orders his tomb is offered to the reader as an individual, but also to some uncertain extent as a representative of his period and nationality—of, as Ruskin wrote in his famous appreciation of the poem, 'the Renaissance spirit,—its worldliness, inconsistency, pride, hypocrisy, ignorance of itself, love of art, of luxury, and of good Latin'.[35] His feeling about the mother of his children, for instance, seems peculiar: it is expressed only as admiration of her beauty, and remains, even in his last breath, inseparable from his rivalry with Gandolf: 'As still he envied me, so fair she was!'[36] This strangely inflected love could be understood as an idiosyncracy of the Bishop's, or as typical of 'Italian Renaissance' aestheticism, competitiveness, etc. Questions about how much, and of what, a character is representative may be asked of any description or imaginative recreation of a personality, and indeed are intrinsic to the notion of character itself, for while someone's 'character' is particular to him or her, the 'characteristics' ('envious', 'typically Renaissance') of which it is said to be made up must be general, otherwise they could not function as descriptive terms. In Browning's monologues, such questions are posed with remarkable intensity. On the one hand, the speakers are strongly delineated as individuals, as the titles usually indicate: not 'A Typical Italian Renaissance Bishop', but 'The Bishop Orders his

---

[35] Ruskin, *Works*, vi. 449.   [36] 'The Bishop Orders his Tomb', 122.

Tomb <u>at</u> <u>St</u> <u>Praxed's</u> <u>Church'</u>; not 'A Painter' (as in Augusta
Webster's Browningesque monologue), but 'Andrea del Sarto'.
On the other hand, the poems' locations are no less vividly indicated, so that we are prompted to wonder how far the single characters making their pregnant speeches are spokespeople for their
eras and nations, to what degree they may be explained by adducing 'the Renaissance spirit' or saying 'ay, but the man is Italian'. In
'The Bishop Orders his Tomb', the uncertainty is left as a puzzle
for the understanding and a stimulus to the imagination; later
poems, however, specifically investigate how the character of an
individual may manifest or differ from the character of his society.

'Fra Lippo Lippi' is set in Florence in the mid-fifteenth century,
a time when the city had abandoned many of its earlier republican
liberties and had given itself up to the protection of Cosimo dei
Medici, who then established the dynasty which was to remain
dominant for the following two centuries. According to the book
which, in Browning's time, was the authoritative history of Italy,
Cosimo 'expressed no democratic opinions'; under his regime 'a
close aristocracy possessed itself of the whole direction of the
state'.[37] The oppressive side of Cosimo's rule is apparent from the
beginning of the poem and indeed provides its occasion, for Lippo
has been arrested by night-watchmen for breaking curfew, and
speaks so as to charm them into restoring his freedom. Contrasting
sets of values are quickly established. On the one hand, the Medici
and the Church, together with their preferred kind of painting
which makes the faithful scorn material pleasures and sets them
'praising'; on the other, Lippo's rebelliousness, sexual profligacy,
and apparently proto-democratic commitment to representing
'every sort' of person in his art.[38] The powers that be, it seems at
first, keep him physically and spiritually enslaved:

> And I've been three weeks shut within my mew,
> A-painting for the great man, saints and saints
> And saints again. . . .[39]

However, as his speech develops, there appears a contradictory
view of the relation between political power and his personal and

---

[37] J. C. L. de Sismondi, *History of the Italian Republics; or, the Origin, Progress, and Fall of
Italian Freedom* (Longman, Orme, Brown, Green and Longmans, and John Taylor, 1832;
new edn., 1838), 225, 246.   [38] 'Fra Lippo Lippi', 190, 145.

[39] Ibid. 47–9.

artistic exuberance. The first step he takes towards securing his liberty from the night watch is, after a mischievous delay, to reveal his connection to the absolutist ruler of the city:

> . . . Who am I?
> Why, one, sir, who is lodging with a friend
> Three streets off—he's a certain . . . how d' ye call?
> Master—a . . . Cosimo of the Medici,
> I' the house that caps the corner. Boh! you were best![40]

As often when he is imagining especially pointed verbal moments in the Italian poems, Browning's idiom veers towards the foreign language, 'how d' ye call' being a word-for-word translation of 'come si chiama'. The postponed mention of Cosimo's magic name hints that Lippo may enjoy the sense of having power in reserve; that he may take a momentary masochistic pleasure from the 'gullet's gripe' which he knows will be released as soon as he alludes to the man who has the whole city in his grasp. By using the word 'friend' he strategically talks up his relationship with his patron; but then it is in the nature of the personal rule of despots to flatter underlings into feeling like friends. The ambivalence gathered around that word (just *how much* of a friend?) expands into a greater uncertainty about the relationship between State power and individual freedom, for Lippo cannot make up his mind whether he feels liberated or enslaved by his connection with Cosimo:

> I'm my own master, paint now as I please—
> Having a friend, you see, in the Corner-house![41]

—he says later, flatly contradicting his earlier account of himself as imprisoned in his mew, serving the great man's will.

Lippo is clearly not an establishment figure like the Bishop who orders his tomb. In some respects he is openly rebellious against the social and religious canons of sixteenth-century Florence. On the other hand, though, his liberty to assert his individual desires is dependent on the patronage of the city's ruler. From this point of view, it seems that his behaviour would be better characterized as 'naughty' than as 'radical'; his profligacy, like the Bishop's, looks like the sort of thing that may be tolerated as a favour by any

---

[40] 'Fra Lippo Lippi', 14–18.   [41] Ibid. 226–7.

oppressive regime. The detailed interrelations of power, art, and personality which the poem brings to our attention must complicate the opinion advanced by John Woolford that for Browning 'the Renaissance was revolutionary in the sense that whatever its social forms it was implicitly egalitarian and democratic in its art'.[42] 'Social forms', it appears in 'Fra Lippo Lippi', cannot be so readily discounted. Their influence goes deep into the painter's personality and his art: it is evident in the balance of self-assertion against subservience in the first line: 'I AM poor brother Lippo, by your leave!'; it is implicit in the ingratiating rhetoric which he keeps up throughout; and it appears again in the self-consciously charming description of the painting in which he imagines that a 'little lily thing' will get him off the hook in heaven by speaking 'the good word for me in the nick', just as he has continually managed to speak the good word for himself to the authorities on earth.[43] As critics have made plain, Browning's Lippo is not the decadent figure presented in A. F. Rio's *De la poésie chrétienne*;[44] but he is not straightforwardly 'egalitarian' either. His delight in rebelliousness relies on the continued existence of the structures against which he rebels, a paradox which is reproduced in his paintings.

'Andrea del Sarto' is set in 1525, about seventy or eighty years after 'Fra Lippo Lippi', at a time of French incursions into Italy, and two years before the expulsion of the Medici and a temporary restoration of popular government.[45] The poem does mention the presence of 'Paris lords' in Fiesole, but otherwise it is not noticeably interested in high-political events, concentrating instead on Andrea's social and economic circumstances.[46] Where Lippo was reliant on a patron, Andrea earns his own living. Lippo's much-broken vow of chastity gives way to Andrea's marriage—a progression which will have been highlighted for Browning by the fact that the nun with whom Lippo eventually set up house (and, once a dispensation had been gained by a good word in the nick, did in fact marry) had the same name as Andrea's wife: Lucrezia. These changes echoed developments in artistic style, for as Browning would have read in Mrs Jameson's *Memoirs of the Early*

---

[42] Woolford and Karlin, *Robert Browning*, 183.

[43] 'Fra Lippo Lippi', 1, 385–6.

[44] David J. De Laura, 'The Context of Browning's Painter Poems: Aesthetics, Polemics, Historics', *PMLA*, 95 (1980), 379.

[45] Sismondi, *History of the Italian Republics*, 344.　　　[46] 'Andrea del Sarto', 146.

Italian Painters (1845) Andrea 'carried to . . . perfection' the 'particular style of grandeur and breadth in the drawing of his figures, the
grouping, and the contrast of light and shade' which Lippo had
'invented': in the words of Browning's Andrea, ' 't is easy, all of
it!'[47]

   Since Andrea has achieved so much of what Lippo only desired,
we might expect that he would seem to himself and us a freer man.
In fact, he presents himself as more of a slave to the newly free
market than Lippo ever was to his monastery, let alone his patron:
'I'll work then for your friend's friend, never fear, | Treat his own
subject after his own way'. With astonishing subtlety, the poem
shows us a mind for whom the world, his own life, even his wife,
register as works of art, and therefore as commodities: 'You smile?
why, there's my picture ready made'. His words to her confuse her
with a painting:

> . . . oh, so sweet—
> My face, my moon, my everybody's moon,
> Which everybody looks on and calls his,
> And, I suppose, is looked on by in turn,
> While she looks—no one's: very dear, no less.[48]

This is not merely (as it has been called) an expression of 'Andrea's
weary jealousy',[49] for the reason why 'everybody' can look on
Lucrezia's face and possess it is that, as he has just said, she serves
as his model. The lines probe how this fact worms its way into his
love for her: it seems that the imaginative elaboration from her
face to the moon (which everyone can see) to the thought of
everyone sharing his pleasure and wanting to possess her image, if
not her, is a way of explaining how sweet he finds her; but then 'I
suppose' introduces the thought that, Galatea-like, the paintings
might take on life and she look back out of them, in which case
he would be prostituting her directly rather than, as at present,
relying on her charms to gain himself commissions. It may be that
he takes some grim pleasure in this prospect (it would be, after all,
a triumph for his art) but, if so, he interrupts it at 'no one's',

---

[47] Mrs Jameson, *Memoirs of the Early Italian Painters and of the Progress of Painting in Italy*,
2 vols. (Charles Knight, 1845), i. 113–14; 'Andrea del Sarto', 67.
[48] 'Andrea del Sarto', 5–6, 33, 28–32.
[49] Leonee Ormond, 'Browning and Painting', in Isobel Armstrong (ed.), *Robert Browning*
(G. Bell and Sons, 1974), 192.

perhaps because the line of thought turns painful as it arrives at the question of who really possesses her affections, perhaps because she bridles at the imputation. He returns to what would be a bland adjective of praise, 'dear', were it not that the drift of his ruminations taints the word with the money that her painted face will earn.

Imagining his wife as a work of art, Andrea has something in common with the Duke of Ferrara. Both men are punctilious— the painter's thought of altering a picture by Raphael, 'That arm is wrongly put . . . and I could alter it' is like Ferrara's wish to tell his Duchess 'here you miss, | Or there exceed the mark'— and they similarly accept the established order of things, although the Duke, of course, thinks of himself as imposing it, whereas Andrea is content to be imposed upon: 'So free we seem, so fettered fast we are!'—he remarks, words which sound to him like a universal truth but which may well strike the reader as a reflection on his particular circumstances.[50] It is odd, therefore, that what he feels himself to be subjected to is not a master but the apparent liberties of owning his home, earning his living and, as his penultimate line emphasizes, freely loving his wife: 'Because there's still Lucrezia,—as I choose'.[51] Paradoxically, the time when he felt most free, at least in the exercise of his art, was when he was in the service of a monarch: 'I surely then could sometimes leave the ground'. Francis I offered him what felt like comradeship: 'One arm about my shoulder, round my neck': this is like Lippo calling Cosimo dei Medici his 'friend', only Andrea seems to revel in the power which the King has over him:

> I painting proudly with his breath on me,
> All his court round him, seeing with his eyes,[52]

The echo of 'Two in the Campagna' ('I would I could . . . | See with your eyes . . . | | No') at once highlights the erotic aspect of this description and suggests that Andrea, with his art of subduing people into his paintings, putting them in their places, is likely to feel at home in the court of an absolutist monarch. But no: 'Too live the life grew, golden and not grey', and he returns to Lucrezia

[50] 'Andrea del Sarto', 111–15, 51; 'My Last Duchess', 38–9.
[51] 'Andrea del Sarto', 266.   [52] Ibid. 151, 156, 158–9.

in 'the grange whose four walls make his world'.[53] While this poem, like 'Fra Lippo Lippi', traces many connections between its speaker's personal life, his art, and his political circumstances, it establishes no formulaic parallels between them, instead alerting us to the variety of ways in which people can understand their places in society, perhaps feeling at liberty in what might to another look like servitude, perhaps taking pleasure in the grip of fetters which they themselves have helped to forge.

The continuities between the two great painter poems suggest that they might be thought of as episodes from a story of art; but they turn out to be episodes of such complexity that any story into which they will fit can have no clear direction or moral. Like 'The Bishop Orders his Tomb at St Praxed's Church', they offer resistance to historical narrative; to the judgemental accounts of Italian art offered by A. F. Rio and Mrs Jameson, to the profound and subtle story told by Ruskin, and even to Browning's own grand narrative of artistic progress and its relation to politics, 'Old Pictures in Florence'. In this poem, as we saw in Chapter 3, classical statues of 'Theseus', 'Niobe', etc. are said to promote submission in people who look at them: 'You learned—to submit is a mortal's duty'; while early Renaissance artists, with their determination to 'paint man man, whatever the issue!' make a revolutionary discovery of human potential. 'Andrea del Sarto' and 'Fra Lippo Lippi' were almost certainly composed in the same year as this work and share many of its concerns, but they refuse to be flattened into the swift narrative which it advances. Chronologically, Lippo and Andrea come later than the artists celebrated in 'Old Pictures in Florence', and we might therefore expect to understand them as continuing the revolution begun by Giotto and his contemporaries. Certainly, Lippo shares the desire to 'paint man man'. On the other hand, his idea of what constitutes 'man' is different from his predecessors', for they wish ' "To bring the invisible full into play! | Let the visible go to the dogs— what matters?" ' In the much-canvassed terms adopted by Browning in his essay on Shelley, they are 'subjective' artists, whereas Lippo and Andrea, with their love of physiques, are 'objective'. In 'Fra Lippo Lippi', correspondingly, Giotto figures as

---

[53] 'Andrea del Sarto', 168, 170.

one of the painters of 'soul' as opposed to 'flesh' whom 'the Prior and the learned' support, and against whom Lippo thinks of himself as rebelling.[54] By his time it is their art that has come to be associated with the religious and political establishment.

Lippo and Andrea might be brought into relation with the scheme of 'Old Pictures in Florence' if we evoke the dialectic of objective and subjective movements proposed in the essay. A series of artists dedicated to the pursuit of 'universal meaning' must be succeeded by 'another sort of poet', who will provide 'new substance by breaking up the assumed wholes into parts of independent and unclassed value'; this movement in turn will eventually fade as a result of its 'very sufficiency for itself', and a new subjective artist will be called for.[55] Lippo, one is tempted to say, is just such 'another sort of poet', while in Andrea the movement reaches exhaustion; only, the scheme does not exactly fit, for the early Italians, 'subjective' though they doubtless would have to be called, also break up assumed wholes in the manner of 'objective' artists, averting their eyes from 'the Truth of Man, as by God first spoken' and becoming 'self-acquainters . . . whatever the issue!' The classical statues likewise combine 'subjective' and 'objective' traits, as they manifest both 'Soul (which Limbs betoken) | And Limbs (Soul informs) made new in marble'. The sentence from the 'Essay' which has most relevance to Browning's painter poems is the great statement of the recurrent need for new interpretation and new creation: 'the world is not to be learned and thrown aside, but reverted to and re-learned'.[56] Each of his works makes a bid to understand its particular bit of the world, but no sooner is it finished than objections present themselves, the terms of the enquiry shift, and a new work is required to reach out towards the truth whose complexity will inevitably exceed its grasp.

Although 'Old Pictures in Florence' is connected to Browning's ideas about the interrelations of art, individuality, and political conditions, and to the monologues which present very detailed examples of such interrelations, it does not provide the key to them. Set on a 'warm March day' when Florence looks like 'the sights in a magic crystal ball', it consciously and happily

---

[54] 'Old Pictures in Florence', 151–2; *Browning: The Poems*, ed. Pettigrew, i. 1001; 'Fra Lippo Lippi', 189, 182, 184, 174.

[55] *Browning: The Poems*, ed. Pettigrew, i. 1004.

[56] 'Old Pictures in Florence', 85, 147–8, 87–8; *Browning: The Poems*, ed. Pettigrew, 1003.

indulges in a simple version of issues which 'Fra Lippo Lippi' and 'Andrea del Sarto' show to be more complicated. When, in its closing stanzas, it equates the early painters with the 'Art' which will blossom in Italy if ever 'Freedom' returns there in the form of a united republic, it is revelling in exactly the sort of peroration, the contrasting of 'fructuous and sterile eras' which it foresees for the republican parliament.[57] 'Old Pictures in Florence' makes explicit reference to *Casa Guidi Windows*, and echoes its subject-matter and rhyme-scheme, but has none of the earlier work's high seriousness. Indeed, it seems rather to tease Barrett Browning's poem, although her husband may not quite have admitted to himself that that was what he was doing. What she takes as a prophecy, to him looks like a daydream. This may owe something to the state of Italian politics in 1853, since (as we saw in Chapter 5) for several years after the failure of the 1848 revolutions the prospect of Italian unity looked distant indeed. However, it is also the case that, although a strong supporter of the Risorgimento, he was more wary than she of the coercive force of even republican political rhetoric, and of the nationalist historiography which tended to abolish the otherness of the past in its eagerness—as Clough had written—to 'reconcile ancient and modern'.[58] 'Old Pictures in Florence' clearly manifests Browning's conviction that forms of art and political systems are interrelated, that the history of Italian painting therefore gives grounds for hoping the Risorgimento will succeed, and that the unification of Italy will have some kind of beneficial effect on artistic production; but its jokeyness no less evidently conveys an understanding that in reality these matters will be far less simple than they appear in the crystal ball of a spring morning.

STYLES OF LIFE

Ever since his first trips to Italy in 1838 and 1844, Browning had lamented what seemed to him the weakness of much Italian poetry. As he wrote in the courtship correspondence, 'Italy is stuff for the use of the North, and no more: pure Poetry there is none, nearly as possible none, in Dante even—materials for Poetry in the

[57] 'Old Pictures in Florence', 4, 12, 261–2, 269.
[58] See above, Chapter 6.

pitifullest romancist of their thousands, on the contrary.'[59] Under pressure from Elizabeth Barrett he soon retracted the slur on Dante, and twenty years later his disappointment had narrowed to the contemporary: 'I never read a line in a modern Italian book that was of use to me,—never saw a flash of poetry come out of an Italian *word*: in art, in action, *yes* . . . I always said, they *are* poetry, don't and can't *make* poetry . . .'. These reflections may seem troubling to a politically correct consciousness: one late twentieth-century critic uses them to indict Browning for 'blind and suffocated smugness', and rages that 'a more unlovely counterpoint of mercantile colonialism and settled racism would be hard to imagine'.[60] Certainly Browning expresses himself bluntly in what were after all private letters, but the indignant modern critic neglects to quote the lines immediately following 'don't and can't make poetry', which read: '—& you know what I mean by *that*,—nothing relating to rhymes and melody and *lo stile*: but as a nation, politically, they are most interesting to me,—I think they have more than justified every expectation their best friends formed of them,—and their rights are indubitable . . .'[61] Browning's remarks in fact suggest a complex train of thought about the relation between Italy's political condition and the state of its literature. What he means by 'poetry' is the vivid pictorial evocation and dramatic interest so evident in his own verse: he is not blindly denying the existence of any kind of good writing in Italy, but making an observation about genre which is in fact well grounded, for one can read widely in Leopardi, Foscolo, Giusti, Niccolini, Guerrazzi, Carducci without finding much to call 'poetry' in this peculiar Browningesque acceptation. To say that Italians '*are*' that particular kind of 'poetry' is to make a generalization about national character which is quite different from the similar-sounding opinions of those for whom—as we saw in Chapter 4—poetry meant elegy. In the letter, as in 'Old Pictures in Florence', reflections on Italian art lead directly to politics, and it is reasonable to assume that as Browning writes to his friend he takes for granted the argument he had advanced in the public arena of the poem, that an explanation for the depressed state of

---

[59] *Brownings' Correspondence*, x. 184.
[60] Robert Viscusi, ' "The Englishman in Italy": Free Trade as a Principle of Aesthetics', *Browning Institute Studies*, 12 (1984), 1–28.   [61] *Dearest Isa*, 238.

contemporary Italian culture is to be sought in its political condition, with the censorship and educational restrictions imposed by
the Austrian Empire and its client regimes. Browning was not
being racist when he judged that in the mid-nineteenth century
there was no 'pure poetry' in Italy, for he held to the belief
expressed in 'Old Pictures in Florence', that 'Pure Art's birth is still
the republic's'.[62]

As he turned Italian subjects into 'pure poetry', representing
vigorous Italian characters and vivid Italian scenery in his writing,
Browning must have had a thought somewhere in his mind that
he was helping to bring Italy into cultural existence, and that he
was thereby in some not very well-defined way supporting the
Risorgimento. Although he took no steps to have his verse translated into Italian, and his contacts with Italian writers were frankly
exiguous, the very abstract view of political and cultural evolution
which, as we saw in Chapter 4, is advanced in *Sordello* and *Casa
Guidi Windows* would have allowed him to think that somehow
his work was making a contribution to that general progress of
humanity of which, to his eyes as well as those of his wife and
many others, the Risorgimento was the clearest contemporary
example. His Pure Art would promote the birth of the republic.
This likely feeling of continuity between his writing and Italian
politics gives a particular inflection to the now generally-accepted
view that Browning's dramatic monologues should be thought of
as a broadly democratic kind of writing because the contextualization of the imagined voice opens it, as Isobel Armstrong says, 'to
interrogation'.[63] Armstrong has provided a thorough grounding
for this position in the intellectual environment of Browning's
youth. However, given the multifaceted and shifting connections
between style and politics which emerge from 'Fra Lippo Lippi',
'Andrea del Sarto', and 'Old Pictures in Florence', it seems
unlikely that this is the only light in which Browning's work
appeared to him, and to his contemporaries, during the two and a
half decades in which his energies were concentrated on the
monologue form.

Browning's first dramatic monologues, 'Johannes Agricola in
Meditation' and 'Porphyria's Lover', present to the reader two
distinctly circumscribed consciousnesses, the one solipsistic, the

---

[62] 'Old Pictures in Florence', 272.   [63] Armstrong, *Victorian Poetry*, 117.

other mad. Although they certainly thereby displace the lyric voice, opening it to question, they do this at the cost of establishing a metaphorical relationship between their own form and the confined circumstances of the represented characters. As the speakers circle around themselves in their ABABB rhymes, happy in their isolation, it is as though they know themselves to be enclosed by the aesthetic state in which Browning presents them; as though the verse-form is a figure of the 'Madhouse Cells' under which title the poems were printed in *Dramatic Lyrics*. As Browning moved the focus of his attention to Italy, the uncanny correlation between poetic form and psychological or social confinement remained. In 'Pictor Ignotus' the verse shadows the compulsive self-restraint which, the speaker tells himself, prevented him from joining the narrative of artistic progress:

> . . . No bar
> Stayed me— . . .[64]

he observes, no bar save the limitation of his own self-distrust, which, the arrangement of the verse prompts us to observe, is represented by the bar of line-end plus rhyme at which his voice now continually turns back. The Italian origin of the word 'stanza'—where it means room—is peculiarly apt to these poems which usually are not divided into stanzas: each of them is, rather, a single long stanza; they are like 'These endless cloisters and eternal aisles' to which Pictor Ignotus has condemned himself with a life sentence. Not all the poems, certainly, ask us to understand their form in this way: 'The Englishman in Italy', say, and 'Up at a Villa—Down in the City' have no particular feeling of confinement about them; but then those are not works in which the speaker is very distinctly characterized, or dramatic circumstances very vividly implied. In the most consummate examples of the form, not coincidentally those which are set in Italy, the boundaries of the verse seem to manifest the limits of the speaker's mind. The Duke of Ferrara, as we saw in Chapter 3, is at ease in the bonds of his verse as he lays down the law for his auditor and indeed everyone beneath him. Fra Lippo, though, chafes at boundaries, and the representation of this aspect of his personality calls out from Browning one of his most virtuoso pieces of writing, the passage

---

[64] 'Pictor Ignotus', 2–3.

where Lippo describes his excursion out of his 'mew' into the freedom of the streets:

> . . . I could not paint all night—
> Ouf! I leaned out of window for fresh air.

The arrangement of those lines, 'Ouf!' suggesting the opening of shutters or a leaning out over the window-sill, implies a consonance between the borders of the verse and the walls of the Medici palace, an edifice of power which exerts its discipline also on Lippo's consciousness. The regularity which has been imposed on his existence is at once disturbed by a flurry of rhythm:

> There came a hurry of feet and little feet,

and the dignity of blank verse is invaded by the irregular form of the song which floats up to him:

> *Flower o' the broom,*
> *Take away love, and our earth is a tomb!*

The dactylic rhythm of that capricious ditty is soon animating Lippo's thoughts and his action;

> Scarce had they turned the corner when a titter
> Like the skipping of rabbits by moonlight,—three slim shapes,
> And a face that looked up . . . zooks, sir, flesh and blood,
> That's all I'm made of! . . .

The second of these lines has thirteen syllables, outrageously overflowing its limits, as Lippo does too when he leaps out of the window.

> . . . I came up with the fun
> Hard by Saint Laurence, hail fellow, well met,—
> *Flower o' the rose*
> *If I've been merry, what matter who knows?*
> And so as I was stealing back again
> To get to bed and have a bit of sleep
> Ere I rise up to-morrow and go work
> On Jerome knocking at his poor old breast
> With his great round stone to subdue the flesh,
> You snap me of the sudden. . . .[65]

---

[65] 'Fra Lippo Lippi', 49–50, 51, 53–4, 58–61, 66–75.

The italicized snatch of lyric decorously draws a veil over what he actually got up to when he 'came' up with the fun. Thereafter, the rhythm changes: it is completely obedient to the metre in the fifth and sixth lines quoted, the iambic plod suggesting a post-coital flatness; and towards the end of the passage the gathering of stressed monosyllables ('poor old breast', 'great round stone') makes Lippo's voice sound wearily oppressed. The near rhyme of 'breast' with 'flesh' newly asserts the boundaries which he had previously breached: Elizabeth Barrett Browning would certainly have felt them to impose 'the despotism of the final emphasis'.[66] Of course Lippo is playing up his story for the benefit of his audience, but the social constraints to which he is returning are real enough. If we are to understand how they feel to him we must recognize that the struggle between his impulses and his obligations appears in the conflict between the freedom of the language and the law of the verse.

As he is swept into sexual liberty by a waft of lyric, Lippo momentarily breaks out of the dramatic monologue genre which frames and distinguishes his identity; but he returns to it as he always must, only no doubt to break out of it again, for his is a life of brinkmanship. When he is in his mew, he says, he sucks 'his lips in tight'. That is all Browning makes of the obvious potential for a pun in Lippo's name (of which the painter himself, speaking Italian, would not have been aware); still, it is enough to offer us an image of him as being continually as it were on the lip of his own identity and occasionally overflowing it, giving himself up to 'the world', as he says when the italicized lyric returns and his 'whole soul revolves, the cup runs over'.[67] Pictor Ignotus, by contrast, has taken care that his 'cup' should never have been 'spilt'; and Andrea del Sarto too is content to remain within the established boundaries of his identity, his reach never exceeding his grasp.[68] This style of life is figured in the setting of his poem—for whereas Lippo leaps out of his window, Andrea uses his to frame himself and his wife in a picture of marital harmony—and also in the appearance of his voice within the verse, for whereas Lippo runs over his lines, Andrea remains tranquil within his, their endings generally corresponding to syntactical pauses, and his

---

[66] See above, Chapter 4. [67] 'Fra Lippo Lippi', 243, 247, 250.
[68] 'Pictor Ignotus', 23.

voice frequently coming to a halt three syllables short of the line-end, as though he lacks the vigour even to approach the lip of his cup. The handling of form in these poems offers us an understanding of personality primarily in terms of conflict between impulse and limitation, while the dramatic circumstances alluded to by the speaking voice ask us to observe the varying degrees in which the limitation at issue is produced by social, economic, and political factors. The variables interact in many different ways: Fra Lippo Lippi presents himself as being all impulse, and as having restrictions imposed upon him from outside. Andrea del Sarto is so at home within his limits that he can conceive of an impulse that might threaten them only as a theoretical possibility, 'in heaven, perhaps'.[69] By its very nature, representing a speaking voice in a dramatic context and in verse, the monologue form investigates the relation between the self and the limits which are constitutive of its identity, but by which it may also feel itself to be constrained.

The forms of oppression imagined in *Men and Women* are very various: psychological, marital, religious, social, and so on. The volume does not announce itself as having very much to do with high politics. And yet, scattered throughout the book are references which nudge a reader's attention towards the political condition of the Italy in which most of its poems were written: there is 'the king' who is 'shot at' in ' "De Gustibus—" ', the 'three liberal thieves' who again 'were shot' in 'Up at a Villa—Down in the City (As Distinguished by an Italian Person of Quality)', the mention in 'A Toccata of Galuppi's' of 'Venice and her people, merely born to bloom and droop', as well as the explicit treatments of political violence in 'Instans Tyrannus' and 'The Patriot'.[70] The absolutist regimes in Italy loom as a shadowy metaphor for the domestic tyrannies which are generally in the foreground of the volume. If we allow our imaginations to dwell on this connection, much in the book can be drawn into affiliation with it: the fantasies of control in 'Mesmerism' and 'A Woman's Last Word', the enjoyment of quiescence evinced in a line such as 'BEAUTIFUL Evelyn Hope is dead', the thought of the earth having been put 'to sleep' in 'A Lovers' Quarrel', the lives

[69] 'Andrea del Sarto', 260.
[70] ' "De Gustibus—" ', 35–6; 'Up at a Villa—Down in the City', 44; 'A Toccata of Galuppi's', 40.

which, in 'The Statue and the Bust', suffer 'Arrest'.[71] The monologue form itself arrests characters, fixing them in the moment of
their enunciation, and usually in a context of privacy (Lippo, of
course, speaks to public authorities, but then he is in trouble). G.
K. Chesterton suggested that *The Ring and the Book* was 'the epic
of free speech';[72] the speakers in *Men and Women* are manifestly
un-free, their words circumscribed by what is generally the intimacy of their occasion and by the pressure of the silent interlocutor. From this point of view, the monologues look less
pro-actively democratic, and more like the product of a mind
focused on a country where, as the Brownings' acquaintance
Edward Dicey noted in a book of political commentary, there was
'no public life', no freedom of speech, heavy restrictions on movement, a country ruled by a group of regimes which (as the
Brownings saw it) sought to stall the progress of history.[73] This is
a poetry, not (as one critic has suggested) 'of the future',[74] but of
an arrested present. We have seen Italy being configured as elegy,
and as prophecy; for Browning it was the location *par excellence* of
the dramatic monologue, a form in which the self appears isolated,
circumscribed, in private, and outside narrative.

Even the poem which is as close as Browning ever allowed
himself to get to a general utterance on the human condition has
its roots in a reflection on Italian politics. 'Two in the Campagna',
with its minimal characterization of its protagonist and very
general dramatic context, is as lyric as it is possible for a dramatic
monologue to be. This tantalizing generic identity puts readers in
a position similar to that of the speaker: he longs to claim that he
is lyrically at one with another person, but is unable to; we are on
the verge of configuring his words as universal lyric truth, but are
pushed back:

ix.

I would I could adopt your will,
　　See with your eyes, and set my heart
　Beating by yours, and drink my fill

---

[71] 'Evelyn Hope', 1; 'A Lovers' Quarrel', 74; 'The Statue and the Bust', 170.

[72] Chesterton, *Robert Browning*, 173.

[73] Edward Dicey, *Rome in 1860* (Macmillan, 1861), 19.

[74] Herbert F. Tucker, Jr., *Browning's Beginnings: The Art of Disclosure* (Minneapolis:
University of Minnesota Press, 1980), 3.

> At your soul's springs,—your part my part
> In life, for good and ill.
>
> x.
> No. . . .[75]

These lines have a peculiar history, for they began life in *Luria*, Browning's martial tragedy of 1846, in a scene where a North African, Husain, describes to his compatriot Luria, commander of the Florentine army, what it would be like attempting to join the ethnic community of Florence:

> Priests, greybeards, Braccios, women, boys and spies,
> All in one tale, each singing the same song,
> How thou must house, and live at bed and board,
> Take pledge and give it, go their every way,
> Breathe to their measure, make thy blood beat time
> With theirs—or—all is nothing—thou art lost—
> A savage . . .[76]

The echoes of this scene in 'Two in the Campagna' are diffuse: 'the fire that fed on earth | Now turns to heaven' becomes 'where heaven looks from its towers'; Luria's character, 'the soul that never can take rest' reappears in 'must I go | Still like the thistle-ball, no bar, | Onward', while the elusive thought which floats across the Campagna, 'everywhere on the grassy slope | I traced it' began as follows:

> . . . as I looked on Life,
> Still everywhere I tracked this, though it hid
> And shifted, lay so silent as it thought,
> Changed shape and hue yet ever was the same.
> Why 'twas all fighting, all their nobler life![77]

Anticipating the Freudian theory of sublimation, Husain looks at the gracious habits of Florentine civilization, and sees in them only displaced or refined forms of conflict. In his view, the good of life is to let one's instincts run free, while all the Florentines would do is shackle them:

> . . . take thee with thine instincts up,
> Thy battle-ardours, like a ball of fire,

---

[75] 'Two in the Campagna', 41–6.   [76] *Luria*, IV. 124–30.
[77] Ibid. IV. 153–4, 144, 179–83; 'Two in the Campagna', 30, 52–4, 19–20.

And class them, and allow them place and play
So far, no farther . . .[78]

(Lines which pre-empt 'You that are just so much, no more' in 'Two in the Campagna'.) Luria, on the other hand, delights in subjecting himself to the foreign civilization:

. . . the thrill
Of coming into you, and changing thus—
Feeling a soul grow on me that restricts
The boundless unrest of the savage heart![79]

Since Florence is 'northern' to Luria, and therefore asks to be compared to Britain, these lines might look fulsomely imperialist, were it not that their vision is disappointed: over-subtle Florence betrays its admirer, who is left mourning the collapse of his 'life's illusion'. Luria remains certain that the progress of civilization is admirable, and that the aim of life is to dedicate oneself to it, thereby restraining the unrest of the savage heart; what was illusory was the hope that his ideal would be realized in the actual behaviour of the city-state. Just because Florence is on the side of progress, he discovers, does not mean that her every act will be just. The disparity between ideal and real must be accepted resignedly, and can be bridged only in imagination: as another character has suggested, Florence 'Is a contrivance to supply a type | Of Man which men's deficiencies refuse'.[80] The actual life of the city will always fall short of its imagined existence as 'type'; but it is the 'type', the ideal image of the city and its potential, which commands its citizens' loyalty.

The wholesale resurgence in 'Two in the Campagna' of vocabulary and arguments from this part of *Luria* suggests that the analogy between love for a person and allegiance to a polity went deep into Browning's imagination. In earlier poems with explicit relevance to the Risorgimento, he had probed the similarity between the two kinds of attachment by setting up conflicts between them. In *Pippa Passes*, a boyish patriot abandons his mother and the prospect of betrothal to risk his life for 'Italy, Italy, my Italy!': one kind of desire is straightforwardly substituted for the other.[81] 'The Italian in England' charts a more complicated development of feeling. The

---

[78] *Luria*, IV. 140–3.   [79] 'Two in the Campagna', 37; *Luria*, 321–4.
[80] Ibid. IV. 266; III. 184–5.   [81] 'Pippa Passes', III. 120.

experienced revolutionary represented in the poem is struck by
the beauty of the woman who saves him, but at once translates it
into a political idiom, saying that she manifests 'Our Italy's own
attitude'; he stifles any possibility of romance by configuring her as
a child of Italy, and therefore his sister: 'I, the son | As you the
daughter of our land!'[82] The poem looks carefully into the
processes by which individual loves can be overwhelmed by devotion to 'the Cause' (as Claude would put it), and that devotion
then itself imaginatively assume the form of a familial or romantic
relationship. The origins in *Luria* of 'Two in the Campagna' similarly but tacitly suggest a comparison between the place in human
identity of love and of attachment to a national community: in
both cases, we are partly given up to the other entity, partly not:
'Nor yours nor mine, nor slave nor free!'; in both cases, we may
know the attachment to be a good thing, even the best thing, and
yet sometimes, even simultaneously, repine at it.[83] More than this,
the connection to *Luria* suggests that 'Two in the Campagna'
should be taken as hinting that the speaker's understanding of his
own condition—and perhaps even the condition itself—is historically contingent. He not only is, but recognizes himself to be,
living at a time in which the 'Infinite' is strongly distinguished
from the 'finite' and the two seem not to meet; in which, therefore, it has become impossible to feel at one with the State, with
another person, or even with yourself.

In the *Men and Women* monologues, there is no triumphant
coming-together as at the end of *Aurora Leigh* (when Romney is
precisely made to see through Aurora's eyes), and none of the
standing-up-in-unison envisaged in *Casa Guidi Windows*. In part,
this is because Browning was never attracted to that sort of
redemptive vision: the tendencies of his imagination, and his views
about the function of poetry, were different. But a further contributory factor is that his imagination was focused on a world from
which those possibilites were absent: Italy in the early 1850s. In
1859, however, this situation began to change: Piedmont and
France instigated a war with Austria which, although it was soon
ignominiously brought to an end by Napoleon III, resulted in an

---

[82] 'The Italian in England', 59, 86–7; see Daniel Karlin, 'The Sources of the Italian in
England', *Browning Society Notes*, 14/3 (Winter, 1984–5), 23–43.
[83] 'Two in the Campagna', 38.

expansion of Victor Emmanuel's territory and influence. In March 1860, provisional governments in Tuscany and Emilia voted to merge with Piedmont; in May, Garibaldi landed in Sicily and conquered the south of Italy, while Piedmontese armies invaded Umbria. Except for Venice and Rome, the whole of Italy was at last united: in January 1861 the first Italian parliament met in Turin.[84]

Browning was quite aware of the role played in these developments by *realpolitik* and dynastic self-interest. Nonetheless, he also discerned in them the workings of an ideal, as he explained in a letter of 1861 which compares events in Italy to the beginnings of the American Civil War:

I think English judgement of the Northern procedures has been wrong from the beginning,—just as of the French procedures (will you let me say) in Italy: our people expected in both cases that the pure & simple *right* in the case would be declared & rigorously carried out without one let or stop or diplomatical fetching of circuits—'Italy shall be free, & Slavery abolished, absolutely, at once & forever.' At the first hesitation in face of difficulties, we cried out, 'Italy will not be freed, nor slavery extinguished, after all'—& our sympathy stopped & irritation began—as if the *spirit* of all we would have sympathized in were not actively alive all the time, & taking the crooked road to what, in this poor world, is only reached by a straight one 'as the crow flies,'—far above our heads, and rather near the heaven.[85]

In the broad terms suggested by this letter, it will have seemed to Browning that Italy, 'stuff for the use of the north', had thrown off its Austrian masters; that the materials which used to lie around his feet had risen up. One piece of stuff in particular had leapt to his attention, the *Old Yellow Book*, which he lit upon in the summer of 1860, at the high point of nationalist excitement. As he recalled in the work which it made possible, *The Ring and the Book*, the discovery seemed an operation of '*spirit*' (and a typically crooked one at that) for he was guided to it by 'a Hand | Always above my shoulder'.[86] The lump of Italian material, which providence had placed under his government, was arranged by him in quite a new way. *The Ring and the Book* is a narrative poem which ranges

---

[84] Candeloro, *Storia dell'Italia Moderna*, iv. 315–535.
[85] *Browning to his American Friends*, 88.   [86] *RB* I. 40–1.

beyond the local circumstances of the monologues in *Men and Women*, imaginatively connecting two parts of Italy which at the time of its writing were still to be unified, Tuscany and Rome. It presents in one work the voices of eleven different Italians. A small indication as to the significance of this fact may be garnered from Sidney Dobell's *The Roman* (1850), a vehemently pro-Risorgimento poetical effusion, which includes a droll representation of Italian disunity. At an inn, one character enquires,

> Which man here
> Tells the best tale?

And hears the reply:

> *Many*.   I. I. I. I. I. I.[87]

The speakers in *The Ring and the Book* are both unified and at variance. Like the Florence admired by Luria and hated by Husain, they are 'All in one tale'; but unlike that unanimous city, they are not 'all singing the same song'. The form of *The Ring and the Book* is designed to investigate community; to understand how it is that its many different characters, with their many diverse circumstances, opinions, and interests, may all nonetheless share in the same story.

ROME-WORK

As Browning was beginning to write his enormous poem, George Meredith published a novel, *Vittoria* (1866–7), in which a signal for revolution in 1848 is provided by an allegorical opera:

The quick-witted Italians caught up the interpretation in a flash. 'Count Orso' Austria; 'Michiella' is Austria's spirit of intrigue; 'Camillo' is indolent Italy, amorous Italy, Italy aimless; 'Camilla' is YOUNG ITALY![88]

If Browning read Meredith's tale, he will have been newly alerted to an aspect of the events described in the *Old Yellow Book* which, as Flavia Alaya argues in a campaigning article, had perhaps already struck him:

A Roman girl of ambiguous lineage (the old Italy, 'Juliet among nations') is forced into a repressive marriage with a foreign nobleman ambitious of

---

[87] Sidney Dobell, *The Roman* (R. Bentley, 1850), 55.
[88] George Meredith, *Vittoria* (Chapman and Hall, 1889), 173.

shoring up his shaky dynasty (the Austrian tyrant); but prompted finally by the stirring of new life within her (Young Italy), she seeks liberation through both her own (revolutionary) defiance of the accepted order and the sympathetic intervention of others (the foreign libertarian powers). Ah, the everlasting pattern of romance!

Alaya presents this Risorgimento allegory as being the peculiar invention of Elizabeth Barrett Browning: the point of its inclusion in *The Ring and the Book* being, therefore, that Browning wished to reiterate her 'faith' in the 'mystery' of 'Italian unity' which both poets thought to be 'the archetype of human solidarity itself'.[89] As we have seen, however, Barrett Browning's understanding of the Risorgimento was by no means that simplistic, and the work of her husband is even more circumspect about the homogenizing pressures exerted by nationalism. In *The Ring and the Book*, the massive detail in which the Italy of the 1690s is imagined, together with the intricate portrayal of the many different characters, keeps any thought of allegory at bay. Meredith's librettist, goaded into ingenuity by Austrian censorship, pursues his coding into every detail of the plot: Count Orso's attachment to one part of his estate, for instance, is 'an allusion to the Austrian argument that the plains of Lombardy are the strategic defensive lines of the Alps'.[90] In Browning's work there are no such parallels to be discovered. What is remarkable about *The Ring and the Book* is that it so consistently does not activate the potential for allegory or symbolism which is so obviously present in its narrative.

With its emphasis on judicial practice and its interest in the Pope, *The Ring and the Book* would certainly have struck contemporary readers as having broad relevance to issues raised by the unification of Italy.[91] Nonetheless, to my eye, there are only two places where the Risorgimento has left a demonstrable mark on the work's verbal texture. One of these is Pompilia's recollection of the discovery that she was pregnant:

---

[89] Alaya, 'The Ring, the Rescue, & the Risorgimento', 24, 33–4.

[90] Meredith, *Vittoria*, 181.

[91] On judicial practice, see W. E. Gladstone, *Two Letters to the Earl of Aberdeen on the State Prosecutions of the Neapolitan Government* (John Murray, 1851); Dicey, *Rome in 1860*, 55–98; and (Ruffini), *Dr Antonio*; on the Pope, see Charles T. Phipps SJ, 'Adaptation from the Past, Creation for the Present: A Study of Browning's "The Pope" ', *Studies in Philology*, 65 (1968), 702–22.

> . . . Up I sprang alive,
> Light in me, light without me, everywhere
> Change! A broad yellow sun-beam was let fall
> From heaven to earth,—a sudden drawbridge lay,
> Along which marched a myriad merry motes,
> Mocking the flies that crossed them and recrossed
> In rival dance, companions new-born too.
> On the house-eaves, a dripping shag of weed
> Shook diamonds on each dull grey lattice-square,
> As first one, then another bird leapt by,
> And light was off, and lo was back again,
> Always with one voice,—where are two such joys?—
> The blessed building-sparrow! . . .[92]

Pompilia's generally tranquil voice becomes suddenly vigorous, chaotically observant, as the appearance of a new life within her awakens her attention to the liveliness in nature, which she describes with her characteristic ingenuousness: 'a myriad merry motes', 'The blessed building-sparrow!' What strikes her in particular is the kinship amongst creatures, of whom she now realizes herself to be one: flies are 'companions'; the birds speak 'with one voice'. She discovers that she is involved in a narrative: whereas previously life had been a 'blank', now she has somewhere to go, a drawbridge to march along. The Risorgimento appears in her account of her destination:

> I have my purpose and my motive too.
> My march to Rome, like any bird or fly![93]

'My <u>march</u> to Rome, <u>like</u> <u>any</u> <u>bird</u> <u>or</u> <u>fly</u>'? It seems very strange, until we remember that at the time of *The Ring and the Book*'s composition and publication Rome was the only part of Italy not included in the new Italian Kingdom; in 1860 it had been the goal of Garibaldi and his thousand, as magazines reported: 'on embarking at Genoa their cry was "A Roma! A Roma!"' When the Kingdom had been formed without its obvious capital, as *The Times* had noted in 1861, 'the Italians' were dissatisfied, thinking that there could be no unity 'without Rome . . . and . . . clamouring to march upon it'.[94] In 1862 and 1867 Garibaldi, acting on

---

[92] *RB* VII. 1223–35.   [93] *RB* VII. 1245–6.
[94] John Sale Barker, 'Italian Unity and the National Movement in Europe', *Macmillan's Magazine*, 3 (Nov. 1860), 79; *The Times* is quoted in W. S. Chambers, *Garibaldi and Italian Unity* (Smith, Elder and Co., 1864), 167.

his own initiative, had again tried and failed to take the city. Pompilia's talk of marching and a drawbridge in itself prompts thoughts of soldiery, so that it would not have been outrageous for a reader in 1869 to make a mental addition to the line 'My march to Rome, like any bird or fly', appending 'or indeed like Garibaldi'.

The more so as images of spring, and of springing up, were much wielded by supporters of the Risorgimento, among them Elizabeth Barrett Browning as we saw in Chapters 4 and 5. A passage oddly similar to Pompilia's awakening occurs in Dobell's *The Roman*, where the mysterious monk named Vittorio Santo (which means Holy Victory) has spent the night among some ruins and wakes at dawn:

> . . . There came
> Soft lightning on my soul, and by a voice
> Ineffable, and heard not with the ears,
> 'ROME'. At that sound a thousand thousand voices
> Spread it through all things. Each imperial column,
> Each prone grey stone, touch'd by the eloquent winds,
> Heard it and gave it back. Trees, woods and fountains
> In musical confusion, leaves, buds, blossoms—
> Even to small flowers unseen, with voices smaller
> Than treble of a fay—atoms of sound
> Whereof a thousand falling on one ear,
> The unwitting sense should count them troubled silence—
> Birds, brooks and waterfalls,—all tongues of dawn,
> The very morning hum of summer time,
> Swell'd the sweet tumult; . . .
>
> . . .
>
> . . . all the earth
> Shook with the sounding ardour, and methought
> My flush'd soul, drunk with zeal, leap'd high and shouted,
> ROME![95]

After the drama and specificity of the Browning, Dobell's diction is imprecise and his assonance monotonous. Nonetheless, the proximity between the two descriptions shows that the idiom of Pompilia's awakening could readily be attached to the Risorgimento. The circumstances in which the two passages occur, however, are importantly different. To Dobell's revolutionary, what speaks through nature is a mystical ideal, something like a Hegelian Spirit, to whose mission he ecstatically dedicates his life. Nation and nature are as one: this is a starkly literal version of the radical organicist idea—which I described in Chapter 2—that nations were 'the natural organization of humanity'. George Eliot gave expression to similar thoughts in *The Spanish Gypsy* (1868): the Roma people, we are told, have no organized religion, but 'in the silent bodily presence feel | The mystic stirring of a common life | Which makes the many one'—a feeling experienced by the protagonist, Fedalma, when she discovers that she is of gypsy birth:

> . . . in my blood
> There streams the sense unspeakable of kind,
> As leopard feels at ease with leopard. . . .[96]

Nation is here conflated with race, and race with biological species, so that allegiance to the nation is presented as a natural imperative which overcomes all other obligations and feelings, even love. This brazenly reductive notion is all the weirder coming from the author who, in *Daniel Deronda* (1876), was to look so acutely into the many divergent and sometimes conflicting factors by which an ethnic identity is made up: it should perhaps be taken as a salutary example of the strange things that can happen when people who are not poets set themselves to writing poetry.

Pompilia's discovery of a unifying force in nature gestures towards such enthusiastic visions of nationhood, but also holds itself apart from them. The same happens when Caponsacchi responds to her appeal:

> . . . it was the first Spring.
> By the invasion I lay passive to,
> In rushed new things, the old were rapt away;
> Alike abolished—the imprisonment
> Of the outside air, the inside weight o' the world
> That pulled me down. . . .
>   . . .
> Into another state, under new rule
> I knew myself was passing swift and sure;[97]

---

[96] George Eliot, *Collected Poems*, ed. Lucien Jenkins (Skoob Books, 1989), 301, 307.
[97] *RB* VI. 946–51, 964–5.

The choice of vocabulary—'invasion', 'abolished', 'imprisonment', 'state', 'rule'—guides readers to associate the collapse of the
old moral order of Caponsacchi's existence with a political revolution; but this glimpse of large vistas soon disappears as his
thoughts turn to specific questions of his duty to his Church and
how best to manage the escape.

The Ring and the Book shows two Italians from the seventeenth
century developing independence and resolve of the kind that
Barrett Browning and others had long urged on their nineteenth-
century compatriots. In the first flush of revolution in 1859, the
Florentine newspaper *Monitore Toscano* had instructed its readers,
'con la *Indipendenza* voi volete giungere alla *Libertà*; il primo fonda-
mento di essa si è il sentimento di governarci in gran parte da noi
stessi': if Browning's work had been written by then, its hero and
heroine might have been adduced as examples of what the journalist had in mind.[98] Defying the established order, Pompilia and
Caponsacchi act on an 'impulse', one which prompts, not self-
assertion, but 'self-sacrifice': Caponsacchi risks his life for Pompilia,
Pompilia risks hers for her child.[99] This too echoes a common
emphasis of Risorgimento rhetoric: 'hurrah for the glorious army
of martyrs', as Claude sneers in *Amours de Voyage*.[100] It seems, then,
that as the personalities and motivations of his two central characters evolved in Browning's imagination, the model of heroism
promoted by the Risorgimento guided his thoughts, leaving a visible mark on the two passages quoted above. No contemporary
reviewer mentioned the work's bearing on Italian unification, but
if any readers did notice it, they could have thought that Pompilia
and Caponsacchi were, like Sordello, heralds of the future, and that
the Risorgimento had come about because more and more people
were feeling and acting in the same '*spirit*'. The Pope opens the way
for such a reflection when he describes Pompilia's escape as an
exemplary rebellion against the established order which had for so
long been accepted as 'The standing ordinance of God on earth'.[101]
Equally, however, here, as in the 'The Bishop Orders his Tomb'
and the other historical monologues, the time-lag holds the story
apart from contemporary events, making it stand in a critical as
much as an expository relation towards them. A reader is at liberty

---

[98] *Monitore Toscano*, 98 (29 Apr. 1859), 1.
[100] See above, Chapter 6.

[99] *RB*. VII. 1600; VI. 999.
[101] *RB* X. 1068.

to judge that the impulse to self-sacrifice is one thing in a personal
relationship such as Pompilia and Caponsacchi's, and quite another
in mass political movements like the war and revolutions of
1859–60. On this view, the couple's behaviour would represent a
moral ideal from which the Risorgimento, as it takes the 'crooked
road' of high politics, must necessarily deviate; and the work
would suggest a warning to those who conflate individual
redemption with subjection to the demands of a nation. *The Ring
and the Book* is an environment in which readers can follow up
many such possibilities, so as better to understand the distinctive-
ness of themselves and their own times as much as their continuity with others and with the past.

THE READER AND THE BOOK

'Do you see this Ring?' To that startling first half-line, a reader
seeing in front of him or her not a ring but a book, must answer
'no'—only it then transpires that by our act of reading we are
somehow to turn the book into a ring, as Browning has in his
imagination made a ring out of the materials in the *Old Yellow
Book*. We are left in no doubt that Guido is guilty, not only of the
murders (about which there has in any case never been any uncertainty) but of the worst motives that have been ascribed to him.
Nonetheless, the structure of the work, in which each character
presents an account of him or herself, is designed to make us peculiarly aware of our activity of interpretation. To form a ring is to
find a way through the book, and each of us will do this in diverse
ways, being moved to different degrees by different lines. The very
fact that the main question about the plot has been answered right
at the outset throws the emphasis onto those details about which
we may happily agree to differ:

> Gallop and go five minutes, and you gain
> The Roman Gate from where the Ema's bridged:
> Kingfishers fly there: how I see the bend
> O'erturreted by Certosa which he built,
> That Senescal (we styled him) of your House![102]

These words of Guido's vividly, and I think affectingly, evoke the
sensibility of an aristocrat for whom the beauty of nature

[102] *RB* XI. 10–14.

('Kingfishers fly there'), something anyone can love, is inseparable from the enjoyment of a gallop on a good horse and admiration for the expensive religious foundation built by a fellow noble (who is styled 'That Senescal' presumably because of his hospitality). Certainly Guido is here anxious to ingratiate himself with his interlocutors, but the feeling in the lines rings true to me, not that I therefore think he should be pardoned, far from it, only that I will understand him slightly differently from someone who forms another impression of the lines. And so on. All the monologues in the work are readings: Half-Rome, The Other Half-Rome, Tertium Quid, the lawyers and the Pope all obviously offer interpretations; but the central figures also interpret themselves and one another. This is the basic structural difference between *The Ring and the Book* and other nineteenth-century narrative poems, or indeed novels. From the one story, each character makes his or her own ring, which Browning 'binds' together with the others to form his book: 'As right through ring and ring runs the djereed | And binds the loose'.[103] Each reader is then invited to take his or her place alongside the other interpreters who are in the book already.

The imaginative community created by the work, therefore, does not speak in the unison of lyric. *Aurora Leigh* asks reader after reader to join in the song with which it ends, and envisages the community of feeling thereby created spreading throughout the nation and beyond. The characters grouped together in Browning's poem, although all involved in the same story, have widely differing views about it. This arrangement puts *The Ring and the Book* in a testing, half-critical relation to the idea—so attractive to Elizabeth Barrett Browning and repulsive to Arthur Hugh Clough—that a nation is a community of sympathy which poetry should foster. Browning may have read in the *Monitore Toscano* in 1859 a typical nationalist resolution: 'facciamo alla fine un fascio di tante forze divise e disordinate, e l'Italia abbia una sola voce e un braccio solo' (the 'fascio'—bundle—being the image that was later appropriated by Mussolini).[104] He presents his reader with a 'fascio' of Italians many of whom are unknown to one another, none of whom address any of the others directly, some of whom are deadly enemies, and all of whom have distinct voices.

---

[103] *RB* I. 467–8.   [104] *Monitore Toscano*, 99 (30 Apr. 1859), 1.

In the face of the calls for national unison trumpeted by revolutionaries and seconded, however circumspectly, by Barrett Browning, *The Ring and the Book* presents an emphatic picture of human diversity, while at the same time focusing on something that brings its various characters, sometimes unwillingly, sometimes unwittingly, together: not a song, not even a narrative in which they all have a part, but a public issue about which each of them has a different opinion.

As he reviews the different testimonies, the Pope says that he uses a sense like that of touch to discover the quality of each: 'habitude that gives a blind man sight | At the practised finger-ends of him', leading him to the point where he can say 'I stand firm'. This image shadows Browning's description of himself in Book I 'feeling' his way into the story as he reads it while walking through Florence, and reappears in Innocent's vision of the future when people's lives will no longer be governed by obedience to the decrees of Church and aristocracy. Deprived of such constraints, he thinks, many people will 'fall away'; but

> Surely some one Pompilia in the world
> Will say, 'I know the right place by foot's feel,
> I took it and tread firm there; wherefore change?'[105]

Primarily, the Pope is imagining what moral life will be like in a world bereft of or liberated from absolute religious and political authority: people will no longer have laws revealed to them, but will be left feeling their way as though blind. However, his words also touch on the limitation of sight which is enforced by reading, when one's fingers hold up a barrier in front of one's eyes, which are then used, not as organs of vision in their own right but as servants to the eye of the mind. It is by reading that the Pope has discovered where he stands in the dark circumstances of the Franceschini case, and by reading that we do likewise. Browning here follows up his own line of thought about the role of poetry in a time of nation-building: not to extend sympathies à la Elizabeth Barrett Browning, nor like Clough to resist such a development with satire, but to present readers with characters from whom they must recognize that they differ but whom they also may comprehend. By developing a feel for these

---

[105] *RB* X. 1248–9, 1259; I. 506; X. 1876, 1885–7.

other people in all their diversity we better realize where we stand ourselves.

Browning thought of his work as creating for his readers an environment just as murky and challenging as that foreseen by the Pope. As he wrote in the famous letter to Ruskin, who had complained about the difficulties of *Men and Women*:

We don't read poetry the same way, by the same law; it is too clear . . . You ought, I think, to keep pace with the thought tripping from ledge to ledge of my 'glaciers', as you call them; not stand poking your alpenstock into the holes, and demonstrating that no foot could have stood there;—suppose it sprang over there?[106]

This explanation bears mainly on the stylistic features of grammatical ellipsis, rhythmical irregularity, and dramatic implication which flummoxed many nineteenth-century readers; it also anticipates Pompilia's technique for reading the world, finding 'the right place by foot's feel'.

For the reader of a poem, what is the equivalent of the Pope's 'habitude', his sense of touch?—'foot' gives a hint, for a poet is unlikely to use that word without thinking of metrical feet. Occasionally but strikingly in *The Ring and the Book*, as in the earlier monologues, the characters' varying conceptions of law, and of its bearings on their valuations and behaviour, are suggested by the relation between the freedom of the language and the law of the verse in the poetry which Browning writes for them. Guido boasts of his allegiance to the established order, in his first monologue claiming that he was selflessly devoted to it, and in his second admitting to having been motivated entirely by self-interest. His social ideal is described in a series of clauses of almost identical construction, in verse which is heavily subjected to what Elizabeth Barrett Browning called 'the despotism of the final emphasis':

> Rome rife with honest women and strong men,
> Manners reformed, old habits back once more,
> Customs that recognize the standard worth,—
> The wholesome household rule in force again,
> Husbands once more God's representative,
> Wives like the typical spouse once more . . .[107]

[106] Woolford and Karlin, *Robert Browning*, 257.   [107] *RB* V. 2039–44.

Infringements of order assume the opposite shape, as when he rages about his wife's social origins:

> Pompilia, I supposed their daughter, drew
> Breath first 'mid Rome's worst rankness, through the deed
> Of a drab and a rogue, was bye-blow bastard-babe
> Of a nameless strumpet, passed off, palmed on me
> As the daughter with the dowry. Daughter? Dirt
> O' the kennel! Dowry? Dust o' the street! Nought more,
> Nought less, nought else but—oh—ah—assuredly
> A Franceschini and my very wife![108]

The grammatical parataxis, lexical violence, and rhythmical irregularity of the middle six lines of this passage (two of which have twelve syllables and three of the others eleven) are what his spouse's provenance sounds like to his ears. The neatness of his preferred order is made bitter to him here when all Pompilia's ectopia is brought home into the dignity of his own name and his own, regular line: 'A Franceschini and my very wife!' Like Fra Lippo, Guido expresses himself through a conflict between freedom and form, the struggle in his voice suggesting the violence of his character, which in turn bears the mark of a society divided between oppressors and oppressed. However, since he likes monotony, and since the laws—as he thought—were set up to gratify him, he gives his allegiance to the opposite side.

Pompilia's voice finds its feet in an utterly different way:

> I felt there was just one thing Guido claimed
> I had no right to give nor he to take;
> We being in estrangement, soul from soul:
> Till, when I sought help, the Archbishop smiled,
> Inquiring into privacies of life,
> —Said I was blameable—(he stands for God)
> Nowise entitled to exemption there.
> Then I obeyed,—as surely had obeyed
> Were the injunction 'Since your husband bids,
> Swallow the burning coal he proffers you!'
> But I did wrong, and he gave wrong advice
> Though he were thrice Archbishop,—that, I know!—
> Now I have got to die and see things clear.[109]

---

[108] *RB* V. 768–75.   [109] *RB* VII. 721–33.

The nearest analogue to the movement of this verse elsewhere in Browning is 'Andrea del Sarto', only where the perfect painter's voice characteristically falls short of the limits of its form, Pompilia's happily fills them up. Even at this most painful moment in her testimony there is no strife between the law of the verse and the spoken accentuation of the words: the swelling objection beginning 'as surely had obeyed' is conveyed merely by repetition, a violent image and the first foot trochee substitution (entirely to be expected in pentameters) at 'Swallow'. Very occasionally, elsewhere in her monologue, Pompilia's speech does disrupt the metre, as in her solemn, touching, and perhaps slightly nervous first line: 'I am just seventeen years and five months old.' But, on the whole, the rhythm of her voice coincides harmoniously with the prescription of the form, expressing itself through slight alterations of pace and emphasis ('I felt there was just one thing'), through idiosyncracies of phrasing ('We being in estrangement', 'privacies of life'), or by gentle syntactic surprises, as in the last three lines of the passage quoted, where the sentence might happily stop after 'advice', or after 'know!—', but in each case carries on. This is nothing like the wholesale infringement and imposition of metrical law through which Guido makes himself heard. We might relate the tranquil movement of Pompilia's verse to the fact that she is about to die and sees things clear; but it seems also to suggest the disposition to obedience which has marked her whole life and which appears in her submission to the archbishop. The strongest evidence that her resistance to Guido was provoked, as she says, by an 'impulse to serve God | Not save myself,—no— nor my child unborn' is that impulse so thoroughly coincides with obedience in the verse Browning writes for her.[110] Even the occasional slight irregularities contribute to this impression, for they are like the loveliest architectural ornament, in Ruskin's description; that which manifests 'a *self*-restrained liberty', in 'voluntary submission to divine law': 'some portion of the design slightly breaks the law to which the rest is subjected . . . the value of this type . . . consist[s] . . . in the acknowledgement *by* the ornament of the fitness of the limitation; . . . as being pleased . . . to have so beautiful a law suggested to it, and one which to follow is so justly in accordance with its own nature'.[111]

---

[110] *RB* VII. 1600–1.   [111] Ruskin, *Works*, ix. 304–5.

Pompilia is offered to the reader as an ideal of virtue, but not as
a heroine. She is not like Aurora Leigh. Many readers will find her
naïve, too ready to forgive, exasperating. Browning's achievement
is to imagine a character whom we must recognize to be truly
virtuous and yet at the same time may very well not like, so that
the circle which each of us inscribes on our imaginative journey
through the poem will probably be different from hers. Tracing
such a circle, each of us joins the interpreters who are already in
the work; however, we are not therefore brought into their
community, not only because they after all exist only in the mind,
but because they are Italians in the seventeenth century, and we
are from a later time, and probably English or American. The
poem takes no steps towards a melding of Italianness and
Englishness in the manner of *Aurora Leigh*; on the contrary, like
the Italian monologues, it relies on our feeling there to be a difference between that other country and our own. In the monologues, the national otherness of the speaker serves, as we saw, to
enforce a recognition of the otherness of each of us from one
another, whatever our nationality. In *The Ring and the Book*,
although the distinctions between the speakers are still strongly
marked, what confronts us is, not an individual, but a group.
Readers are prompted, therefore, to ask, when they free themselves from the work and turn to look at the world around them,
what group they belong to, and to what degree it is a unity, what
its limits are, and where they stand in it. That great reader of
Browning, G. K. Chesterton, understood this well when he
suggested as an analogue to the events in this poem which so
subtly investigates Italian nationhood, an episode in the risorgimento of another oppressed nation: 'some *cause célèbre* of our day,
such as the Parnell Commission': ' "Half-London" would be the
arguments of an ordinary committed and sensible unionist', 'The
"Other half-London" would be the utterance of an ordinary
educated and sensible Home Ruler', ' "Tertium Quid" would be
some detached intellectual, . . . possibly Mr. Bernard Shaw'.[112]

---

[112] Chesterton, *Robert Browning*, 161.

PART III

TENNYSON'S BRITAIN

8

EVER-BROADENING ENGLAND

Tennyson, 'always an enthusiast for Italian freedom'—as his son records—was also an enthusiast for the British Empire, a regime which denied the right of self-determination to the many indigenous peoples under its sway. A surprising accommodation, perhaps, yet not an unusual one, for the Risorgimento was so compelling to English imaginations that it was harnessed by many mutually contradictory causes: extension of the franchise (Garibaldi was honorary president of the National Reform League); the coming Republic (Swinburne); monarchical constitutionalism (the *Quarterly Review*); even apocalyptic prophecy. When the strictly Nonconformist parents of Edmund Gosse sat down to their favourite activity of interpreting the Book of Revelation, they found 'direct statements regarding Napoleon III and Pope Pius IX and the King of Piedmont, historic figures which they conceived as foreshadowed, in language which admitted of plain interpretation, under the names of denizens of Babylon and companions of the Wild Beast'.[1]

For Tennyson, the Risorgimento and the British Empire were both instances of unification; and unification was in his mind almost universally a good. He wished the Empire to grow ever more cohesive, even to the point of becoming a single nation: 'I hope that I may live to see England and her Colonies absolutely one, with as complete a reciprocity of the free gifts of God, as there is between one county and another in the mother-country.'[2] At the front of his mind as he wrote those words was probably the

---

[1] *Memoir*, ii. 1; Beales, 'Garibaldi in England', 212; Swinburne, *Songs Before Sunrise*, 10–30; *Quarterly Review*, 110/219 (July 1861), 216; Edmund Gosse, *Father and Son: A Study of Two Temperaments* (1907), ed. Peter Abbs (Harmondsworth: Penguin, 1983), 78–9.

[2] *The Letters of Alfred Lord Tennyson*, ed. Cecil Y. Lang and Edgar F. Shannon Jr., 3 vols. (Oxford: Oxford University Press, 1982–90), iii. 55.

ideal of intra-imperial free trade, for in other respects—as he was
well aware—the mother country was in itself far from being
'absolutely one'. 'In Wales, in Scotland and in Ireland there is
Celtic blood and Celtic languages utterly unintelligible to us are
still spoken', as the Cambridge historian J. R. Seeley noted in
1883.[3] Distinctions of 'blood', of course, have no physiological
basis, and it is therefore difficult to gauge exactly what Victorians
meant when they used the language of race—a matter to which I
will return. Linguistic disparities were, however, both real and
marked, as were religious differences, with the prevalence of
Roman Catholicism in Ireland, Nonconformity in Wales, and
Presbyterianism in Scotland distinguishing those countries from
England which, though substantially Anglican, contained much
denominational variety. There were administrative inconsistencies
too, such as Scotland's separate banking system and legal code; and
there were already distinct football and rugby associations.[4]
Commentators were quick to hypostasize such disparities into
contrasting national characters, the English being defined, according to *Blackwood's* in 1829, by 'independence' and 'brutality' as
against the 'sagacity' and 'cunning' of the Scottish and the
'gallantry' and 'faithlessness' of the Irish—enduring stereotypes
which then, as now, could be more or less embroidered according
to the fancifulness of the writer.[5]

At the beginning of the century, it seems that an over-arching
British identity coexisted fairly happily with feelings of Welshness,
Englishness, and Scottishness (though never Irishness); but as the
United Kingdom advanced into the time of nation-building this
compromise came under strain. Scotland remained predominantly
happy with the Union; but in Ireland there was resistance to
British rule throughout the century, with the population increasingly conceiving of itself as an oppressed nationality in the style of
Italy, although Catholics were loath to model their ambitions on
the Risorgimento because of its anti-Papal tendencies. In Wales,
persistent unrest began to develop into something like a national
movement during the 1860s; there, Italy was more readily adopted

[3] J. R. Seeley, *The Expansion of England* (Macmillan, 1883), 48.
[4] Hoppen, *The Mid-Victorian Generation*, 515–6, 526.
[5] Alexander Walker, 'Characters of the English, Scots, and Irish', *Blackwood's Edinburgh Magazine*, 26/99 (Nov. 1829), 824.

as an example.[6] Responding to these developments, Matthew Arnold in 1867 promoted the idea of a homogeneous Kingdom-wide national identity: an 'Englishman's . . . Welsh and Irish fellow-citizens'—he lamented—'are hardly more amalgamated with him now than they were when Wales and Ireland were first conquered, and the true unity of even these small islands has yet to be achieved'.[7] When the title 'The United Kingdom of Great Britain and Ireland'—so awkwardly combining a recognition of difference with an assertion of unity—had been launched in 1800, the dominant meaning of 'United' was political: it alluded to the new unity of the State. The 'true unity' which interested Arnold, however, was cultural: he wanted to see the unified State produce a single, united nation.

In making his proposals for national amalgamation, Arnold had an eye to the larger territories of the Empire, as his phrase 'the true unity of even these small islands' makes plain. Thoughts such as Tennyson's, that colonies might become as close-knit as counties, drew some plausibility from the development of steam navigation: surveying the prospects for imperial unity in 1839, Herman Merivale (later under-secretary for India) had declared resound-ingly, if optimistically, that the remotest quarters of the earth were now 'placed at once . . . within our immediate reach'.[8] Nonetheless, it was obvious that the Empire included far greater geographical, linguistic, religious, cultural and—as the Victorians saw it—'racial' differences than the British Isles. In consequence, the ideal of national unity, which was already creating problems for the not-very-united Kingdom, gave rise to even starker diffi-culties when it influenced people's thoughts about the Empire. In *The Expansion of England* (of which Tennyson gave a copy to Gladstone in 1883),[9] J. R. Seeley argued that the Empire should be considered a 'Greater Britain'—a phrase he had borrowed from the title of a book by Charles Dilke (1868). Greater Britain or expanded England?—it is only the first of the volume's many uncertainties. The Empire, Seeley claims, is held together by

---

[6] Colley, *Britons*, 361–3; D. George Boyce, *Nationalism in Ireland*, 2nd edn. (Routledge, 1991), 183; Reginald Coupland, *Welsh and Scottish Nationalism: A Study* (Collins, 1954), 227; John Davies, *A History of Wales* (Harmondsworth: Penguin, 1994), 417.

[7] Arnold, *Complete Prose Works*, iii. 392.

[8] Herman Merivale, *Introduction to a Course of Lectures on Colonization and the Colonies* (Longman, 1839), 15.   [9] *Memoir*, ii. 301.

'community of race, community of religion, community of inter-est'. However, he soon notices that, like the United Kingdom, the Empire includes other 'races'; and he therefore alters 'community of race' to the less ambitious 'common nationality'. 'A good many French and Dutch and a good many Caffres and Maories may be admitted without marring the ethnological unity of the whole', he proposes; the Empire is, he now says 'a vast English nation'. Tennyson would have approved. However, Seeley's idea of the empire-as-nation excludes India, which, he submits, 'does not make part of Greater Britain in the same sense', for its 'subject or rival nationalities', being alien in 'race', 'religion', and 'traditions', 'cannot be perfectly assimilated'. At this point, the model of nationhood to which his ideas are always drawn makes it difficult for him to justify continued imperial government. In combination with the Hindu religion, British rule is, he suggests, likely to foster the development of an Indian national consciousness: 'if there could arise in India a nationality-movement similar to that which we witnessed in Italy, the English Power could not even make the resistance that was made in Italy by Austria, but must succumb at once.' Confronted by this incompatibility between nationhood and empire, his argument subsides: Indian affairs, he admits, are 'difficult to understand or to form an opinion about'; he concludes with the lame view that 'for the present we are driven both by necessity and duty to a closer union', despite all his previous reasoning to the effect that such a union could be neither very intimate nor very lasting.[10]

The line which Seeley draws between India and the rest of the Empire had long been observed in the practice of imperial admin-istration. Following a report by Lord Durham in 1839, 'responsi-ble' government—in which the executive was held accountable to a locally elected legislature—was granted to Canada (1848) and then in piecemeal fashion to most of the other settlement colonies over the following decade.[11] Having large populations of English and British origin, these colonies were thought to deserve the typically English right of limited self-government. Paradoxically,

[10] Seeley, *The Expansion of England*, 8, 11, 50, 75, 11, 46, 184–5, 227, 301, 306.

[11] Denis Judd, *Empire: The British Imperial Experience, 1765 to the Present* (Harper Collins, 1996), 52–3; Hoppen, *The Mid-Victorian Generation*, 158–9. See also A. G. L. Shaw, 'British Attitudes to the Colonies, *ca.* 1820–1850', *Journal of British Studies*, 9/1 (Nov. 1969), 71–95; C. C. Eldridge (ed.), *British Imperialism in the Nineteenth Century* (Macmillan, 1984), 59–61.

however, the exercise of that right was likely to make them ever more distinct from the mother-country, and so put the ideal of empire-as-nation under threat. In the early 1860s, the academic and journalist Goldwin Smith went so far as to propose outright independence for the settlement colonies, a step which, he argued, would not damage the kind of imperial unity that really mattered: 'that connexion with the Colonies, which is really a part of our greatness—the connexion of blood, sympathy, and ideas—will not be affected by political separation. And when our Colonies are nations, something in the nature of a great Anglo-Saxon federation may, in substance if not in form, spontaneously arise out of affinity and mutual affection.'[12] Smith's commitment to the ideal of nationhood is explicit in his suggestion that the colonies should become nations; but, though veiled, it is no less present in the description of his proposed 'federation' which, as a 'connexion of blood, sympathy and ideas . . . affinity and mutual affection' is merely the empire-as-nation under another name and without a corresponding State apparatus. The terminological finesse is necessary to hide the conflicts of identity that would be only too apparent if he were to say that each ex-colony was to be a 'nation' on its own, but at the same time to be united in 'nationhood' with others. Lord Dufferin, the Governor of Canada, likewise had it both ways when, in 1873, he wrote to Tennyson about 'the ardour of Canadian Nationality': 'amongst no people have I ever met . . . a more legitimate pride in all those characteristics which constitute their nationality'—while also remarking, without any hint of contradiction, 'I find they cling with fanatical tenacity to their birthright as Englishmen, and to their hereditary association in the past and future glories of the mother country'.[13] The expansion of England left the country's identity difficult to describe in terms of nationhood, for the ideal of national unity, given such prestige by the Risorgimento, was ill-adapted to the multiple and conflicting allegiances produced by colonization.

With regard to India, the possibility of Anglicization—perhaps leading to self-government—had during the first half of the century been frequently canvassed in theory though not very intensely pursued in practice. After the Uprising (or Mutiny) of

---

[12] Goldwin Smith, *The Empire: A Series of Letters Published in 'The Daily News', 1862, 1863* (John Henry and James Parker, 1863), 6.   [13] *Memoir*, ii. 143–4.

1857 even the thought of such a prospect was largely abandoned, as the London government brought the subcontinent under more direct control, imposing a form of rule which was blazoned to the world with the declaration of Victoria as Empress in 1876.[14] Precisely because India was now understood to be starkly un-English, it was yoked by administrative structure and ceremonial symbolism all the more closely to England. In 1864, George Trevelyan expressed what was by then a common opinion: 'such is the incompatibility of sentiment and custom between the European and the native, that even the firmest friends of the latter allow that a complete amalgamation is quite hopeless.' Even now, however, some vestiges of an ideal of common nationhood remain: 'as time goes on', he suggests, European and indigenous populations will 'live side by side with mutual sympathy and self-respect, and work together heartily for the same great ends'. Twenty years later, Sir James Fitzjames Stephen returned to the notion of Anglicization, thinking it 'not improbable that in the course of time, though I think it will be a long time, native habits of life and ways of thought will give way to, and be superseded by, those of Europe', and that, as with the settlement colonies, this growth in Englishness would be crowned by the supremely English and yet paradoxically de-anglicizing gift of self-government.[15]

These ruminations were conceptually—and often geographically—far removed from the day-to-day business of imperial rule. Stephen might have been less optimistic had he heeded the Indian nationalist Dadabhai Naoroji's complaint of the imperial government's 'repeated breach of pledges to give the natives a fair and reasonable share in the higher administration of their own country'.[16] In practice, officials imposed the line between English and non-English all the more forcefully as its position became less certain. As Homi Bhabha has put it, in imperial India, 'to be

---

[14] Ronald Hyam, *Britain's Imperial Century, 1815–1914: A Study of Empire and Expansion*, 2nd edn. (Macmillan, 1993), 133–41; *The Oxford History of the British Empire*, iii: *The Nineteenth Century*, ed. Andrew Porter (Oxford: Oxford University Press, 1999), 395–445.

[15] George Otto Trevelyan, *The Competition Wallah* (Macmillan, 1864), 444, 446; J. F. Stephen, 'Foundations of the Government of India', *Nineteenth Century*, 14 (Oct. 1883), 558.

[16] Dadabhai Naoroji, 'The Pros and Cons of British Rule' (1871), W. Theodore de Bary (ed.), *Sources of Indian Tradition*, 2 vols. (New York: Columbia University Press, 1964), ii. 114.

Anglicized' was '*emphatically* not to be English'.[17] In the less pressured circumstances of the British Isles, however—in the books and articles that Tennyson read and heard discussed, the intellectual climate that he inhabited—to be Anglicized was *perhaps* to be English. That Indians might become more English or partly English or parody the English, and that Canadians, Australians, New Zealanders might become less English or even foreign, made the question of what constituted Englishness more vexed than it would in any case have been if England were confined to the United Kingdom. While Italy, and later Germany, were becoming more cohesive, England was doing the opposite. England, Britain, the United Kingdom, Greater Britain—or, in Tennyson's phrase 'ever-broadening England': how was the nation to be defined, and what, if any, were its limits?[18]

Tennyson's son records of his father that 'one of the deepest desires of his life was to help the realisation of the ideal of an Empire', in which 'the most intimate union of every part' would coincide 'with a heightening of individuality to each member'.[19] He leaves it unclear whether indigenous peoples are to be included in 'the most intimate union', and on what terms; an uncertainty which was grandly illustrated when, in 1886, representatives both human and material were brought to London from the furthest reaches of the Empire for the Colonial and Indian Exhibition. As they observed the displays of Angora goats from South Australia, a 'typical Indian Palace', Guianans 'employed in weaving hammocks', etc., the English may predominantly have had a feeling of confrontation with the Other; but they may also have felt some expansion of their own identities. Certainly, the opening ceremony sent out mixed signals: the Queen sat, in aggressively imperial fashion, on a throne 'taken at the capture of Lahore'; on the other hand, the second verse of the national anthem was sung in Sanscrit—by then recognized as having a common root with European languages—suggesting the adoption of India into the empire-as-nation.[20] The hymn

---

[17] Bhabha, *The Location of Culture*, 87.
[18] 'To the Queen [Idylls of the King]', 30.   [19] *Memoir*, ii. 223 n.
[20] Frank Cundall, *Reminiscences of the Colonial and Indian Exhibition* (William Clowes and Sons, 1886), 60, 81, 27, 9.

Tennyson wrote to be performed at the opening diplomatically includes both these possibilities.

> Britain's myriad voices call,
> 'Sons, be welded each and all,
> Into one imperial whole,
> One with Britain, heart and soul!
> One life, one flag, one fleet, one Throne!'
> Britons, hold your own![21]

One possible interpretation is that Britain's 'Sons' qualify as 'Britons' when they become 'One with Britain', so that 'Britons, hold your own!' is a call to the whole Empire to stand up for itself, most likely against the growing threat from France. This is the empire-as-nation. Another possibility is that Britain's 'Sons' remain distinct from 'Britons', so that the last line envisages a defensively imperial Britain holding on to its charges like a nervous nanny. Tennyson had deployed the same soft-focus technique in a poem written for Queen Victoria's birthday four years earlier:

> To all the loyal hearts who long
>   To keep our English Empire whole!
> To all our noble sons, the strong
>   New England of the Southern Pole!
> To England under Indian skies,
>   To those dark millions of her realm![22]

It is unclear whether 'our English Empire' means 'the Empire which consists of us English' or 'the Empire, consisting of other peoples, which we English possess'; and whether 'those dark millions of her realm' means 'those dark millions who make up the realm which is England under Indian skies' or 'the dark millions who are governed by those English people who live in India'. We cannot tell whether the 'New' of 'New England' owes its initial capital to its position in the line or to its being part of a proper name; whether, that is, 'the strong | New England of the Southern Pole' is a 'new England (just a continuation of the old)' or 'New England (a distinct new entity to replace the lost New England in America)'. It is impossible to determine whether

---

[21] 'Opening of the Indian and Colonial Exhibition by the Queen', 35–40.
[22] 'Hands All Round (1882)', 13–18.

'England under Indian skies' is that part of England which just happens to be under Indian skies—as distinct from, say, Cornish ones—or a hybrid place importantly different from plain England, 'England-under-Indian-skies'.

These poems certainly manifest diplomatic craft, some might say guile. They hide the disparity between views of India as possession and as constituent of the empire-as-nation; they conceal the discrepancy between an idea of the colonies as expanded England and the growth of colonial self-government. In concocting these fudges, they show that, because of the Empire, Englishness had developed to an extreme degree that intrinsic haziness of national identity which I described in Chapter 2. As we saw, national identities are made up of a composite of different factors: language, history, geography, food, etc. The elements which amalgamate to form one nation's identity may therefore differ, and receive diverse emphases, from those which combine in another; and indeed a single nation may very well be imagined in varying ways by its different members. The version of nationalism adopted by Bismarck in Germany emphasized blood and soil, as extreme right-wing nationalists in many different countries have continued to do ever since. In Italy, Mazzini focused on language, geography, and history, adding excitement in the form of a nebulous 'Mission'. In the view of recent theorists in France, 'the French national idea' is that of 'a legal and political pact between free and equal individuals', a suggestion which, in its universalist ambitions, simply ignores the cultural factors which conceptions of nationhood generally embody: it is in fact a definition of the State.[23] In nineteenth-century England, the national identity could not satisfactorily be based on language, for English was spoken in the United States; it could not focus primarily on land, for England was ever-broadening. Both those elements nonetheless do enter into imaginings of the English nation; but for Tennyson, and for many of his contemporaries, their role was subsidiary to two other factors which the English could carry with them overseas, and perhaps impart for the ends of Anglicization: the liberty afforded by the Queen and the mother of Parliaments, and, above all, the 'English national character'.

---

[23] Julia Kristeva, *Nations without Nationalism*, trans. Leon S. Roudiez (New York: Columbia University Press, 1993), 40; cf. Gil Delannoi and Pierre-André Taguieff, *Théories du Nationalisme: Nation, Nationalité, Ethnicité* (Paris: Kimé, 1991), 13, 33.

Interest in the character of the English had quickened in the shadow of the 1832 Reform Act. Bulwer Lytton introduces his *England and the English* (1833) by suggesting that 'those changes which have wrought such convulsions in states, have begun by revolutions in the *character* of nations . . . The English of the present day are not the English of twenty years ago'—a claim which, with its assumption that there is a homogeneous 'nation' at the origin of political change, is characteristic of a time of nation-building. The limited extension of the franchise which had been granted in 1832 began the process of shifting political power from English gentlemen to Englishmen at large who would use their votes as their characters dictated. In such circumstances, it would obviously be reassuring for a reformist aristocrat such as Bulwer Lytton to discover that the values of the nation were the same as those of his class. So, indeed, he does: 'the root of all our notions, as of all our laws, is to be found in the sentiment of property', he observes, and he emphasizes (acutely) 'that Passion for the Unsocial, which we dignify with the milder epithet of the Domestic'.[24] Accounts of national character are generally more stipulative than ethnographic, but *England and the English* is remarkably so, having as its purpose the expansion of a class identity into the identity of a nation. Such, overwhelmingly, is the intent of descriptions of English nationality in the mid-nineteenth century. Tennyson's 'Briton' has a bold front, 'common sense', 'Saxon pith of nerve' and wants no truck with 'the popular breath'; in *Alton Locke* (1850), Charles Kingsley writes of 'the true English stuff . . . the stuff which has held Gibraltar and conquered at Waterloo—which has created a Birmingham and a Manchester, and colonised every quarter of the globe', and makes his working-class protagonist find it epitomized in a boat of undergraduates competing in the Bumps at Cambridge.[25]

In the second half of the century, such definitions of national character frequently overlapped with theories of race. In *The Visions of England* (1881–2), F. T. Palgrave advances a comparatively welcoming conception of the English as a 'race, of many races well compact', but it was more common to emphasize the

---

[24] Edward Lytton Bulwer, *England and the English*, 2 vols. (R. Bentley, 1833), 4, 7, 12.

[25] 'Hail Briton!', 41, 68, 76; Charles Kingsley, *Alton Locke, Tailor and Poet: An Autobiography* (1850; Macmillan, 1876), 104.

difference between the English, possessed of pith of nerve, etc., and less reliable inhabitants of the United Kingdom, supposedly Celts.[26] In an article of 1870 entitled 'The Origin of the English Nation', the historian E. A. Freeman took a familiar line when he asserted 'we are a Low-Dutch people, who left our old home in the course of the fifth and sixth centuries and found ourselves a new home by conquest in the Isle of Britain. That island, lately a Roman Province, had been a short time before left to itself, and was in a state of utter anarchy and disorganization'. From this point of view, the Empire overseas was only an extension of that smaller empire which the English had already established in the British Isles, and the question of what would become of India was the same question as what was becoming of Wales and Ireland, only larger. As Freeman went on: 'we are Englishmen, sprung from the old stock which changed Britain into England, as it has, before and since, planted other Englands elsewhere.'[27] The possibility of double vision created by this idea was taken up by Tennyson in *Idylls of the King*, a work which tells the story of an empire in ancient Britain, while having an eye to the British Empire in the modern world.

For some writers, races were clearly defined, the divisions between them unbridgeable: 'human character, individual and national, is traceable solely to the nature of that race to which the individual or nation belongs', proposed Robert Knox with blithe internal contradiction ('individual *and* national'?) in 1850; 'to me', he continued, 'the Caledonian Celt of *Scotland* appears a race as distinct from the Lowland Saxon of the same country, as any two races can possibly be: as negro from American; Hottentot from Caffre; Esquimaux from Saxon.'[28] For those who managed to hold such opinions, the only way for the English to be ever-broadening was for them to exterminate other peoples: 'when the European comes into contact with any other type of man, that other type disappears ... Let us not shade our eyes, and pretend not to see this result', wrote J. A. Roebuck in 1849 (Knox, by contrast, thought the English could not long survive in tropical

---

[26] Francis T. Palgrave, *The Visions of England*, 2 vols. (privately printed, 1881–2), 4.

[27] Edward A. Freeman, 'The Origin of the English Nation (Part III)', *Macmillan's Magazine*, 22 (May, 1870), 31, 46.

[28] Robert Knox, *The Races of Men* (Henry Renshaw, 1850), pp. v, 14.

climes).[29] However, racial terms were not everywhere employed with such cruel absoluteness. Matthew Arnold, always master of the slippery phrase, was in this area particularly elusive. In *On the Study of Celtic Literature* (1867) 'Celtic' and 'Saxon' begin as racial categories: the Celts, we learn, originated 'in the heart of Asia'. Because of such remarks, he has been accused of reducing cultural and political conflict to 'the workings of a permanent racial difference'.[30] However, as the argument progresses, his terms shift so as to signify characteristics which are cultural, not racial, and which therefore can be learned.[31] When he urges the necessity of 'fusion' between the English 'race' and the Celts, what he has in mind is not a programme of forced marriages but the development of 'a unity of spirit': the resulting 'new type' of Englishman, 'more intelligent, more gracious, and more humane' is not a racial hybrid but the product of an education such as might be obtained from his proposed Professor of Celtic at Oxford.[32]

Tennyson was attracted to the language of race, but he shared Arnold's confusion about its meaning. In conversation during his later years he was capable of startling prejudice ('niggers are tigers, niggers are tigers', he was heard to mutter during discussion of Governor Eyre in 1865) and of clinical racist speculation: ' "the Celtic race does not easily amalgamate with other races, as those of Scandinavian origin do, as for instance Saxon and Norman, which have fused perfectly" '.[33] In his verse, however, the word 'race' wanders away from the circumscribed categories to which theorists such as Knox would fix it, sometimes expanding to include everyone ('the kindly race of men'), sometimes contracting to a family ('the race of Aylmer'), while racial terms can be juggled with happy abandon, as in his poem of welcome to Princess Alexandra of Denmark, who married the Prince of Wales in 1863:

[29] J. A. Roebuck, *The Colonies of England* (J. W. Parker, 1849), 138; Knox, *The Races of Men*, 107.

[30] Arnold, *Complete Prose Works*, iii. 292; Robert J. C. Young, *Colonial Desire: Hybridity in Theory, Culture and Race* (Routledge, 1995), 60–1.

[31] See Cannon Schmitt, *Alien Nation: Nineteenth-Century Gothic Fictions and English Nationality* (Philadelphia: University of Pennsylvania Press, 1997), 121.

[32] Arnold, *Complete Prose Works*, iii. 395, 392.

[33] Norman Page (ed.), *Tennyson: Interviews and Recollections* (Macmillan, 1983), 80; *Memoir*, ii. 338.

> . . . Saxon or Dane or Norman we,
> Teuton or Celt, or whatever we be,
> We are each all Dane in our welcome of thee,[34]

Even if, as he came increasingly to assert in old age, 'race' was an important influence on personality, he is likely to have thought its manifestations sporadic and its presence difficult to fix with any certainty. A remark of Lady Tennyson's gives evidence of a relaxed attitude towards racial definitions: 'I too am partly a Celt I believe and so you will believe from my indignations.'[35] Her husband, too, generally puts 'race' second to the characteristics whose presence it is sometimes adduced to explain: from the early 'English Warsong', where England—in contrast to France—is said to have no room for the 'hollow at heart'—'He is weak! we are strong; he a slave, we are free'—to 'The Defence of Lucknow' (1879), where 'race' appears less as a virtue in its own right, than as an origin of the moral qualities by which the national identity is primarily defined: 'English in heart and in limb, | Strong with the strength of the race to command, to obey, to endure'.[36] In the conclusion to *The Princess*, the 'Tory member's eldest son' praises the English for 'Some sense of duty . . . faith . . . reverence . . . patient force . . . manhood'.[37] Even during the scare about a possible French invasion in 1852, it is not a 'race'—nor even a coast-line—that appears to be under threat:

> God save the nation,
> The toleration,
> And the free speech that makes a Briton known.
> Britons, guard your own.[38]

Nation, toleration, free speech: as it seems to Tennyson, the English nation is distinguished primarily, not by place, nor language, nor race, but by character, along with the political principles in which character seems to be manifest.

Elizabeth K. Helsinger has proposed that for Tennyson, as for 'the nineteenth century' in general, a nation 'must be able to imagine itself in a certain kind of space, a space that is located and bounded, demarcated by natural and political boundaries separating

---

[34] 'Tithonus', 29; 'Aylmer's Field', 577; 'A Welcome to Alexandra', 31–3.
[35] *Letters of Alfred Lord Tennyson*, ii. 289.
[36] 'English Warsong', 11, 30; 'The Defence of Lucknow', 46–7.
[37] *The Princess*, 'Conclusion', 52–7.   [38] 'Britons, Guard Your Own', 27–30.

it from other nations, as opposed, for example, to the space without fixed borders through which the state embodied in a monarch could once be imagined to move'.[39] The 'rural scenes' which she goes on to discuss were certainly important to English national identity, as the frequent attempts to recreate familiar landscapes in India, Tasmania, Malaysia, etc. abundantly prove. However, Tennyson's England, unlike Mazzini's Italy, was not 'bounded'; on the contrary, it was 'ever-broadening'. The degree of England's involvement with its Empire distinguished it from every other European country in the time of nation-building, and exerted unique pressure on its national identity. Hence the importance for Tennyson, for England in the nineteenth century, and indeed England thereafter, of the notion of character.

This conception of nationhood had an unnerving consequence, for if English nationality was character, each person's claim to it rested on his or her inner life. The English were therefore peculiarly vulnerable to a recursive line of thought which has been well described by Slavoj Žižek:

If I identify myself as an Englishman, I distinguish myself from the French, Germans, Scots, Irish, and so on. However, in the next stage, the question is raised of who among the English are 'the real English', the paradigm of Englishness; who are the Englishmen who correspond in full to the notion of English? . . . the final answer is of course that *nobody* is fully English, that every empirical Englishman contains something 'non-English'.[40]

For Tennyson, the battle of Englishness was fought in India, in Ireland, and also within the mind of each English person. When he adjures his co-nationals to 'fear the neighbourhood | Of that unstable Celtic blood | That never keeps an equal pulse', he means both that they should beware of their neighbours, the French and the Irish, and that they should endeavour to control the dangerous Celtic elements which, as Lady Tennyson knew, might very well inhere in their personalities.[41] England required the subjugation of the Celt within. Writing about the Risorgimento, Clough and both Brownings—with their different

---

[39] Elizabeth K. Helsinger, *Rural Scenes and National Representation: Britain, 1815–1850* (Princeton: Princeton University Press, 1997), 15.

[40] Slavoj Žižek, *For They Know Not What They Do: Enjoyment as a Political Factor* (Verso, 1991), 110.   [41] 'Hail Briton!', 18–20.

emphases and angles of attack—all focus on the conflicts and consonances between individuals and different kinds of socio-political order. Writing about England, Tennyson takes for granted that continuity between individual and national identity which Clough so relentlessly questioned. The disturbances and resolutions with which Tennyson is concerned occur at once within individual lives and within the nation; not between one sphere and the other. As we will see, *The Princess* tells simultaneously of a reconciliation between two individuals and two elements within ever-broadening England, while *Idylls of the King* is inseparably the story of an empire and of an individual. In Tennyson's words: 'by King Arthur I always meant the soul'.[42]

[42] *Poems of Tennyson*, ed. Ricks, iii. 260.

9

THE EMPIRE OF THE
IMAGINATION

REALMS OF GOLD

'The poet in a golden clime was born', wrote the young
Tennyson, although he was himself born in Lincolnshire, a clime
at best verdant, at worst dank.[1] In support of his claim to the
foreign nationality of at least his imagination, he could have
offered much of his earliest writing, in which the lushest displays
of his burgeoning poetic powers were occasioned by thoughts of
'Babylon', 'Bassorah', 'Hindostan', and 'Persia':

> . . . Anatolia, and the fane
> Of Belus, and Caïster's plain,
> And Sardis . . .

The incantational listing of those exotic names focuses attention
on their sounds and general implications, not the specific places to
which they refer. They are—the ordering of the sequence
momentarily suggests—an ABC of the Orient, and the star which
beams over them 'so gorgeously and far' might well be the star of
Tennyson's genius, asserting its dominion over the realm of
language.[2] If a Browning dramatic monologue resembles a room
or cloister into which we peer, these poems, deploying all the
resources of phonetic evocation to draw readers into enjoyment of
them, are like the many rivers they describe ('Ganga', 'Nile',
'Indus'); they ask us to drift along with the current of them, to be
carried down their 'stream of gold'.[3] Arthur Hallam was soon to
describe Tennyson as a poet of 'sensation', weaving 'a sort of

---

[1] 'The Poet', 1. [2] 'Persia', 38–40, 37. [3] Ibid. 54, 63, 52.

magic', 'full of deep and varied melodies'.[4] The essence of that kind of writing was to be found in the verse of golden climes.

Since they present eastern and southern lands as realms of imagination and sensory delight, these works evidently inhabit the broad cultural formation of orientalism, in which the West is constructed as the centre of reason and clarity, an ego to the orient's id. For one modern critic, to say 'inhabit' is to put the matter mildly: 'the ultimate threat to remote spaces comes from Tennyson himself . . . The poetic spirit is the advance guard of capitalism and imperialism, and cannot escape this involvement.'[5] This makes it seem that Tennyson's luxuriant descriptions are as straightforwardly complicit in the extension of empire as the gung-ho tales of Captain Marryat or G. A. Henty. Even in the most youthful poems, however, his golden climes differ from the orientalist stereotype. Instead, his exotic locations possess an imposing history; great cities that have flourished and been destroyed, civilizations that have risen and declined, and which make the British Empire look rather small. This grand and melancholy perspective is drawn directly from Byron; once he was at Cambridge, however, Tennyson's representations of distant realms became more his own, and the association between his writing, sensation, and the tropics both more marked and more enquiring. Invaders of what at first seems to be a paradise island, the sailors in 'The Lotos-Eaters' are certainly in the 'advance guard' of imperialism; but Tennyson's representation of them offers little encouragement to prospective colonialists. He shows quite explicitly that they have given in to a lure of sensual indulgence; unnervingly for the reader, the poem reproduces that temptation in the pleasures of its verse. There can be few more entrancing lines of poetry than those which describe the music that has entranced the Lotos-eaters:

> Music that gentlier on the spirit lies,
> Than tired eyelids upon tired eyes;[6]

The delight taken and offered here is more intellectual than that of 'Persia', for coexisting with the lulling phonetic melody ('-lier'

---

[4] *The Writings of Arthur Hallam*, ed. T. H. Vail Motter (New York: Modern Language Association of America, 1943), 186–7.

[5] Alan Sinfield, *Alfred Tennyson* (Oxford: Blackwell, 1986), 39, 50, 53.

[6] 'The Lotos-Eaters', 50–1.

sinking into 'lies', 'tired' on both its appearances stretching out to
fill the space of two syllables, as though spoken through a yawn) is
the startling leap of mind which is embodied in the synaesthetic
image. The suggestion that the music of poetry lulls reason and
virtue to sleep comes up against a recognition that, in order to
notice that suggestion, our eyes and our minds must be wide
awake. This awareness distinguishes the experience offered by
'The Lotos-Eaters' from that offered by the Lotos-eaters. The
poetry of 'sensation' here is of a more complicated kind than that
described by Hallam, for to understand the poem is to see that its
'magic' must be at once felt and resisted.

   The mixed feelings—about poetry, about the senses, and about
the exotic—which appear in the stylistic tension of 'The Lotos-
Eaters' are given discursive elaboration in 'Timbuctoo'. As it
reflects upon the search for the city of its title, which had not been
discovered when it was written, and which for Europeans therefore existed only in rumour and imagination, the poem does
express a thought not unlike 'the poetic spirit is the advance guard
of capitalism and imperialism': the Spirit of Fable, we are told,
teaches 'man . . . to attain | By shadowing forth the Unattainable'.
However, as we read on, the Spirit ceases to look like the herald
of anything worth having: it dwells in 'the intricate and
labyrinthine veins | Of the great vine of *Fable*' which, although
'Deep-rooted in the living soil of truth', produces 'complicated
glooms' and 'cool impleachèd twilights' in which people take
'refuge'.[7] Writing on the same theme, Arthur Hallam had argued
in characteristically up-beat fashion that the imagination fills
unknown places such as Timbuctoo with visions of 'Love, and
Truth, and all that cannot die', all of which are thoroughly 'minis-
trant on good'.[8] Tennyson's sombre image implies a less happy
role for the imaginings in which his poem has itself indulged. Even
when the obscurities of the vine of '*Fable*' are cleared away by
'*Discovery*', unveiling the real city, there is little to rejoice in:
'Black specks amid a waste of dreary sand, | Low-built, mud-
walled, Barbarian settlements'. It seems that the 'Unattainable'
shadowed forth by the Spirit of Fable really is unattainable, and
that people's actual achievements—including the extension of
empire—will inevitably fall short of their dreams. For Tennyson,

---

[7] 'Timbuctoo', 192–3, 217–18, 221, 223–4, 222.   [8] Hallam, *Writings*, 41, 43.

the discovery of Timbuctoo leads to none of the flowerings of civilization or free trade which arise from a similar venture in Harriet Martineau's *Dawn Island* (1845); on the contrary, after the Spirit's departure, 'all was dark!'[9]

Even at the basic level of paraphrase, therefore, these early, exotic poems turn out to be inquisitive about—and tendentially critical of—the orientalist formation which, being written in England in the 1820s and 1830s they could not help but inhabit. Their most remarkable quality, however, is that stylistic detail continually draws attention to the fact that, like most of his readers, Tennyson could visit the locations of these works only in his imagination. He had not been to Persia when, in his mid-to-late teens, he wrote 'Persia'; and indeed he was never to go there: the nearest he ever came to the tropics was Lisbon. The element of literary self-awareness, latent even in the earliest verse, becomes explicit in 'Recollections of the Arabian Nights', a poem which makes available to the reader's imagination the recollection of an experience which was in the first place imagined, having taken place as the speaker read the *Arabian Nights*. Strangely, Arthur Hallam enlists this work in his argument that Tennyson is one of the poets 'of sensation' remarkable for the subtlety and variety of the 'impressions . . . produced on their imaginations by the real appearance of Nature'; he praises the poem for its 'images of exquisite accuracy', despite the fact that neither he nor Tennyson had ever seen the environment in which it knowingly pretends to occur.[10] A recurrent feature of the images is, on the contrary, their artificiality. Grass is like 'damask-work', blooms are 'braided', palm-trees are 'pillared', boughs form a 'dome', rillets are 'diamond', flowers wear 'tiars' (tiaras), and so on: with her 'ebony' hair, 'brow of pearl' and 'argent-lidded eyes', the Persian girl in the penultimate stanza resembles nothing so much as the personification of an inlaid sewing box.[11] The work is less 'a perfect gallery of pictures', as Hallam would have it, than a perfect gallery of pictures of pictures.[12]

'Recollections of the Arabian Nights' admits and puts to expressive use what had always been true of the poems set in

---

[9] 'Timbuctoo', 240, 243–4, 248.　　　　　　[10] Hallam, *Writings*, 187, 193.

[11] 'Recollections of the Arabian Nights', 28, 29, 39, 41, 48, 64, 138, 137, 135.

[12] Hallam, *Writings*, 193.

exotic places: that they show the impression produced on Tennyson by the imaginative experience of reading. While the earliest works do not themselves reflect on this fact, the poems written after 1827 do. Tennyson's insistence that the description of a waterfall 'Slow-dripping veils of thinnest lawn' in 'The Lotos-Eaters' had been drawn from 'Nature herself' does not prevent it from combining with the 'slumbrous <u>sheet</u> of foam' and the '<u>woven</u> copse' to give a distinctly domestic feel to the island, implicitly comparing it to a cosy four-poster.[13] This draws attention to the fact that the poem has been elaborated in the imagination by someone sitting at home in England reading the *Odyssey*, and might therefore have been titled 'Recollections of Homer'. A few years earlier, when he had prefaced 'Timbuctoo' with a couplet ascribed, falsely, to 'Chapman' Tennyson was alluding, not to anything in the works of Chapman himself, but to Keats's sonnet 'On First Looking into Chapman's Homer'. Standing 'upon the Mountain which o'erlooks | The narrow seas', Tennyson's speaker is like Keats's Cortez, staring 'at the Pacific'. Like Keats, the 'realms of gold' in which he has been travelling are the realms of literature.[14]

Even 'Anacaona', at first sight the most reprehensibly orientalist of these works, urges the reader towards a critical appraisal of the sort of dream which it itself quite knowingly embodies. It is, again, a 'recollections' poem, for Tennyson had found his subject in the pages of Washington Irving's *History of the Life and Voyages of Christopher Columbus*. The island queen who has lived on in his mind, 'Warbling in the bloomed liana', 'Wantoning in orange groves | Naked and dark-limbed and gay, | Bathing in the slumbrous coves' has very obviously been adapted to the requirements of desire: pornographically half-veiled by the lines is an indication of where the undergraduate Tennyson and his Cambridge contemporaries (all of course male) doubtless dreamed of bathing their lianas.[15] It seems that this implication did not occur to the pure-minded Arthur Hallam, who was keen to see the work published; Tennyson, however, forbad exposure of what he called 'that black b— Anacaona and her cocoa-shadowed *coves* of

---

[13] 'The Lotos-Eaters', 11, 13, 18; *Memoir*, i. 259.
[14] 'Timbuctoo', 1–2; Keats, 'On First Looking into Chapman's Homer', 12, 1.
[15] 'Anacaona', 1, 5–7.

niggers—I cannot have her strolling about the land in this way—
it is neither good for her reputation nor mine'.[16] While it is itself
frankly racist, his remark also shows he was aware that 'Anacaona'
presents its reader with a fantasy of imperial exploitation. While
straightforward indulgence in the fantasy remains possible, reflec-
tive readers, who notice how the writing so evidently panders to
male desire, will be set thinking about the relation between the
imaginative treatment of Anacaona which is before them and her
unhappy end at the hands of the Spanish. Like 'The Lotos-Eaters',
though in a sourer manner, the poem is designed both to attract
and to repel: the luxuriant images beckon us to enjoy them, but
the insistence, the monotony of their attentions pushes us away.
The 'white men' who appear towards the end of the work look
like fairy-tale representatives of Tennyson and his audience,
'kingly in apparel, | Loftily stepping with fair faces'; as the queen
Anacaona sings for them, the poem 'Anacaona' sings for us. They,
however, silence her, and we . . . ?—we silence the poem when
we reach its end. By eliding the details of her murder, which he
knew from Irving's book, Tennyson produces an unsettling
suggestion about the relationship between cultural exploitation
and imperial violence: it is as though her demise has somehow
been caused by our act of reading.[17]

The portrayal of Tennyson as 'the ultimate threat to remote
spaces' fails to register the complexity of these works. A contrasting view of them as showing the role of 'corrupt European civilization' in destroying 'the idyllic life led by the native inhabitants
of exotic places' is likewise too simple.[18] The poems offer their
readers what are, quite knowingly, imaginative constructs of the
exotic, repositories for all the possibilities of life which seemed to
be excluded from Tennyson's Britain. They therefore set up an
implicit comparison between physical escape to a geographical
elsewhere and mental escape into the realms of the imagination;
and by doing that, they enquire into the ways in which a person's
psychological order is affected by the order of the society he or she
inhabits. To dream of Anacaona or the Lotos is to retreat into an

---

[16] *Poems of Tennyson*, ed. Ricks, ii. 308.

[17] 'Anacaona', 65, 75–6; Washington Irving, *A History of the Life and Times of Christopher
Columbus*, 4 vols. (Paris: A. and W. Galignani, 1828), iii. 407.

[18] Susan Shatto, 'The Strange Charm of "Far, Far Away": Tennyson, the Continent and
the Empire', in Michael Cotsell (ed.), *Creditable Warriors* (Ashfield Press, 1990), 123.

antisocial realm of self-gratification, and there to indulge the un-
English elements which, as we saw in the last chapter, lurk within
every English person. Equally, the venting of such impulses in
imagination may allow people to be all the more English in their
actual behaviour. The poems both are, and are about, the dreams
on whose suppression the maintenance of the English character
depends.

This aspect of Tennyson's tropical verse, essential though inex-
plicit in all the examples of the genre written after 1827, is made
plain in a lyric of 1833: 'warmer sky' and 'purple seas' offer a
tempting prospect which, the speaker says, he would take up were
it not that he thinks free speech to be more important than the
liberty to wander and wonder.[19] Five years later, the speaker of
'Locksley Hall', whose libidinal impulses have been denied the
scope of marriage, reacts more violently both to the lure of the
tropics and to the contrasting imperative to identify with the
values of his nation: 'I will take some savage woman, she shall rear
my dusky race' he fantasizes (perhaps in the wake of an uncritical
reading of 'Anacaona'); only to repress the vision with iron
resolve: 'Fool, again the dream, the fancy! but I *know* my words
are wild'.[20] Like *Amours de Voyage*, the poems which I have been
discussing investigate the pressures exerted on an individual by
attachment to a nation, as well as the opposing forces which
Clough presented in the more respectable guise of 'individual
culture'. In Clough's poem, the lines of conflict are mainly drawn
between Claude, the single human being, and the social expectations by which he is surrounded. The struggles which interest
Tennyson, by contrast, take place within a personality, for in his
view—as we saw in the last chapter—to build a national identity
was to build a character.

After the passing of the Reform Bill (1832), and Hallam's death
(1833), Tennyson's imagination generally turned away from the
realms of gold, and confined itself to works which securely manifest the communal Englishness elaborated in 'Hail Briton!' and
'Love thou thy land', the Englishness of 'common sense',
'Reverence', 'sober-suited Freedom', and so on.[21] The 'English
Idyls' have been well described as upholding 'the linked orders of

---

[19] 'You ask me, why, though ill at ease', 26, 4.   [20] 'Locksley Hall', 168, 173.
[21] 'Hail Briton!', 41, 44; 'You ask me, why, though ill at ease', 6.

a rural social hierarchy and a "nobly simple" English poetics'.[22] Consequently, they register the problems of identity and cohesion which were central to the time of nation-building mainly by shutting them out. In *The Princess* (1847), Tennyson again ventures on golden climes, exploring the relationship between someone of 'Southern' and someone of 'Northern' nationality. As its influence on *Aurora Leigh* would suggest, this work is much concerned with the unity and disunity of 'ever-broadening England'.

DREAM NARRATIVE: THE PRINCESS

A reader of Tennyson's early, tropical verse is nudged into understanding that the poems are creatively aware of their own fictionality; readers of *The Princess* have the self-conscious fictionality of its central narrative proclaimed to them. The story told by the group of undergraduates in the ruins of an abbey on a summer's day is a dream not only of the south. In addition to the fantastical southern princess—who is in the tradition of Anacaona although more warmly dressed—there is a fantastical northern prince, and the fantasy of a *rapprochement* between the two. Instead of the venting in imagination of un-English impulses, there is a melding in imagination of the English and the Other. The Prologue maps out these large, symbolic ramifications of a narrative whose central and explicit subject is 'the higher education of women'.[23] Admitted to the grounds of Vivian Place on an open day are representatives of the masses, 'the multitude, a thousand heads', who, like Ida's women in her palace, are there for the purpose of education. We are encouraged, therefore, to find in the story of the Princess's revolt and reconciliation a warning to Chartists, Saint-Simonians, or anyone else who would challenge the established social order from below. In the house itself, a display of ethnographic artefacts leads our thoughts towards another tendentially rebellious area of ever-broadening England. There are the fruits of empire— 'Laborious orient ivory'—and its spoils: 'cursed Malayan crease, and battle-clubs | From the isles of palm'.[24] As Coventry Patmore

---

[22] Helsinger, *Rural Scenes*, 77.
[23] *Memoir*, i. 249; for the poem's bearing female education, see John Killham, *Tennyson and The Princess: Reflections of an Age* (Athlone Press, 1958).
[24] *P*, Prologue, 57, 20–2.

observed in a review, however, the pursuit of these implications is not straightforward, for the main narrative 'at first appears to have not the remotest connexion with the matters obviously hinted at in the "prologue" '.

Patmore went on to propose a full-scale allegorical reading, in which Ida represents 'the passive or feminine principle of the intellect' and the Prince the 'powers of higher activity and authority'; the story of their relationship is connected to the world of the Prologue, he suggests, because 'the all important characteristic of the age we live in' is 'the vast struggle which has long been in progress against authority of every possible kind'.[25] While so rigid an interpretation is evidently reductive, it remains true that the story is handled in such a way as to guide a reader's mind in the direction of, if not allegory, at least a hazier, 'parabolic' understanding of the sort that Tennyson proposed for *Idylls of the King*.[26] The two countries which make up the narrative's world are referred to only as 'North' and 'South', the initial capitals suggesting that those words should be taken as names as well as locations. This bare nomenclature imparts a schematism to the poem's geography, opening the way for a series of hints that the two countries should be seen as spatial representations of the two genders. Ida was born in the South, but when she starts acting out what in the poem's standards are her masculine ideas she moves to a palace right on the frontier between the two States; in consequence, having travelled far south to Gama's court, the Prince's party then has to ride 'many a long league back to the North' in order to catch up with her.[27] In the liminal area she has made her own, Ida is left free to pursue her ambition of equalizing the genders; and the Northern men are at liberty to parody it by cross-dressing. At the vertices of North and South, by contrast, gender has imposed itself strongly: the King of the Northerners is 'rough', much given to roaring, and promotes an unembarrassedly basic variety of patriarchy: 'Man is the hunter; woman is his game.'[28] The Southern King, Gama, has contrasting verbal habits, and must submit to having his and his sons' gender altered by the operation of metaphor: ' "Boys!" shrieked the old king, but vainlier than a hen

---

[25] (Coventry Patmore), 'Tennyson's *Poems—The Princess*', *North British Review*, 9/17 (May 1848), 65–9.   [26] *Memoir*, ii. 127.

[27] *P* I. 147, 166.   [28] *P* I. 86; V. 147.

| To her false daughters in the pool'. 'Not like a king', the Prince has earlier observed, clearing a space for the unwritten thought, 'but like a queen'.[29] This is different from the play with gender which takes place on the border because it is not willed: Gama and his family live in something like a climate of femininity which has affected their growth, promoting Ida and stunting her father, who is reduced to a 'little dry old man'.[30]

However, the apparent conflation of gender and nationality founders with the description of Gama's sons, who are huge: 'nor ever had I seen | Such thews of men', the Prince marvels. They are required to be super-manly in this way because they must be allowed to defeat the Prince in the tournament without too catastrophically diminishing him. Tennyson attempts to harmonize this requirement of the plot with his gendered geography by giving the enormous southerners some feminine touches: 'lightly pranced | Three captains' shifts the delicacy of movement from their horses to the men themselves; they are then compared to stars; their armour is said to be nicely 'washed with morning', and about the eldest, Arac, clings the 'shadow of his sister'.[31] Nonetheless, in their presence the tentative allegory disappears. This fading-in-and-out of an implication is characteristic of Tennyson's 'parabolic' mode, and is what distinguishes it from allegory proper. The method's virtue is that it draws attention to the way in which different categories of understanding overlap— in this case, to the fact that national identities included gendered elements, while differences between the genders could be thought analogous to those between nationalities—without forcing the two terms into a false relationship of absolute equivalence.

The flexible layering of gender and nationality in the world of *The Princess* brings the poem into contact with the issue of relations, within the Empire, between 'southern' and 'northern' nations. The effeminate Gama (whose name directs our thoughts towards India in the wake of Vasco da Gama) manifests that 'want of truthfulness' which British administrators typically found in Indians: he leaves the Prince 'nettled that he seemed to slur | With garrulous ease and oily courtesies | Our formal compact', a remark

---

[29] *P* V. 318–19; I. 117. 'Queen' took on the meaning 'homosexual' in the 'late C19', according to Eric Partridge, *A Dictionary of Slang and Unconventional English*, ed. Paul Beale (Routledge and Kegan Paul, 1984). [30] *P* I. 116.
[31] *P* V. 245–6, 244–5, 254, 248.

which, with the implicitly racist feeling gathered around 'oily', precisely evokes the budding of misunderstanding between representatives of different ethnic groups.[32] Ida's racial type is the subject of an insinuation: she looks, we are told, 'liker to the inhabitant | Of some clear planet close upon the Sun, | Than our man's earth'. Therefore she is dark-skinned, we might assume, especially as the description has a root in the words of the Prince of Morocco in the *Merchant of Venice*, who tells Portia, 'Mislike me not for my complexion, | The shadowed liuerie of the burnisht sunne, | To whom I am a neighbour, and neere bred' (he then goes on to compare himself favourably to 'the fairest creature North-ward borne', an avatar of Tennyson's Prince). However, the word 'clear', in the account of the Princess, pushes against this implication, as do the succeeding lines which veer away from skin-colour into the uncontentious terms of 'grace and power', and include no more details of her appearance.[33] Inter-racial marriages often featured in contemporary imperialist melodramas:[34] while his imagination does reach out in that direction, it appears that Tennyson—the author of 'Locksley Hall'—was not able to envisage such a prospect with equanimity.

Cross-dressing, the Prince and his companions likewise take a step in the direction of contemporary melodrama, in which transvestism often featured both as a means of airing anxieties about the effects on personal identity of contact with the Other and as a mechanism by which a narrative of the extension of power could be advanced.[35] On the nineteenth-century stage, as on Shakespeare's, disguise could be used to figure the pervasiveness and cunning of established political rule. In the melodramas, bands of British frequently appeared, like the Prince and his two friends, as ' "we happy few"—outnumbered and therefore in the right'.[36] Like characters from a novel by Captain Marryat (*Masterman Ready* was published in 1841), the protagonists of Tennyson's boys' own adventure demonstrate the pluck and occasional duplicity necessary

---

[32] Trevelyan, *The Competition Wallah*, 259; *P* I. 161–3.

[33] *P* II. 21–3, 24; *The Merchant of Venice*, II. i: *Shakespeares Comedies, Histories, & Tragedies*, 185.

[34] Heidi J. Holder, 'Melodrama, Realism and Empire on the British Stage', in J. S. Bratton *et al.*, *Acts of Supremacy: The British Empire and the Stage, 1790–1830* (Manchester: Manchester University Press, 1991), 132.   [35] Ibid.

[36] J. S. Bratton, 'British Heroism and the Structure of Melodrama', in Bratton (ed.), *Acts of Supremacy*, 25.

for the successful imperialist. They search out the weak point in the Princess's regime, their own co-national Psyche; urging her childhood memories and 'ancient ties', they persuade her to recognize the priority of her original ethnic identity over her new loyalty to Ida. That bridgehead gained, they secure Blanche with a promise of advancement as though she were a dissatisfied potentate in the court of a Maharajah: 'I find you here but in the second place . . . | I offer boldly: we will set you highest'. At a later stage, when the Northern King has arrived with reinforcements, the Prince shows an aptitude for strategy on a grander scale, advising his father against starting a battle because it would cause resentment amongst the local population: ' "lest from the abuse of war . . . | A smoke go up through which I loom to her | Three times a monster." ' *The Princess*'s lessons in statecraft would not have been out of place in Machiavelli's *The Prince*.[37]

This imperial aspect of the narrative expands on the hint made by the ethnographical collection in the Prologue, and suggests a topical relevance to colonial policy. The 1840s saw a change of mood about the degree to which Britain should be involved in the running of its colonies. In 1839, Lord Durham's *Report on the Affairs of British North America* had recommended that Canada should be allowed greater powers of self-rule: these were conceded gradually during the early years of the decade until full cabinet government for domestic matters was formally established in 1848. As we saw in the last chapter, the policy was gradually extended to most of the white colonies, but not to the Empire's black and Asian subjects. Durham expected that his proposals would lead to 'a perfect subordination' of the colonies to the mother country once they realized that their interests lay in that direction. Tennyson agreed: as his son records, 'he gloried in the work done by Lord Durham and in the form of Colonial Government initiated by him in Canada'. Die-hard Tories, on the other hand, were furious at what seemed to them a weakening of Britain's power.[38] Ida's rejection of the 'formal compact' which

---

[37] *P* II. 245; III. 141–3; V. 120–5. The echo between the two titles is noted in Christopher Ricks, *Tennyson*, 2nd edn. (Macmillan, 1989), 179, where it is related to Prince Albert.

[38] *The Report of the Earl of Durham, Her Majesty's High Commissioner and Governor General of British North America: A New Edition* (Methuen and Co., 1902), 208; *Memoir*, i. 185 n.; *The Report of the Earl of Durham*, xvi.

bound her to the Prince, and her bid for total independence, might be a Tory nightmare about the consequences of allowing the colonies freedom of the sort that Gama has afforded to her.[39] On the other hand, the Prince, who urges reverence for the established order while at the same time recognizing Ida's aspirations for development, might be a fairy-tale Lord Durham. These parallels need not have been present to Tennyson's consciousness as he wrote the poem; they may not even have occurred to any contemporary reader. What they do show, however, is the degree to which Tennyson's mind conceived of relations between men and women and between Britain and the colonies in overlapping terms. To think of one was inevitably to bring in the other. The version of gender-relations offered in the Prince's visionary speech, 'Not like to like, but like in difference', though 'in the long years liker must they grow', anticipates the model of empire which Tennyson was to promote with increasing vigour as he advanced in years: 'the most intimate union of every part of our British Empire . . . with a heightening of individuality to each member'.[40] Certainly the comparison cannot be pressed too far: it would be misplaced, because too specific, to connect (say) the physiological differences between men and women to the supposed disparities between different 'races'. The Prince leaves it diplomatically unclear just how much 'liker' Man and Woman are to grow in future years, and just how thorough is to be the corresponding merger between North and South, and indeed just how precise is the analogy between these two prospects. On both levels the immediate terms of the relationship seem comparatively liberal. Prince and Princess both discover that they need one another in order to become truly themselves, although with his image of Woman as 'music' to Man's 'noble words', the Prince suggests that he will retain a controlling voice in the otherwise equal partnership.[41] With regard to the Empire, this implies a union rather like that which Arnold was later to propose for the United Kingdom in *On the Study of Celtic Literature*.

As he gathered his thoughts in the months before he began sustained work on *The Princess*, Tennyson can hardly have failed to

---

[39] *P* I. 163.   [40] *P* VII. 262–3; *Memoir*, ii. 223 n.

[41] *P* VII. 270.

notice an instance of cross-dressing which was much in the news. In June 1843 *The Times* carried very full reports of the so-called 'Rebecca Riots' which had been taking place in Wales. Under the leadership of 'Rebecca', a man in women's clothes, agricultural workers attacked toll-gates and workhouses, both of which they considered to be unjust sources of taxation. The origin of 'Rebecca' is mysterious, but certainly he/she developed into an impressive figure of anarchy, the transgression of the order of gender shadowing the attacks on the order of society. The riots may well have added something to Tennyson's thoughts as he wrote of the Prince and his companions donning 'female gear' so as to transgress Ida's boundaries, and he may perhaps have associated *The Times*'s 'redoubtable Rebecca' with his own Ida, 'Grand, epic, homicidal'.[42] More striking, however, is the similarity between the language directed at 'Rebecca' by members of the establishment and the Prince's speech to Ida. One Mr Hall, a barrister representing some of the agitators, published in *The Times* a letter to 'Rebecca', in which he attributed the unrest to 'ignorance, which prevents you from being able to guide in its proper course the great and irresistible force which you possess. A hundredth part of your strength, properly applied, will do more for you, and without risk, than a thousand times your power wasted in the absurdities you have lately indulged in. Be guided by me. Do what I tell you, and you must be victorious in the end.'[43] Before long, events began to develop along the lines Mr Hall suggested. A Government Commission was established; Rebecca's grievances were heard within the pale of the law; some concessions were made, and order was re-established. It was the same strategy of compromise for the sake of containment that had been adopted by Lord Durham in Canada, and that was soon to be deployed by Tennyson's Prince. 'Come, | Yield thyself up: my hopes and thine are one', as he says, securing Ida's obedience by adopting a reduced and deferred version of her aspirations.[44] The fact that Ida has previously defeated him, which makes her a more successful threat to authority than either Rebecca or the Canadian rebels, only goes to enforce the poem's ideological contention. As it appears from the narrative, she—and all the rebellious forces for

---

[42] *The Times*, no. 18329 (22 June 1843), 5–6; *P* I. 196; Prologue, 219.
[43] *The Times*, no. 18331 (24 June 1843), 7.   [44] *P* VII. 342–3.

which she is a figurehead—must always yield to the Prince and everything he represents, for the necessity of obedience is inscribed within her: 'something wild within her breast, | A greater than all knowledge, beat her down'.[45]

Like *Aurora Leigh*, a work which it greatly influenced, *The Princess* has an obvious ideological project, but of a contrasting tendency. Although both poems tell stories of compromise, *Aurora Leigh*'s two protagonists end up in a feminine space outside the established social order, *The Princess*'s under masculine guidance within it. Barrett Browning asks us to identify with Aurora—a second Ida—and to give our allegiance to the more liberal pattern of life which she initiates in Italy. It is as though we and the Prince were all to end up joining Ida's university and sharing her vision of freedom broadcast over all the world. Tennyson expects his readers to adopt the point of view of the Prince, his narrator, who is left unnamed (like his father) so as to promote familiarity. For 'the Prince' read 'our Prince'; whereas 'Princess Ida' is a foreign creature who must be given a specific label. Urging us to take sides in this way, the poem also encourages us to feel that an aesthetically pleasing conclusion to the work will require the fulfilment of the Prince's hopes. It is therefore true of Tennyson's poem, as has been said of Renaissance plays, that 'the form itself . . . helps to contain the radical doubts it . . . provokes'.[46] As with Shakespeare's histories, we can speak of *The Princess* as 'appropriating' the 'practices' of political power, the Prince's strategies towards the Princess reproducing those of the government towards Canada and towards Rebecca, not necessarily because Tennyson was explicitly thinking of those particular cases, but because the poem is 'implicated' in the processes by which the established order is maintained.

However, the relationships which can exist between readers and texts are different from those which may pertain between members of a theatre audience and a play that is being performed. As we have seen, other nineteenth-century poets drew attention to the part-public, part-private nature of reading as a way of raising questions about individuals and groups, Clough in particular assessing the value of 'individual culture' by configuring reading as an invasion of privacy. Tennyson, on the other hand, disavows as

---

[45] *P* VII. 222–3.   [46] Greenblatt, *Shakespearean Negotiations*, 65.

much as possible the private aspect of his text, asking his readers to think of themselves as members of a community. The crowds at Vivian Place offer us an image of our own entry into the garden of Tennyson's imagination, and when we follow the privileged party into the ruined abbey, we are asked to identify with the set of acquaintances who then form both audience and actors of a lyrico-narrative performance. This is different from the unconventional family of readers imagined in *Aurora Leigh*, and different also from the *Ring and the Book*'s construction of its readers as a society of distinct individuals whose views are likely to differ as much as those of the work's many narrators. Tennyson's narrative does have different speakers, but his early idea that they should be distinctly characterized, and that their differences should be related to identifiably distinct phases in the story, has entirely disappeared. As it stands, the suggestion of the narrative form is that individuals become one in the narration of the story, which therefore assumes the collective status of myth. In Browning's terms, we are 'All in one tale, each singing the same song'.[47]

Essential to this effect is the poem's concentration on royals. *Aurora Leigh*, *Amours de Voyage,* and *The Ring and the Book* all give voice to characters from the bourgeoisie as well as from the gentry; indeed, the relation between aristocratic and middle-class values is in each work a central concern. With Marian Erle, *Aurora Leigh* takes a further step down the social scale: however idealized one judges her character to be, at least it is there, and plays a major part. The only roles in *The Princess* that are neither aristocratic nor royal are cameos, and caricatured ones at that: 'mine host' in part I, and the 'eight mighty daughters of the plough' who are on security duty in part IV.[48] This means that Tennyson's poem operates according to a different system of representation. Browning and Clough broadened the boundaries of their realms of verse to include—roughly—the sort of people who would have been given the vote by the Reform Act of 1832; and Barrett Browning went a stage further. Members of different ranks of society were represented in those poems by people like themselves. In the terms of rhetoric we can call this 'metonymical' representation; in terms of politics, 'democratic' (though guardedly so in the cases of Browning and Clough). *The Princess*, by contrast, offers its readers

---

[47] See above, Chapter 7.   [48] *P* I. 171; IV. 528.

symbolic or monarchical representation. We are invited to
become subjects, preferably of the North—but of the South if we
must—and to recognize Prince and Princess as representing our
thoughts, interests, and desires symbolically, in the way monarchs
represent their people.

   If we had been following *The Times*'s reports of Rebecca in the
last week of June 1843, on Thursday 29th we would have found
that she had been knocked off the page by an account of 'THE
MARRIAGE OF HER ROYAL HIGHNESS THE PRINCESS AUGUSTA' to the
Grand Duke of Mecklenburgh Strelitz. Prominent throughout this
report is order of the kind that Rebecca was committed to disturb-
ing. Diagrams represent the positions taken up by different ranks
in the procession, 'the way being marshalled by Garter King of
Arms and the Heralds'; different elements of the ritual take place
in different locations, and the movements between them are carefully noted; as for gender, the behaviour of Duke and Princess
foreshadows the end of Tennyson's poem: 'the bridegroom
evinced great self-possession, and gave the responses in a firm and
audible tone. The responses of the bride were not heard.'[49]
Enacted on that day was a pageant of order at the heart of empire,
standing symbolically in contrast to the upheavals in Canada, in
Wales, and indeed upheavals anywhere, and of any kind.

   In *The Princess*, both rebellion and reconciliation have the broad
symbolic scope of a royal wedding. They are connected to social
unrest, to the Empire, and even—so lines inserted in 1850 maintain—the French, who with their perpetual revolutions are 'Like
our wild Princess with as wise a dream'.[50] This multiplicity of relevance is achieved at the cost of precision; but its virtue is in the
light it casts on the ideological interconnections between different
elements within the social whole. The narrative argues that the
fulfilment of individuals, both women and men, is to be found in
marriage of the kind that will be lived out by Ida and the Prince;
and that the endurance of such relationships requires the establishment of a similar union within the United Kingdom; and that the
success of that union in turn requires a similar unification of the
Empire. The story, therefore, advances a very powerful—because
nebulous—version of the analogy between marital and political
union which I described in Chapter 3. To this web of implication,

---

[49] *The Times*, no. 18335 (29 June 1843), 4–5.   [50] *P*, Conclusion, 69.

we can add Patmore's suggestion about psychology, although his allegorical rigour must be abandoned. *The Princess* envisages an accommodation between the rebellious, Southern, feminine, imaginative forces which Tennyson had investigated in his early exotic poems, and the harmonious order of both individual and society—the one relying on the other—which he had elaborated in 'Love thou thy land'.

By presenting the central narrative as a tale told by a group of undergraduates whose socio-political assumptions are freed, on a summer's afternoon, from much challenging contact with the actual, Tennyson prompts his readers to recognize that the story takes place in what we might call a realm of ideological abstraction. The narrative is concerned, not with particular southern and northern countries, but with South and North; not with a distinctively characterized man and woman, but with Prince and Princess, Man and Woman. Readers are asked to think of themselves as being drawn together in allegiance to and admiration of the central myth, as being turned into members of a community of feeling like the audience of a Renaissance theatre. However, the fact that the narrative reaches us in print rather than on stage, so that we have to *imagine* ourselves into the position of members of an audience, rather than just finding ourselves there, means that the poem, as it urges us to accept its values also makes quite clear to us that that is what it is doing. It need not follow that, as one critic has suggested, The Princess should be read as 'skeptical if not critical' of the ideal of reconciliation which it offers;[51] only that it makes plain to readers that what is being offered is, precisely, an ideal which, in being removed from the real, has connections to it which are all the more multifarious.

A NATIONAL TEXTURE

Released from the constraints of realism, the central narrative of *The Princess* occupies a space of formal and generic liberty. The scribe who is said to have 'drest it up poetically' explains that he has 'moved as in a strange diagonal' between heroic and burlesque; the structure of the work itself establishes two other generic poles between which the narrative makes its conciliatory way.[52] Already

---

[51] Helsinger, *Rural Scenes*, 97.   [52] *P*, Conclusion, 6, 27.

in the first edition blank-verse lyrics were at three climactic points
incorporated into the body of the narrative; from the third edition
onwards the insertion of rhymed verses between the different parts
of the tale, to be sung by the women of the party, sets up a frame
of association between gender and genre upon which the story
then elaborates. The women sing 'Between the rougher voices of
the men, | Like linnets in the pauses of the wind', thereby intro-
ducing a suggestion which is seconded in the narrative: when
Psyche rises 'upon a wind of prophecy' she soon has it taken out
of her sails: 'as when a boat | Tacks, and the slackened sail flaps'.[53]
Ida too has the 'passion of the prophetess' and intends to 'trim our
sails' so as to forge ahead into the future; and she is similarly let
down.[54]

The Prince is the story's narrator, but the perfect equation
between gender and genre which that implies is complicated by
the fact that from the outset he is associated with the tendentially
lyric qualities of love and reminiscence. When, on the geological
expedition, he sings his lyric of the swallow, Ida rebukes him (or
her, as she still takes him to be), for producing 'A mere love-
poem!'[55] Ida herself—like the Barrett Browning of *Casa Guidi
Windows*—prefers a different mode of verse, prophecy, which,
although directed to the future, rather than the present or the past,
is still a variety of lyric. It is as though her neglect of the other
possible tenses of what *The Princess* assumes to be woman's natural
genre has obliged the Prince to occupy them. The ineptitude of
his singing, however, suggests that they do not suit him; when, in
part VII, Ida discovers herself through reading lyrics of love, there
is no longer a need for him to desert his commanding narrative
role.

The end of the story, however, is not an unmitigated triumph
for the narrative genre. Like *Aurora Leigh*, the tale comes to an end
in the present tense of speech. In the Prince's closing words to Ida
the distinction between narrative and lyric subsides:

> . . . Dear,
> Look up, and let thy nature strike on mine,
> Like yonder morning on the blind half-world;
> Approach and fear not; breathe upon my brows;

[53] *P*, Prologue, 237–8; II. 154, 168–9.   [54] *P* IV. 122, 51.
[55] *P* IV. 108.

In that fine air I tremble, all the past
Melts mist-like into this bright hour, and this
Is morn to more, and all the rich to-come
Reels, as the golden Autumn woodland reels
Athwart the smoke of burning weeds. . . .[56]

This describes a single moment—so far, so lyric—yet one through which the processes of time, narratively linking past, present, and future, appear to travel. Exceptionally strong phonetic cohesion makes the words continue into one another: 'Melts mist-like' (as though they themselves were melting), or 'mist . . . this . . . this | is . . . rich', or 'morn . . . more . . . all . . . Autumn . . . Athwart'. The vision and the movement of the verse combine to suggest a stasis which persists through change, in the manner of the lines about nationhood which I discussed in Chapter 3: 'Love thou thy land, with love far-brought | From out the storied Past, and used | Within the Present, but transfused | Through future time by power of thought'.

Tennyson may have taken some hints towards this reconciliation of lyric and narrative genres from a work he had certainly read: Henry Taylor's long 'dramatic romance' in verse, *Philip Van Artevelde* (1834), which narrates the utter failure of a revolt against established power, and whose ideological position is in consequence staunchly Tory.[57] Mid-way through the many hundred pages of dramatic blank verse, there occurs a rhymed lyrical 'interlude' which represents '*an interwoven thread | Of feminine affection fancy-fed*'. This soon turns out to have been sung by Elena, '*an Italian Lady*' who then becomes romantically involved with Philip, the revolutionary protagonist. Her influence is disastrous; the implication being that as Taylor has kept his lyric interlude clearly separate from the dramatic blank verse in which '*matters masculine*' are dealt with, so women, especially ones from dubious southern places such as Italy, should keep away from politics.[58] The remarkable imaginative force which Tennyson imparts to his more generous, progressive-and-yet-conservative vision may have drawn some impetus from his disagreement with Taylor. Certainly he made similar, though more profound and subtle, connections between genre, gender, and political stance.

[56] *P* VII. 329–37.   [57] See Armstrong, *Victorian Poetry*, 100–1.
[58] Henry Taylor, *Philip Van Artevelde: A Dramatic Romance*, 2 vols. (Edward Moxon, 1834), i. 264; ii, p. iii; i. 287.

Other linguistic unifications are achieved in the Prince's remarkably assimilative final lines. In his essay 'The Influence of Italian upon English Literature', Arthur Hallam had observed that rhyme 'appears to be the creation of Southern climates: for the Southern languages abound in vowels, and rhyme is the resonance of vowels, while the Northern overflow with consonants and naturally fall into alliteration'.[59] The Northern Prince shows himself to be a master of internal rhyme, marrying it happily to the alliteration which, in Hallam's view, is more natural to him ('breathe . . . brows . . . bright . . . burning', 'melts mist- . . . morn . . . more'). Elsewhere in his essay, when discussing a passage of Shakespeare, Hallam proposes that 'the equipoise of Southern and Northern phraseology creates a natural harmony, a setting of full base to keen treble', and goes on to say that he looks with reverence 'to the bonds by which the Law of the Universe has fastened me to my distant brethren of the same Caucasian race; to the privileges which I, as an inhabitant of the gloomy North, share in common with climates imparadised in perpetual summer'.[60] By 'Southern and Northern phraseology' he means words derived respectively from the romance languages and from Anglo-Saxon. Hallam was writing at the very beginning of a widespread surge of interest in English etymology and its relation to national history. Soon, the Philological Society of London was founded (1842): in 1859 it resolved to produce a new English dictionary, now the *OED*. Soon, Hallam's and Tennyson's friend R. C. Trench published *On the Study of Words* (1851) and *English Past and Present* (1855), and F. Max Müller his *Lectures on the Science of Language* (1861–4).[61] In the retrospective light of these developments, Hallam's analysis looks rudimentary. Nonetheless, the *Memoir* shows that Tennyson made a similarly blunt distinction with regard to the language of the *Idylls*: 'if he differentiated his style from that of any other poet, he would remark on his use of English—in preference to words derived from French and Latin.'[62]

Tennyson's linguistic preferences, however, had not always been the same. In his review of *Poems, Chiefly Lyrical* (1830),

---

[59] Hallam, *Writings*, 222.   [60] Ibid. 215–16.
[61] See Hans Aarsleff, *The Study of Language in England, 1780–1860* (Athlone Press, 1967; repr. 1979), 230–47.   [62] *Memoir*, ii. 133 n.

Hallam had with reason praised the volume for its employment of all the elements of the 'compound language': 'we see no signs in what Mr Tennyson has written of the Quixotic spirit which has led some persons to desire the reduction of English to a single form, by excluding nearly the whole of Latin and Roman derivatives'—precisely the spirit by which Tennyson was later to be animated.[63] His earliest poems relish the presence in the language of that southern phraseology which was largely to be exiled from the *Idylls*: 'Immense, sublime, magnificent, profound!' for instance, or 'Dome on Dome repose in placid light | Imperially beautiful'.[64] Those Romance words bring with them a feeling, less of southernness, than of grandeur: the first quotation describes Niagara Falls, while the second gives a view of Moscow. However, when such words are used in a southern context, their own southernness becomes more notable a trait. For instance: 'Tressèd with redolent ebony, | In many a dark delicious curl'. Since the poem is set in the world of the Arabian Nights, and these lines describe a 'Persian girl', we are encouraged to remark on the aptness of the metaphor, ebony being an oriental wood, and perhaps also on the origins of 'redolent' and 'delicious' which have a phonetically exotic lilt about them as well as being etymologically Latinate.[65] The words' meanings and rhythms combine with their derivations to produce a southern 'feel'. The gauging of such a 'feel' would ideally require a critic who, like the 'well-educated gentleman' described by Ruskin in *Sesame and Lilies* (though preferably less fraught with class prejudice) 'is learned in the *peerage* of words; knows the words of true descent and ancient blood, at a glance, from words of modern canaille; remembers all their ancestry, their intermarriages, distant relationships, and the extent to which they were admitted, and offices they held, among the national noblesse of words at any time, and in any country'.[66]

In the strongly polarized world of *The Princess*, it seems reasonable to expect, not that southern and northern phraseology will be massed, as it were, in different armies (in any case a linguistic impossibility), but that the distinction between them might, on particular occasions, take on expressive salience. It does appear that

---

[63] Hallam, *Writings*, 198.
[64] 'On Sublimity', 78; 'The Invasion of Russia by Napoleon Buonaparte', 30–1.
[65] 'Recollections of the Arabian Nights', 138–9, 134.
[66] Ruskin, *Works*, xviii. 65.

northern words cluster around the Northern king, as for instance
when he deals with the gift from the South:

> . . . he started on his feet,
> Tore the king's letter, snowed it down, and rent
> The wonder of the loom through warp and woof
> From skirt to skirt; . . .[67]

('Letter' here is the only clear Latinate; 'rent' arrived via old
French in the twelfth century, though as a monosyllable it already
had the beginnings of an English character, which will have
increased with age.) There are plenty of Romance words that
Tennyson could have selected if he had wished to give a different
feel to this description: 'he rose erect, dismembered the letter,
released the pieces on the air, sundered the textured miracle from
border to border, marge to marge' (to give an extreme version);
that he has opted almost entirely for northern phraseology, that he
has gone out of his way to employ 'snow' and 'skirt' metaphori-
cally (the latter suggesting the Northern king's habitual misogyny),
and that he has given 'to start' something like its Old English
meaning of 'to leap', suggests that the northernness of the language
should be felt as having expressive force. Gama employs a contrasting diction:

> . . . we esteem you for it.—
> He seems a gracious and a gallant Prince,
> I would he had our daughter: for the rest,
> Our own detention, why, the causes weighed,
> Fatherly fears—you used us courteously—
> We would do much to gratify your Prince—
> We pardon it; and for your ingress here[68]

'Gracious' rather than 'well-mannered'; 'gallant', not 'brave';
'detention' (first use, *c.*1570, probably direct from Latin) instead of
the less southern 'imprisonment' (already in Middle English);
'courteously', not 'kindly'; 'gratify' (*c.*1540), not 'please' (Middle
English); 'pardon', not 'forgive'; 'ingress', not 'inroad': all clearly
drawn from the southern reaches of the language.

Ida also has occasional outbreaks of southern phraseology: 'We
give you welcome: not without redound | Of use and glory to
yourselves ye come', as she says to the freshers, with a pomposity

[67] *P* I. 59–62.   [68] *P* V. 203–9.

which seems unusual even for the principal of a college.[69] In his youth, Tennyson had found such Miltonic diction straightfor-wardly impressive: 'O thou omnipotent Love whose boundless sway | And uncontrolled dominion boweth down | The Spirits of the Mighty'.[70] No longer. One of the students in the Prologue, had 'clamoured' for the heroine of their tale to be 'some great Princess, six feet high, | Grand, epic, homicidal'; Ida's magnilo-quent first words reach back to and seem to fulfil that vision, inseparably Latinate and mock-heroic.[71] This opening suggestion, however, is not sustained. It may just possibly be that we should be struck by a cluster of harmonious Latinates at the end of the lyric by which she is finally overcome:

> Myriads of rivulets hurrying through the lawn,
> The moan of doves in immemorial elms,
> And murmuring of innumerable bees.[72]

In the light of Hallam's remark about climates imparadised in perpet-ual summer it seems apt that so many of the words productive of so summery a vision should be of Romance origin; but obviously the feel of this writing owes more to phonetics than to etymology.

In *English Past and Present*, Trench describes the creation of the English language as one of 'the great acts of that nation to which we belong'; 'love of our language', he says, 'is but the love of our own country expressing itself in one particular direction'. It is not surprising, therefore, that his description of the language should draw its terms from a particular conception of the English nation. Of the translators of the Authorized Version of the Bible, he observes: 'they gave to the Latin side of the language its rights, though they would not suffer it to encroach upon and usurp those of the Teutonic part of the language.' This was a particularly happy compromise because 'Anglo-Saxon' is the 'foundation' of the English language, its 'basis'; and as such is a force for stability: 'wherever the passion of a poem is of that sort which *uses, presumes,* or *postulates* . . . ideas, without seeking to extend them, Saxon will be the "cocoon" . . . which the poem spins for itself.' Latinates, on the other hand, suggest 'the motion of the feeling'.[73] English, the

---

[69] *P* II. 28–9.
[70] 'The Devil and the Lady', 14–16.
[71] *P*, Prologue, 218–19.
[72] *P* VII. 205–7.
[73] R. C. Trench, *English Past and Present: Five Lectures* (John W. Parker and Son, 1855), 1–2, 26, 16, 22.

compound language, embodies a typically 'English' compromise
between stasis and change.

Trench does not mean his distinctions to be taken absolutely; and
Tennyson's imagination was of course alert to many other aspects of
words in addition to their etymology. Nonetheless, if, as he well
might, Trench had looked into *The Princess* when he was composing his volume, he would have found evidence in support of his
claims. In the Conclusion (from the third edition onwards) one of
the story-tellers looks across the channel towards the upheavals of
1848: 'mock heroics stranger than our own; | Revolts, republics,
revolutions'.[74] The Parisian wild dreams have that ring of comical
over-ambition which previously had characterized the Princess,
grand, epic, homicidal. In this context one can certainly hear the
Romance words pressing into the language, asserting their rights
with dangerously subversive force: 'révoltes, républiques, révolu-
tions'. This speaker, the 'Tory member's eldest son', deploys a line
of (mostly) solid English diction against the Latinate threat: 'the
rulers and the ruled', 'duty', 'faith' (via Old French, *c.*1300) 'reverence' (via Old French, *c.*1290), 'laws', 'manhood'.[75] But the narrator, who has more moderate views, acts like the Authorized
Version, welcoming southern phraseology into his language, while
surrounding it with words whose rights have been solidly established
since the Middle Ages (the Latinates are underlined):

> 'Have <u>patience</u>', I <u>replied</u>, 'ourselves are full
> Of <u>social</u> wrong; and maybe wildest dreams
> Are but the needful <u>preludes</u> of the truth:
> For me, the <u>genial</u> day, the happy crowd,
> The <u>sport</u> half-<u>science</u>, fill me with a faith'.[76]

Trench would have found a more delightful accommodation of
basis and motion in the Prince's words, which I make no apology
for quoting a second time:

> <u>Approach</u> and fear not; breathe upon my brows;
> In that <u>fine</u> <u>air</u> I <u>tremble</u>, all the <u>past</u>
> Melts mist-like into this bright <u>hour</u>, and this
> Is morn to more, and all the <u>rich</u> to-come
> Reels, as the golden <u>Autumn</u> woodland reels
> Athwart the smoke of burning weeds. . . .

---

[74] *P*, 'Conclusion', 64-5.   [75] Ibid. 50, 53-7.   [76] Ibid. 72-6.

A contributory factor, albeit a minor one, to the harmonious feel of these lines is that all the words of Romance origin have been in the language since at least the fourteenth century. A comparatively modest extension of rights, therefore; but still a more liberal regime than that which will hold sway in *Idylls of the King*.

The Brownings in their poems about Italy, and Tennyson in *The Princess*, a poem having to do with England, both handle verse in a way that establishes a contrast between different elements and then makes expressive use of the relationship between them. For the Brownings, the most absorbing interaction was that between the law of the verse and the freedom of the language. This, they manipulated to many ends; among them, a shadowing of conflicts and collaborations between liberty and political structure, issues exemplified pre-eminently by the Risorgimento. Tennyson's writing suggests contrasts, not between form and language but—in so far as those two aspects of a piece of writing can be separated—within each of them. There is the distinction between lyric and narrative, and then the melding of the two together; the polarity between northern and southern phraseology, and then the weaving of both into a single texture. What the three poets share, in this regard, indicates that their formal sensibilities were all creatively responsive to the time of nation-building; the disparity between Tennyson and the Brownings, on the other hand, suggests that they conceived of national unity in different ways. For Tennyson, unity did not mean the achievement of harmony between the people and the State; he simply did not conceive of politics in those terms, imagining instead a community of affection and loyalty: 'Love thou thy land'. As it seemed to him, national unity meant continuity between past, present, and future, which is to say a melding of lyric and narrative. It meant a *rapprochement* between different populations: upper and lower classes, Saxons and Celts, the northern and southern peoples within the Empire, all of whom might be brought together into one texture like northern and southern phraseology. It was, not the achievement of a form, but the creation of a character. Neither in the case of the Brownings, nor in that of Tennyson, is it possible to draw a clear distinction between formal sensibility

and political understanding. That the Brownings thought of
verse as a conflict between law and freedom predisposed them
to understand the Risorgimento in the same way. Equally,
political conditions affected the significances they attached to
those elements of their verse. In Tennyson's case, the liking for
evenness of texture which is evident throughout his writing will
have prompted him to look for and value similar qualities in the
world around him. And, equally, the shifting geographical
borders of the British state, the expanding limits of representation, the absence of a written constitution, all these political
factors will have encouraged him to think of the society for
which he was writing as a texture rather than a form. In consequence, the style of *The Princess*, like its symbolic narrative, is
adapted to the circumstances of ever-broadening England.

In his concern with bringing disparate vocabularies together,
Tennyson is like Clough; but whereas the *Bothie* reproduces the
words actually spoken by different groups of people ('topping',
'slan leat'), Tennyson's negotiations occur at the more abstract
level of etymology. *The Princess*, therefore, carries no implications
about the rights and wrongs of the progressive standardization of
'book-English' which was occurring because of increased ease of
travel and the spread of school education—as the dialect poet
William Barnes lamented in a volume, published in 1848, which
Tennyson possessed.[77] Tennyson's admiration for Barnes's verse,
as well as his own experiments in dialect such as 'The Northern
Farmer', shows that he held no brief for the standardization of
English. Nonetheless, there is at least one writer who would have
felt *The Princess*'s way with diction to be culturally coercive. James
Clarence Mangan, a poet associated with Young Ireland, had
recognized the un-English propensities of Tennyson's early exotic
verse, and had developed his own line in southernness of imagining, producing fake translations from oriental languages which
delight in word-play and uncertain identities. Tennyson would
have been amused, but not surprised, if he had read Mangan's 'To
the Ingleezee Khafir, Calling Himself Djaun Bool Djenkinzun'.
This 'Djaun Bool' (John Bull), we are told, reviles 'IRAN's
nation and race': a note informs us 'Iran, as our readers may be

---

[77] William Barnes, *Poems of Rural Life in the Dorset Dialect: With a Dissertation and Glossary*, 2nd edn. (John Russell Smith, 1848), 1.

aware, is the ancient name of Persia', the point being to remind us that Erin is the ancient name of Ireland.[78] If Mangan had read *The Princess*, he would have spotted that the lyrics of Ida's land are imitated from the Persian; but he is not likely to have smiled at the discovery.

[78] *The Collected Works of James Clarence Mangan*, ed. Jacques Chuto, 4 vols. (Blackrock, Co. Dublin: Irish Academic Press, 1996–9), iii. 34, 449.

10

THE MARRIED STATE:
IDYLLS OF THE KING

A NEW–OLD TALE

Tennyson's Arthur is not a historical figure: in that, he differs from Browning's Guido Franceschini and Tennyson's own Queen Mary. Neither is he a fictional character who inhabits a specific historical moment: he is not like Browning's bishop who orders his tomb. *Idylls of the King*, Tennyson said, 'is not the history of one man or of one generation, but of a whole cycle of genera-tions'; it is 'New-old, and shadowing Sense at war with Soul'.[1] To complain, as Gerard Manley Hopkins did, that the work is 'incor-rect' in its rendering of the 'detail and keepings' of the Middle Ages is to judge it against a wrong expectation, for it is not set in the Middle Ages; to regret, like Christopher Ricks, that in the *Idylls* 'Tennyson did not achieve an imaginative recreation of the past', is too readily to assume that the past was what he wished to represent.[2]

The uncertain temporal co-ordinates of the *Idylls* were estab-lished by the first part of the work to have been composed, 'Morte d'Arthur', written in 1833–4 and published in 1842. The start of this poem is designed to produce nothing like the shock of Browning's beginnings. The scene and characters are introduced by an impersonal narrator. When Arthur speaks, his idiom has none of the individuality of tone or peculiarity of reference we would expect in a Browning version; indeed, in diction and rhythm his language is indistinguishable from the narrator's, and, we soon discover, from Sir Bedivere's. As though to emphasize

---

[1] *Memoir*, ii. 127; 'To the Queen [*Idylls of the King*]', 37.
[2] Ricks, *Tennyson*, 257.

the lack of (to resurrect a once fashionable term) 'polyglossia', each voice is given the same line to speak in turn: 'Clothed in white samite, mystic, wonderful' says King Arthur at line 31, words which are exactly repeated by the narrator at line 144, and then by Sir Bedivere fifteen lines further on. Although the conversation reported in the poem occurs between two characters, it is not located in a space that they think, or that we take, to be private. King Arthur:

> 'The sequel of today unsolders all
> The goodliest fellowship of famous knights
> Whereof this world holds record. . . .'[3]

This is not news to his interlocutor. From the height of their slightly archaic, epic language ('goodliest', 'whereof'), the characters seem to be addressing themselves to anyone who cares to attend. Although their world is held apart from ours, therefore, it is not marked as distinctly different in the manner of Browning's Italy.

As its title suggests, 'Morte d'Arthur' is (in the terms I proposed in the last chapter) a 'recollections' poem. Just as 'Anacaona' does not reproduce the Anacaona described in Irving's *History of the Life and Voyages of Christopher Columbus*, but changes her into a figure of fantasy, so 'Morte d'Arthur' represents, not Malory's Arthur, but an idea to which he has given rise. The self-conscious fictionality of Tennyson's poem is the more evident because Malory's *Le Morte d'Arthur* (like the *Mabinogion*, which was to be the other major source for *Idylls of the King*) is itself not a history, but a work which blends invention and record in the nebulous tincture of myth. Like *The Ring and the Book*, *Idylls of the King* has its origin in old writing; but whereas Browning's source was a historical document from the late 1690s, Tennyson's materials had no such connection to a particular time. The *Idylls* continue a tradition which Malory continued from his sources, which themselves derived . . . it is not clear from where. Herbert Tucker is therefore right to assert, in the course of a scrupulous discussion, that 'the subject of "Morte d'Arthur" is cultural tradition' and to draw attention to the 'avowedly legendary character' of what Tennyson 'means to transmit to modern readers'. However, his description

---

[3] 'Morte d'Arthur', 14–16.

of the work as representing 'the moment at which a history passes into a tradition' mistakenly implies that we are being shown a historical Arthur who lived before the stories of him began.[4] The poem cannot be so securely anchored. It reaches back through the mists of time, which have no discernible boundary. It takes place in the endlessly repeated moment at which one rendering of tradition gives way to another; equally (depending on how a reader reacts), its moment is like that of 'The Lady of Shalott', the endlessly repeated moment at which tradition becomes subject to interpretation.[5]

During the year in which 'Morte d'Arthur' was composed, Tennyson wrote other poems on figures from myth. 'Tithonus' and 'Ulysses' are, of course, 'recollections' poems (they both derive from both Homer and Dante) and, like 'Morte d'Arthur', they both reach back, not to a time, but through time. Having 'become a name', Ulysses is a myth in his own lifetime; what he desires—'To sail beyond the sunset', 'To follow knowledge . . . | Beyond the utmost bound of human thought'—resembles the long, mysterious life of myth; his experience of travelling around the world, as a result of which, he says, 'I am a part of all that I have met' suggests the wide dissemination of the self which is achieved by the circulation of writing, and especially of published books.[6] Tithonus, immortal and yet ageing, even more evidently partakes of the condition of a text. In the poised words of Eric Griffiths, 'the essence of pleasure in reading "Tithonus" rests on the very changelessness which pains its speaker; the poem, like Aurora herself, renews its beauty reading by reading.'[7] We might rather say that Aurora is like that perilous abstraction 'the reader', who rises above the poem in 'silence', lighting it with imaginative sympathy as the goddess's 'eyes brighten' to illuminate Tithonus; and in the same way as 'the reader'—which means reader after reader after reader—is endlessly renewed, so Aurora is fresh every morning, while the text, like Tithonus, lies there, ageing although always the same.[8] Grieving for Arthur Hallam, Tennyson wrote poems which describe what they themselves possess: a life unusually, but not eternally, prolonged through time.

[4] Herbert F. Tucker, *Tennyson and the Doom of Romanticism* (Cambridge, Mass.: Harvard University Press, 1988), 318, 320.　　　　　　　[5] See above, Chapter 1.
[6] 'Ulysses', 11, 60, 31–2, 18.　　　　　　　[7] Griffiths, *The Printed Voice*, 140.
[8] 'Tithonus', 44, 38.

Like Ulysses and Tithonus, King Arthur should be understood, not as a historical person represented according to mythical or epic conventions, but as a character who inhabits the slow timescale of myth. Unlike those classical figures, however, he is British, and so brings with him a feeling of locality. Trans-historical, and yet not trans-cultural, his existence is like the imagined endurance of the nation itself. The expansion of 'Morte d'Arthur', primarily a work of personal mourning, into *Idylls of the King*, primarily (as we will see) a work about national unity, suggests the deep relation between grief and nineteenth-century feelings of nationhood, both dwelling on the past, both longing to discover continuities between it and the present. 'Morte d'Arthur', and the *Idylls* as a whole, are designed to produce in their readers that 'ghostly intimation of simultaneity across homogeneous, empty time', a feeling of 'as-it-were ancestral "Englishness" ' which, as we saw in Chapter 1, attach to the words 'Earth to Earth, ashes to ashes, dust to dust'.[9] Indeed, many of Arthur's phrases, as general in application as they are lapidary in form, are not unlike quotations from liturgy: 'This is a shameful thing for men to lie'; 'Authority forgets a dying king'; 'a man may fail in duty twice, | And the third time may prosper'; 'The old order changeth, yielding place to new'; 'God fulfils himself in many ways'; 'the whole round earth is every way | Bound by gold chains about the feet of God' and so on.[10] These grand statements may be thought the more impressive because of the empty, eerie landscape into which they are uttered: here is a resolve which survives the collapse of the entire civilization to the maintenance of which it was committed, and by the existence of which it was sustained. Equally, we may reflect that it is the absence of social pressures around Arthur which allows him to enunciate so many abstract moral apophthegms in such a resounding manner.

The Ring and the Book challenges readers to establish an imaginative relationship between the particular historical moment which it represents and their own. 'Morte d'Arthur' challenges them to reach an imaginative accommodation between the particularities of their own time and its grand, comparatively timeless abstraction. When it was published, 'Morte d'Arthur' was, like the

---

[9] Anderson, *Imagined Communities*, 144–5.
[10] 'Morte d'Arthur', 78, 121, 129–30, 240, 241, 254–5.

central narrative in *The Princess*, introduced and succeeded by passages which, located securely in the nineteenth century, act as half-way houses for readers entering and leaving the strange realm of the poem itself. The closing verses, describing a dream provoked by 'Morte d'Arthur', in which the King appears as a sea-captain before metamorphosing by free association (as ship sails to port) into a 'modern gentleman | Of stateliest port' have been described by Christopher Ricks as 'inanely' suggesting 'that Prince Albert can be seen as Arthur come again', 'nakedly inviting Swinburne's unforgettable thrust, "Morte d'Albert" '.[11] Any such fixed equation as Arthur = Albert would doubtless be trite, but there would be no less foolishness in refusing to draw any connection at all between Arthur's world and the world in which and for which the poem was written—not that such considerations would much have bothered Swinburne, a writer very little interested in the public reaches of the imagination. The dream is in any case not offered as a key by which Arthur can be translated into the nineteenth-century. It associates him with a descendant, firstly of his martial aspect, and then of his courteous one; only to be dissipated by the church bells which suggest a further analogue for the King who will not die: Christ. This last thought echoes the discussion preceding the recitation, in which there had been talk of 'the general decay of faith'; an issue which enters into 'Morte d'Arthur' from many angles.[12] There is the King's ten-line adjuration, greatly expanded from a hint in Malory, that Sir Bedivere should pray for his soul. There is the vow of obedience which Bedivere twice breaks and, at the third attempt, fulfils. More profoundly, there is the question as to whether belief in Arthur's existence would not be better assured by the preservation of Excalibur as 'record', and 'relic', rather than by the mere telling of stories, 'empty breath | And rumours of a doubt'.[13] That Tennyson's poem exists, of course, shows that Arthur was right to trust the second option. Nebulously summoned up here is the hint of a comparison between religious faith and the imaginative suspension of disbelief which is a condition of reading works of fiction, or indeed works of myth such as 'Morte d'Arthur'. Casting away Excalibur, the 'relic', Bedivere commits the memory of his King

---

[11] 'The Epic [Morte d'Arthur]', 294–5; Ricks, *Tennyson*, 131.
[12] 'The Epic [Morte d'Arthur]', 18.   [13] 'Morte d'Arthur', 98–100.

to the spoken and written word. This is a Protestant emphasis; but it should also leave us pondering the likeness between the faith perpetuated in a religious community, and the beliefs (in a broader sense) shared by members of a nation, to whose existence, as it appeared in the nineteenth century, literature was fundamental. That likeness is particularly salient in a country, such as England, which is possessed of a national Church.

These considerations bring 'Morte d'Arthur' into proximity with an allegorical scheme for his projected Arthurian epic which Tennyson had penned sometime in the 1830s, and which included the entry 'K. A. Religious Faith', along with 'Excalibur, war', 'The Round Table: liberal institutions', and several others.[14] To readers versed in the allegories of Langland, Spenser, or Bunyan, this key will seem to anticipate a work rather different in character from 'Morte d'Arthur'; and Tennyson had indeed experimented with other ways of handling the Arthurian legends. In addition to 'The Lady of Shalott' and the blithe monologue 'Sir Galahad'—published in the same volume as 'Morte d'Arthur' in 1842—there had been at least the beginnings of a 'Ballad of Sir Lancelot' which, to judge from J. M. Kemble's account, was to have been distinctly Spenserian in manner. As Guinevere and her lover ride through a forest, they are rebuked by 'Merlin with spindle shanks, vast brows and beard and a forehead like a mundane egg'; at Lancelot's reply, 'Merlin, who tropically is Worldly Prudence, is of course miserably floored. So are the representatives of Worldly Force, who in the shape of three knights, sheathed, Sir, in trap from toe to toe, run at Sir L. and are most unceremoniously shot from their saddles like stones from a sling.'[15] Like Spenser's Orgoglio or Ignorance, Merlin with his egg-head and the knights with their armour made of rock are in part visual images. This is a development from the symbolic mode of 'The Lady of Shalott'. The lady is not herself a poet, a mind, a labourer, or whatever else she might be taken to mean; rather she is in a relation of likeness (a metaphorical relation) to those other entities because of her activity and situation. Merlin and the three knights also have a metaphorical relation to what they signify. The difference is that their meanings are univocal, and they bear their likenesses on their bodies; both alterations being necessary

---

[14] *Memoir,* ii. 123.   [15] *Poems of Tennyson,* ed. Ricks, i. 545.

to meet the requirements of the more complex narrative in which they appear.

In the 1842 *Poems*, Tennyson published only a 'Fragment' of the projected ballad, from which all traces of allegory have been excised.[16] The reason may be that in 'Morte d'Arthur' he had found a different way of bringing into his verse abstract significances of the kind listed in his skeletal key. In the 'Morte', Arthur does have to do with 'Religious Faith', but he does not signify it in the same way as Merlin signifies 'Worldly Prudence' in the 'Ballad'. Arthur is a faithful man: we might say that he partakes of faith, and therefore has a metonymical relationship to it. However, this is not constant. On the one hand, he is susceptible to uncertainty: 'all my mind is clouded with a doubt'.[17] On the other, there are times when he speaks with the voice of faith, as when he berates Sir Bedivere for not doing his bidding, or when he urges the benefits of prayer. At these moments, he seems to be faith's incarnation. This primarily metonymical, if variable, mode of signification extends through *Idylls of the King* as a whole, although occasionally, as we will see, there are instances of allegory in the style of the 'Ballad of Sir Lancelot'. Tennyson expected his readers to take pleasure in the shifting layers of meaning. His well-known remark that 'poetry is like shot-silk with many glancing colours' refers, not to Empsonian verbal ambiguity, but to alterations of perspective of the kind that make Arthur, in the 'Morte' seem to be most importantly sometimes a king, sometimes faith, sometimes plain man.[18] By the time Tennyson began concentrated work on the *Idylls* in the mid-1850s, his thoughts about his King had altered somewhat. Now, he generally associated him with conscience, and developed an implicit but ubiquitous analogy between the authority of conscience and political rule.

KING AND CONSCIENCE

As drifts generally do, the 'parabolic drift' of the *Idylls* comes and goes. Sometimes, the Arthur-as-conscience analogy is suggested but not imposed, as when the depraved Ettarre says of her King, 'I never heard his voice | But longed to break away', words that may refer equally well to the dislike of one human being for

---

[16] *Poems of Tennyson*, ed. Ricks, i. 544.   [17] 'Morte d'Arthur', 258.
[18] *Memoir*, ii. 127.

another. Sometimes, the parabolic drift is overwhelming, as when
Bellicent tells of her youthful friendship, in which the future King
appears out of nowhere, at first comforting her when she has been
unjustly punished, but then as she grows up becoming 'Stern . . .
and then I loved him not', behaviour which is distinctly more
typical of a conscience than of a child.[19] On yet other occasions,
the drift recedes entirely: Arthur's proclamation of a joust in
'Lancelot and Elaine' cannot be understood as anything other than
the proclamation of a joust. Of all the *Idylls'* many changes of drift,
the most abrupt occurs in 'Guinevere'. The Queen's conversation
with the novice seems naturalistic, and prepares us to think of
Arthur as a cuckolded husband. On his arrival, however, he
berates his wife with a severity and lack of self-doubt which would
be hardly conceivable—let alone exemplary—in a human being.
His forgiveness is no less puzzling:

> . . . and I,
> Lo! I forgive thee, as Eternal God
> Forgives: . . .[20]

On a naturalistic reading, this 'leaves us as breathless as a man who
boasts of his own humility'.[21] If we evoke the analogy with
conscience, on the other hand, Arthur's speech turns into an
outpouring of self-disgust; his recognition that Guinevere's lips are
'Lancelot's: nay, they never were the King's' implies—
movingly—that the self can never really love virtue, and will
always pine after the glamorous and the charming; his confidence
that 'before high God' she will 'spring' to him and 'claim' him
expresses faith that there is a heaven in which it will be possible to
be pure. Yet, even as we are in the midst of assembling this parabolic reading it is snatched away from us. Having forgiven her
(having forgiven himself, we want to say) he tells Guinevere: 'do
thou for thine own soul the rest', returning her and him to the
status of independent, self-motivating individuals.[22]

Such interpretive short-circuits pose a question about the
nature and extent of individuality. Sometimes, the characters are

---

[19] 'Pelleas and Ettare, 247–8; 'The Coming of Arthur', 353.

[20] 'Guinevere', 540–2.

[21] John D. Rosenberg, *The Fall of Camelot: A Study of Tennyson's Idylls of the King*
(Cambridge, Mass.: Harvard University Press, 1973), 129.

[22] 'Guinevere', 549, 561–2, 542.

viewed as persons in their own right; sometimes, as elements of a larger being. This larger being is Arthur's regime which, if we ride the parabolic drift, becomes a whole person having Arthur for his or her conscience. The *Idylls*, therefore, enquire into the idea, recurrent in political philosophy from Plato to the twentieth century, that a well-governed State is like a person, with the various sections of society assuming the roles of different faculties, organs, or limbs.

In 1838, Gladstone (then Tennyson's acquaintance, later his friend) had produced his own version of the old analogy: 'the state is a person, having a conscience', he had claimed, drawing on Hooker's *Ecclesiastical Polity*, and then developing the argument in terms characteristic of the time of nation-building: 'national influences form much of our individual characters. National rewards and punishments, whether by direct or circuitous visitation, influence and modify the individuals who form the mass. National will and agency are indisputably one, binding either a dissentient minority, or the subject body, in a manner that nothing but the recognition of the doctrine of national personality can justify.'[23] By following a circular line of reasoning, he concluded that the proper exercise of government required the continuance of the Church of England as an established Church. A State was like a person; a person had a conscience; therefore a State should have an Established Church to provide spiritual guidance for its citizens, hence making its resemblance to a person more complete.

When Arthur binds his knights by 'strait vows to his own self', compelling them to 'reverence the King, as if he were | Their conscience, and their conscience as their King', he founds a realm which is in a high degree like a personality.[24] Assuming influence over his subjects' spiritual lives, he arrogates to himself the functions of a Church. Like English monarchs since Henry VIII , he is at once a political and a religious leader; indeed, it may be that we should think of him as fulfilling Coleridge's programme that the State 'should display a transition into the character of a church': with its 'spire to heaven', Camelot certainly looks as much like a cathedral as a court.[25] In Malory, the Church has separate powers, and there

[23] W. E. Gladstone, *The State in its Relations with the Church* (John Murray, 1838), 9, 38.
[24] 'The Coming of Arthur', 261; 'Guinevere', 465–6.
[25] Coleridge, *On the Constitution of Church and State*, p. ix; 'Gareth and Lynette', 302.

is some vestige of this arrangement in the *Idylls*, where Dubric, at the marriage of Arthur and Guinevere, is described as 'Chief of the church in Britain'. Thereafter, the Church disappears. The consequent blurring-together of political and religious authority allows Arthur to be associated simultaneously with two key moments in British history. Achieving independence from 'Rome, | The slowly-fading mistress of the world', he is like the medieval chieftains who resisted imperial taxation; but he is equally like a Reformation churchman asserting the primacy of conscience.[26] This dual function goes some way towards justifying, even on the naturalistic level, his treatment of his wife in 'Guinevere': he speaks to her, not only as husband, or king, but as the voice of her religion.

In the spring and summer of his rule, Arthur's subjects are good and happy in so far as they obey him, which is to say in so far as they recognize themselves to be constituents within the greater personality which is the State. The first four *Idylls*, therefore, are those which respond best to allegorical keys of the sort proposed by some Victorian reviewers: 'if Arthur represents the Soul or the Ideal, Lancelot represents the Imagination, Merlin the Intellect, Guinevere the Heart, Vivien the Flesh.'[27] Sir Gareth, impetuous and joyful, is like the embodiment of, say, 'delight', which 'snobbishness', personified by Lynette, holds in contempt. His quest, compelling him to conquer knights who—in a radical departure from Malory—explicitly represent the temptations of youth, maturity, and old age, as well as the fear of death, is like the disciplining of such an emotion to bear up under the trials of existence. That he borrows Lancelot's horse and shield in order to overcome 'Death' suggests the importance of imagination in sustaining a belief in immortality.[28] With a bit of effort, the events which Tennyson has reproduced from Malory can be brought into the same scheme: the defeat of Sir Kaye is like delight's emancipation from the pleasures of the stomach; the Baron who is saved from being drowned in the oily mere . . . well, perhaps he represents a depressive sort of feeling. Here, as with the appearance of Gama's sons in *The Princess*, we reach the limits of the area that Tennyson has made susceptible to parabolic interpretation.

---

[26] 'The Coming of Arthur', 453, 503–4.
[27] (Annie E. Keeling), 'Tennyson's King Arthur', *London Quarterly Review*, no. 169, n.s. 49 (Oct. 1895), 84.   [28] 'Gareth and Lynette', 1347.

Sir Geraint, in the succeeding pair of idylls, looks like a representative of, say, 'devotion', who at the beginning of the story lacks a proper object and therefore oversleeps. In the course of 'The Marriage of Geraint' he overcomes 'pride', which is embodied explicitly in Edyrn the Sparrowhawk ('I was up so high in pride | That I was halfway down the slope to Hell', as he later admits—an emphasis absent from the source, which this time is the *Mabinogion*). Geraint then attaches himself to Enid, who seems to personify attentive observation: that she is 'Arrayed and decked' by Guinevere 'as the loveliest, | Next after her own self, in all the court' suggests the importance of visual perception to the warm feelings which are represented by Guinevere. In the next stage of his adventures, Geraint starts to act like an emotion run out of control, first of all suspecting Enid's fidelity, and then driving her ahead of him into a wild region of unpredictable behaviour: he is, we are told, as a man 'when his passion masters him'.[29] True to her function, Enid notices and warns him of dangers to which he would otherwise be blind. He declines into sensuality, represented by Limours (l'amour) and then succumbs to despair (Doorm), before returning to his proper, subsidiary role in Arthur's court. In these idylls, as in 'Gareth and Lynette', there are elements (the three tall knights, the horses driven along by Enid) which find no counterpart in the psychological map which the reader is nonetheless encouraged to sketch in. This—as we saw with regard to *The Princess*—is the difference between Tennyson's parabolic mode and strict allegory. Nonetheless, the clear indication is that Gareth, Enid, and Geraint are happy when they accept the roles that Arthur prescribes for them. When they do this, the propensities of each of them (joy, perceptiveness, devotion, etc.) flourish, so that they come to resemble the various faculties of a personality duly obedient to the prescriptions of conscience. Since Arthur's State is like a person, the activities of its members give rise to parabolic suggestions of the sort that I have been pursuing.

In the succeeding idylls, however, the resemblance of State to person progressively fades. Balin, prey to 'violences', is another knight-as-passion; but he ceases to obey Arthur and gives himself up to his own agency, behaving in a manner which therefore cannot be understood in terms of the State personality, and ending

---

[29] 'Geraint and Enid', 789–90; 'The Marriage of Geraint', 17–18; 'Geraint and Enid', 43.

up completely outside it, i.e. dead.[30] Merlin likewise abandons his
position as the representative of 'intellect', and turns into nothing
more than a lascivious old man. Elaine is never brought into the
Arthurian system because Lancelot refuses to love her: in consequence, she too eludes parabolic interpretation. All these bids for
independence on the part of characters who ought to recognize
their subservience to Arthur have immediate and disastrous consequences. By the time of 'The Last Tournament', however, it
appears that Tristram, whose role in the State personality should
be that of 'proficiency', or perhaps 'plausibility', has learned to
function quite adequately according to his own materialist lights.
'Use and skill' are enough to win the Tournament, he says: the old
requirements of purity and loyalty no longer obtain. The thoughts
and perceptions of such a man are beautifully rendered in the
decription of his ride towards Lyonnesse:

> Before him fled the face of Queen Isolt
> With ruby-circled neck, but evermore
> Past, as a rustle or twitter in the wood
> Made dull his inner, keen his outer eye
> For all that walked, or crept, or perched, or flew.
> Anon the face, as, when a gust hath blown,
> Unruffling waters re-collect the shape
> Of one that in them sees himself, returned;
> But at the slot or fewmets of a deer,
> Or even a fallen feather, vanished again.[31]

Like an animal, he is preternaturally sensitive to the stimuli around
him, which he registers as a pool responds to a gust of wind, or as
the even, iambic surface of the verse gives way to the rhythmical
disturbance of 'rustle', 'twitter', 'fallen feather'. When his brain is
not occupied with these perceptions, it reverts to the other motive
of his actions, his desire for Isolt. This is the mind of someone who
has made his all out of what, according to the *Idylls*, should be only
subordinate elements of a character. He might be a primitive man,
not yet schooled in the ways of faith and self-repression; but his
place in the history of Camelot makes it clear that he is, rather, the
product of a high degree of civilization—a Swinburne, say, or a
Pater—who has vowed himself to the delights of sense, thereby

---

[30] 'Balin and Balan', 201.   [31] 'The Last Tournament', 198, 363–72.

reeling 'back into the beast'. He ought to accept his place in the State personality, but instead believes himself to be an autonomous individual. The Round Table dissolves as such behaviour spreads: here, as in Gladstone's volume, 'private judgement . . . threatens to desecrate and degrade the whole function of political government'. In the last two *Idylls*, as we have seen, a consistent parabolic suggestion reappears, but that is because the State personality has been reduced to its barest elements: Arthur, Guinevere, Bedivere—the last knight 'in whom should meet the offices of all'—and Modred the face of mortality.[32]

Arthur's is an absolutist regime: he is like Browning's Duke of Ferrara, but with the important difference that, since he embodies conscience, his commands are always good. His rule is therefore not an equivalent of absolutism as it operated in history; rather, it is an abstract representation of government that can be brought into relation with many different actual political systems. Tennyson's early note, 'The Round Table: liberal institutions', seems incompatible with the behaviour of Arthur's knights: they go around killing people, and certainly do not stand for election. However, it would be mistaken to conclude that the first thought about the Round Table had been replaced with a second thought of an equally specific nature (perhaps, 'The Round Table: *ancien regime*'), for when they came to be written the *Idylls* took on broader and hazier connotations. Arthur embodies an ideal of virtuous rule which may be realized in a good king, a good parliament, a good landlord, or a person with a good conscience. Like *The Princess*, the *Idylls* tell a comparatively abstract story which, precisely because it is abstract, has manifold implications. They narrate, not any specific political developments, but the decline of reverence, the growth of self-satisfaction. Certainly, as Tennyson looked around him at the world in which he lived, he found evidence for such decay in working-class unrest and the growth of agitation in Ireland; but he understood these developments to be examples of a more general moral corruption. The *Idylls* are his most elaborate exposition of the understanding of politics in terms of character which I outlined in Chapter 8.

Of the several contemporary political issues with which the *Idylls* establish a relation, one is the growth of the British Empire.

---

[32] 'The Last Tournament', 125; Gladstone, *The State*, 127; 'The Passing of Arthur', 293.

As V. G. Kiernan has suggested, 'Arthur's expanding kingdom is
. . . a small empire, subjugating or overawing less civilized areas
and bringing them within the pale of Christian manners', the
connection with the activities of the British Empire being the
more evident because Arthur 'has an exceptionally fair complexion, as if to tipify the white man'.[33] In fact, Arthur is whiter than
white, 'fair | Beyond the race of Britons and of men': fairer than
'men' because he is pre-eminently virtuous; 'fairer than 'Britons'
to suggest the light colouring of Anglo-Saxons by contrast with
Celts.[34] In the traditional sources, Arthur is himself a Briton who
fights against the Anglo-Saxon invaders. In Tennyson's work,
these intruders, and the place they established, 'England', are never
mentioned; but Arthur comes (according to the most authoritative
rumour) from across the sea, looks foreign, and has the qualities of
virtue, sternness, and so on generally associated with the Anglo-
Saxons. The *Idylls* share E. A. Freeman's view that the British
Empire in the world is a continuation of the English empire in the
United Kingdom;[35] but they go further, associating Arthur not
only with white as against black and Asian, and Anglo-Saxon as
against Celtic, but with masculine as against feminine, and
conscience as against all the other elements of a personality. At any
point, one of these implications is likely to be exerting greater
imaginative pressure on the narrative than the others. 'Merlin and
Vivien' has most to do with the threat of the feminine; 'The
Coming of Arthur' with the origins of conscience; and 'Balin and
Balan' with the cohesion of the United Kingdom.

In 1831, when Tennyson and Arthur Hallam had 'interchanged
thoughts on the political state of the world', they had been worried
by 'Ireland especially, which is "the most volcanic point." '[36] Over
the ensuing decades, events lived up to their fears: there was the
famine, and the rebellion of 1848; then, in the 1850s, there was a
resurgence of systematic agitation in the shape of the national
Tenant League, and, later that decade, the beginning of the
Fenians' violent separatist campaign, which soon spread to
Canada. 'T. rages against the Fenians', William Allingham noted
in his diary for 1867.[37] The following year, Gladstone was elected

[33] V. G. Kiernan, *Poets, Politics and the People*, ed. Harvey J. Kaye (Verso, 1989), 141.
[34] 'The Coming of Arthur', 329–30.   [35] See above, Chapter 8.
[36] *Memoir*, i. 82.
[37] Hoppen, *The Mid-Victorian Generation*, 559–90; *William Allingham's Diary*, 167.

prime minister largely for his policy on the Irish question: 'my mission is to pacify Ireland', he had declared; in 1869 he oversaw the disestablishment of the Anglican Church of Ireland, an act which Tennyson deplored: 'we look with anxiety to the Irish Church Bill . . . Any severance of Church and State is, we think, above all things to be deprecated, as fostering the common tendency to look upon parts of man as man instead of the whole being,' Hallam Tennyson wrote at the time.[38] Meanwhile, sustained composition of the *Idylls* had got under way. The first instalment of the work, consisting of 'Enid' (later divided into 'The Marriage of Geraint' and 'Geraint and Enid'), 'Vivien' (later retitled 'Merlin and Vivien'), 'Elaine' (later 'Lancelot and Elaine') and 'Guinevere', was published in 1859, having been composed over the previous three years. This volume, with its concentration on personal relationships, looks more like a response to *Men and Women* than the kernel of a work epic in ambition. When Tennyson returned to his Arthurian endeavour a decade later, he brought martial topics to the fore, publishing in 1869 a book which contained 'The Coming of Arthur' and 'The Passing of Arthur', as well as 'The Holy Grail' and 'Pelleas and Ettarre'. If he felt a contrast between the treachery (as he saw it) of the Fenians, and the patriotism newly imparted to the *Idylls* by this volume ('Strike for the King and live!'—as the knights sing), he kept the thought private. It may be that when he wrote 'The Last Tournament', printed in a magazine in 1871, Isolt's 'Irish hair and Irish eyes' seemed to him newly dangerous in the light of contemporary developments, but again, that thought does not impress itself noticeably on the text. 'With the publication of "Gareth and Lynette" in 1872', Hallam Tennyson recalls, 'my father thought that he had completed the cycle of the "Idylls" '—ten episodes (for 'Enid' was as yet undivided) being after all a reasonable number— 'but later he felt that some further introduction to "Merlin and Vivien" was necessary, and so wrote "Balin and Balan" '.[39] This oddly afterthought-of final *Idyll* was composed between 1872 and 1874, a time of high interest in Irish matters: in 1870 Isaac Butt had founded the Home Government Association, and sixty home rulers were returned in the general election of 1874. Tennyson

---

[38] Boyce, *The Irish Question and British Politics 1868–86*, 19–31; *Memoir*, ii. 57.
[39] 'The Coming of Arthur', 487; 'The Last Tournament', 403; *Memoir*, ii. 121.

will undoubtedly have been incensed by these developments, which went against all his convictions about national and imperial unity: as he exclaimed after Gladstone's conversion to Home Rule a decade later, 'I love Gladstone, . . . but I hate his Home-rule policy.'[40]

Three decades earlier, Tennyson had considered bringing Irishness into the union of characters effected by *The Princess*: according to his early plan for the story-tellers to have distinct personalities, the débâcle in the tent was to have been narrated by 'a wild November fool':

> Twice had he been convened and once had fought
> A bargeman—he was Irish out of Clare.
> For every prize he wrote and failed in all,[41]

('Clare' being indistinguishably the Irish county and the Cambridge college.) Although these lines were dropped, Tennyson may nonetheless have felt that the final version of his poem contained some trace of Ireland, for the rhyming lyrics, added in 1850, had largely been composed during a visit there in 1848. As his host, Aubrey de Vere, noted in his recollection: 'it was a time of political excitement, and Ireland was on the brink of that silly attempt at rebellion which put back all her serious interests for a quarter of a century.' If Tennyson thought there to be a consonance between Ireland's silly attempt at rebellion and Ida's, the lyrics were a calmative response, for they brought into *The Princess*'s formal and ideological union those 'lyrical . . . qualities' which were all he could find to like in the Irish character.[42]

Some such idea seems to have occurred to his host, for when de Vere wrote 'Insifail' (1861), 'a National chronicle cast in poetic form' he found, as he explained in the Dublin edition of 1863, that 'the character of Irish History'—presumably as being intermittent and usually melancholy—'rendered it natural that its illustration should be chiefly lyrical'.[43] Nonetheless, he did manage also to produce a narrative depiction of Ireland's history in 'The Sisters; or, Weal in Woe: An Irish Tale' (1861). The fate of the siblings Mary and Margaret, we are told, 'Shadow'd a phantom image of

---

[40] Ibid. ii. 462.   [41] *Poems of Tennyson*, ed. Ricks, iii. 588.
[42] *Memoir*, i. 289; *William Allingham's Diary*, 199.
[43] Aubrey de Vere, *Inisfail: A Lyrical Chronicle of Ireland* (Dublin: James Duffy, 1863), p. xxvi.

my country, | Vanquish'd yet victor, in her weal and woe'. Margaret, the elder of the two, has a 'quick eye, and serviceable hand' and a name for 'industry'; she prospers, and soon comes to rule 'serene | A wire-fenced empire'; evidently, therefore, she is a 'shadow' of England, which de Vere later calls Ireland's 'sister' nation. Mary, by predictable contrast, is impractical, but compensates for this shortcoming with a 'visionary and pathetic grace'. At the famine she emigrates, first to Liverpool, then to the east coast of America, whence she is driven by 'a wayward instinct' to the west coast, where she enters a nunnery. News that her sister is married and her grandmother ill, however, summons her home, where she in turn falls ill. As she lies dying, the sisters rediscover their love for one another: 'Once more | Her sister was her sister!'. 'Unlike fortunes | Had placed at angles those two lives that once | Lay side by side', the narrator reflects; but now 'The prosperous from the unprosperous sister sought | Heart-peace'. Envisaging the material extinction of his nation but the persistence of its spirit, De Vere anticipates Arnold's *On the Study of Celtic Literature*, although, being a convert to Roman Catholicism, he has a clearer idea of the form that the spirit should take: as a mysterious vision proclaims in 'Inisfail', 'Thy Country is risen and lives on in thy faith'.[44]

'Balin and Balan' is unusually little dependent on Malory, drawing from him only some hints towards the character of Balin, the dual fratricide at the end of the story and the brawl in Pellam's castle. In the other *Idylls*, Tennyson typically simplifies his wandering originals; in 'Balin and Balan' he wrote a narrative of his own, and made his tale of two brothers beginning with 'B' both significantly echo and significantly differ from de Vere's tale of two sisters beginning with 'M'. Balin embodied Tennyson's view of Irish national character just as surely as Mary embodied de Vere's: he is 'the Savage', prone to 'moods' and 'madness'; as Tennyson said of the Irish in 1867, 'Kelts are all mad furious fools!' A draft which describes his hair as a 'most strange red' makes the connection even more clearly.[45] Balin's attack on Arthur's 'thrall' may also have been thought typical of an Irishman, for according

[44] Aubrey de Vere, *The Sisters, Inisfail, and Other Poems* (Longman, Green, Longman and Roberts, 1861), 13, 15–17, 41, 23, 32, 302.
[45] 'Balin and Balan', 51, 137, 225; *William Allingham's Diary*, 167; *Poems of Tennyson*, ed. Ricks, iii. 375.

to a pamphlet entitled *Irish Seditions* which later came into Tennyson's possession, 'he is a brutal tyrant to those whom he deems his social inferiors' (Kiernan adduces Tennyson's 'country-men in India, who', he says, 'were much given to beating their servants').[46] Balan, like Margaret, contrasts with his sibling, although in a different way, exerting spiritual restraint upon him: 'I . . . | Had often wrought some fury on myself, | Saving for Balan'.[47] The two of them look like shadows, not of England and Ireland but, if of anything, of Ireland and the Anglican Church. When Arthur overthrows the brothers and summons them to Camelot he is bringing them under his rule: like Ireland in 1800, they become part of a united kingdom. Tennyson does not drop heavy hints like de Vere's 'industry' and 'empire', but there are some suggestive oddities of phrasing: the brothers, 'added to their Order lived | A wealthier life than heretofore'; it was 'so rich a fellowship'—comments which would, admittedly, be fanciful if applied expressly to nineteenth-century Ireland, but which nonetheless gesture in the direction of economics.[48] Balan's depar-ture from Camelot on his quest to King Pellam is like Irish dises-tablishment: like the Church of Ireland he is left on his own to do combat with someone who, with his affectation of holiness and devotion to 'Thorns of the crown and shivers of the cross' looks distinctly like a personification of Catholicism (Hallam Tennyson called him 'the type of asceticism and superstition').[49] Heading off in the direction of spirituality, Balan's wanderings are like Mary's; but Tennyson protestantly disapproves of what the Catholic de Vere sets up as an ideal. Like Margaret, Balin is left behind, as, politically, Ireland remained part of the British State.

Deprived of his brother's restraining influence, Balin feels increasingly out of place. Observing Lancelot's gentility, he groans:

> . . . 'These be gifts,
> Born with the blood, not learnable, divine,
> Beyond *my* reach . . .'[50]

---

[46] Anon., *Irish Seditions; Their Origin and History from 1792–1880: Ireland's Curse—England's Trouble* (Diprose and Bateman, 1883), p. iv; Kiernan, *Poets, Politics and the People,* 141–2. [47] 'Balin and Balan', 59–61.

[48] Ibid. 88–90, 144. [49] Ibid. 108; *Poems of Tennyson,* ed. Ricks, iii. 385.

[50] 'Balin and Balan', 170–2.

Exactly what, in Tennyson's view of the matter, a well-meaning Celt might feel when confronted with the gifts of British civilization. As a means of improving himself he asks, and is granted, permission to wear the Queen's 'crown-royal' on his shield. This is like Ireland demanding, and being given, Home Rule:

> The crown is but the shadow of the King,
> And this a shadow's shadow, let him have it,
> So this will help him of his violences![51]

With characteristic blindness to the failings of others, but uncharacteristic casualness about the emblems of his kingship, Arthur makes his gift with what sounds like a politician's calculated understatement: Home Rule?—but it's only a shadow of legislative independence. The results of this concession are not happy: struck by self-doubt, Balin leaves Arthur's court, taking 'the self-same track as Balan', and ending up in the Catholic and slanderous environment of Pellam's castle. Goaded into violence by his treatment there, he casts off the 'priceless cognizance' that links him to the Queen, and as a result engages in the doubly fatal conflict with his brother.[52] In a later poem, 'The Voyage of Maeldune', which was 'intended to represent . . . the Celtic genius', Tennyson performs a series of variations on this theme. Wandering like Balin and Balan, although across the sea, the voyagers arrive at successive pairs of contrasting islands, finding on most of them some reason to start a brawl, until they reach the isle of the 'Double Towers' which, because of a perpetual earthquake, 'shocked on each other and butted each other'. This, as Hallam Tennyson notes, is 'symbolical of the contest between Roman Catholics and Protestants'; in line with Tennyson's view of 'the Celtic genius', Maeldune's men take sides: 'the one half slew the other'. The relevance to Home Rule of this, and of Balin and Balan's analogous demise, is made clear by an entry in Allingham's diary for 1884: 'W.A. . . . "suppose England tried leaving them to themselves." T.—"Civil War!" '[53] It may be that the long-delayed publication of 'Balin and Balan' was prompted by a sense of its aptness to Irish affairs: by 1884 when it appeared (the year when

---

[51] 'Balin and Balan', 196, 199–201.   [52] Ibid. 285, 424.

[53] *Poems of Tennyson*, ed. Ricks, iii. 62; 'The Voyage of Maeldune', 105, 108; *Poems of Tennyson*, ed. Ricks, iii. 66; 'The Voyage of Maeldune', 114; *William Allingham's Diary*, 325.

Tennyson made that comment to Allingham about civil war), Ireland was again a pressing topic: Parnell had become leader of the Home Rule party in 1880; the Phoenix Park murders occurred two years later; and in 1886, Gladstone finally brought his Home Rule Bill into Parliament.

If Tennyson were to read the foregoing paragraphs, it is possible that he would complain, as he did of some contemporaries, that I have 'explained some things too allegorically', having taken his 'hobby, and ridden it too hard'.[54] Yet even if the connection with de Vere was unconscious, and even if it did not actually occur to Tennyson that (say) Balan's role is like that of the Church of Ireland, he would undoubtedly have agreed that Balin is an Irish sort of character, and that his story shows how such a character will behave if it is not kept under suitable government. Like *The Princess*, therefore, 'Balin and Balan' is an archetypal narrative which articulates and explores the relationship between different characteristics. It, too, is an ideological abstract, manifesting in a generalized form a pattern of thought and feeling which could be projected on to events in Ireland or any analogous situation in which 'parts of man' were looked upon as 'man instead of the whole being'. In *The Princess*, the mythical genre—and therefore ideological comprehensiveness—of the central narrative is explained by the balmy circumstances of the narration: the story-tellers reveal their guiding prejudices all the more starkly for being relaxed after their pleasant picnic. For its similar qualities, *Idylls of the King* offers the implicit justification that it derives from ancient legends: these stories, the work says to its readers, are the ideological core of the national tradition to which you belong.

This challenging abstractness is perhaps the most fundamental difference between Tennyson's *Idylls* and a work by which they were in many respects anticipated: Bulwer Lytton's *King Arthur* (1849). Tennyson had crossed swords with Lytton in the 1830s, and it seems that his old enemy's incursion into Arthurian territory helped to reawaken his own interest in it.[55] Lytton's *King Arthur* is in rhyming stanzas, and belongs to the romance tradition of Spenser and Ariosto rather than the epic line in which Tennyson situated himself: it takes its materials from fabliaux rather than from

---

[54] *Memoir*, ii. 126–7.
[55] Charles Tennyson, *Alfred Tennyson* (Macmillan, 1949; reissued 1968), 224–5.

Malory and the *Mabinogion*. Nonetheless, it does have designs on
being a Great National Work for the nineteenth century: having
ranged through many digressions in its narration of Celtic Arthur's
resistance to Saxon invasions, the poem concludes with his
marriage to 'Genevieve', daughter of the Saxon King, and the
creation of a 'common throne'. This is a cursory—and explicitly
racialized—version of the end of *The Princess*. Lytton's ambitions
extend to allegory: his Arthur, like Tennyson's, is 'Nature's
masterpiece, perfected Man', and his adventures on occasion turn
into a pilgrim's progress. He enters 'Death, that dim phantasmal
EVERY WHERE', drawing from the experience the happy conclusion
that 'An instant flits between life's latest sigh | And life's
renewal;—that it is to die!' No less unmistakably, other parts of the
work satirize contemporary politics: Sir Gawaine is captured by
Vikings whose guiding principle is revealed to be (in the work's
best-known line) 'THE GREATEST PLEASURE OF THE GREATEST
NUMBER'; they intend to cook him, because 'No pleasure like a
Christian roasted slowly, | To Odin's greatest number can be
given'. Imprisoned, Gawaine endeavours to teach socialist princi-
ples to a dog: 'free dogs, themselves unbound, | With all who
would be free should fraternise'. Once this approach has failed, he
discovers a principle dear to economic liberalism: 'Our selfish
interests bid us coalesce.'[56]

These parts of Lytton's *King Arthur* are allegorical in the strictest
sense, for each figure is unequivocally a reference to something
else: Vikings = utilitarians, the dog = the people. This means that
the work fails to give the impression of occupying an imaginative
space of its own, instead offering its readers a series of coded
remarks about the world they know already. The characters in
Idylls of the King are not reducible to a code. Like *The Ring and the
Book*, Tennyson's work holds itself apart in a realm of verse that
can be drawn into varying relations with the world of the reader;
but whereas Browning's imagined elsewhere is historically specific
and is described according to the conventions of realism,
Tennyson's is a place of myth. As soon as we think we have identified a character as a representation of this or that psychological or
political entity, or indeed of an individual human being, the

---

[56] Sir E. Bulwer Lytton, *King Arthur*, 2 vols. (Henry Colburn, 1849), ii. 301, 298, 294,
205–6, 65, 72, 74.

resemblance disappears before our eyes. John D. Rosenberg has suggested that this persistent fluidity of meaning 'is essentially a defense of the truth of dreams, in which symbol, setting, and character are alternate manifestations of each other and an act can be simultaneously good and evil, ecstatic and terrifying'.[57] However, Tennyson is not Yeats: in the *Idylls*, although the precise scope of reference of an action may be uncertain, its moral valuation is always clear. Guinevere's infidelity may be taken as a psychological condition, a wife's betrayal of her husband, or as the sign of a disloyalty endemic in the State; but whichever interpretation is uppermost, the act itself is always evil. *Idylls of the King* is at once the history of a State, the story of a marriage, and the narrative of an individual life. The perpetually shifting perspective which makes one level always give way to another and then to another, suggests that what matters to an individual, to a marriage, and to the State is essentially the same. It suggests also that the one is dependent on the other, so that a virtuous self requires and is necessary to a virtuous marriage, and that virtuous marriages support and rely on a virtuous polity. The interweaving of these threads of meaning is what most marks out the *Idylls* as inhabiting a time of nation-building. In Arthur's regime, there is no conflict between what is good for the individual and what is good for the nation, or between what is good for the nation, and what is good for the State: this is a conservative vision of organic national unity in the tradition of Burke. However, the *Idylls* narrate what appears to be the inevitable destruction of that ideal by the forces of disloyalty, which manifest themselves variously as sensuality, adultery, and rebelliousness—rebelliousness like that of the Fenians who were, in Tennyson's view, not a national movement in their own right, but a disruptive element within the character of ever-broadening England.

A WORLD OF WORDS

The Round Table is established by a speech act. The State which is brought into being by this act includes a rule about language. Vowing to reverence their King as their conscience, their conscience as their King, the knights commit themselves to

---

[57] Rosenberg, *The Fall of Camelot*, 103.

rendering fixed and unambiguous the relationship between signifier, signified and referent, be they speaking of a thing, an action, or a thought. Arthur's reign creates an area of security which is insepara- bly physical, moral, and linguistic. A knight who disobeys him, like Sir Gawain in 'Lancelot and Elaine', or Sir Bedivere in 'The Passing of Arthur', betrays both his King and himself: 'Man's word is God in man'. From this point of view, the worst aspect of Guinevere's adul- tery is that it breaks her marriage vow. When Sir Tristram says 'we sware but by the shell', blithely taking for granted the disparity between his word and his actions, Arthur's reign is doomed.[58]

The King's attachment to plain speech leads him to prefer solid- looking vocabulary: monosyllables, and words of Anglo-Saxon derivation. He begins married life on nothing like the terms of dictional tolerance which had been established for Princess Ida by her Prince:

> And Arthur said, 'Behold, thy doom is mine.
> Let chance what will, I love thee to the death!'
> To whom the Queen replied with drooping eyes,
> 'King and my lord, I love thee to the death!'[59]

Of these thirty-six words, only one ('replied') is not of Anglo- Saxon derivation, and only four are not monosyllables. The oath he makes his knights swear has the same character: he

> Bound them by so strait vows to his own self.[60]

The broad direction of the *Idylls'* linguistic tendencies had been set by 'Morte d'Arthur', where the comparatively high proportion of words derived from Anglo-Saxon makes sense as contributing, in a general way, to the poem's stern and distant character. That early work, however, is not so wary of Latinates as the rest of the *Idylls*, written much later, were to be. Arthur's second word in the 'Morte', 'sequel', has a distinctly foreign feel to it and is banished from the other *Idylls*. Then, he was quite happy to use the verb 'to perform'; he never employs it again. He speaks of Sir Bedivere's 'mission', a word which reappears only in the dictionally and morally dubious landscape of Earl Doorm, accompanied by 'perilous' and 'turbulence'.[61] In the later *Idylls*, some Latinates,

---

[58] 'The Coming of Arthur', 132; 'The Last Tournament', 270.
[59] 'The Coming of Arthur', 466–9.   [60] Ibid. 261.
[61] 'Morte d'Arthur', 14, 67; 'Geraint and Enid', 527, 525, 521.

such as 'reverence' and 'authority', are central to Arthur's rule: here, as in *The Princess,* factors other than etymology must be taken into account when judging the 'feel' of a word (after all, both 'round' and 'table' have Romance roots).[62] Generally, Arthur keeps his southern phraseology on a tight rein:

> . . . he spake and cheered his Table Round
> With large, divine, and comfortable words,[63]

'Large' is drawn back towards its obsolete meanings 'munificent' and 'copious'; 'comfortable', too, requires its old sense of 'encouraging' which, in Tennyson's day, persisted only in the prayer-book phrase 'comfortable words' used to introduce the passages of scripture read out after absolution (*OED*).

In this realm of plain, primitive, and sacred speech, outbreaks of dictional ambiguity, rhythmical uncertainty, and vocabulary of Romance derivation are to be viewed with mistrust. Earl Limours, the 'all-amorous Earl', with his 'pliant courtliness', 'Femininely fair and dissolutely pale' is Arthur's linguistic antithesis. His conversation is all that one would expect from someone whose very name suggests a Latinate pun: he 'took the word and played upon it, | And made it of two colours'.[64] Geraint is well on the way towards Limours's state of Latinity even before he leaves his own castle:

> . . . a prince whose manhood was all gone,
> And molten down in mere uxoriousness.[65]

At the end of his trials, on the other hand, he recovers his masculine, monosyllabic and predominantly Anglo-Saxon weight:

> They called him the great Prince and man of men.[66]

Arthur establishes a realm of semantic, etymological, and rhythmical solidity within a world of linguistic chaos. Obedience to him is the more necessary because the grounds of his rule are uncertain:

> 'Confusion, and illusion, and relation,
> Elusion, and occasion, and evasion'[67]

---

[62] 'Guinevere', 465; 'The Coming of Arthur', 260.   [63] Ibid. 266–7.
[64] 'Geraint and Enid', 360, 278, 275, 291–2.
[65] 'The Marriage of Geraint', 59–60.   [66] 'Geraint and Enid', 960.
[67] 'Gareth and Lynette', 281–2.

Merlin's words, inseparably Latinate and riddling, tally with his ambiguous character as both Arthur's mentor and a connoisseur of the dangerous regions beyond the King's knowledge. In the light of the dictional negotiations in *The Princess*, we might expect that as disloyalty spreads through Arthur's kingdom, southern phraseology will make incursions into Tennyson's page. This does not happen. The work remains predominantly Anglo-Saxon in dictional character throughout. Tennyson, that is to say, keeps faith with Arthur when all his knights except Sir Bedivere are lost to him. Even when the King departs his world, the *Idylls* retain his stamp:

> . . . he saw, the speck that bare the King,
> Down that long water opening on the deep
> Somewhere far off, pass on and on, and go
> From less to less and vanish into light.
> And the new sun rose bringing the new year.[68]

(One Latinate: 'pass'.) Tennyson asks us to commit our sensibilities to this restricted diction, as Arthur's knights bind themselves to his strait vows. Many readers have refused. Elizabeth Barrett Browning went (characteristically) to the heart of the difficulty: 'the colour, the temperature, the very music, left me cold'—words which revealingly echo Guinevere's indifference towards her King: 'I yearned for warmth and colour which I found | In Lancelot'.[69] The *Idylls* are written in opposition to all those glamorous, tempting reaches of language, feeling, and the world which Tennyson had loved to dream of in the early exotic poems, and whose accommodation with the duties of Englishness he had contrived to imagine in *The Princess*. The experience of reading *Idylls of the King* is the reverse of the experience of reading 'The Lotos-Eaters': we are challenged, not to resist the seductive beauty of the verse, but to love it despite, nay, because of its plainness.

Written piecemeal over several decades, published here and there ('The Last Tournament' in a magazine, 'Balin and Balan' in *Tiresias and Other Poems*), the *Idylls* came before their original public, not as a single united work, nor even (like *The Ring and the Book*) as a serial, but as episodes, appearing at long intervals and in

---

[68] 'The Passing of Arthur', 465–9.
[69] Ricks, *Tennyson*, 254; 'Guinevere', 642–3.

unpredictable order. Critics have since catalogued thematic parallels and patterns of imagery, and argued that the *Idylls* therefore
achieve triumphant unity of form.[70] To the work's first readers,
this proposal would have carried even less conviction than it does
today. For them, the *Idylls* can have possessed unity, not in the
sense of a discrete structure, but only in the sense of uniformity, of
consistent ethical concern and dictional character. When Elizabeth
Barrett Browning told her story of Aurora's, and Romney's,
disenchantment with the established social and political order, she
shaped her poem so that it, too, broke with formal convention.
The Ring and the Book asks its readers to find their own paths
through its material as Pompilia discovered her own moral direction; the 'repulsive' fragmentariness of *Amours de Voyage* gives
formal expression to Claude's distrust of unification both matrimonial and national. Tennyson's consideration of the kind of unity
that was appropriate to his work on Arthur will have been guided
by the kind of unity that he thought Arthur himself represented: a
unity of personality. Wherever and whenever they came across
one of the *Idylls*, contemporary readers will have recognized it, as
Arthur's knights were known, by its 'state | And presence', its
distinguished and reliable bearing.[71] The mental processes which
gave rise to this similarity are too nebulous to be followed with
accuracy. Nonetheless, it seems safe to say that Tennyson's feeling
about what constituted 'unity' appeared in, and was itself shaped
by, and created interrelations between, his thinking about his
nation, about Arthur's kingdom, and about his own realm of verse,
all of which are understood primarily in terms of character.

   None of the long poems I have discussed is a work of art
conceived as an object, whose form is to be observed and admired.
They all ask readers to enter into their realms of verse, and each
(as we have seen) imagines that residency on different terms. The
Idylls make no attempt to ingratiate themselves with their readers:
they do not extend the hand of friendship like *Aurora Leigh*; they
do not welcome all and sundry into their domain like *The Princess*.
Rather, they are just there, as though they have no need to make
an effort, since, being the story of conscience, they occur within
each of us; and because, being the story of a nation, they are what

---

[70] Rosenberg, *The Fall of Camelot*, 13, 31–3, 134.
[71] 'Lancelot and Elaine', 181–2.

we already inhabit. This thought (conjectural, I admit) may help to explain something strange about the work's imagery. In *Idylls of the King* the similes (as even Ricks accepts) are 'triumphs'.[72] The odd thing is that almost without exception they compare human thoughts and actions to events in a nature bereft of human presence. For example:

> . . . The Queen
> Looked hard upon her lover, he on her;
> And each foresaw the dolorous day to be:
> And all talk died, as in a grove all song
> Beneath the shadow of some bird of prey;
> Then a long silence came upon the hall,
> And Modred thought, 'The time is hard at hand.'[73]

That is beautifully handled, the move into the image being prepared for by the hint of vision in 'foresaw', and occurring at just the instant when the members of the court retreat into their own imaginings. Who is the bird of prey?—we might wonder, for a moment; only for the answer to be given us as we step back from the grove into the hall.

However, the verse's transitions from culture to nature and back again are not always contrived with such elegance:

> Aimed at the helm, his lance erred; but Geraint's,
> A little in the late encounter strained,
> Struck through the bulky bandit's corselet home,
> And then brake short, and down his enemy rolled,
> And there lay still; as he that tells the tale
> Saw once a great piece of a promontory,
> That had a sapling growing on it, slide
> From the long shore-cliff's windy walls to the beach,
> And there lie still, and yet the sapling grew:
> So lay the man transfixt. . . .[74]

The apparent redundancy of the comparison makes one wonder why Tennyson stretched his syntax so awkwardly to bring it in. Local aptness appears to be secondary to the cumulative effect of such images, which is to link the *Idylls'* myths about English national character to the landscape in which that character primarily resides. For people who have read the work, the sight of a landslide can

---

[72] Ricks, *Tennyson*, 259. 　　　　[73] 'Pelleas and Ettarre', 591–7.
[74] 'Geraint and Enid', 157–66.

summon up Geraint's encounter; when birds fall silent, they may think of Modred. The *Idylls* endeavour to inspirit the English countryside with recollections of key moments in a national mythology.

That—I think—was Tennyson's intention for his images; but they carry with them another implication which he may not have recognized. Arthur's rule is a dominion of spirit over the natural world; and nature in the end defeats his ambition that his people should be pure: 'Great Nature through the flesh herself hath made | Gives him the lie!'—as Vivien says.[75] Each simile enacts in microcosm the *Idylls'* great subject: the defeat of civilization; the turning away from culture to nature, from an ideal of perfected humanity to enjoyment of the beast within.

For Tennyson, living in a time of nation-building, human perfection required national unity. Among the tantalizing stories which Merlin recounts to Vivien before giving himself into her power, is one about a song sung by a young knight 'when first the question rose | About the founding of a Table Round'. The song expresses a desire for unity: 'such a song, such fire for fame' (and so on) 'That when he stopt we longed to hurl together, | And should have done it . . .' only, the hart with golden horns which they were hunting then appeared, and they set out chasing after it 'Through the dim land; and all day long we rode | Through the dim land . . .' until it vanished.[76] It was essential to nineteenth-century nationalism that there should exist an ideal of national unity, in which individuals would be utterly fulfilled. It was no less essential that this ideal should not be attainable, but should dwell tantalizingly in the future, in the past, and in the imagination, so that life, both political and personal, would be an endless falling-short. The possibilities and constraints, miseries and delights of this way of thinking—of this way of being—were, as we have seen, much and variously explored by Tennyson's contemporaries in their poems which mediate between the realms of the imagined and the actual. The *Idylls* starkly represent the impossibility of attaining an ideal of personal and national unity which they nonetheless urge their readers to pursue. As Merlin says at the end of his anecdote of failed endeavour: 'such a noble song was that'.

---

[75] 'Merlin and Vivien', 50–1.
[76] Ibid. 407–26. The last words of this paragraph are from line 431.

CODA: AFTER THE REALMS OF VERSE

The Brownings, Tennyson, and Clough all wrote poems having to do with matrimony, and found a variety of narrative possibilities in their common theme. *The Princess*, *The Bothie*, and *Aurora Leigh* tell of the achievement of a union; *Amours de Voyage* of a failed courtship; *Idylls of the King* and *The Ring and the Book* of unhappy marriage and separation. All these works establish connections between their stories about personal unification and a public arena in which unity is also at issue; but, again, they make these links in different ways. *Amours de Voyage* is set during an actual nationalist revolution, so that comparisons between personal and political ardour are brought explicitly into play. In *Idylls of the King*, the marriage of Arthur and Guinevere is in a nebulously symbolic relation to the unity of their kingdom, while the detailed historical positioning of *The Ring and the Book* is designed to attack those generalizing habits of the imagination upon which Tennyson relied. Finally, the poems all explore consonances between aesthetic and political forms, so that readers who enter into their realms of verse experience restraints and liberties, and patterns of cohesion and disintegration, which echo the concerns of their narratives.

For all these poets, stylistic preference and political opinion belong together in a continuum of thought and feeling; but in each of them the continuum incorporates different elements, drawing them together in different ways. The Brownings' interest in exploiting conflicts between the law of the verse and the freedom of the language both fosters and expresses their thinking about antagonisms between liberty and law on a national scale. However, Arthur Hugh Clough, whose political views were similar to theirs, writes in a different manner. Like Tennyson, he envisages unity primarily in terms of dictional texture; but the association between this conception of style and Burkean organic community—so important to Tennyson—is absent from his verse. Reading this generation of poets, therefore, we can discern various imaginative and stylistic propensities which come into contact with politics, but in such distinct ways, and with such diverse results, that it is impossible to formulate strict generalizations about their workings in the period as a whole. Rather, we should think in terms of potential associations being activated in particular circumstances.

Of course, not all mid-nineteenth-century poets, not even all major mid-nineteenth-century poets, exploited the group of creative possibilities which so occupied the Brownings, Clough, and Tennyson. Matthew Arnold held his verse back from the public issues to which they were attracted ('the Time Stream' in which you 'plunge and bellow', as he put it to Clough) allowing these to appear only in the distant background of 'Empedocles on Etna', and to cast only a pale shadow on his imitation classical tragedy, *Merope* (1857).[1] William Barnes found sufficient inspiration in Dorset life and landscape. Nonetheless, the interrelations between poetic form and stories of marital and national union which Tennyson, Clough, and the Brownings all in their diverse ways explored are peculiar to the mid-nineteenth century. Forty years earlier, forty years later, the same conjunctions do not appear.

In Chapters 3 and 7 I gave some indication of how the roots of this mid-nineteenth-century convergence can be traced in Byron and Wordsworth; a similarly sketchy account of how it fared in the work of later authors may help to frame the achievement of the poetry which has been the subject of this volume. Swinburne was excited by the unification of Italy and devoted to Mazzini: in *A Song of Italy* (1867) and *Songs Before Sunrise* (1871) he printed hundreds of pages of verse on Risorgimento themes. This writing, however, is not at all concerned to measure individual liberty against the claims of nationhood, or to gauge events of the present in relation to a putatively national past. Such issues would to Swinburne have seemed irredeemably prosaic: 'art knows nothing of time . . . servant of fact . . . she cannot in any way become', as he declared, thereby shutting out from his consideration all the discrepancies between 'hope and fact' which had interested

---

[1] *Letters of Matthew Arnold to Arthur Hugh Clough*, 95.

Elizabeth Barrett Browning.[2] Swinburne calls for the members of a nation to unite themselves utterly and all (in Browning's phrase) sing the same song: 'an hundred cities' mouths in one'.[3] As we saw in Chapter 2, he personifies the State as 'mother', and takes pleasure in imagining total submission to her commands: 'she alone and none other, | Shall cast down, shall build up, shall bring home'.[4] In his view, such obedience is a condition of liberty, for liberty means being freed from individuality, released into a continuum of sensation: 'How long till thralls live free?'—he asks 'England': 'How long till all thy soul be one with all thy sea?'[5]

Swinburne was the readier to hold such opinions, and the better able to embody them in writing, because, in the practice of his art, he discerned no conflict between the law of the verse and the freedom of the language. In an essay which takes issue with Patmore's formulation in the course of an attack on Browning, he maintains that for the true poet, 'laws' of form 'are current and ingrained in the very flesh and blood with which he works—burnt into his nerves and brain'; they exert upon him no greater pressure than moral law upon 'a man who cannot sin'.[6] His own verse creates the feeling of such an identity between freedom and law by characteristically producing rhythms which are either so variable as to suggest no underlying metrical norm ('Laus Veneris'), or so regular as hardly to depart from the prescription of the metre ('Prelude' to *Songs Before Sunrise)*. Writing of this kind does not ask its readers to gauge a relationship between voice and form, or to observe the creation of a dictional texture. Unlike Browning's monologues, or Tennyson's recollection poems, Swinburne's lyrics of national unity maintain no distance between themselves and the reader, asking us, rather, to abandon ourselves to their chorus of praise.

Yeats had a similar understanding of 'the purpose of rhythm': 'to prolong the moment of contemplation . . . to keep us in that state of perhaps real trance, in which the mind liberated from the pressure of the will is unfolded in symbols'.[7] Verse shaped to such

[2] A. C. Swinburne, *William Blake: A Critical Essay* (J. C. Hotten, 1868), 90.
[3] Swinburne, *A Song of Italy* (John Camden Hotten, 1867), 55.
[4] 'Dedication: To Joseph Mazzini', *Songs Before Sunrise*, p. vi.
[5] 'A Marching Song', *Songs Before Sunrise*, 186.
[6] *New Writings by Swinburne*, ed. Cecil Y. Lang (1964), 50–1.
[7] W. B. Yeats, *Essays and Introductions* (Macmillan, 1961), 159.

an aim may register with acuity impressions of the ambivalent aftermath of nationalist self-sacrifice ('A terrible beauty is born') or the blank motivations of heroism ('In balance with this life, this death'); but since it is not itself felt to be negotiating between freedom and constraint, individuality and convention, it cannot frame the questions which preoccupied Clough, the Brownings, and Tennyson.[8] The same must be true of a poet of free verse, such as Ezra Pound, for whom the act of writing will by definition not feel like an interaction between individual impulse and given form. In harmony with this style (cause and consequence can again not be distinguished) Pound is not interested in investigating the political, ethnic, and temporal constraints which operate on people's lives, preferring to dismiss these as 'provincial', and counteract them with versions and translations from medieval Italian and Chinese.[9] In his long poem, *The Cantos*, which is in many ways indebted to Browning, the attention to historical and national difference which characterized his predecessor disappears: Sigismundo Malatesta and Confucius speak indiscriminately to the present and to the world.

Many books have been and will be written about the political bearings of the poetry of Yeats and Pound: my brief remarks are intended only to suggest that they asked different questions about politics from the writers of the realms of verse, and in different ways. Partly, this is due to brute historical factors: by the time of the First World War, nationhood was hardly so attractive and puzzzling an idea as it had been half a century before. Equally, though, it was because they had a different understanding of what verse was and how it related to its readers.

In the last third of the twentieth century, as nation-building once more compelled the imaginations of people in Britain and Ireland, poets again adopted some of the modes of writing and imagining which characterized Tennyson, the Brownings, and Clough. The non-communicative couple in Paul Muldoon's 'Sushi' are descendants of Andrea and Lucrezia del Sarto, as the similarity between the two first lines announces:

---

[8] 'Easter, 1916', 80; 'An Irish Airman foresees his Death', 16. Quoted from W. B. Yeats, *The Poems*, 2nd edn., ed. Richard J. Finneran (Macmillan, 1981).

[9] See *Ezra Pound: Selected Prose, 1909–1965*, ed. William Cookson (Faber and Faber, 1973), 160.

'Why do we waste so much time in arguing?'

But do not let us quarrel any more;[10]

In Muldoon's poem, the silent reverie of the male character falls, not into blank verse like the speech of Andrea, but into half-rhymes which give a feeling of inevitability to the development of his thoughts. The only full rhymes are when the voice of his partner breaks in upon his musings: this might suggest that she is pulling him back towards his role in the couple as in the couplet; it might equally show that his mind and hers spontaneously chime. The uncertainty reaches its culmination when his and the poem's last word, 'Eriugena', reaches all the way back to her word in the first line, 'arguing', producing an unnerving coincidence of self, personal relationship, and artistic form which is distinctly reminiscent of Browning.

In a later poem, 'Wire', nationalist politics provide the occasion for another reflection on individuality and its limits. Here, the form of the solitary speaker's cerebration is more constrained, for the poem is a sestina, the sevenfold iteration of the six rhyme-words suggesting the inescapable resurgence of memories. Stumbling upon 'a makeshift hide or shooting-box' in Connecticut, he has the thoughts and fears that such a discovery would provoke in Northern Ireland. Words he thought he had left behind return:

> the hard-line
> yet again refusing to toe the line,
> the bullet and the ballot box,

The clichés of political rhetoric work their way into his mind to such an extent that he ducks down as if he himself 'were on the run'.[11] The psychological residue of political violence, although more subtle in its workings, seems no less oppressive than State control as portrayed in an earlier poem, 'The Boundary Commission', which is in two equal stanzas, perhaps suggesting that its language has been split in the same way as the institution named in the title has divided a village. On the other hand, the

[10] Paul Muldoon, *New Selected Poems, 1968–1994* (Faber and Faber, 1996), 126; Browning, 'Andrea del Sarto', 1.

[11] Muldoon, *Hay* (Faber and Faber, 1998), 94–5.

words themselves fall into two groups of quatrain half-rhymes as though inviting the separation. The query about the interaction between imposed and inherent form which is raised by the structure of the verse appears again in the central image: 'a shower of rain' divides 'Golightly's lane' (a personal name to contrast with the impersonal title); 'It might have been a wall of glass | That had toppled over'.[12] The weather creates a natural border; but the comparison makes it look like the result of violence, of a bomb shattering a shop window. As it moves from rain to glass, from nature to culture (the reverse of Tennyson's practice in *Idylls of the King*), the image suggests an inevitability in the hardening of ethnic diversity into conflict; equally, it may carry a lament for a time when the protagonist could see rain without thinking of shattered windows.

The difficult relation between identities felt as inherent and those felt to be imposed is again at issue in Kate Clanchy's 'The Bridge Over the Border'. On a stopped train, the female speaker remembers a time when, in the same place, she was subjected to the attentions of an American who 'saw a country in my eyes', configuring her as—we might say—a Scotland of women in the manner of Barrett Browning or of Tennyson. Then, too, she remembered something, another bridge, which she had been crossing in pursuit of another man until she had stopped to look at swallows,

> . . . drawn
> to Africa, or heat, or home, not knowing
> which, but certain how. . . .

Like Pompilia's reaction to her pregnancy, this image hints at a comparison between national identity and a natural homing instinct. However, the swallows seem to the speaker like 'crosses on stock-market graphs', the move from nature to culture here, as in the Muldoon, drawing attention to factors in the construction of nationhood, in this case economic compulsion. The poem's last line has about it a feeling of redemption: 'and I stared, as if panning for gold'; but 'gold' harks back through the stock-market to the 'filmic, golden light' which had prompted the American's declaration in the first place while a busker plucked out '*Scotland the*

---

[12] Muldoon, *New Selected Poems*, 38.

Brave.[13] In fluid sentences which elude the stanzas' grasp, 'The Bridge Over the Border' describes a flight away from an extraneous, phoney-seeming national identity into memory and the personal life. However, those realms provide no better grounds in which to secure a sense of selfhood.

'The Boundary Commission', a poem about Ireland, and 'The Bridge Over the Border', a poem about Scotland, both owe debts to that most English of post-war lyrics, 'The Whitsun Weddings'. Larkin's verse itself echoes the 'The Lotos-Eaters' as it describes a train's 'slow and stopping curve' through 'the tall heat', 'All afternoon'. The succeeding events would have seemed to Tennyson no less familiar than the atmosphere in which they occur: weddings, at each station the departure of a new couple, so that in all, on that journey, 'A dozen marriages got under way'. The unifying scope of marriage in *The Princess* and *Aurora Leigh* is here made almost comically literal, as the couples are brought together unawares into the same social and poetic form, and board that most Victorian of contributions to national unity, a train. They journey to the national capital:

> . . . We slowed again,
> And as the tightened brakes took hold, there swelled
> A sense of falling, like an arrow-shower
> Sent out of sight, somewhere becoming rain.[14]

In so far as the arrows are like sperm, the image is about the transmutation of desire into new life. In so far as they are exemplary of battle—they recall in particular the arrow-shower at Agincourt in Olivier's 1944 film of *Henry V*—they ask us to think about the wars and other forms of violence underlying the community in which the couples will live their lives, and about the processes by which the results of such conflicts are made to appear as natural as rain (although not, we are reminded by 'The Boundary Commission', if you live in Northern Ireland). It would be too easy to say that rain is the ideal of nationhood and arrows its reality: nations require violence, but they also create a sense of belonging from which people may draw comfort, even inspiration; just as, although sex is a biological imperative, people

13 Kate Clanchy, *Samarkand* (Picador, 1999), 1.
14 Philip Larkin, *Collected Poems*, ed. Anthony Thwaite (Faber and Faber, 1988), 114–16.

nonetheless feel love. If we take the arrows as alluding to the Second World War, the 'somewhere' is the here inhabited by the newly-weds and perhaps also by the speaker. If we take them as suggesting endeavour in the present, directed towards an uncertain future, the 'somewhere' is a 'somewhere far off' like that into which Arthur departs at the end of *Idylls of the King*. Either way, among the manœuvres by which they are converted into rain are the doings of imagination, including Larkin's poem itself. As it conducts its knowing idealization of England, 'The Whitsun Weddings' acts like the poems of the Brownings, Tennyson, and Clough, enquiring into the processes in which it is itself involved, and thereby mediating between individuals and their nation, between the now, the future, and the past: between here and 'somewhere'.

WORKS CITED

Works mentioned in passing in the body of the text, but not cited in the notes, are not included in this list. Essays first printed anonymously in Victorian periodicals are listed under the name of the journal in which they appeared. Place of publication is London unless otherwise stated.

AARSLEFF, HANS, *The Study of Language in England, 1780–1860* (Athlone Press, 1967; repr. 1979).

ACTON, JOHN EMERICH EDWARD DALBERG, FIRST BARON ACTON, *Essays on Freedom and Power* (Thames and Hudson, 1956).

ALAYA, FLAVIA, 'The Ring, the Rescue, & the Risorgimento: Reunifying the Browning's Italy', *Browning Institute Studies*, 6 (1978), 1–41.

ALLINGHAM, WILLIAM, *William Allingham's Diary*, ed. Geoffrey Grigson (Centaur, 1967).

ALTHUSSER, LOUIS, *Essays on Ideology* (Verso, 1984).

ANDERSON, BENEDICT, *Imagined Communities: Reflections on the Origin and Spread of Nationalism*, 2nd edn. (Verso, 1991).

Anon., *The Admirable Letter of the Count de Montalembert, to the Rev. —, Member of the Cambridge Camden Society, on the Architectural, Artistical, and Archaeological Investigations of the Puseyites* (Cambridge: J. B. Thompson, 1844).

Anon., 'The Briton's Lament for Italy', *New Monthly Magazine*, 2 (1821), 17.

Anon., 'Bravo, Mazzini', *Punch*, 17 (1849), 35.

Anon., *Irish Seditions; Their Origin and History from 1792–1880: Ireland's Curse—England's Trouble* (Diprose and Bateman, 1883).

ARMSTRONG, ISOBEL, *Language as Living Form* (Brighton: Harvester, 1982).

—— *Victorian Poetry: Poetry Poetics, and Politics* (Routledge, 1993).

ARMSTRONG, JOHN A., *Nations Before Nationalism* (Chapel Hill, NC: University of North Carolina Press, 1982).

ARNOLD, MATTHEW, *The Complete Prose Works of Matthew Arnold*, ed. R. H. Super, 11 vols. (Ann Arbor: University of Michigan Press, 1960–77).

—— *The Letters of Matthew Arnold to Arthur Hugh Clough*, ed. H. F. Lowry (Oxford: Oxford University Press, 1932).

—— *The Poems of Matthew Arnold*, 2nd edn., ed. Kenneth and Mirian Allott (Longman, 1979).

ASHFORD, JOHN, *Italy's Hope: A Tale of Florence* (J. F. Hope, 1857).

BAILEY, PETER, *Popular Culture and Performance in the Victorian City* (Cambridge: Cambridge University Press, 1998),

BAKHTIN, M. M., *Speech Genres and Other Late Essays*, trans. Vern W. McGee (Austin, Tex.: University of Texas Press, 1986).

BARKER, JOHN SALE, 'Italian Unity and the National Movement in Europe', *Macmillan's Magazine*, 3 (Nov. 1860), 71–80.

BARNES, WILLIAM, *Poems of Rural Life in the Dorset Dialect: With a Dissertation and Glossary*, 2nd edn. (John Russell Smith, 1848).

BEALES, DEREK, *England and Italy, 1859–60* (Thomas Nelson and Sons, 1961).

—— 'Garibaldi in England: The Politics of Italian Enthusiasm', John A. Davis and Paul Ginsborg (eds.), *Society and Politics in the Age of the Risorgimento* (Cambridge: Cambridge University Press, 1991).

—— *The Risorgimento and the Unification of Italy* (George Allen and Unwin, 1971).

BEETZ, KIRK H., *Tennyson: A Bibliography, 1827–1982* (Scarecrow, 1984).

BHABHA, HOMI K., *The Location of Culture* (Routledge, 1994).

BIAGINI, EUGENIO F., *Liberty, Retrenchment and Reform: Popular Liberalism in the Age of Gladstone, 1860–1880* (Cambridge: Cambridge University Press, 1992).

Blackwood's Edinburgh Magazine, 85 (Mar. 1859), 350–65: 'Italy: Her Nationality or Dependence' (J. B. Atkinson).

—— 90 (Oct. 1861), 463–78: 'Social Science' (J. B. Atkinson).

BLAGDEN, ISA, *Agnes Tremorne*, 2 vols. (Smith, Elder and Co., 1861).

BLESSINGTON, COUNTESS OF (ed.), *The Keepsake for 1846* (1845).

The Book of Common Prayer (Oxford University Press, n.d.).

BOYCE, D. GEORGE., *The Irish Question and British Politics 1868–86* (Macmillan, 1988).

—— Nationalism in Ireland, 2nd edn. (Routledge, 1991).

BRATTON, J. S., et al., *Acts of Supremacy: The British Empire and the Stage, 1790–1830* (Manchester: Manchester University Press, 1991).

BREUILLY, JOHN., *Nationalism and the State* (Manchester: Manchester University Press, 1985).

BROWNING, ELIZABETH BARRETT, *Aurora Leigh*, ed. Margaret Reynolds (Athens, Oh.: Ohio University Press, 1992).

—— *Casa Guidi Windows*, ed. Julia Markus (New York: Browning Institute, 1977).

—— *The Complete Works of Elizabeth Barrett Browning*, 6 vols., ed. Charlotte Porter and Helen A. Clarke (New York: Thomas Y. Crowell and Co., 1900).

BROWNING, ELIZABETH BARRETT, *An Essay on Mind, With Other Poems* (James Duncan, 1826).

—— *Hitherto Unpublished Poems and Stories*, 2 vols. (Boston: Bibliophile Society, 1914).

—— *The Letters of Elizabeth Barrett Browning*, 2 vols., ed. Frederick G. Kenyon (Smith, Elder and Co., 1897).

—— *The Letters of Elizabeth Barrett Browning to Mary Russell Mitford, 1836–54*, ed. Meredith B. Raymond and Mary Rose Sullivan, 3 vols. (Winfield, Kan.: Wedgestone Press, 1983).

—— and BROWNING, ROBERT, *The Brownings' Correspondence*, ed. Philip Kelley, Ronald Hudson, and Scott Lewis (Winfield, Kan.: Wedgestone Press, 1984–).

BROWNING, ROBERT, *Browning to his American Friends: Letters between the Brownings, the Storys and James Russell Lowell 1841–1890*, ed. Gertrude Reese Hudson (Bowes and Bowes, 1965).

—— *Dearest Isa: Robert Browning's Letters to Isabella Blagden*, ed. Edward C. McAleer (Austin, Tex.: University of Texas Press, 1951).

—— *The Poems*, ed. John Pettigrew, 2 vols. (Harmondsworth: Penguin, 1981).

—— *The Poems of Browning*, ed. John Woolford and Daniel Karlin (Longman, 1991–).

—— *The Poetical Works of Robert Browning*, general ed. Ian Jack (Oxford: Clarendon Press, 1983–).

—— *The Ring and the Book*, ed. Richard D. Altick (Harmondsworth: Penguin, 1981).

—— *Robert Browning and Julia Wedgwood: A Broken Friendship as Revealed in their Letters*, ed. Richard Curle (John Murray and Jonathan Cape, 1937).

—— *Robert Browning's Prose Life of Strafford*, introduction by C. H. Firth (Kegan Paul, Trench, Trübner and Co., for the Browning Society, 1892).

—— 'The Tomb at St Praxed's', *Hood's Magazine*, 3/3 (Mar. 1845), 237.

—— and BROWNING, ELIZABETH BARRETT, *The Letters of Robert Browning and Elizabeth Barrett Barrett, 1845–6*, 2 vols. ed. Elvan Kintner (Cambridge, Mass.: Harvard Univerity Press, 1969).

BULWER: see 'Lytton'.

BURKE, EDMUND, *Reflections on the Revolution in France* (1790), ed. Conor Cruise O'Brien (Harmondsworth: Penguin, 1968).

BYRON, GEORGE GORDON, Lord, *Byron's Letters and Journals*, 12 vols., ed. Leslie A Marchand (John Murray, 1973–82).

—— *Lord Byron: The Complete Poetical Works*, 7 vols., ed. Jerome J. McGann (Oxford: Clarendon Press, 1980–93).

Cambridge Camden Society, *Report of the Cambridge Camden Society* (Cambridge: printed for the society, 1840).

CANDELORO, GIORGIO, *Storia dell'Italia Moderna*, 2nd edn., 11 vols. (Milan: Feltrinelli, 1988–91), vols. i–v.

CARLYLE, THOMAS, *Critical and Miscellaneous Essays*, 5 vols. (Chapman and Hall, 1899).

—— *On Heroes, Hero-Worship and the Heroic in History* (Chapman and Hall, 1897).

CASTAN, CORA, 'Structural Problems and the Poetry of *Aurora Leigh'*, *Browning Society Notes*, 7/3 (1977), 73–81.

CHAMBERS, W. S., *Garibaldi and Italian Unity* (Smith, Elder and Co., 1864).

CHESTERTON, G. K., *Robert Browning* (Macmillan, 1913).

CLANCHY, KATE, *Samarkand* (Picador, 1999).

CLOUGH, ARTHUR HUGH, *The Correspondence of Arthur Hugh Clough*, ed. Frederick L. Mulhauser, 2 vols. (Oxford: Clarendon Press, 1957).

—— *The Poems of Arthur Hugh Clough*, 2nd edn., ed. F. L. Mulhauser (Oxford: Clarendon Press, 1974).

—— *Poems and Prose Remains of Arthur Hugh Clough*, ed. Blanche Clough, 2 vols. (Macmillan, 1869).

—— *Selected Prose Works of Arthur Hugh Clough*, ed. Buckner B. Trawick (University, Ala.: University of Alabama Press, 1964).

COLERIDGE, SAMUEL TAYLOR, *Biographia Literaria: Or Biographical Sketches of My Literary Life and Opinions*, 2 vols., ed. James Engell and W. Jackson Bate (Princeton: Princeton University Press, 1984).

—— *On the Constitution of Church and State*, ed. John Colmer (Princeton: Princeton University Press, 1971).

COLLEY, LINDA, *Britons: Forging the Nation, 1707–1837* (New Haven: Yale University Press, 1992).

—— 'Whose Nation? Class and National Consciousness in Britain, 1750–1830', *Past and Present*, 113 (Nov. 1986), 97–118.

COOPER, HELEN, *Elizabeth Barrett Browning, Woman and Artist* (Chapel Hill, NC: University of North Carolina Press, 1988).

COUPLAND, REGINALD, *Welsh and Scottish Nationalism: A Study* (Collins, 1954).

CRAWFORD, MABEL SHERMAN, *Life in Tuscany* (Smith, Elder and Co., 1859).

CUNDALL, FRANK, *Reminiscences of the Colonial and Indian Exhibition* (William Clowes and Sons, 1886).

DAVID, DEIRDRE, *Intellectual Women and Victorian Patriarchy: Harriet Martineau, Elizabeth Barrett Browning, George Eliot* (Macmillan, 1987).

DAVIES, JOHN, *A History of Wales* (Harmondsworth: Penguin, 1994).

DELANNOI, GIL and TAGUIEFF, PIERRE-ANDRÉ, *Théories du Nationalisme: Nation, Nationalité, Ethnicité* (Paris: Kimé, 1991).

DE LAURA, DAVID J., 'The Context of Browning's Painter Poems: Aesthetics, Polemics, Historics', *PMLA*, 95 (1980).

DICEY, EDWARD, *Rome in 1860* (Macmillan, 1861).

DICKENS, CHARLES, *Little Dorrit*, ed. Harvey Peter Sucksmith (Oxford: Clarendon Press, 1979).

—— *The Nonesuch Dickens: Collected Papers*, ed. Arthur Waugh *et al.* 2 vols., (Nonesuch Press, 1937).

—— *Pictures from Italy* (1846), ed. Kate Flint (Harmondsworth: Penguin, 1998).

DOBELL, SIDNEY, *The Roman* (R. Bentley, 1850).

DONALDSON, SANDRA, *Elizabeth Barrett Browning: An Annotated Bibliography of the Commentary and Criticism, 1826–1990* (G. K. Hall, 1993).

DONNE, JOHN, *The Elegies and The Songs and Sonnets*, ed. Helen Gardner (Oxford: Clarendon Press, 1965).

DURHAM, EARL OF, *The Report of the Earl of Durham, Her Majesty's High Commissioner and Governor General of British North America: A New Edition* (Methuen and Co., 1902).

Edinburgh Review, 55/110 (July 1832), 362–97, 'Political Condition of the Italian States' (William Empson).

—— 63/125 (Apr. 1836), 225–39, 'The Oxford Malignants and Dr. Hampden' (Thomas Arnold).

—— 93/190 (Apr. 1851), 498–534, 'The Defeat of Italy' (Henry Lushington).

ELDRIDGE, C. C. (ed.), *British Imperialism in the Nineteenth Century* (Macmillan, 1984).

ELIOT, GEORGE, *Collected Poems*, ed. Lucien Jenkins (Skoob Books, 1989).

—— *Middlemarch*, ed. David Carroll (Oxford: Clarendon Press, 1986).

—— *George Eliot: Selected Critical Writings*, ed. Rosemary Ashton (Oxford: Oxford University Press, 1992).

ELIOT, T. S., *On Poetry and Poets* (Faber and Faber, 1957).

EMPSON, WILLIAM, *Some Versions of Pastoral* (1935; Hogarth Press, 1986).

EVERETT, BARBARA, *Poets in their Time: Essays on English Poetry from Donne to Larkin* (Oxford: Clarendon Press, 1991).

Foreign Quarterly Review, 11/21 (Jan., 1833), 29–72, 'Modern Rome and the Papal Government' (André Vieusseux).

FORSTER, MARGARET, *Elizabeth Barrett Browning* (Vintage, 1998).

FREEMAN, E. A. 'The Origins of the English Nation (Part III)', *Macmillan's Magazine*, 22 (May 1870), 31–46.

FREUD, SIGMUND, *Civilization and its Discontents*, ed. James Strachey (Hogarth Press, 1975).

GALLENGA, ANTONIO (pseud. Luigi Mariotti), *Italy in 1848* (Chapman and Hall, 1851).

GASKELL, ELIZABETH, *North and South* (1855), ed. Angus Easson (Oxford: Oxford University Press, 1982).

GELLNER, ERNEST, *Nations and Nationalism* (Oxford: Blackwell, 1983).

GILBERT, SANDRA M., 'From *Patria* to *Matria*: Elizabeth Barrett Browning's Risorgimento', Angela Leighton (ed.), *Victorian Women Poets: A Critical Reader*, (Oxford: Blackwell, 1996), 24–52.

GISSING, GEORGE, *By the Ionian Sea: Notes of a Ramble in Southern Italy* (Chapman and Hall, 1901).

GIUSTI, GIUSEPPE, *Opere di Giuseppe Giusti*, ed. Nunzio Sabbatucci (Milan: UTET, 1976).

GLADSTONE, W. E., *Gleanings of Past Years, 1843–78* (John Murray, 1879).

—— *Two Letters to the Earl of Aberdeen on the State Prosecutions of the Neapolitan Government* (John Murray, 1851).

—— *The State in its Relations with the Church* (John Murray, 1838).

GOODE, JOHN, '1848 and the Strange Disease of Modern Love', John Lucas (ed.), *Literature and Politics in the Nineteenth Century*, Methuen, 1971), 45–76.

—— '*Amours de Voyage*: The Aqueous Poem', Isobel Armstrong (ed.), *The Major Victorian Poets: Reconsiderations*, (Routledge and Kegan Paul, 1969), 275–97.

GOSSE, EDMUND, *Father and Son: A Study of Two Temperaments*, ed. Peter Abbs (Harmondsworth: Penguin, 1983).

GREENBERG, ROBERT A., 'Ruskin, Pugin, and the Contemporary Context of "The Bishop Orders his Tomb" ', PMLA, 84/6 (Oct. 1969) 1588–94.

GREENBLATT, STEPHEN, *Shakespearean Negotiations: The Circulation of Social Energy in Renaissance England* (Oxford: Clarendon Press, 1988).

GRIFFITHS, ERIC, *The Printed Voice of Victorian Poetry* (Oxford: Clarendon Press, 1989).

HABERMAS, JÜRGEN, *The Structural Transformation of the Public Sphere: An Inquiry into a Category of Bourgeois Society*, trans. Thomas Burger and Frederick Lawrence (Cambridge: Polity Press, 1989).

HALLAM, ARTHUR, *The Writings of Arthur Hallam*, ed. T. H. Vail Motter (Modern Language Association of America, New York, 1943).

Handbook for Travellers in Central Italy including the Papal States, Rome, and the Cities of Etruria (John Murray, 1843).

Hansard's Parliamentary Debates (London).

HARDY, BARBARA, *The Advantage of Lyric: Essays on Feeling in Poetry* (Athlone Press, 1977).

HAYTER, ALETHEA, *Mrs Browning: A Poet's Work and its Setting* (Faber, 1962).

HEGEL, G. W. F., *The Philosophy of History*, trans. J. Sibree (1899; repr. New York; Dover Publications, 1956).

—— *Vorlesungen über die Philosophie der Geschichte*, ed. T. Litt (Stuttgart: Philipp Declam, 1989).

HELGERSON, RICHARD, *Forms of Nationhood: The Elizabethan Writing of England* (Chicago: University of Chicago Press, 1992).

HELSINGER, ELIZABETH K., *Rural Scenes and National Representation: Britain, 1815–1850* (Princeton: Princeton University Press, 1997).

HEMANS, FELICIA, *The Works of Mrs Hemans*, 7 vols., (Edinburgh: Blackwood, 1839).

HOBBES, THOMAS, *Leviathan*, ed. Richard Tuck (Cambridge: Cambridge University Press, 1991).

HOBSBAWM, ERIC, *Nations and Nationalism since 1780: Programme, Myth, Reality*, 2nd edn. (Cambridge: Cambridge University Press, 1992).

HOPPEN, K. THEODORE, *The Mid-Victorian Generation, 1846–1886* (Oxford: Clarendon Press, 1998), 200.

HOUGHTON, WALTER E., and SLINGERSLAND, JEAN (eds.), *The Wellesley Index to Victorian Periodicals*, new edn. CD-ROM (Routledge, 1999).

HUMBOLDT, WILHELM VON, *Ideen zu einem Versuch, die Gränzen der Wirksamkeit des Staats zu bestimmen* (Breslau: Eduard Trewendt, 1851).

—— *The Sphere and Duties of Government*, trans. J. Coulthard (Chapman, 1854).

HUTCHINSON, JOHN, and SMITH, ANTHONY D., *Nationalism* (Oxford: Oxford University Press, 1994).

HYAM, RONALD, *Britain's Imperial Century, 1815–1914: A Study of Empire and Expansion*, 2nd edn. (Macmillan, 1993).

Illustrated London News.

IRVINE, WILLIAM, and HONAN, PARK, *The Book, the Ring and the Poet: A Biography of Robert Browning* (Bodley Head, 1974).

IRVING, WASHINGTON, *A History of the Life and Times of Christopher Columbus*, 4 vols. (Paris: A. and W. Galignani, 1828).

JAKOBSON, ROMAN, *Language in Literature* (Cambridge, Mass.: Harvard University Press, 1987).

JAMES, HENRY, *Italian Hours*, ed. John Auchard (University Park, Pa.: Pennsylvania State University Press, 1992).

—— *William Wetmore Story and his Friends*, 2 vols. (Thames and Hudson, 1903).

JAMESON, MRS, *Memoirs of the Early Italian Painters and of the Progress of Painting in Italy*, 2 vols. (Charles Knight, 1845).

JUDD, DENIS, *Empire: The British Imperial Experience, 1765 to the Present*, (Harper Collins, 1996), 52–3.

JUMP, JOHN D. (ed.), *Tennyson: The Critical Heritage* (Routledge and Kegan Paul, 1967).

KARLIN, DANIEL, *The Courtship of Robert Browning and Elizabeth Barrett* (Oxford: Clarendon Press, 1985).

—— 'The Sources of the Italian in England', *Browning Society Notes*, vol. 14/3 (Winter, 1984–5), 23–43.

KEATS, JOHN, *The Poems of John Keats*, ed. Miriam Allott (Longman, 1970).

(KEBLE, JOHN), *Tract 89: On the Mysticism Attributed to the Early Fathers of the Church*, 2nd edn. (J., G., and F. Rivington, 1842).

—— *The Christian Year*, 67th edn. (John Henry and James Parker, 1860).

KEMILAINEN, AIRA, *Nationalism: Problems Concerning the Word, the Concept and Classification* (Jyväskylä: Studia Historica Jyväskyläentia 3, 1964).

KIERNAN, V. G., *Poets, Politics and the People*, ed. Harvey J. Kaye (Verso, 1989).

KILLHAM, JOHN, *Tennyson and The Princess: Reflections of an Age* (Athlone Press, 1958).

KING, HARRIET ELEANOR HAMILTON, *The Disciples* (Henry S. King and Co., 1873).

—— *Letters and Recollections of Mazzini*, (Longmans, Green and Co., 1912).

KINGSLEY, CHARLES, *Alton Locke, Tailor and Poet: An Autobiography* (1850; Macmillan, 1876).

KNOX, ROBERT, *The Races of Men* (Henry Renshaw, 1850).

KRISTEVA, JULIA, *Nations without Nationalism*, trans. Leon S. Roudiez (New York: Columbia University Press, 1993).

LANDON, LETITIA ELIZABETH, *The Improvisatrice and Other Poems*, (Longman, Rees, Orme, Brown and Green, 1831).

LANGBAUM, ROBERT, *The Poetry of Experience: The Dramatic Monologue in Modern Literary Tradition*, 3rd edn. (Chicago: University of Chicago Press, 1985).

LARKIN, PHILIP, *Collected Poems*, ed. Anthony Thwaite (Faber and Faber, 1988).

LATHAM, EDWARD, *Famous Sayings and their Authors*, 2nd edn. (Swan Sonnenschein, 1906).

LEAVIS, F. R., *New Bearings in English Poetry: A Study of the Contemporary Situation* (1932; Harmondsworth: Penguin, 1972).

LEWIS, LINDA M., *Elizabeth Barrett Browning's Spiritual Progress: Face to Face with God* (Columbia, Miss.: University of Missouri Press, 1998).

LITZINGER, BOYD and SMALLEY, DONALD (eds.), *Browning: The Critical Heritage* (Routledge and Kegan Paul, 1970).

LLOYD, DAVID, *Nationalism and Minor Literature: James Clarence Mangan and the Emergence of Irish Cultural Nationalism* (Berkeley and Los Angeles: University of California Press, 1987).

London Quarterly Review, 169, n.s. 49 (Oct. 1895), 76–95, 'Tennyson's King Arthur' (Annie E. Keeling).

LYTTON, E. BULWER, LORD LYTTON, *England and the English*, 2 vols. (R. Bentley, 1833).

—— *King Arthur*, 2 vols. (Henry Colburn, 1849).

LYTTON, E. BULWER, LORD LYTTON, *Rienzi* (1835; J. M. Dent, 1911).

MCGANN, JEROME J., *The Beauty of Inflections: Literary Investigations in Historical Method and Theory* (Oxford: Clarendon Press, 1985).

MAIDEN, MARTIN, *A Linguistic History of Italian* (Longman, 1995).

MANGAN, JAMES CLARENCE, *The Collected Works of James Clarence Mangan*, ed. Jacques Chuto, 4 vols. (Blackrock, Co. Dublin: Irish Academic Press, 1996–9).

MANZONI, ALESSANDRO, *I promessi sposi* (1840–2), trans. as T*he Betrothed and History of the Column of Infamy*, ed. David Forgacs and Matthew Reynolds (J. M. Dent, 1997).

MARTIN, ROBERT BERNARD, *Tennyson: The Unquiet Heart* (Oxford: Clarendon Press, 1983).

MARX, KARL, *Critique of Hegel's Philosophy of Right*, ed. Joseph J. O'Malley (Cambridge: Cambridge University Press, 1970).

—— *Karl Marx: Selected Writings*, ed. David McLellan (Oxford: Oxford University Press, 1977).

MAZZINI, GIUSEPPE, *Life and Writings of Joseph Mazzini*, 6 vols. (Smith, Elder and Co., 1864–7).

MEREDITH, GEORGE, *Vittoria* (Chapman and Hall, 1889).

MERIVALE, HERMAN, *Introduction to a Course of Lectures on Colonization and the Colonies* (Longman, 1839).

MICHELET, JULES, *Histoire de la Révolution française*, 5 vols. (Paris: Chamerot, 1847–50).

MILL, JOHN STUART, *On Liberty and Other Essays*, ed. John Gray (Oxford: Oxford University Press, 1991).

MILTON, JOHN, *The Works of John Milton*, general ed. Frank Allen Patterson (New York: Columbia University Press, 1931–8).

Monitore Toscano (Florence).

(MOORE, THOMAS), *The Fudge Family in Paris, edited by Thomas Brown, the Younger*, 2nd edn. (Longman, Hurst, Rees, Orme and Brown, 1818).

MORETTI, FRANCO, *Modern Epic: The World System from Goethe to Garcia Marquez*, trans. Quintin Hoare (Verso, 1996).

MULDOON, PAUL, *New Selected Poems, 1968–1994* (Faber and Faber, 1996).

—— *Hay* (Faber and Faber, 1998).

MYERS, ERNEST, *The Defence of Rome and Other Poems* (Macmillan, 1880).

NAOROJI, DADABHAI, 'The Pros and Cons of British Rule' (1871), in W. Theodore de Bary (ed.), *Sources of Indian Tradition*, W. Theodore de Bary, 2 vols. (New York: Columbia University Press, 1964).

North British Review, 9/17 (May 1848), 43–72, 'Tennyson's *Poems—The Princess*' (Coventry Patmore).

NUSSBAUM, MARTHA C., *Love's Knowledge: Essays on Philosophy and Literature* (New York: Oxford University Press, 1990).

ORMOND, LEONEE, 'Browning and Painting', in Isobel Armstrong (ed.), *Robert Browning* (G. Bell and Sons, 1974).

PAGE, NORMAN (ed.), *Tennyson: Interviews and Recollections* (Macmillan, 1983).

PALGRAVE, FRANCIS T., *The Visions of England*, 2 vols. (privately printed, 1881–2).

PARTRIDGE, ERIC, *A Dictionary of Slang and Unconventional English*, ed. Paul Beale (Routledge and Kegan Paul, 1984).

PATMORE, COVENTRY, *Coventry Patmore's 'Essay on English Metrical Law': A Critical Edition with Commentary*, ed. Sister Mary Augustine Roth (Washington: Catholic University of America Press, 1961).

PAULIN, TOM, *Minotaur: Poetry and the Nation-State* (Faber and Faber, 1992).

PEMBLE, JOHN, *The Mediterranean Passion: Victorians and Edwardians in the South* (Oxford: Clarendon Press, 1987).

PERUTA, FRANCO DELLA, *Società e classi popolari nell'Italia dell'ottocento* (Palermo: EPOS, 1985).

PHELAN, JOSEPH PATRICK, 'Elizabeth Barrett Browning's *Casa Guidi Windows*, Arthur Hugh Clough's *Amours de Voyage* and the Italian National Uprisings of 1847–9', *Journal of Anglo-Italian Studies*, 3 (1993), 137–52.

—— 'Radical Metre: The English Hexameter in Clough's *Bothie of Toper-na-Fuosich*', *Review of English Studies*, NS 50/198 (1999), 166–87.

PHIPPS, CHARLES T., S.J, 'Adaptation from the Past, Creation for the Present: A Study of Browning's "The Pope" ', *Studies in Philology*, 65 (1968), 702–22.

POPE, ALEXANDER, *The Poems of Alexander Pope*, ed. John Butt (Methuen, 1963).

PORTER, ANDREW (ed.), *The Oxford History of the British Empire, Volume iii: The Nineteenth Century* (Oxford: Oxford University Press, 1999).

POUND, EZRA, *Ezra Pound: Selected Prose, 1909–1965*, ed. William Cookson (Faber, 1973).

Quarterly Review, 83/166 (Sept. 1848), 552–84. 'Whiteside on Italy' (Edward Cheney).

—— 105/209 (Apr. 1859), 527–64, 'Foreign Affairs – War in Italy' (W. E. Gladstone).

—— 110/219 (July 1861), 208–47, 'Cavour' (A. H. Layard).

—— 130/259 (Jan. 1871), 71–92, 'Count Bismarck, Prussia, and Pan-Teutonism' (John Wilson).

RADER, RALPH W., 'The Dramatic Monologue and Related Lyric Forms', *Critical Inquiry*, 3/1 (Autumn, 1976), 131–53.

RICKS, CHRISTOPHER, *Tennyson*, 2nd edn. (Macmillan, 1989).

ROEBUCK, J. A., *The Colonies of England* (J. W. Parker, 1849).

ROSENBERG, JOHN D., *The Fall of Camelot: A Study of Tennyson's Idylls of the King* (Cambridge, Mass.: Harvard University Press, 1973).

RUDMAN, HARRY W., *Italian Nationalism and English Letters* (G. Allen and Unwin, 1940).

(RUFFINI, GIOVANNI), *Dr Antonio: A Tale: By the Author of Lorenzo Benoni* (Edinburgh: Thomas Constable, 1855).

RUSKIN, JOHN, *The Works of John Ruskin*, 39 vols., ed. E. T. Cook and Alexander Wedderburn (George Allen, 1903–12).

SCHAMA, SIMON, *Citizens: A Chronicle of the French Revolution* (Harmondsworth: Penguin, 1989).

SCHMITT, CANNON, *Alien Nation: Nineteenth-Century Gothic Fictions and English Nationality* (Philadelphia: University of Pennsylvania Press, 1997).

SCOTT, PATRICK GRIEG, *The Early Editions of Arthur Hugh Clough* (New York: Garland, 1977).

SEELEY, J. R., *The Expansion of England* (Macmillan, 1883).

SETON-WATSON, HUGH, *Nations and States: An Enquiry into the Origins of Nations and the Politics of Nationalism* (Methuen, 1977).

SHAKESPEARE, WILLIAM, *Shakespeare's Comedies, Histories, & Tragedies: Being a Reproduction of the First Folio Edition, 1623* (Oxford: Clarendon Press, 1902).

—— *The Riverside Shakespeare*, 2nd edn., ed. G. Blakemore Evans (Boston: Houghton Mifflin, 1997).

SHANNON, EDGAR F., 'Poetry as Vision: Sight and Insight in "The Lady of Shalott" ', *Victorian Poetry*, 19 (1981), 207–23.

SHATTO, SUSAN, 'The Strange Charm of "Far, Far Away": Tennyson, the Continent and the Empire', Michael Cotsell (ed.), *Creditable Warriors* ed. Michael Cotsell (Ashfield Press, 1990), 113–29.

SHAW, A. G. L., 'British Attitudes to the Colonies, *ca.* 1820–1850', *Journal of British Studies*, 9/1 (Nov. 1969), 71–95.

SHELLEY, PERCY BYSSHE, *Shelley's Prose: or, The Trumpet of a Prophecy*, ed. David Lee Clark (Albuqerque, N. Mex.: University of New Mexico Press, 1966).

SINFIELD, ALAN, *Alfred Tennyson* (Oxford: Blackwell, 1986).

SISMONDI, J. C. L. DE, *History of the Italian Republics; or, the Origin, Progress, and Fall of Italian Freedom*, new edn. (Longman, Orme, Brown, Green and Longmans, and John Taylor, 1838).

SMITH, ANTHONY D., *National Identity* (Harmondsworth: Penguin, 1991).

SMITH, DENIS MACK, *The Making of Italy, 1796–1866* (Macmillan, 1968).

—— *Mazzini* (New Haven: Yale University Press, 1994).

SMITH, GOLDWYN, *The Empire: A Series of Letters Published in 'The Daily News', 1862, 1863* (John Henry and James Parker, 1863).

SPRINGER, CAROLYN, *The Marble Wilderness: Ruins and Representation in Italian Romanticism, 1775–1850* (Cambridge: Cambridge University Press, 1987).

STAËL, MADAME DE, *Corinne ou l'Italie* (1807; Paris: Gallimard, 1992).

STEPHEN, J. F., 'Foundations of the Government of India', Nineteenth Century, 14 (Oct. 1883), 541–68.

SWINBURNE, A. C., *New Writings by Swinburne*, ed. Cecil Y. Lang (1964), —— *A Song of Italy* (J. C. Hotten, 1867).

—— *Songs Before Sunrise* (F. S. Ellis, 1871).

—— *William Blake: A Critical Essay* (J. C. Hotten, 1868).

TAYLOR, BARBARA, *Eve and the New Jerusalem: Socialism and Feminism in the Nineteenth Century* (Virago, 1983).

TAYLOR, DENNIS, *Hardy's Metres and Victorian Prosody* (Oxford: Clarendon Press, 1988).

TAYLOR, HENRY, *Philip Van Artevelde: A Dramatic Romance* (Edward Moxon, 1834).

TENNYSON, ALFRED LORD, *The Letters of Alfred Lord Tennyson*, ed. Cecil Y. Lang and Edgar F. Shannon Jr., 3 vols. (Oxford: Oxford University Press, 1982–90).

—— *The Poems of Tennyson*, 2nd edn., ed. Christopher Ricks, 3 vols. (Longman, 1987).

TENNYSON, CHARLES, *Alfred Tennyson* (Macmillan, 1949; reissued 1968).

TENNYSON, EMILY LADY, *Lady Tennyson's Journal*, ed. James O. Hoge (Charlottesville, Va.: University Press of Virginia, 1981).

TENNYSON, G. B., *Victorian Devotional Poetry: The Tractarian Mode* (Cambridge, Mass.: Harvard University Press, 1981).

TENNYSON, HALLAM LORD, *Alfred Lord Tennyson: A Memoir: By his Son*, 2 vols. (Macmillan, 1897).

THORPE, MICHAEL (ed.), *Clough: The Critical Heritage* (New York: Barnes and Noble, 1972).

The Times.

TOSH, JOHN, *A Man's Place: Masculinity and the Middle-Class Home in Victorian England* (New Haven: Yale University Press, 1999).

TRENCH, R. C., *English Past and Present: Five Lectures* (John W. Parker and Son, 1855).

TREVELYAN, G. M., *Garibaldi's Defence of the Roman Republic* (Longmans, Green and Co., 1907).

—— *Garibaldi and the Thousand* (Longmans, Green and Co., 1909).

TREVELYAN, GEORGE OTTO, *The Competition Wallah* (Macmillan, 1864).

TROLLOPE, THOMAS ADOLPHUS, *Filippo Strozzi: A History of the Last Days of the old Italian Liberty* (Chapman and Hall, 1860).

—— *Tuscany in 1849 and in 1859* (Chapman and Hall, 1859).

TUCKER, HERBERT F., Jr, *Browning's Beginnings: The Art of Disclosure* (Minneapolis: University of Minnesota Press, 1980).

—— *Tennyson and the Doom of Romanticism* (Cambridge, Mass.: Harvard University Press, 1988).

TULLY, JAMES (ed.), *Meaning and Context: Quentin Skinner and his Critics* (Cambridge: Polity Press, 1988).

VERE, AUBREY DE, *Inisfail: A Lyrical Chronicle of Ireland* (Dublin: James Duffy, 1863).

—— *The Sisters, Inisfail, and Other Poems* (Longman, Green, Longman and Roberts, 1861).

VERGA, GIOVANNI, *I Malavoglia*, ed. G. Carnazzi (Milan: Rizzoli, 1978).

VISCUSI, ROBERT, ' "The Englishman in Italy": Free Trade as a Principle of Aesthetics', *Browning Institute Studies*, 12 (1984), 1–28.

WALKER, ALEXANDER, 'Characters of the English, Scots, and Irish', *Blackwood's Edinburgh Magazine*, 26/9 (Nov. 1829), 818–24.

Westminster and Foreign Quarterly Review, 53/104 (Apr. 1850), 57–85, 'The Liberty of Rome' (W. J. Linton).

WHITE, HAYDEN, *The Content of the Form: Narrative Discourse and Historical Representation* (Baltimore: Johns Hopkins University Press, 1987).

WILLIAMS, RAYMOND, *Culture and Society: Coleridge to Orwell* (1958; Hogarth Press, 1993).

—— *The Long Revolution* (Harmondsworth: Penguin, 1965).

WOOLF, STUART, *A History of Italy 1700–1860: The Social Constraints of Political Change* (Methuen, 1979).

WOOLFORD, JOHN, and KARLIN, DANIEL, *Robert Browning* (Longman, 1996).

WORDSWORTH, WILLIAM, *The Prelude*, ed. J. C. Maxwell (Harmondsworth: Penguin, 1971).

—— and COLERIDGE, SAMUEL TAYLOR, *Lyrical Ballads 1805*, ed. Derek Roper (Plymouth: Northcote House, 1987).

YEATS, W. B., *Essays and Introductions* (Macmillan, 1961).

—— *The Poems*, 2nd edn., ed. Richard J. Finneran (Macmillan, 1981).

YOUNG, ROBERT J. C., *Colonial Desire: Hybridity in Theory, Culture and Race* (Routledge, 1995).

ŽIŽEK, SLAVOJ., *For They Know Not What They Do: Enjoyment as a Political Factor* (Verso, 1991).

INDEX